To Ben,
Whose work and service to students is *always* at the core.

Your good friend,
Kirk

17 Sept. ~~2005~~ 2008

Required text, Prosem I, F'11 (PsyDoc/C115)

Routledge
Taylor & Francis Group
270 Madison Avenue
New York, NY 10016

Routledge
Taylor & Francis Group
2 Park Square
Milton Park, Abingdon
Oxon OX14 4RN

Routledge is an imprint of Taylor & Francis Group, an Informa business

Printed in the United States of America on acid-free paper
10 9 8 7 6 5 4 3 2 1

International Standard Book Number-13: 978-0-415-95471-6 (Hardcover)

Library of Congress Cataloging-in-Publication Data

Existential-integrative psychotherapy : guideposts to the core of practice / edited by Kirk J. Schneider.
p. ; cm.
Includes bibliographical references.
ISBN-13: 978-0-415-95471-6 (alk. paper)
ISBN-10: 0-415-95471-1 (alk. paper)
1. Existential psychotherapy. 2. Integrative psychotherapy. I. Schneider, Kirk J.
[DNLM: 1. Psychotherapy--methods. 2. Existentialism. WM 420 E95m 2007]

RC489.E93E95 2007
616.89'14--dc22 2007007149

Visit the Taylor & Francis Web site at
http://www.taylorandfrancis.com

and the Routledge Web site at
http://www.routledge.com

Contents

Preface

This book opens a new chapter in existential-mainstream collaborations on practice. Drawing on the foundations of my original existential-integrative text, *The Psychology of Existence*, co-authored with the late Rollo May (1995), this book advances the therapeutic conversation to a new generation of students and practitioners. This is a generation that has witnessed the ascendancy and subsequent dilution of influence by the managed care and standardization movements in psychology, and a parallel rise in new, more diversified practices. While these practices do not yet dominate the therapeutic landscape, they are increasing in salience, as this book attests.

This book, accordingly, represents both an update and expansion on the clinical chapters in *The Psychology of Existence*; it also signals an urgent plea. It is a plea to the psychotherapy community to wake up and recognize *existential* dimensions of diversified practices; for without the existential — the understanding of a person's relation to being — such practices too often devolve into adjustment rituals, rarified or removed "strategems," that quell but do not necessarily transform. This book, then, is a repository — both impassioned and broad — of existential dimensions of diverse practices. These dimensions are applied to a remarkable array of approaches, theories, and clinical populations, and they demonstrate, convincingly, in my view, that existential-mainstream collaboration is not only desirable, but imperative, if we are to advance the cause of whole and substantive transformation of lives. Among the domains that are addressed in this text are existential-integrative practices with racial and ethnic minorities, gays and lesbians, single women, children, clients with severe disturbances, older persons, alcoholics, phobic clients, and clients who are dying. Equally, the book illustrates the compatibility of existential sensibilities with a variety of ostensibly contrasting theoretical orientations. These include the integration of existential practices with cognitive-behavioral, psychoanalytic, religious, and even short-term orientations and interventions.

In sum, this book accentuates the value of an existential *attitude* across cultures, diagnoses, and orientations. To the extent that students develop this attitude, they will be worthier and more complete facilitators. What is this attitude that bolsters so much of the core of what we practitioners prize? It is presence — deep, abiding, and emancipatory — and it is one of the avowed tragedies of our contemporary era that precisely these elements are neither nurtured nor prized in standardized training and service facilities throughout our land.

This book will illuminate the value of presence, depth, and emancipatory practices across a diversity of settings and methodologies, and it will provide to both the developing trainee and the interested practitioner step-by-step skill repertoires to guide and cultivate their ministrations. At the same time, however, this book is not simply a how-to manual designed to systematize integrative therapeutic practice. By contrast, it is a compendium of discovery that, in keeping with its existential-integrative philosophical base, provides guideposts to therapy's inmost domains.

Finally, this book owes its incarnation to many caring and dedicated souls within the existential-integrative therapeutic community, but first and foremost to my great teachers, Rollo May (1909–1994) and James and Elizabeth Bugental. They never shrank from bold inquiry or the advocacy of bold inquiry. May was the original inspiration for this existential-integrative undertaking, and James Bugental and his remarkable wife, Elizabeth, were my hands-on facilitators in existential-integrative practice. To each, I convey my unwavering gratitude.

Second, I am indebted to the participants in this volume who sacrificed their time, energy, and even professional comfort zones to plow new fields in therapeutic theory and application. You have my enduring appreciation.

Third, I am grateful to the acquisition editor, George Zimmar, for his own daring vision, as well as commitment to this undertaking.

Kirk J. Schneider

Introduction

Existential-Integrative Psychotherapy: A New Era

In his landmark book, *Existence*, Rollo May outlined one of the boldest psychological agendas of the 20th century. Existential psychology, he wrote,

> does not purport to found a new school as over against other schools or to give a new technique of therapy as over against other techniques. It seeks rather, to analyze the structure of human existence — an enterprise which, if successful, should yield an understanding of the reality underlying all situations of human beings in crisis. (1958, p. 7)

Believe what one will about the ambitiousness of May's proposal, today we can see that it is both relevant and prophetic. Contemporary existential psychotherapy, for example, is neither a school nor a systematic doctrine; yet it has had a steady and enduring impact on a variety of psychological practices. Indeed, existential psychotherapy is in the ironic position of being one of the most widely influential yet least officially embraced orientations on the professional scene (see Norcross, 1987; Yalom, 1980), or as leading researcher John Norcross (1987) put it, "the existential orientation frequently underlies clinical practice without explicit recognition or awareness" (p. 42).

These words are even more relevant today, some 20 years after Norcross's declaration. Consider, for example, the recent burst of interest in existentially oriented practices among therapists who do not traditionally identify themselves as existential. Among the existentially oriented themes that these therapists now espouse are mindfulness, attunement to the here and now, deepening the emotional scene, and cultivating tolerance for, rather than preemptive restructuring of, uncomfortable affects (e.g., see the contributions by Fosha, Bunting & Hayes, and Wolfe, Part 3).

The ambivalent reception of existential psychotherapy among professionals is echoed by an equally mixed reaction among students. While substantial numbers of psychology majors are intrigued (and often profoundly moved) by isolated existential themes, they are perplexed by the therapeutic approach as a whole and comments such as the following are not infrequent: "The readings in existential psychology are fascinating, but how do you apply them?" or "I feel like the material touches something very deep in me and the lives of my clients; I just don't know how or why."

How can we account for these wildly divergent attitudes among scholars? How is it that one of the most potent sources for the comprehension of psychological phenomena is at the same time one of the most difficult to coherently discuss or apply? Part of the answer surely lies in the complexity of the project itself. Any approach that aims to "understand the reality underlying all . . . human beings in crisis" is bound to be an elusory one. Part of the problem, however, rests with us existentially oriented practitioners ourselves. Although we have made valiant theoretical and therapeutic contributions (see, for example, Bugental, 1976, 1987; Cooper, 2003; May, Angel, & Ellenberger, 1958; Yalom, 1980), we have yet to cohesively integrate them for practical clinical use. We have also spent much of our energy in the reactive rather than proactive mode of discourse, as Norcross (1987) observed two decades ago:

> In the past . . . existential therapy has often been defined *against* other therapies; that is, in a reactive or negative manner. . . . In the future, existential therapy must move toward a definition *for* something; that is, in a proactive or positive manner. In so doing, its identity must be firmly rooted in a coherent and useful theoretical structure. (p. 63)

But even more important, Norcross declared, "existential therapists' practices must be examined with *particular reference to therapy process and outcome*" [italics added] (p. 63).

While some in the existential community may bristle at Norcross's plea, they would do well, I believe, to accord it careful attention. How much longer, for example, can existential therapy afford to maintain the position of an elite, underutilized movement? How much longer can existential-oriented practitioners accept the incorporation and resultant dilution of their ideas by theoretical traditions at cross-purposes with them? Finally, how much longer can existential theorists justify informality, obscurity, and disunity simply to oppose rigidity?

Fortunately, thanks to some recent meta-analyses — as well as qualitative studies of process and outcome — this state of affairs is shifting. It can now be stated with a modicum of confidence, for example, that existential-experiential practices match, and in some cases outperform, a variety of mainstream (e.g., cognitive behavioral) strategies and practices (Ackley, 1997; Elliott, 2002; Elliott & Greenberg, 2002; see also the "common factors" research in Wampold, 2001). Furthermore, there are now a variety of payment alternatives, including medical savings accounts, sliding fee scales, and government-subsidized payment plans, that can help to support such longer-term existential-experiential practices, and consumers, apparently, are in alignment with these developments (Consumer Reports, 1995; Miller, 1996; Schneider, 1998a).

Today we stand at the threshold of a new consciousness in psychology. It is a consciousness of psychology's rich and complex texture and its many-layered "truths." The quantitative-experimental tradition in psychology, for example, is increasingly acknowledging the validity of qualitative nonexperimental designs and approaches (Williams, 1992; APA Presidential Task Force on Evidence-Based Practice, 2006). It is in the area of psychotherapy integration, however, that psychology's broadened outlook is especially salient. The impetus for this movement is the proposition, supported by growing evidence (e.g., Beutler & Clarkin, 1990; Norcross, 1986; Wampold, 2001), that while all of the major therapeutic orientations are effective, their effectiveness could be enhanced by coordinating which approaches, under what conditions, achieve optimal results.

Recent developments in psychoanalysis also suggest a widened stance. I refer particularly to the shift from biologically derived models of human development to interpersonally based positions. This shift includes a more personal and empathic view of therapeutic relationships and a more generous conception of the self (see the contributions by Portnoy and Stolorow, Chapter 12). Recent advances in attachment theory, neurobiology, and cognitive science also reflect this widened stance (see the contributions by Fosha and Bunting & Hayes, Part 3).

These trends, coupled with the increased awareness of the limitations of manualized, symptom-oriented therapies (Ackley, 1997; Elkins, 2007; Westen, Novotny, & Thompson-Brenner, 2004), all point to the need for a more comprehensive model of practice.

The implications of the above cannot be overstated, for they signal a revised conception of existence. The question is: What paradigms will lead us in organizing this revision, and upon which traditions — both philosophical and empirical — will they draw? While many candidates can and should emerge for this task, existential psychotherapy, I believe, is in a particularly suitable position to do so. The basis for this contention is twofold: existential psychotherapy's stated position of comprehensiveness and its direct descent from artistic and literary sources — contexts renowned for their depth.[1]

The premise of this book, accordingly, is that existential psychotherapy is in a prime position to lead the next wave of reform in clinical practice. Not only would such a development benefit therapeutic consumers (e.g., by elevating the quality of their healing), but it would also complement the increasingly interdisciplinary profession as a whole (APA Presidential Task Force on Evidence-Based Practice, 2006).

To summarize, existential psychotherapy is both complementary to and integrative of other practice modalities. Not only is it concerned with the clinical influences of biology, environment, cognition, and social relations, but it is also concerned with "the full network of relations," as Merleau-Ponty (1962) put it — including those with transpersonal features — that inform and underlie those modalities.

Let us take the case of Diane, for example, to illustrate this integrative view. For years, Diane has felt empty inside, hollow — and for years she has masked over those feelings. She has consumed herself with drugs, gorged herself with food, and inflated herself with falsehoods. But when the shades close at night, or when the partying ceases, the hollowness in Diane returns — and with increasing ferocity.

Diane is exasperated when she steps into my office on this misty evening. She is 40, depressed, and isolated.

She has tried many *treatments*, she tells me bitingly, but they invariably fall short of the mark. To be sure, she is quick to elaborate, they do help to a point. They serve to *maintain* her, or "get her through the night." They help her to change habits, for example, or to chemically alter her mood. They give her thought exercises and practical, rational advice. They reward her when appropriate and discourage her when necessary.

They help her to learn the *reasons* for her despair, and the distortions, consequently, of having misunderstood those reasons.

But the hollowness in Diane remains, she declares to me, and no matter how many ways she thinks about or acts differently toward that experience, she cannot fundamentally alter it.

Existential therapy could help to break this pattern, I think, as Diane sits across from me. It could work in *conjunction* with the other therapies, *deepening* her hard-won gains. For example, in addition to helping Diane *think* more logically about her hollowness, I would also work with her to *explore* that hollowness — to see what it is about, to immerse herself in it, and to experience its (immediate, kinesthetic, and affective) dimensions.

The more she can work with these dimensions, I would propose, the less they will threaten her and the more she can range freely within them. She can then be freed from the vicious cycle of compartmentalized therapies to seek richer meanings of a longer term in her life — and she can forgo her compensatory masks.

The problems of Diane and her oversimplified "cures" — indeed the problems of mainstream psychology — are but microcosms of a societywide epidemic. It is an epidemic of part-methods treating part-lives, of quick fixes and easy solutions that console, but fail to genuinely *confront*, human problems.

The signs of this epidemic are legion: The erosion of the environment is traceable to get-rich-quick methods of industrial disposal. Impression management, trickle-down economics, and "you're with us or against us" are the ongoing watchwords of presidential politics. Great procurements of revenue are spent on an agile and indomitable military (while funds for health care, the homeless, and job training dwindle).

Divisiveness and violence become increasingly acceptable problem-solving strategies.

Given the above, what is my position — the existential-integrative position — in psychotherapy,[2] and how will it be used throughout this text? First, the existential-integrative position is a revaluation of the oversimplified and one-dimensional thinking that, in my experience, permeates conventional portrayals of the human being. I perceive two basic dangers in the conventional approach — a tendency to both unduly reduce and exaggerate the human condition (Schneider, 2004). On the reductionist side, I see an increasing trend toward conceiving of human beings as machines — precise processors of information who can readily accommodate to an automated, routinized lifestyle. With respect to exaggeration, I am concerned about trends in our field that depict the human being as a demigod (one who can predict and control both internal and external environments) and trends that shun the challenges of human vulnerability.

Finally, I am concerned about more recent trends, such as extreme elements of poststructural psychology, which appear to spurn the shared or foundational aspects of the human being in favor of a kind of cavalier relativism.

Beyond these critical analyses, however, the existential-integrative position also proposes a vision. While I have already hinted at this vision psychotherapeutically, I now present a more comprehensive statement.

Existential-integrative psychology is that confluence of artistic, philosophical, and clinical disciplines that employ what might roughly be called a phenomenological method of arriving at an understanding of human existence. While existential-integrative psychology does not *exclude* other research methodologies from its purview, as we shall see, it views phenomenology as its apotheosis. Formulated by Edmund Husserl (1931) and updated by Maurice Merleau-Ponty (1962), the phenomenological method attempts to grasp the fullness of a given human experience in as rich a language or mode of expression as possible. The phenomenological method combines the artistic approach of immersing oneself in and empathizing with a given experience with the scientific approach of systematically organizing and sharing an experience with a professional community. To illustrate the uniqueness of the phenomenological approach to experience, consider the following comparison. First, I present a phenomenological description of an agoraphobic patient who observes his neighborhood from his house.

> The houses . . . gave the impression of being closed up, as if all the windows were shuttered, although he could see this was not so. He had an impression of closed citadels. And, looking up, he saw the houses leaning over toward the street, so that the strip of sky between the roofs was narrower than the street on which he walked. On the square, he was struck by an expanse that far exceeded the width of the square. He knew for certain that he would not be able to cross it. An attempt to do so would, he felt, end in so extensive a realization of emptiness, width, rareness and abandonment that his legs would fail him. He would collapse. . . . It was the expanse, above all, that frightened him. (van den Berg, 1972, p. 9)

Now consider an excerpt from the conventional description of agoraphobia (without panic disorder) given in the fourth edition of the *Diagnostic and Sta-*

tistical Manual of Mental Disorders (American Psychiatric Association [APA], 1994).

> Agoraphobia: Anxiety about being in places or situations from which escape might be difficult (or embarrassing) or in which help may not be available in the event of having an unexpected or situationally predisposed Panic Attack or panic-like symptoms. Agoraphobic fears typically involve characteristic clusters of situations that include being outside the home alone; being in a crowd or standing in a line; being on a bridge; and traveling in a bus, train, or automobile. (p. 396)

These excerpts reveal divergent empirical considerations of the same phenomenon. While the latter emphasizes the *exterior* features of agoraphobia — those that can be observed, measured, and specified, the former stresses the *interior* features of the experience — those that can be felt, intuited, and symbolized.

It is out of this personalist-phenomenological tradition, accordingly, that existential-integrative psychology arose. It is out of the desire to base theory on intimate, qualitative data that existential-integrative psychology evolves and exerts its influence (see May, 1958; Mendelowitz & Schneider, 2008).

While existential-integrative psychologists vary to some degree with respect to their interpretations of data such as the above, a consensus has formed around three central themes.

The first core finding is that *human being* (or consciousness) is suspended in mystery, only degrees of which are accessible to reflection. Put another way, consciousness is suspended between two vast and primordial poles: freedom and limitation. The freedom polarity is characterized by will, creativity, and expressiveness, and the limitation polarity is typified by natural and social restraints, vulnerability, and death.* While this thesis may appear commonsensical at first, we will see how complex and subtle it can be and how profoundly it can affect our understanding of psychosocial functioning. The freedom-limitation polarity, for example, forms the template for a revised theory of the psychodynamics of functional and dysfunctional behavior: the productive and unproductive dimensions of choice, self-direction, and desire on the one hand, and discipline, order, and accommodation on the other. We will see how traditional psychological views have tended to dichotomize along the freedom-limitation continuum and how the existential-integrative tradition (through art and philosophy) has anticipated and attempted to counter such dichotomizations.*

The second core existential-integrative finding is that dread of either freedom or limitation (due generally to past trauma) promotes extreme or dys-

* This thesis will be elaborated upon in terms of its clinically relevant features — expansion, constriction, and centering — in Part 2, "Theory of the Existential-Integrative (EI) Approach."

functional counterreactions to either polarity. A boy who associates limit setting with abuse, for example, is likely to counteract those feelings with a willful, aggressive orientation. Conversely, a woman who associates freedom with unmanageable power and responsibility is likely to become reticent and withdrawn. Many stories from classic myth or literature illustrate this conception. In Goethe's *Faust*, for example, Faust's bargain with the devil for unlimited power is a reaction to the despair and boredom of his ascetic life. Conversely, Ivan Ilych (from the Tolstoy classic) is so petrified by the uncontrollability and complexity associated with his freedom that he becomes a prisoner of propriety in order to escape.

The final core finding is that confrontation with or integration of freedom and limitation (across numerous spheres of functioning) is enlivening and health promoting. This finding can be illustrated by the person who has learned to accept his or her multifaceted nature and who is thus capable of engaging freedom and limitation more or less as the circumstance demands rather than because of intimidation or panic. Such a person is able to see the beauty of her or his paradoxical situation as well as its tragedy and is thereby inclined to be flexible rather than rigid about life's predicaments. Finally, he or she acknowledges the power of both polarities and spurns efforts to defuse or minimize them (see Becker, 1973; May, 1981; Schneider, 1990/1999).

An example of this sort of person is the man or woman who can allow himself or herself to be both bold and tender, creative and disciplined, and exploratory and committed in key life areas. After Faust's deflation, for example, he was able to appreciate the options of his ordinary existence, such as his love for the village girl, Gretchen. Following Ilych's realization of the preciousness of life, he found the courage to expand and transform his social role. (For a fuller discussion of the literary and mythic implications of existential-integrative psychology, see May, 1991, and Schneider & May, 1995).

In summary, existential-integrative psychology aims to articulate that which is central and vital to human experience. These shared foundation structures are based on the subjective and intersubjective investigations of phenomenology.

To repeat, the three core dimensions of the human psyche to emerge from such investigations are:

1. Human being is suspended in mystery, only degrees of which are accessible to consciousness. Freedom is characterized by will, creativity, and expressiveness; limitation is signified by natural and social restraints, vulnerability, and death.
2. Dread of freedom or limitation (usually due to past trauma) promotes dysfunctional or extreme counterreactions to either polarity (i.e., oppressiveness or impulsivity).
3. Confrontation with or integration of the polarities promotes a more vibrant, invigorating life design. This life design is exemplified by

> increased sensitivity, flexibility, and choice. It is also characterized by fullness: the humility and wonder or, in short, awe of our cosmic condition.

Now let us return to the existential-integrative psychotherapy upon which the theory serves as foundation. This book is divided into three parts: a discussion of the recent and future trends of existential-integrative practice, the guideposts to an existential-integrative approach to therapy, and case illustrations of existential-integrative practice.

The book opens with recent and future trends in existential-integrative therapy. This discussion centers on the role of existential-integrative therapy in the face of the so-called cognitive and biological revolutions, as well as recent counterreactions to those developments — such as trends in social constructivism and transpersonal psychology. The case of Karen serves to animate this discussion and demonstrate its clinical relevance. The section concludes with a bridge-building essay by two clinical graduate students — "A Student Point of View: Existential Psychotherapy From Within the Training Process."

The next part, "Guideposts to an Existential-Integrative (EI) Approach," is the core theoretical statement of the book. It outlines an existential-integrative approach to practice. Drawing upon related but less comprehensive existential-integrative purviews (e.g., Bugental, 1987; May, 1958, 1981; Schneider, 1990/1999), this outline addresses six levels of therapeutic intervention: the physiological (medical), the environmental (behavioral), the cognitive, the psychosexual, the interpersonal, and the experiential. Each level, moreover, is understood as a liberation condition (or offering) attending to ever-widening spheres of psychophysiological injury.[3] The chief aims of the framework are twofold: to provide a coherent overview of existential-integrative liberation and to clarify when, how, and with whom given liberation approaches may be appropriate in this (aforementioned) context. Practical, illustrative skill-building exercises are provided at the close of this section.

Finally, the book closes with a resplendent and — to my knowledge — unprecedented array of existential-integrative case studies. These case studies, authored by leading authorities in mainstream as well as humanistic orientations, guide readers through a wide swath of existential-integrative practices. Moreover, these practices are highlighted by an impressive range of ethnically and diagnostically diverse clinical populations and fresh applications of approach.

In closing, let me take a moment to share my continued zeal over one of the pivotal and original features of this book — its stress on *integration*. Never before, to my knowledge, has an existential text attempted to reach out to so many disciplines, settings, and client populations, and rarely has such a work been so focused on the multifaceted concerns of graduate-level practitioners. The part on recent and future trends combines the perspectives of both experienced professionals and graduate students and also provides an interdisciplinary case study. The part on existential-integrative theory integrates a diversity of *procedural* orientations, and the part on case illustrations embraces a rich (culturally and diagnostically mixed) range, reported by an equally diverse set of practitioners.

If there is one group to whom I continue to owe the impetus for this existential ecumenism, it is the clients and trainees who have been served by it, and I am grateful for their appeals.

Notes

1. It is one of the sad ironies of our field that people like Rollo May had to enroll in nonpsychology graduate programs (like those of theology or literature) in order to study the whole person. While some disaffected students eventually come back to psychology's fold, as did Dr. May, how many do not? How much intellectual talent is discouraged by the vested interests of mainstream psychology and the commercialized culture to which it is obliged? But this state of affairs is changing, as this volume attests, and I hope more will welcome it. (See also Mendelowitz & Schneider, 2008, for a summary of new developments in existential psychology's depth tradition.)
2. Existential-integrative psychology represents both a broadening of the traditional existential view (e.g., to include mainstream psychological perspectives) and a blending of two other existentially oriented psychologies — humanistic existentialism and existential psychoanalysis. Although humanistic existentialism (represented by such theorists as Carl Rogers and Fritz Perls) and existential psychoanalysis (represented by thinkers such as Ludwig Binswanger and Medard Boss) have many features in common, there are several points on which they differ. While humanistic existentialism emphasizes optimism, potential, and (relatively) rapid transformation, existential psychoanalysis underscores subconsciousness, uncertainty, and (relatively) gradual transformation. Moreover, whereas humanistic existentialism emphasizes individual growth, existential psychoanalysis stresses social, spiritual, and philosophical growth.

   Existential-integrative psychology, on the other hand, attempts to make room for all of these dimensions, neither over- nor underestimating their value (see Yalom, 1980, or May, 1958, for an elaboration of this discussion).

   Finally, while it is true that existential psychology is, by definition, integrative (see Merleau-Ponty, 1962), rarely is this connection made explicit. Here I attempt to redress this significant oversight.
3. Although terms such as *intervention*, *psychophysiological*, and the like are frequently considered reductionist and therefore inadequate by existential theorists, there are several reasons why I use them in this text: (1) to reach a diverse and mainstream readership, (2) to limit abstruse or ungainly jargon, and (3) to ease readers' transition to more sophisticated coinages that they can readily pursue if they so desire.

   Therefore, from this point on, terms such as the above are to be viewed as transitional — means to more complicated ends.

   More will be said on this subject in Part 2.

References

Ackley, D. C. (1997). *Breaking free of managed care.* New York: Guilford Press.

American Psychiatric Association. (1994). *Diagnostic and statistical manual of mental disorders* (4th ed.). Washington, DC: Author.

APA Presidential Task Force on Evidence-Based Practice. (2006). Evidence-based practice in psychology. *American Psychologist, 61,* 271–285.

Becker, E. (1973). *Denial of death.* New York: Free Press.

Beutler, L., & Clarkin, J. (1990). *Systematic treatment selection: Toward targeted therapeutic interventions.* New York: Brunner/Mazel.

Bugental, J. (1976). *The search for existential identity: Patient-therapist dialogues in humanistic psychotherapy.* San Francisco: Jossey-Bass.

Bugental, J. (1987). *The art of the psychotherapist.* New York: Norton.

Consumer Reports. (1995, November). Mental health: Does therapy help? *Consumer Reports,* 734–739.

Cooper, M. (2003). *Existential therapies.* London: Sage.

Elkins, D. (2007). Empirically-supported treatments: The deconstruction of a myth. *Journal of Humanistic Psychology, 47,* (4).

Elliott, R. (2002). The effectiveness of humanistic therapies: A meta-analysis. In D. J. Cain & J. Seeman (Eds.), *Humanistic psychotherapies: Handbook of research and practice* (pp. 57–81). Washington, DC: American Psychological Association.

Elliott, R., & Greenberg, L. S. (2002). Process-experiential psychotherapy. In D. J. Cain & J. Seeman (Eds.), *Humanistic psychotherapies: Handbook of research and practice* (pp. 279–306). Washington, DC: American Psychological Association.

Husserl, E. (1931). *Ideas: General introduction to pure phenomenology* (W. Gibson, Trans.). New York: Macmillan.

May, R. (1958). The origins and significance of the existential movement in psychology. In R. May, E. Angel, & H. Ellenberger (Eds.), *Existence: A new dimension in psychiatry and psychology* (pp. 3–36). New York: Basic Books.

May, R. (1981). *Freedom and destiny.* New York: Norton.

May, R. (1991). *The cry for myth.* New York: Norton.

May, R., Angel, E., & Ellenberger, H. (Eds.). (1958). *Existence: A new dimension in psychiatry and psychology.* New York: Basic Books.

Mendelowitz, E., & Schneider, K. J. (2008). Existential psychotherapy. In R. Corsini & D. Wedding (Eds.), *Current psychotherapies* (8th ed.) (pp. 295-327). Belmont, CA: Thompson/Brook Cole.

Merleau-Ponty, M. (1962). *Phenomenology of perception.* (C. Smith, Trans.) London: Routledge.

Miller, I. J. (1996). Managed care is harmful to outpatient mental health services: A call for accountability. *Professional Psychology: Research and Practice, 27,* 349-363.

Norcross, J. (Ed.). (1986). *Handbook of eclectic psychotherapy.* New York: Brunner/Mazel.

Norcross, J. (1987). A rational and empirical analysis of existential psychotherapy. *Journal of Humanistic Psychology, 27,* 41–68.

Schneider, K. J. (1998a). Toward a science of the heart: Romanticism and the revival of psychology. *American Psychologist, 53,* 277–289.

Schneider, K. J. (1998b). Existential processes. In L. S. Greenberg, J. C. Watson, & G. Lietaer (Eds.), *Handbook of experiential psychotherapy* (pp. 103–120). New York: Guilford.

Schneider, K. J. (1999). *The paradoxical self: Toward an understanding of our contradictory nature* (2nd ed.). Amherst, NY: Humanity Books. (Original work published 1990)

Schneider, K. J. (2004). *Rediscovery of awe: Splendor, mystery, and the fluid center of life*. St. Paul, MN: Paragon House.

Schneider, K. J. & May, R. (1995). *The psychology of existence: An integrative, clinical perspective*. New York: McGraw-Hill.

van den Berg, J. (1972). *A different existence: Principles of phenomenological psychology*. Pittsburgh: Duquesne University Press.

Wampold, B. E. (2001). *The great psychotherapy debate: Models, methods, findings*. Mahwah, NJ: Erlbaum.

Westen, D., Novotny, C. M., & Thompson-Brenner, H. (2004). Empirical status of empirically supported psychotherapies: Assumptions, findings and reporting in controlled, clinical trials. *Psychological Bulletin, 130*, 631–663.

Williams, R. (1992). The human context of agency. *American Psychologist, 47*, 752–760.

Yalom, I. (1980). *Existential psychotherapy*. New York: Basic Books.

Part 1

Recent and Future Trends in Existential-Integrative Psychotherapy

In this section, I examine four recent and future developments in psychotherapy that have both informed and instigated existential-integrative practice: the cognitive revolution, developments in biopsychology, and the trends toward transpersonal and social constructivist reformation. I examine the nature of these formulations, trace their application to a clinical case, and consider their relevance to existential-integrative practice. Finally, in the last half of this section, I feature a student contribution. This contribution elucidates the recent and emerging challenges of existentially oriented clinical graduate students. Specifically it anatomizes the demands faced by these (and other) students but also, and equally, the rich rewards of adopting an intensive existential-integrative "alternative."

1
From Segregation to Integration

The world of psychotherapy, as noted earlier, is changing, and existential psychotherapy is on the cusp of that change. In the years since *Existence*, there have been at least four dramatic developments in psychotherapy, and each has reshaped the field. Cognitive psychotherapy, for example, brought welcome attention to the autonomy of the human intellect; biopsychology revealed untold physiological and behavioral interconnections (Beck, 1976; Thompson, 1973). In more recent years, transpersonal (or transcendental) psychotherapy and postmodernist philosophy (in the form of social constructivist approaches) have ushered in even bolder paradigmatic shifts (Wilber, Engler, & Brown, 1986; Bernstein, 1986; Gergen, 1991; Epting & Leitner, 1994). For example, transpersonal psychotherapy inspired (and in some cases revived) an interest in alternative healing methods, Eastern and Western meditative traditions, and paranormal phenomena. Social constructivist approaches, correspondingly, relativized and thereby broadened therapeutic and cultural notions of truth. Within the context of a culturally sensitive framework, all perceptual phenomena are legitimated by this framework, and none can be said to be inherently superior to any other.

However, there has been a price for these reformative developments, and the outlines of that price are becoming clear. First, I refer to contemporary therapy's increasing specialization. We will soon be, if we are not already, threatened by a chaos of competing practices. Second, we are threatened by the limitations inherent in the respective points of view. While they are salient within their own domains, they tend to be simplistic or devitalizing when applied beyond those domains. (See, for example, the concerns expressed by May, 1967; Wampold, 2001; Wertz, 1993; Westen, Novotny, & Thompson-Brenner, 2004.)

Put plainly, we need a therapeutic foundation that will do justice to both our diversity and our particularity, our freedom and our limits. Such a foundation would view human beings in their fullness while carefully acknowledging their tragedy and incompleteness. It would honor our biological and mechanical propensities, but not at the cost of compromising our capacity to create and transcend ordinary consciousness. What, specifically, would such a foundation look like? Consider the following vignette* for an illustration:.

> Karen is a 37-year-old, middle-class female. She has a husband and a 15-year-old son who plays Little League baseball. Ordinary in most respects, Karen has one outstanding trait: She is 424 pounds.
>
> What is a 424-pound world like? Karen reflects:
>
> I weighed [myself on] the freight scale at Johnson's Trucking terminal. I couldn't buy clothes even in large-size women's specialty shops because their sizes stopped at 52 and I was a size 60. My wardrobe consisted of three caftans which I had specially made: one — navy, black, and brown — sewn straight up the sides with openings for my head and arms. I wore slip-on sandals in summer and winter because I couldn't bend over to lace sneakers up and dress shoes buckled under my weight. I didn't own a coat, but that didn't matter since I was hardly ever out of the house anyway. In the morning, I'd maneuver myself out of bed, go to the kitchen, get my stash of food, and settle into my chair in the living room, comforted by the assurance that food was all around me. My days were filled with the drone of soap operas in the background. I lived my life vicariously through my husband and children. They became my arms and legs and my windows to the outside world. When I went anywhere, I drove. The car became part of my insulation, my armor, my protection. I used to drive around town eating, stuffing down anger, guilt, hurt — eating until nothing mattered any more. (Roth, 1991, p. 173)

Let us imagine how a team of contemporary psychologists might understand Karen's condition and what this understanding implies for the integrative vision referred to above.

From the behavioral standpoint, for example, Karen's obesity would probably be understood as a function of her environment. Rearrange her surroundings, behaviorists would contend, and you will significantly modify her compulsion. In particular, they would pin her problem on the wealth of junk foods she keeps around her house (which serve as conditioned stimuli), her consumption of food while engaging in other behaviors (such as television viewing), and her perception of foods as positive (or negative) reinforcers. To redress these concerns, behaviorists would try to help Karen reduce or eliminate the problematic stimuli and replace them with stimuli that are more adaptive.

Physiological psychologists, by contrast, would look to Karen's brain, central nervous system, and cell metabolism for their answers. They might conjecture that deficits in her ability to metabolize her food, for example, ren-

* This vignette is modeled on the case of Karen Russell, who is eloquently described by Geneen Roth (1991, pp. 172–184). Where I have speculated about her condition, I have noted that I have done so

der her physiologically predisposed to obesity. Depending on the severity of her predisposition, they might recommend a combination of drugs, dietary restrictions, and surgical procedures. To the extent that Karen was able to lose weight without severe measures, physiological psychologists might suggest that she lose weight gradually through a carefully modified diet and a regular form of aerobic exercise (such as walking).

Cognitive therapists, on the other hand, would concentrate on the relationship between Karen's thought patterns and her malady. In particular, they would try to help Karen understand the connection between her faulty beliefs, assumptions, and expectations and her maladaptive behavior. They might point out, for example, that when she is lonely she believes she will always be lonely, and this generalization leads to the faulty belief that food is the only alternative to this loneliness. Once Karen can recognize these maladaptive schemas, the cognitive psychologists would contend, she will be able to modify or restructure them, and hence her behavior.

Let us pause a moment and reflect on Karen's apparent response to such regimens: "I have tried to break free from my state of nonexistence hundreds of times," Karen tells us. "I'd been to scores of doctors" (Roth, 1991, p. 174). Like many compulsive eaters, moreover, it is a good bet that Karen was helped by some of these doctors — at least temporarily. For example, Karen was probably able to reprogram her life through such contacts. In particular, she probably mustered the will needed to keep junk food out of her house, to devise new links between eating and other behaviors, and to develop fresh, more appropriate ways to reward herself. She also probably took appetite suppressants and a variety of nutritional supplements along her recuperative path.

Yet if Karen sounds bitter about these therapies, it is probably because — in spite of their efficacy — in some intimate, vital way, they failed to address her wound. "Exercise, dear," Karen recalled angrily about the advice she had received at one of her weight-control meetings, "Just *push* yourself away from the table three times a day" (Roth, 1991, p. 174).

My own experience with compulsive eaters has convinced me that cognitive-behavioral and physiological treatments can be essential first steps on the path to recovery. They help people understand the importance of reassessing their habits, belief systems, and approaches to food. They educate them about their physiology and the physiology of practice. But most important, perhaps, they prompt clients to begin a process of deep reflection about their lives — who they essentially are and where they are headed — and this, in turn, sometimes leads to fundamental change (Mendelowitz & Schneider, 2008; Schneider, 1990/1999).

"Whenever something hurt too much," Karen recollects, "I would pack up and leave myself because I was afraid that if I experienced the fear, it would eat me alive. I made the commitment to stay with myself, [however, and to] let the fear or hurt wash over me" (Roth, 1991, p. 175).

Until now, we have examined treatment regimens that help Karen and countless clients like her to get a foothold on their compulsions; they teach them *operational* (measurable, specifiable) ways to change their lives. Yet these methodologies tend to address narrow ranges of the problem, failing to touch the "fear" or "hurt," as Karen puts it, that underlie those ranges. Now let us assess methodologies that purport to confront more substantive domains of psychological functioning — those of transpersonalism and social constructivism. How might they foster Karen's emancipation from food?

Transpersonal therapy encompasses those disciplines and practices that address *transcendental* (or nonordinary) states of consciousness. To the extent that transpersonal psychology accepts existential mystery, for our purposes, it provides vital insights into such transcendental phenomena as energy shifts, paranormal and visionary states, religious and spiritual crises, and unitive experiences. To the extent that the discipline spurns existential mystery, on the other hand, it can impose exaggerated or premature solutions on treatment; it can also rob the client of the chance to develop her own solutions and discoveries (for examples see Dass, 1992; Cortright, 1997; May, 1986; Schneider, 1987, 1989; Zweig & Abrams, 1991; and the contribution by Hoffman, Chapter 9).

How would a team of existentially sensitive transpersonalists understand and help Karen? First, they would probably help her evolve to the point where she could begin to ask deeper questions about herself: What does she want in her life? Where is she headed? Who does she ultimately wish to become? "I grew up to believe in an angry God," Karen acknowledges,

> a God who punishes you, a God who is never pleased, for whom only perfection is enough. I went from an angry mother to an angry God to being angry at myself. Diets were an extension of the angry God; I could never be good enough. I would always rebel and feel horrible about myself afterwards. . . .
>
> I realized that I was not that bad and that openheartedness, not punishment, was the way into my problems with food. (Roth, 1991, p. 181)

Next, the transpersonalists might assist Karen (through meditation, for example) to dwell in formerly uninhabitable parts of herself, such as her loneliness or vacuousness. This could have the effect of opening Karen to the deeper meanings of that suffering, and of reconciling her with those meanings. No longer would she feel as compelled to fill her being with food, she would find, but could realize that solace through living.

After three and a half years of sustained meditative therapy, Karen states, "Now I am living. It's the difference between eating my feelings and feeling my feelings" (Roth, 1991, p. 180). "I'm alive," she goes on,

> and . . . feel everything with great vibrancy. I walk in the woods and feel a hushed sense of awe. Driving around in the warm spring rain a few weeks ago, I was spellbound by a double rainbow. . . . Last week at work, I saw some bare oak trees covered with raindrops. I knew they were just raindrops on a naked tree, but to me they were diamonds. (p. 183)

The danger of such a transcendental emphasis, on the other hand, is that it unwittingly implies salvation to Karen, or that it shortsightedly implies a resolution. Anxiety can (and fruitfully does) exist alongside glimpses of divinity, and it is in the dialogue between that people achieve vitality (May, 1981, 1985; Schneider, 2002, 2004; Tillich, 1952). The dialectical features of Karen's struggle, for example, bring a poignancy to her life — a savoring of momentary triumphs — and a wisdom that evolves through humility.

> I wish I could tell you that being a size twelve is all wonderful but I'm finding out that being awake and alive is a package deal. I don't get to go through the line and pick only goodies. On one side is wonder, awe, excitement and laughter — and on the other side is tears, disappointment, aching sadness. Wholeness is coming to me by being willing to explore ALL the feelings.
>
> So . . . 275 pounds later, my life is a mixture of pain and bliss. It hurts a lot these days but it's real. It's my life being lived by me and not vicariously through a soap opera the way it used to be. I don't know where it's all heading, but one thing I know for sure: I'm definitely going. (Roth, 1991, pp. 183–184)

The social constructivist approach to Karen's difficulty, finally, draws upon the premises of postmodernism, which are just now being therapeutically articulated. Broadly speaking, postmodernism holds three basic assumptions: (1) there are no absolute truths, (2) all realities (or stories) are socially constructed, and (3) fluidity among realities is desirable (O'Hara & Anderson, 1991). How, then, might social constructivism comprehend Karen?

First, it would seek to understand Karen's story about her obesity — how she defines it, what issues she believes contributed to it, and which stories she believes might help her to modify her condition. For example, Karen might tell a kind of psychoanalytically oriented story about how she was abandoned as a child, how she rarely received validation, and how food was substituted for companionship (Roth, 1991, p. 178). She might then talk about the diets and weight-loss programs she had failed and the deep sense of something missing in her life. Despite her fears, however, social constructivists are likely to respond to Karen with a sense of optimism at this point, a sense that many future stories are available to her and that she — with their guidance — can choose the one(s) that work.

The nagging and unanswered problem here, of course, lies in the criteria the social constructivists choose. Are resultant changes in Karen's symptomatology, for example, the factors that determine her success, or are they shifts in her subjective world? Are *intuitive narratives* (such as "message" dreams) worthy of the same attention as *intellectual narratives* (such as statistical judgments)? To whom or what can Karen turn in this menagerie?

One answer lies in the growing movement called *technical eclecticism* (Lazarus, Beutler, & Norcross, 1992). Briefly, this movement holds that the diversity of therapies can be unified by empirical means, or by extant studies of technical effectiveness. Review the literature on therapeutic outcome, technical eclecticists suggest, and you will discern the optimal strategies.

The problem with this standpoint, however, is that the therapeutic-outcome literature is dominated by the quantitative-experimental tradition and neglects or ignores the emerging phenomenological analyses of outcome (Gendlin, 1978; Mahrer, 1986). As a result, technical eclecticism tends to have a cognitive-behavioral bias, and existential (or experientially based) approaches receive short shrift (see Part 2 for an elaboration on this point).[1]

Let us return now to the foundational model we have been seeking and review our conclusions thus far. It is clear, first of all, that contemporary schools are effective in key areas and that their cultivation must be encouraged. It is equally clear that psychology is in disarray at present and that specialization is largely to blame. Physiological and cognitive-behavioral approaches work, for example, but to what ends — external adjustment, transient serenity? While such outcomes are important (and indeed crucial) for some clients, are they the standards upon which to ground our entire field? Transpersonal and social constructivist approaches, likewise, are emancipatory, but are they, particularly in their more strident forms, attentive enough to our vulnerable and contingent sides — our creatureliness as well as saintliness? Our capacity to experience life's poignancy as well as plasticity?

As an existentially oriented therapist, I must answer in the negative to these queries and press toward a more fruitful alternative. That existential psychology can provide such an alternative, I believe, is attested to by its *phenomenological* (experiential) database, its freedom-limitation dialectic, and its challenge to people to fully engage that dialectic (see Burston & Frie, 2006).

Furthermore, I believe that the other approaches can thrive within this multidimensional frame. Physiological and cognitive-behavioral models, for example, can be understood as emancipatory transitions (or footholds) on the path to a broader liberation (see the contribution by Fosha, Chapter 12). Transpersonal and postmodern (or eclectic) visions, conversely, can be seen as outermost facilitators of liberation that feed back to and bolster the cognitive-behavioral and physiological processes (see the contribution by Bunting & Hayes, Chapter 10).

This then, is my proposal for an *assimilative integration* model of existential therapy. Assimilative integration accommodates the application of a variety of practices within one overarching framework (Stricker, 2005). While such an approach may sound overly ambitious at points, it is urgent, I believe, to propose it, and I highly encourage an ongoing dialogue regarding its viability.

Accordingly, let me animate this (existential-integrative) alternative and cast it into the marketplace of ideas.

First, I present the views of two clinical graduate students, who explore the role and challenges of existential psychotherapy in academia. Next, in Part 2, I elaborate the theoretical underpinnings of an existential-integrative therapy, and finally, in Part 3, I present a range of existential-integrative case applications.

References

Beck, A. (1976). *Cognitive therapy and the emotional disorders.* New York: Signet.

Bernstein, R. (1986). *Philosophical profiles.* Philadelphia: University of Pennsylvania Press.

Burston, D., & Frie, R. (2006). *Psychotherapy as a human science.* Pittsburgh: Duquesne University Press.

Cortright, B. (1997). *Psychotherapy and spirit: Theory and practice in transpersonal psychotherapy.* New York: SUNY Press.

Dass, R. (1992). *Compassion in action: Setting out on the path of service.* New York: Crown.

Epting, F. R., & Leitner, L. M. (1994). Humanistic psychology and personal construct theory. In F. Wertz (Ed.), *The humanistic movement: Recovering the person in psychology* (pp. 129–145). Lake Worth, FL: Gardner Press.

Gendlin, E. (1978). *Focusing.* New York: Bantam.

Gergen, K. (1991). *The saturated self: Dilemmas of identity in contemporary life.* New York: Basic Books.

Lazarus, A., Beutler, L., & Norcross, J. (1992). The future of technical eclecticism. *Psychotherapy, 29,* 11–20.

Mahrer, A. (1986). *Therapeutic experiencing: The process of change.* New York: Norton.

May, R. (1967). *Psychology and the human dilemma.* New York: Van Nostrand.

May, R. (1981). *Freedom and destiny.* New York: Norton.

May, R. (1985). *My quest for beauty.* Dallas: Saybrook. (Distributed by Norton.)

May, R. (1986). Transpersonal or transcendental? *Humanistic Psychologist, 14,* 87–90.

Mendelowitz, E., & Schneider, K. (2008). Existential psychotherapy. In R. Corsini & D. Wedding (Eds.), *Current psychotherapies* (8th ed., pp. 295–327). Belmont, CA: Thompson/Brook Cole.

O'Hara, M., & Anderson, W. (1991, September). Welcome to the postmodern world. *Networker,* 19–25.

Roth, G. (1991). *When food is love.* New York: Plume.

Schneider, K. J. (1987). The deified self: A "centaur" response to Wilber and the transpersonal movement. *Journal of Humanistic Psychology, 27,* 196–216.

Schneider, K. J. (1989). Infallibility is so damn appealing: A reply to Ken Wilber. *Journal of Humanistic Psychology, 29,* 470–481.

Schneider, K. J. (1999). *The paradoxical self: Toward an understandng of our contradictory nature* (2nd ed.). Amherst, NY: Humanity Books. (Original work published 1990)

Schneider, K. J. (2002). A reply to Roger Walsh. In K. J. Schneider, J. F. T. Bugental, & J. F. Pierson (Eds.), *The handbook of humanistic psychology* (pp. 621–624). Thousand Oaks, CA: Sage Publications.

Schneider, K. J. (2004). *Rediscovery of awe: Splendor, mystery, and the fluid center of life.* St. Paul, MN: Paragon House.

Shedler, J., Mayman, M., & Manis, M. (1993). The illusion of mental health. *American Psychologist, 48,* 1117–1131.

Stricker, G. (2005). Perspectives on psychotherapy integration. *Psychotherapy Bulletin, 40* (4).

Thompson, R. (1973). *Introduction to biopsychology.* San Francisco: Albion.

Tillich, P. (1952). *The courage to be.* New Haven, CT: Yale University Press.

Wampold, B. E. (2001). *The great psychotherapy debate: Models, methods, findings.* Mahwah, NJ: Erlbaum.

Wertz, F. (1993). Cognitive psychology: A phenomenological critique. *Journal of Theoretical and Philosophical Psychology, 13,* 2–24.

Westen, D., Novotny, C. M., & Thompson-Brenner, H. (2004). Empirical status of empirically supported psychotherapies: Assumptions, findings and reporting in controlled, clinical trials. *Psychological Bulletin, 130,* 631–663.

Wilber, K., Engler, J., & Brown, D. (1986). *Transformations of consciousness: Conventional and contemplative perspectives on development.* Boston: New Science Library.

Zweig, C., & Abrams, J. (1991). *Meeting the shadow: The hidden power of human nature.* Los Angeles: Tarcher.

2
A Student Point of View: Existential Psychotherapy From Within the Training Process

While the impact of existential practice on mainstream graduate education has been minimal, there are signs — as this book makes plain — that a trend reversal may be occurring. Spearheading this trend reversal are the growing numbers of disaffected professionals that we have discussed. On a quieter, or grassroots, level, however, a student-based rebellion appears to be coalescing. Aroused by psychology's cultural and theoretical diversity, these students seek commensurately interdisciplinary psychologies. Let us turn now to the ground-level insights of two former graduate students from the California School of Professional Psychology, Alameda/Berkeley (now Alliant International University). Written at the time they were students (1995), albeit slightly updated, this section still stands as a beacon for all who pursue existential therapy training, both within and outside of the academy.

ANN BASSETT-SHORT AND GLENN A. HAMMEL

Ann Bassett-Short, PhD, counseled low-income women at a Manhattan settlement house until shifting her focus toward spirituality and existential psychology. She currently oversees pastoral care at a Quaker meeting on Long Island and advises a conflict resolution program of the American Friends Service Committee. On the side, she is a choral conductor and arranger.

Glenn A. Hammel, PhD, is a neuropsychologist specializing in geriatrics and forensics. He lectures internationally on issues related to elder care and aging parents. He has found a passion in trying to perform clinical assessments that integrate the values and approach of existential psychology with the science and knowledge of neuropsychology. He and his family reside in Sacramento, CA.

As clinical practicum and internship students will attest, training to be a psychotherapist is an undertaking of great proportions. Consider the following scene:

> Your first client is looking at you, waiting for a reply. You wonder to yourself how the two of you will build this new and untried relationship into one that could bear painful intensity and encourage this individual toward a life more intentional, spirited, and distinctly his or her own. Where do you start? You could go in a hundred different directions. Fragments of books, supervision sessions, classroom discussions, and experiences in your own life rush past you. Then you notice your client's eyes — their pain, hope, and fear — and you make your response. Later, you realize that you'll be starting over to some degree with each new client throughout your career. You hope for a day when you've become used to starting over.

When student clinicians find themselves disoriented in the therapy hour, it often has to do with the shifting nature of their beliefs about personality functioning, psychopathology, and the conduct of therapy. Students' efforts to find their clinical identities can certainly be furthered by exploring a theoretical orientation whose values seem especially consonant with their own. Schools of therapy, however, vary in their accessibility and usefulness to students. As we will describe below, we find that existential psychology speaks clearly to student concerns and offers considerable aid in meeting some of training's most difficult challenges.

We feel intimately familiar with the challenges of formal training in clinical psychology. We came to this writing when both of us were nearing the end of our doctoral programs in a freestanding school of professional psychology and were conducting our fifth year of supervised therapy in community settings. Although our education in psychology has been fairly mainstream (largely psychodynamic), we began supplementing our programs early in graduate school with study and supervision in existential psychology. Much of our impetus toward existentialism had to do with us as individuals, not with our being students per se. In fact, to imply that we could speak accurately about ourselves only as students would counter the basic existential assumption that humans are indivisible wholes. To emphasize the relevance existential psychology can have for those in training, however, we will restrict our focus here to issues with which students, in particular, wrestle.

What are these student challenges? One part of evolving professionally entails coming to terms with the extraordinary wealth of verbal and nonverbal information clients often present. Students must find a way to conceptualize what they witness and help the client stay oriented in what appear to be the most valuable directions. A complicating issue is that armed with the insights of graduate school, students too often apply their techniques and knowledge *to* clients instead of working *with* them in shared endeavors. For instance, theory can obscure one's clients if one applies it around them like scaffolding. Scaffolding does provide builders a secure place to stand when working in difficult places and gives architects the opportunity to view an emerging building from new angles. But a builder's rough scaffolding can easily camouflage and be mistaken for the intricate architecture it surrounds. Similarly, students erect theory around the client quickly — often automatically — when they are uncertain and hoping for a surer vantage point, as in the opening vignette. One of the most formidable challenges for beginning therapists, then, is to draw structure from a particular orientation without letting theory obscure the complex, unique individual in front of them.

Existential psychology can help with student concerns and challenges like these through four specific features: (1) a focus on the client's immediate experience, (2) an emphasis on the human capacity for choice, (3) an acknowledgment of the limits of action, and (4) an emphasis on phenomenological formulations.

A Focus on the Client's Immediate Experience

One way in which the student can lose sight of the client as an individual is by giving too little attention to the client's immediate experiences. Students sometimes fail to notice subtle shifts, for example, in the client's emotional intensity, facial expressions, gestures, or the character of the individual's remarks in session. Missing these nuances means losing some of the person's most telling (and fleeting) disclosures. Conversely, attaining some fluency in the client's unique verbal and nonverbal "dialect" can be an important step in hastening the development of a solid therapeutic alliance.

Students can be distracted from this immediacy in many ways. We have already mentioned the danger of becoming preoccupied in session with one's academic knowledge of psychology. Students may also be preoccupied with the future: thinking, for instance, about how they will describe the session now in progress to their supervisor. Some students may also not yet be accustomed to working with a client in great emotional pain; they may find the individual's distress somewhat overwhelming and seek refuge in more emotionally muted explorations. One area that often falls in this category is exploration of the client's history. History gathering certainly has its place and, indeed, is often explicitly required by field placements. Unfortunately, the temptation remains strong to collect the information from clients in ways that reduce clients' immediacy and increase their distance and detachment in session.

Training in existential psychology can help students with its consistent and overarching emphasis on immediacy. In fact, existential therapists emphasize that one does not need to fill in all the blanks about a client's past. Instead, one needs to *know* the client (May, 1958). Yalom (1980) adds that exploring deeply can mean thinking "not about the way one came to be the way one is, but *that* one is" (p. 11). If, during history gathering, one focuses on the individual who experienced the events — and who is experiencing something right now — one is much less likely to lose the person for the details. Lastly, existential psychology's demand that therapists remain attuned to their own ongoing, immediate experiences also encourages students to maintain a here-now focus in session.

An Emphasis on the Human Capacity for Choice

Another student challenge is to retain awareness of the client's capacity for choice. Clients, for instance, sometimes present their lives as intractably sad, downplaying their ability to effect change. Having participated in the therapeutic process comparatively few times (and perhaps having little confidence in their clinical abilities), students may believe such presentations too readily. Existential psychology, however, maintains a clear emphasis on the human capacity for a good measure of choice. Although not all levels of choice are conscious, as Irvin Yalom (1980) points out, individuals often have a larger range of choice than they perceive.

Ironically, the pressure to devalue a client's ability to choose sometimes comes from the field placement itself. Some settings, for example, attribute client responses primarily to transference and view this construct in a way that reduces client responsibility. The implication is that clients were driven to respond as they did by echoes of the past within their unconscious. The student's already heightened tendency to minimize the client's degree of choice is compounded when working in such settings.

The existential definition of *transference*, on the other hand, places more emphasis on the client's capacity to choose. Rollo May (1958) reminds his readers that constructs like transference draw considerable meaning from the client's immediate circumstances in the session. For May to hypothesize that a client is so demanding because she or he is trying to capture her or his father's love "may be a relief and may also be in fact true." But the crux of the matter, May continues, is that the client "is doing this to me in this given moment, and the reasons it occurs at this instant . . . are not exhausted by" how the client and father related (p. 83). In other words, earlier dynamics and displaced feelings cannot completely explain a client's motivations. The client is also motivated by more contemporary reasons. It may be true that this individual has somehow acquired a distorted way of interpreting and interacting with others, but more important is the fact that she or he is right now using that particular style. To some degree, May concludes, the client is choosing to act in that manner to a real person in that room at that minute.

An Acknowledgment of the Limits of Action

Amid all this accent on choice, however, it should not escape consideration that individuals also live within constraints. We suggested earlier that student therapists at times underestimate their clients' capacity for choice. This may in part reflect the very real, limiting circumstances with which their clients often struggle. Many students work in community mental health settings and see extremely low-fee clients, some of whom live in conditions of poverty, homelessness, and intense discrimination. Many other students work in medical milieus where they witness the physical and social constraints that disability or illness place on clients.

Theories that emphasize human potential without a concomitant focus on limitation may inadvertently lead students to blame clients for not changing their outward circumstances. Existential psychotherapists recognize and articulate the onerous press of one's social world. Seemingly vain and hopeless experiences, like those endured by concentration camp prisoners or the mythical Sisyphus (Frankl, 1992; Camus, 1942/1991; May, 1991), for instance, occupy a sobering place in existential thought. Existentialists do not flinch from considering those instances where tangible choices of action are nearly absent.

Existential psychology goes further, though, and emphasizes the transformative power one possesses even in these outwardly hopeless predicaments. Individuals are still capable of choosing the meanings they ascribe to their situation, we are reminded. Writing of his own Nazi captivity, Frankl (1992) asserts that a person can be stripped of all "but one thing: the last of the human freedoms — to choose one's attitude in any given set of circumstances, to choose one's own way . . . [in his case, to avoid being] molded into the form of the typical inmate" (p. 75). Refusing to relinquish this sort of choice in the face of constraint, an existentialist would argue, helps preserve the humanity of the human being.

Students working with clients in severely constrained external circumstances can thus be assured that their awareness of limitation will find expression in existential psychology. Importantly, existential psychology also acknowledges individuals' ability (at least inwardly) to transform their social world. This offers the student a realistic base on which to anchor clinical interventions and a way for both therapist and client to coax meaning from despair.

An Emphasis on Phenomenological Formulations

We have said that part of the challenge of training involves tapping a theoretical orientation when conceptualizing one's clinical work without letting theory obscure the client. Advanced students are expected to use clinical theory in a thorough and formal manner that makes preserving a sense of the client's uniqueness all the more important. These students are frequently asked to integrate the available information about their clients and present "case formulations" in supervision and seminars. The presentations may entail explaining the nature of their clients' defenses, core conflicts, symptoms, level of functioning, personality structure, and diagnostic category. This type of formulation encourages valuable reflection, but the therapist can slip into perceiving the dynamic and unfolding client in a static and self-fulfilling manner.

One's client can become first a "case" and then a "category" ("borderline," for example). What follows from this clinical shorthand is the danger of replacing the individual with a construct ("borderlines tend to . . ."). Yet, to be effective guides, therapists obviously need a coherent understanding of their clients' problems and clear therapeutic strategies. They also need to be able to communicate the basis of their strategies to other clinicians.

An existential approach to formulating client problems and strengths does not ignore diagnostic evaluation or consideration of defenses and conflicts. However, existential formulations are based less on existing clinical and diagnostic categories than they are on the client's phenomenology. The approach emphasizes the personal experience of each client. One attempts to bring a fresh and relatively unbiased mindset to a consideration of the individual's situation.

An existential psychotherapist might begin a formulation by considering questions of the following nature: What is this client's particular pain? How would the client evaluate his or her day-to-day living? What is getting in the client's way? In what ways is this client getting in his or her own way? How is the client right now treating us both? How am I experiencing this client? How well is the client able to notice his or her own reactions as well as those of others? This kind of reflection keeps the focus on the client and therapist in the moment and can thus be especially constructive for students. Creating and presenting formulations during training tends to be quite anxiety provoking. The thought of evaluation is constant and can draw students away from therapeutic concerns into solely intellectual pursuits. Remaining committed to understanding and describing the client's world as she or he experiences it — even when formulating — helps students be sure they are focusing on the architecture, not the scaffolding.

We have mentioned only a few of the challenges students encounter in training to be psychotherapists. First of all, student clinicians must come to terms with the amount of information clients present and must work *with* the client instead of unilaterally applying interventions. Students often turn to a particular theoretical orientation in their training and receive valuable guidance and vantage points. However, they must resist letting theory impede their view of the client as a complex and unique individual. Students also face more specific challenges, like remaining attuned to the client's shifting verbal and nonverbal nuances, maintaining belief in the client's ability to effect change, recognizing a client's external constraints without despair, and formulating client material in ways that summarize without distorting.

As we discussed, existential psychology offers considerable help in meeting these challenges. It does so because of its emphasis on the client's immediate experiencing and its focus on our significant capacity for choice. Further, it distinguishes freedom of action from freedom of interpretation and takes a more phenomenologically based approach to formulation. Put simply, existential psychology anchors students to the individuality of their clients.

Thus far, we have restricted our comments to students in formal training. Yet to speak of the client as an individual is to recognize that therapy with him or her will be a novel experience and will require learning a new dialect. In this way, all clinicians are to some degree students and may find a number of their concerns addressed within existential psychology as well.

Notes

1. The validity of so-called objective measures of psychological functioning (including those used in pre- and posttherapy studies) has cogently been called into question recently (see Shedler, Mayman, & Manis, 1993, for an elaboration.)

References

Camus, A. (1991). *The myth of Sisyphus and other essays* (J. O'Brien, Trans.). New York: Vintage Books. (Original work published 1942)

Frankl, V. (1992). *Man's search for meaning: An introduction to logotherapy* (4th ed., I. Lasch, Trans., Part 1). New York: Beacon.

May, R. (1958). Contributions of existential psychology. In R. May, E. Angel, & H. Ellenberger (Eds.), *Existence: A new dimension in psychiatry and psychology* (pp. 37–91). New York: Basic Books.

May, R. (1991). *The cry for myth*. New York: Norton.

Schneider, K. J. (1990). The worship of food: An existential perspective. *Psychotherapy*, *27*, 95–97.

Yalom, I. (1980). *Existential psychotherapy*. New York: Basic Books.

Part 2
Guideposts to an Existential-Integrative (EI) Approach

The purpose of this section is to provide a theoretical framework for an existential-integrative (EI) approach to therapy. The discussion to follow illustrates one way to understand and coordinate a variety of mainstream practices within an overarching existential framework.[1] The aims of this endeavor are severalfold: to clarify what existential therapists do and how they do it, to broaden the practice options of existential and mainstream therapists, and to elucidate the conditions under which certain practice modalities may have optimal effects. The final aim of this section is to set the table for the rich array of case illustrations to follow. These illustrations both draw on and elaborate the EI model.

Although cited favorably by a growing body of literature (e.g., Cooper, 2003; Cummings & Cummings, 2000; Greenberg, Watson, & Lietaer, 1998; Mendelowitz & Schneider, 2008; Watson & Bohart, 2002), the EI approach remains provisional. It is a preliminary set of guidelines that are based on my own theoretical and therapeutic synthesis (Schneider, 1990/1999, 1998, 2003, 2006). For the purposes of this text, I have broadened this synthesis, integrated it with other therapies, and formalized its implications for practice.

The attempt to formulate an existential-integrative standpoint — although theoretically justified — has exceedingly few precedents in the therapy literature (Beutler & Clarkin, 1990). It remains for future research, therefore — in particular that of the phenomenological variety — to assess and refine it (see Elliott, 2002; Rennie, 2002; Walsh & McElwain, 2002; Wertz, 2002).[2]

How This Section Is Organized

To help readers navigate this lengthy section, I provide the following thumbnail sketch:

First, I set forth the theory of the EI approach — therapy as liberation conditions,[3] consciousness as liberation levels, and experiential consciousness as the culmination of those levels.

Second, I elaborate on the personality dynamics that characterize the experiential (and every other) level — the capacities to constrict, expand, and center oneself — and the functional and dysfunctional implications of those dynamics.

Third, I lay out the therapeutic guidelines implied by the theory — how to discern appropriate liberation conditions, when and how to shift among liberation conditions, and ways to deepen (i.e., move toward) the experiential core of those conditions.

Fourth, I focus on the experiential liberation condition itself. This condition embraces four basic stances: (1) presence, (2) invoking the actual, (3) vivifying and confronting resistance (or self-protections), and (4) the rediscovery of meaning and awe.

I conclude the section, finally, with summaries illustrating the experiential liberation condition, a summary of the decision points leading up to (or away from) the experiential liberation condition, and a set of skill-building exercises designed to apply the experiential liberation condition.

Notes

1. Those wishing to apply this approach should have basic knowledge of clinical theory and practice and be appropriately trained or supervised.
2. Although attempts have been made to integrate so-called existential practices into mainstream or transtheoretical frameworks (e.g., see Prochaska & DiClemente, 1986; Beutler & Clarkin, 1990), few attempts, to my knowledge, have aimed at integrating mainstream approaches into the existential outlook. (See Bugental, 1978, 1987, for fine but brief exceptions; Koestenbaum, 1978, for a philosophical integration; and Barton, 1974, for a synthesis of Freud, Jung, and Rogers.)

   The framework I am about to present, moreover (which I have elsewhere called the *paradox principle* [Schneider, 1990/1999]), possesses at least one more novel feature — an existential metapsychology. I will elaborate upon this metapsychology (e.g., its dynamic and developmental features), discuss its relevance to therapy integration, and apply it to the clinical context.

   Finally, I cannot overstate the need for students to begin appropriately investigating proposals such as the above. I strongly hope they will take up the cause.
3. *Conditions* (which can also be viewed as *offerings*, *stances*, *modalities*, or *strategies*) are to be understood not as therapist-imposed solutions, but as catalysts to eventual client-based discoveries. As we shall see, this axiom holds for each of the liberation modalities, but it is especially salient where clients' responsibility for change is greatest — the experiential modality.

References

Barton, A. (1974). *Three worlds of therapy: Freud, Jung, and Rogers.* Palo Alto, CA: National Press Books.

Beutler, L., & Clarkin, J. (1990). *Systematic treatment selection: Toward targeted therapeutic interventions.* New York: Brunner/Mazel.

Bugental, J. F. T. (1978). *Psychotherapy and process: The fundamentals of an existential-humanistic approach.* Reading, MA: Addison-Wesley.

Bugental, J. F. T. (1987). *The art of the psychotherapist.* New York: Norton.

Cooper, M. (2003). *Existential therapies.* London: Sage.

Cummings, N., & Cummings, J. (2000). *The essence of psychotherapy.* New York: Academic Press.

Elliott, R. (2002). The effectiveness of humanistic therapies: A meta-analysis. In D. Cain & J. Seeman (Eds.), *Humanistic psychotherapies: Handbook of research and practice* (pp. 57–81). Washington, DC: APA Press.

Greenberg, L., Watson, J., & Lietaer, G. (Eds.). (1998). *Handbook of experiential psychotherapy.* New York: Guilford.

Koestenbaum, P. (1978). *The new image of the person: The theory and practice of clinical philosophy.* Westport, CT: Greenwood.

Mendelowitz, E., & Schneider, K. (2008). Existential psychotherapy. In R. Corsini and D. Wedding (Eds.), *Current psychotherapies* (8th ed., pp. 295-327). Belmont, CA: Thompson/Brook Cole.

Prochaska, J., & DiClemente, C. (1986). The transtheoretical approach. In J. Norcross (Ed.), *Handbook of eclectic psychotherapy* (pp. 163–200). New York: Brunner/Mazel.

Rennie, D. (2002). Experiencing psychotherapy: Grounded theory studies. In D. Cain & J. Seeman (Eds.), *Humanistic psychotherapies: Handbook of research and practice* (pp. 117–144). Washington, DC: APA Press.

Schneider, K. J. (1998). Existential processes. In L. Greenberg, J. Watson, & G. Lietaer (Eds.), *Handbook of experiential psychotherapy* (pp. 103–120). New York: Guilford.

Schneider, K. J. (1999). *The paradoxical self: Toward an understanding of our contradictory nature.* Amherst, NY: Humanity Books. (Original work published 1990)

Schneider, K. J. (2003). Existential-humanistic psychotherapies. In A. Gurman & S. Messer (Eds.), *Essential psychotherapies* (pp. 149–181). New York: Guilford.

Schneider, K. J. (Writer). American Psychological Association (Producer). (2006) *Existential Therapy* [Motion picture in the Systems of Psychotherapy Series 1]. (Available from the American Psychological Association, 750 First Street, NE, Washington, DC 20002–4242)

Walsh, R., & McElwain, B. Existential psychotherapies. In D. Cain & J. Seeman (Eds.), *Humanistic psychotherapies: Handbook of research and practice* (pp. 253–278). Washington, DC: APA Press.

Watson, J., & Bohart, A. (2002). Humanistic-experiential therapies in the era of managed care. In K. Schneider, J. Bugental, & J. Pierson (Eds.), *The handbook of humanistic psychology: Leading edges in theory, practice, and research* (pp. 503–517). Thousand Oaks, CA: Sage.

Wertz, F. (2002). Humanistic psychology and the qualitative research tradition. In K. Schneider, J. Bugental, & J. Pierson (Eds.), *The handbook of humanistic psychology: Leading edges in theory, practice, and research* (pp. 247–262). Thousand Oaks, CA: Sage.

3

Theory of the Existential-Integrative (EI) Approach

Therapy as Liberation Conditions/Consciousness as Liberation Levels

The chief aim of existential-integrative (EI) therapy, as Rollo May (1981) put it, is "to set people free" — physically, mentally, and spiritually (p. 19). For our purposes, *freedom* is the perceived capacity for choice within the natural and self-imposed limitations of living. These limitations include (but are not exhausted by) culture, genes, biology, and cosmic destiny, such as earthquakes (May, 1981). The maximization of freedom, then, is the core emphasis of EI therapy; moreover, there are many levels at which such freedom (choice) can be maximized (e.g., the physiological, the cognitive-behavioral, the interpersonal, and so on). There are also a range of proximities (e.g., from the relatively external — physical — to the relatively internal — attitudinal) with which people can experience freedom. Now the great question, of course, is how to facilitate such liberation and under what conditions.

Let us begin our inquiry by considering the following hypothetical position. Human experience (or *consciousness*) can be understood in terms of six (intertwining and overlapping) levels of freedom (see Figure 3.1): (1) the physiological, (2) the environmental, (3) the cognitive, (4) the psychosexual, (5) the interpersonal, and (6) the experiential (*being*). These levels (or *spheres*) of consciousness reflect increasing degrees of freedom within an ever-deepening domain. The outermost (physiological) level, for example, is a simpler and more restrictive manifestation of the environmental level, the environmental level is a simpler and more restrictive manifestation of the cognitive level, and so on.[1]

The range of freedom at any given level is a function of the domain that delineates that level. One's experience of physiological (or *organic*) freedom, for example, is both activated and delimited by one's ancestry, physical disposition, diet, exercise quota, substance use (e.g., drugs or alcohol), and other genetic and biochemical equivalents.

One's experience of environmental freedom is similarly delineated by classical and operant conditioning phenomena (see Skinner, 1953; Wolpe, 1969). To the degree that one can manipulate conditioned and unconditioned stimuli (as in desensitization and graded-exposure procedures) or positive

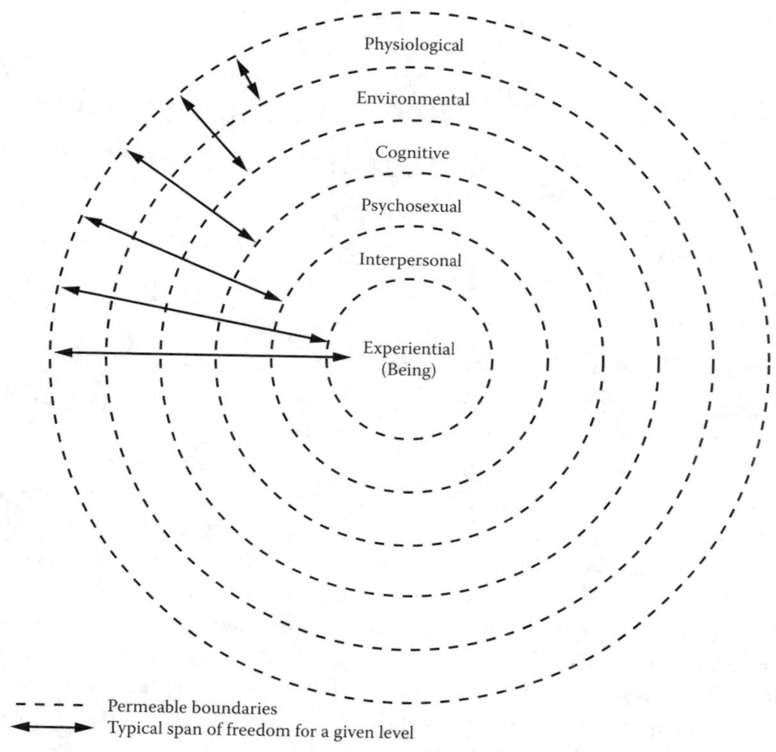

Figure 3.1 Levels or spheres of consciousness. The levels of consciousness are overlapping and intertwined: The differences among them are a matter of emphasis.

and negative reinforcement contingencies (as in reward and avoidance stratagems), one can attain measurable, observable environmental mastery. An example might be rewarding oneself with a vacation for keeping up a high grade average.

Cognitive freedom is demarcated by the principles of logic and rational thought (Beck, 1976; Ellis, 1962). One experiences freedom to the extent that one can identify maladaptive schemas (e.g., beliefs, assumptions, and self-statements); change those schemas through practice; and adopt new schemas based on rational and objective evidence. Some of the strategies one might use to bring about this level of liberation are rational restructuring, positive reframing, social modeling, thought stopping, thought rehearsal, and guided visualization. Using one of these strategies might bring about the recognition that one is not a worthless or hopeless person just because of an unsuccessful conversation with a potential romantic partner, for example.

Until now, I have considered relatively conscious and measurable forms of psychophysiological* liberation. I have considered choice at the level of biochemistry, environmental manipulation, and specifiable thought processes. Now, let us shift our emphasis to comparatively subconscious, nonquantifiable psychophysiological experiences. These experiences are posited to underlie and sometimes subvert the above physiological, environmental, and cognitive levels of freedom (May, 1958; Schneider, 1990/1999).

Freedom at the level of psychosexuality, for example, entails clarification and integration of one's sexual-aggressive past; to the degree that this is not accomplished, one is considered pathogenically vulnerable (Freud, 1927/1963). Liberation at this level means the strengthening of the ego — the capacity to maximize instinct gratification (sexual-aggressive expressiveness) while minimizing a sense of punishment and guilt (superego repressiveness). Imbalances toward either overgratification or repression are considered compulsive and therefore unfree. Psychosexual liberation is facilitated by the psychoanalytic techniques of free association, interpretation of the resistances and transference, intellectual insight, and dream interpretation. The emphasis here is on a cognitive understanding of the relationship between present relationships and past psychosexual conflicts. The therapist serves as a surrogate parent here, clarifying and correcting the client's distorted psychosexual reminiscences. For example, the therapist would help the client understand how the childhood dread of castration might manifest itself as an adult fear of assertiveness.

Freedom at the level of interpersonal relations (such as that illustrated by self-psychology) both acknowledges and transcends freedom at the level of psychosexual relations (Kohut, 1977). The operative dimensions here are interpersonal attachment and separation, not merely drives and social prohibitions. Freedom at the interpersonal level balances individual striving and uniqueness with interpersonal dependence and connectedness. Although interpersonal liberation also stresses the understanding of early childhood dynamics, the specific components of those dynamics differ from the components of psychosexual liberation. They include (but are not limited to) desires for and frustrations with affection, nurturance, validation, encouragement, and social/moral direction. Interpersonal liberation is facilitated not only by intellectual insight but also by re-experiencing the past in the present. The therapist-client relationship is the vehicle for this re-experience, and current separation-attachment issues are focused upon. With time and an appropriately corrective therapeutic experience, the client comes to value her capacity both for separateness and for relatedness and is markedly less coerced by

* Unless otherwise indicated, the *holistic* (complex, ambiguous, and intertwining) nature of terms such as *psychophysiological* is always implied (see Merleau-Ponty, 1962, for an elaboration).

either position. For example, she might re-experience early nurturance deficits and work through the resultant fears, frustrations, and overcompensations associated with this damage.

Forming the core of our spectrum, finally, is what I term *experiential freedom*, which might also be called *being level* or *ontological freedom*. Experiential liberation embraces not only physiology, environmental conditioning, cognition, psychosexuality, and interpersonal relations, but also cosmic or intersituational relations — the whole human being as far as possible (Merleau-Ponty, 1962). Experiential liberation is intersituational in that it pertains not merely to this or that content or period of one's life, but to the preverbal/kinesthetic awarenesses that underlie contents or periods of one's life. Put another way, experiential liberation is a "reoccupation project" — clients are supported to "reoccupy " (e.g., embody) the parts of themselves that have been denied. The more that clients are able to reoccupy themselves, the more they are able to both access and express hitherto estranged dimensions of themselves, and it is these very dimensions that deepen people's appreciation for life (see also Bugental, 1978; Tillich, 1967, p. 109).

Occasionally this appreciation leads to awe — a sense of profound humility, not just before a particular *way* of being, but before being itself; and this humility is also linked with wonder — a capacity to marvel at, explore, and even navigate vast ranges of what had formerly been prohibited to one. The result is that experiential liberation — through awe — can recast an extraordinary range of life difficulties: from the despairing to the grandiose, from the hate filled to the apathetic. The question for the sufferer is: To what degree will experiential liberation lift him out of narrow identifications and fill him with an appreciation for all of life's dimensions — the tragic as well as the transcendent — and enhance, thereby, his capacity to will (Pierson, 2002; Schneider, 2004; Yalom, 1980)?

Experiential liberation is affect centered and has a host of historical influences. It compares favorably, for example, to Merleau-Ponty's (1962) "body-subject," Wilhelm Reich's (1949) "bioenergy," and Morris Berman's (1989) "kinesthetic awareness." Each is centered in the body, and each attends to the relatively nonmediated consciousness that radiates through the body.[2] Experiential liberation, finally, is also client centered — derivative of and pertinent to the client's own particular struggles. This is not to say that the therapist's and society's concerns are dismissed in experiential liberation. Unquestionably, they cannot be dismissed and should be raised responsibly in the course of therapy. However, the ultimate criteria for experiential liberation reside in clients' awarenesses, and it is they who must live with the consequences of those criteria.

One of the best illustrations of experiential liberation is Dante Alighieri's *Inferno*, in *The Divine Comedy* (see May, 1991; Schneider & May, 1995). In this classic parable, Dante finds himself lost in a dark woods. He is alone and middle aged. Soon he encounters Virgil, who will accompany him into his "hell." It is no accident that I use the term *accompany* in connection with Virgil. Virgil does not advise Dante about going into his hell; nor does he attempt to explain that hell to Dante. Furthermore, he does not talk about the hell to Dante. He does not rationally restructure, reprogram, tranquilize, or cheer Dante up about his hell. By contrast, Virgil joins, stays present to, and makes himself available for Dante on his labyrinthine journey.

For me, Virgil epitomizes the experiential therapist. This is because through Virgil's presence, Dante is able to discover the resources within himself to deal with and work through his hell. Put another way, Virgil neither directs Dante nor abandons him, but steadfastly contains, evokes, and reflects Dante back to himself. Virgil holds up a series of mirrors to Dante that help him to see what he struggles with, what blocks him from that struggle, and what resources he can muster to overcome that blockage. Through Virgil, Dante is able to face himself, to face the chaotic and obliterating levels of his suffering, and to "occupy" new ranges of himself (as exemplified by the final installment of *The Divine Comedy: the Paradiso*).

To elaborate, experiential liberation is distinguished by four intertwining and overlapping dimensions: (1) the immediate, (2) the kinesthetic, (3) the affective, and (4) the profound or cosmic. These dimensions form the ground, or horizon, within which each of the aforementioned liberation conditions operates, and they are the context for at least one more clinically significant set of structures. These are, according to phenomenological research, the capacities to constrict, expand, and center one's energies and experiences (Becker, 1973; Binswanger, 1975; Guntrip, 1969; Keleman, 1985; Laing, 1969; May, 1969, 1981; Schneider, 1990/1999, 1993; Tillich, 1952; Yalom, 1980). *Expansion* is the perception of bursting forth and extending psychophysiologically; *constriction* is the perception of drawing back and confining psychophysiologically.* Expansion is associated with a sense of advancing, enlarging, dispersing, ascending, filling, accelerating, or, in short, *increasing* psychophysiological capacities. Constriction, on the other hand, is signified by the perception of retreating, restricting, isolating, falling, emptying, slowing, or, in short, *reducing* psychophysiological capacities. Finally, *centering* is the capacity to be aware of and direct one's constrictive or expansive possibilities.

Constriction and expansion form a potentially infinite continuum, only degrees of which are conscious. Constrictive or expansive dream fantasies

* Although *expansion* is often associated with *freedom*, and *constriction* with *limits*, they are not always synonymous terms. Restraint, focus, and discipline, for example, can be freeing in some contexts; conversely, activism, assertion, and audacity can be limiting (e.g., when compulsively engaged). In the balance of this text, therefore, freedom and limitation are viewed primarily as *contexts* for constriction and expansion, and not their conceptual equivalents.

(e.g., ones in which humiliation or vengeance play a role) may be *sub*conscious. The further one pursues constriction, the closer one gets to a sense of being "wiped away," obliterated. The further one pursues expansion, the closer one gets to an equally excessive perception of "exploding," entering chaotic nonentity (Laing, 1969). (I use the prefix *hyper-* with *constriction* or *expansion* to designate the dysfunctional or unmanageable engagement of either polarity.) *Dread* of constriction or expansion (due mainly to past trauma) fosters extreme or dysfunctional counterreactions to those polarities. This sets up a situation where, for example, expansive grandiosity becomes an escape from, or a counterreaction to, the constrictive belittlement one experienced as a child; or constrictive rigidity becomes an avoidance of the expansive disarray and confusion one experienced in a natural disaster. Confrontation with the constrictive or expansive dreads, on the other hand, can promote renewed capacities to experience the world (e.g., from a standpoint of humility for the grandiose client or from the standpoint of spontaneity for the rigid client).

These two polar eventualities — chaos and obliteration, greatness and smallness — haunt the entire spectrum of freedoms (see Figure 3.2).* They constitute both the dreads and the possibilities underlying physiological excitation (e.g., elation) and inhibition (e.g., tranquility), conditioned recklessness (e.g., conduct disorders) and withdrawal (e.g., phobias), cognitive exaggeration (e.g., overgeneralization) and rigidity (e.g., dichotomous thinking), gluttony (e.g., promiscuity) and psychosexual austerity (e.g., abstinence), and separation (e.g., estrangement) and interpersonal attachment (e.g., dependency).

In sum, experiential liberation is facilitated by careful and sensitive therapeutic invitations to *stay present to* (explore) denied constrictive or expansive parts of oneself. The more these parts manifest anxiety (as opposed to intellectual or detached content), the closer they are purported to be to core constrictive or expansive injuries. The gradual integration of this (preverbal/kinesthetic) material and the sense that one can survive its chaotic or obliterating implications promotes health, vitality, and an enhanced appreciation for spiritual dimensions (e.g., awe, wonder, and connectedness with the cosmos). Although experiential liberation can help to open up extraordinary ranges of possibility, it is not purported to dissolve all conflict or puzzlements. To the contrary, it accepts the dialectical condition *between* self and not-self, freedom and limits, and helps clients to find *optimal* rather than *consummate* meanings (Bugental, 1987; May, 1981; Schneider, 1987, 1989). The implication here is that although there are always more possibilities for constrictive or expansive encounters, we cannot always reach or bear them. It is enough, at this level,

* There is an intimate connection, it seems, between our most gripping anxieties (e.g., greatness, smallness) and the primordial forces of the universe (e.g., the big bang) — and the reports of clients confirm it (Grotstein, 1990; Schneider, 1990/1999, 1993).

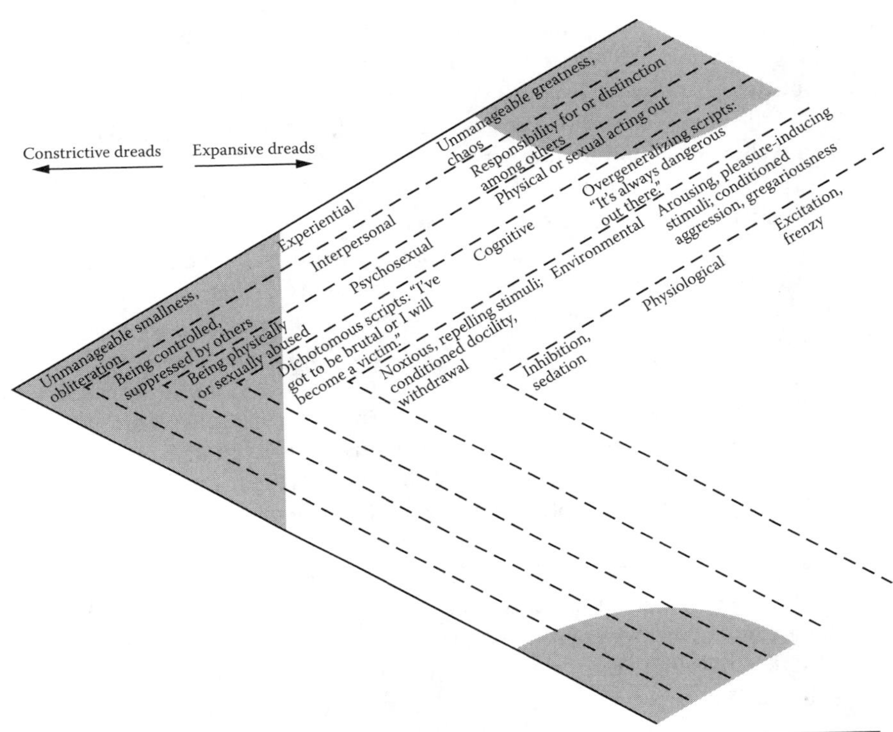

Figure 3.2 Levels of consciousness and associated dreads (cross section of Figure 3.1). These are just a few examples of the dreads (and sometimes fascinations) that can be associated with each of the levels. Shaded sections pertain to regions that many people experience symbolically and subconsciously.

to emancipate key blocks and anxieties to, for example, overcome one's timid, reticent disposition by confronting one's deepest revulsions to brazenness.

Constriction (Smallness) and Expansion (Greatness) as Omnipresent Horizons

Abraham Maslow (1967) once observed that we fear our greatness as well as our lowliness, and this is precisely the core dilemma from the existential-integrative standpoint. As I have suggested, the fears of both constriction and expansion (or their clinically useful synonyms, *smallness* and *greatness*) haunt the entire spectrum of existential freedoms. They are the keys, moreover, to a full existential restoration. Before considering the clinical consequences of these contentions, however, let us attempt to formalize what I have proposed thus far.

1. The human psyche (*consciousness*) is characterized by two polar positions: the capacity to constrict (make oneself small) and the capac-

ity to expand (make oneself great). Constriction and expansion form a continuum, only degrees of which is conscious. For the purposes of the EI framework, consider six positions along this continuum: (a) the physiological, (b) the environmental, (c) the cognitive, (d) the psychosexual, (e) the interpersonal, and (f) the experiential (*being*). Whereas physiological, environmental, and cognitive positions along the continuum are dominated by extrinsic, conscious processing, psychosexual, interpersonal, and experiential modalities are accented by intrinsic and pre- and subconscious mediation.

2. Dread of constrictive or expansive polarities promotes dysfunction, extremism, or polarization, the degree and frequency of which is generally proportional to the degree and frequency of one's dread. Put another way, one will do everything one can, including becoming extreme and destructive oneself, to avoid the constrictive or expansive polarity that one dreads. The dread of physiological expansion (*arousal*), for example, can promote extreme or dysfunctional measures to constrict (*pacify*) oneself. The conditioned fear of enclosures (constriction) can foster excessive efforts to enlarge or expand one's surroundings. The dread of catastrophic (expansive) cognitions can associate with narrow, regimented cognitions. The revulsion from a constricted puritanical upbringing can correlate with an indulgent, expansive adulthood. The horror of a directionless, rootless upbringing, on the other hand, can generate absolutist and fundamentalist tendencies later in life. The terror of being ontologically and cosmically dismissed (*obliterated*), finally, can lead to desperate psychophysiological efforts to manifest ontologically, to be all-important. (This, too often, tragically leads back again to the impoverished position because aspirations of the former magnitude cannot be borne for long; consider, for example, the experiential swings of the manic-depressive or borderline personality.) (See Table 3.1 for an elaboration on these dreads).
3. Stated in terms of the classic psychoanalytic formulation, *drive-anxiety-defense*, this experiential model proposes *awareness of potential for obliteration or chaos-anxiety-defense.* This formulation compares favorably with Yalom's (1980) notion of *awareness of existential "givens"* (i.e., death, freedom, isolation, and meaninglessness)-*anxiety-defense*, with one exception: I view the latter (givens) as secondary to the former (awareness of obliteration or chaos), and I view the former as echoing our central human challenge — the capacity to experience mystery (infinity, being) while being both daunted by and resourceful toward that mystery. For example, I view Yalom's death anxiety as anxiety about how we negotiate infinity (groundlessness, the vast unknown). I view his concern about freedom as a concern about how we handle unbounded expansion, extension, and disarray. I see his

Table 3.1 Some Psychiatric Disorders and Their Associated Dreads

Disorder	Dread
Hyperconstrictive Patterns and the Dread of Ultimate Expansion (Greatness, Chaos)	
Depression	Assertion, stimulation, ambition, standing out, possibility
Dependency	Autonomy, venturing out on one's own, unmanageable responsibility
Anxiety	Potency and its associated risks, responsibilities, strains; also, foolishness, spontaneity, unpredictability
Agoraphobia	Open places, conflict, confusion
Obsessive-compulsiveness	Experimentation, surprise, confusion and complexity, disarray, recklessness
Paranoia	Trusting, reaching out, the confusion, complexity, brutality of relationships
Depressant substance abuse (e.g., Valium, alcohol[a])	All of the above
Hyperexpansive Patterns and the Dread of Ultimate Constriction (Smallness, Obliteration)	
Mania	Confinement, limitation, delay of impulses, devitalization
Antisocial personality	Vulnerability, weakness, victimization
Hysteria	Rejection, insignificance
Narcissism	Inadequacy, unworthiness, impotence
Impulsiveness	Regimentation, routine, emptiness
Claustrophobia	Entrapment, tight or closed places
Stimulant substance abuse (e.g., speed, cocaine)	All of the above
Hyperconstrictive/Expansive Blends	
Passive-aggressivity	On the one hand, belittlement and, on the other, the rage or fury that results from that dread (the combination produces such blunted aggression as sarcasm and dawdling)
Borderline personality	Extreme belittlement, insignificance combined with extreme rage, fury (which leads to both fusion/tyranny and isolation/withdrawal)
Manic depression	Confinement, limitation, and delay, on the one hand, and assertion, stimulation, and ambition on the other
Schizophrenia	Vaporizing (which may lead to disorganized, omnipotence-striving states) and exploding (which may foster obsessive, catatonic-like qualities); schizophrenia associates with constrictive and expansive dreads in their most radical forms

Note: The relationship between the above clinical syndromes and the dreads that may give rise to them is theoretical and provisional. It is based on a small but intriguing body of clinical data, which implicates both temperament and psychological trauma (Schneider, 1990/1999). It remains for future research — especially of a phenomenological nature — to reconsider the soundness of these postulates.

[a] While alcohol is a depressant, it can also, paradoxically, serve to stimulate (*hyperexpand*) via its disinhibiting properties.

concern about isolation, correspondingly, as a reflection of how we handle a sense of cosmic separation, rootlessness — or, on the other hand, how we deal with our sense of cosmic smallness, nothingness. Finally, I view his accentuation on meaninglessness as a reflection of our struggle to make sense of our cosmic nothingness (smallness) and, at the same time, creativity (greatness). I view these givens from other standpoints as well, but predominantly from within the context of constrictive or expansive dread, desire, or resourcefulness (Schneider, 1990/1999, 1993, 2004).

Developmental View

Although the dread of (and compensation for) constrictive/expansive polarities can be seen at every existential level and is integral to the respective liberation of every level, its genesis is far from uniform. Constrictive or expansive dread can arise in a wide variety of spatial, temporal, and dispositional contexts. Let us consider several of the main ones here — acute, chronic, and implicit traumas (Schneider, 1990/1999).

Acute trauma is the perception of an event as immediately contrary and shocking. It is an existential jolt that produces extreme fear. When a child falls ill, for example, a profound alteration in mobility may be experienced. If this alteration is powerful enough, it can alarm the child, not merely at the level of physiology (pleasure-pain), but at the level of her groundedness in the world. It may associate with mortal fears of diminishment, minimization, imperceptibility, and perhaps even dissolution. The intensity of the child's fear is a function of many factors, including (but not limited to) her original psychophysiological disposition (i.e., her hardiness level), the severity of her illness, the cultural and familial contexts in which she contracts the illness, and so on. Discrepancy is the key here. The greater she experiences a discrepancy between her original disposition and subsequent events, the greater is the likelihood that she will deny those subsequent events and hence become experientially debilitated. Such debilitation is likely to manifest itself initially in the form of excessive efforts to expand (e.g., cry out, refuse, defy) her condition of growing immobilization. If these protestations prove comparatively viable, she will be able to maintain her denial of smallness and live out her life in a variety of compensatory fashions. Depending on the severity and subsequent handling of her trauma, accordingly, she is likely to exhibit a range of expansionist traits, from exuberance and feistiness to outright belligerence and imperiousness.

If, on the other hand, the child's attempts to deny her illness are repeatedly and unabatingly rebuffed, then another traumatic cycle may develop — that of *chronic trauma*. Whereas acute trauma focuses on the original dread of constricting (i.e., of becoming immobilized), chronic trauma centers on the counteraction of that dread (fruitless and repeated efforts to become mobilized, expand). The result of this shift is a complete reversal of the original situation. Instead of denying and overcompensating for psychophysiological smallness, the client now does everything she can to render herself small and to avoid psychophysiological greatness.

The third scenario for developing constrictive or expansive trauma is the subtler cycle of intergenerational, or implicit, trauma (see the family systems literature [e.g., McGoldrick & Gerson, 1985] for a fuller discussion of this cycle). *Implicit trauma* is the indirect, vicariously transmitted trauma of family and caretakers. Unlike acute and chronic trauma, implicit trauma is never directly experienced by the affected individuals but is learned, accepted, and stored in their memories. While the basis for implicit trauma is relatively obscure, both initial disposition and modeling appear to play instrumental roles. The implicit-traumatic sequence goes something like this: A family member, say our hypothetical client, experiences acute or chronic trauma. Her trauma (i.e., her fear of immobility) leads, in turn, to compensatory behavior (such as overachieving) designed to thwart the precipitating injury. As this cycle solidifies in our client's personal life, it also begins to filter into her relationships with her children. It is at this point, predictably, that her children develop a risk for implicit trauma. For this to occur, however, two basic conditions must be met: (1) The children must idealize, and thereby strive to emulate, their mother's excesses, and (2) they must display inherent dispositions (e.g., ambitiousness) that comfortably conform to these excesses. Given these prime conditions, accordingly, immobility and smallness can prove far-ranging intergenerational enemies, unwittingly internalized and unknowingly transmitted. Only the broken-hearted casualties, such as those who fail to superachieve, can begin to unravel the contagion (Schneider, 1990/1999). Table 3.2 summarizes the three traumatic cycles.

The operation of the above traumas, as may be evident by now, is confined to neither period nor place, type of polarization (i.e., constrictive/expansive), or existential level (e.g., physiological). Although childhood, because of its comparative vulnerability, is more susceptible to traumatic impacts, such impacts are not restricted to childhood. Trauma originates not in relation to parents, peers, or any other stimulus per se, but in relation to being, to the groundlessness that is our condition. Hence, it is not so much the specific content of the abuse or pain that unnerves us so, but the implications of that content for our being in the world, for our relationship to the universe. It is in this sense that physical and emotional shocks, parents, family myths, and so on symbolize wider networks of alarm — our smallness or greatness before creation itself.

The third principle that has emerged from our existential-integrative formulation is that the confrontation with or integration of constrictive/expansive polarities promotes healing, vitality, and health. This principle also operates at various levels of freedom and can best be understood in terms of these

Table 3.2 Purported Operation of Three Traumatic Cycles

Type of Trauma	Perceived Subject's Disposition	Purported Environmental Demand	Psychological Effect on Subject
Acute	Constrictive	Expansive	↑[a] Constriction
	Expansive	Constrictive	↑ Expansion
	Neutral[b]	Expansive	↑ Constriction
	Neutral	Constrictive	↑ Expansion
Chronic	Constrictive	Expansive	↑ Expansion
	Expansive	Constrictive	↑ Constriction
	Neutral	Expansive	↑ Expansion
	Neutral	Constrictive	↑ Constriction
Implicit	Constrictive	Constrictive	↑/=[c] Constriction
	Expansive	Expansive	↑/= Expansion

[a] ↑ means increased constriction or expansion relative to one's disposition.

[b] *Neutral* means relatively nonpolarized.

[c] ↑/= means about the same or an increased degree of constriction or expansion relative to one's disposition.

Source: Schneider, K. J. (1990/1999). *The paradoxical self: Toward an understanding of our contradictory nature* (p. 85). Amherst, NY: Humanity Books.

levels. For example, constricting lethargy can be dealt with by nutritional regimens designed to release and expand energy. Expansive criminality can be environmentally modified to constrict via aversive and alternative reinforcements. Constrictive timidity, conversely, can be environmentally conditioned to expand (e.g., by confronting the object of dread). Rigid belief systems can be rationally restructured into expansive, adaptive belief systems. Sexually expansive adult behavior can be explained on the basis of sexually constrictive (or expansive) childhood behavior and thus rechanneled. Compulsive isolation (and constricting) can be explained and transcended through emotionally corrective bonding (and expanding). By facing and experiencing one's frailty, finally, one can learn to understand and transform one's pomposity.

Through these means, choice and the capacity for genuine self-encounter broaden while denial and overcompensation shrink. Far from associating with injuries, moreover, smallness and greatness begin associating with growth opportunities. For example, humility can replace docility, discipline can replace obsessiveness, and zest can replace inflation.

Now that we have considered the basic theoretical dynamics of existential-integrative therapy, it is time to put the picture together. It is time to reflect upon how and when to coordinate the EI framework and who or what determines its success.

Notes

1. This structure of consciousness is both provisional and revisable in the light of new evidence. It is a theoretically useful map, in other words, and is in no way intended to be taken as an actual or ultimate territory. In this way, I differentiate the EI structure from other developmental frameworks that imply ultimate or absolute truth as their zenith; my only zenith is mystery.
2. Body consciousness in this context differs from the physiological or organic consciousness I spoke of earlier. Whereas physiological or organic consciousness is relatively simple (i.e., circumscribed, excitatory), body consciousness is relatively complex (i.e., multitextured, sublime); and whereas physiological or organic consciousness is comparatively overt (i.e., measurable), body consciousness is comparatively intimate (i.e., qualitative). (See Merleau-Ponty, 1962, for an elaboration of these points.)

References

Beck, A. (1976). *Cognitive therapy and the emotional disorders*. New York: Signet.

Becker, E. (1973). *The denial of death*. New York: Free Press.

Berman, M. (1989). *Coming to our senses: Body and spirit in the hidden history of the West*. New York: Bantam.

Binswanger, L. (1975). *Being in the world: Selected papers of Ludwig Binswanger* (J. Needleman, Trans.). New York: Basic Books.

Bugental, J. F. T. (1978). *Psychotherapy and process: The fundamentals of an existential-humanistic approach*. Reading, MA: Addison-Wesley.

Bugental, J. F. T. (1987). *The art of the psychotherapist*. New York: Norton.

Ellis, A. (1962). *Reason and emotion in psychotherapy*. New York: Lyle Stuart.

Freud, S. (1963). *A general introduction to psychoanalysis* (J. Riviere, Trans.). New York: Pocket Books.

Grotstein, J. (1990). The black hole as the basic psychotic experience: Some newer psychoanalytic and neuroscience perspectives on psychosis. *Contemporary Psychoanalysis, 18*, 29–46.

Guntrip, H. (1969). *Schizoid phenomena, object-relations and the self*. New York: International Universities Press.

Keleman, S. (1985). *Emotional anatomy*. Berkeley, CA: Center Press.

Kohut, H. (1977). *The restoration of the self*. New York: International Universities Press.

Laing, R. D. (1969). *The divided self: An existential study in sanity and madness*. Middlesex, England: Penguin.

Maslow, A. (1967). Neurosis as a failure of personal growth. *Humanitas, 3*, 153–169.

May, R. (1958). Contributions of existential therapy. In R. May, E. Angel, & H. Ellenberger (Eds.), *Existence: A new dimension in psychiatry and psychology* (pp. 37–91). New York: Basic Books.

May, R. (1969). *Love and will*. New York: Norton.

May, R. (1981). *Freedom and destiny*. New York: Norton.

May, R. (1991). *The cry for myth*. New York: Norton.

McGoldrick, M., & Gerson, R. (1985). *Genograms in family assessment*. New York: Norton.

Merleau-Ponty, M. (1962). *Phenomenology of perception*. London: Routledge.

Pierson, J. (2002). Closing statement. In K. Schneider, J. Bugental, & J. Pierson (Eds.), *The handbook of humanistic psychology: Leading edges in theory, practice, and research* (pp. 669–671). Thousand Oaks, CA: Sage.
Reich, W. (1949). *Character analysis.* New York: Orgone Institute Press.
Reik, T. (1948). *Listening with the third ear.* New York: Farrar, Straus.
Schneider, K. J. (1987). The deified self: A "centaur" response to Wilber and the transpersonal movement. *Journal of Humanistic Psychology, 27,* 196–216.
Schneider, K. J. (1999). *The paradoxical self: Toward an understanding of our contradictory nature* (2nd ed.). Amherst, NY: Humanity Books. (Original work published 1990)
Schneider, K. J. (1992). Therapists' personal maturity and therapeutic success: How strong is the link? *The Psychotherapy Patient, 8,* 71–91.
Schneider, K. J. (1993). *Horror and the holy: Wisdom-teachings of the monster tale.* Chicago: Open Court.
Schneider, K. J. (2004). *Rediscovery of awe: Splendor, mystery, and the fluid center of life.* St. Paul, MN: Paragon House.
Schneider, K. J., & May, R. (1995). *The psychology of existence: An integrative, clinical perspective.* New York: McGraw-Hill.
Skinner, B. F. (1953). *Science and human behavior.* New York: Macmillan.
Tillich, P. (1952). *The courage to be.* New Haven, CT: Yale University Press.
Tillich, P. (1967). *My search for absolutes.* New York: Simon & Schuster.
Wolpe, J. (1969). *The practice of behavior therapy.* New York: Pergamon.
Yalom, I. (1980). *Existential psychotherapy.* New York: Basic Books.

4
Therapeutic Implications of the Theory

The question of coordination within the EI framework immediately raises a related problem: Given the premium placed on authenticity within existential practice philosophy (e.g., Bugental, 1965), how can a therapist coordinate (i.e., help to shape) a way of being with clients? This is a subtle yet critical issue that warrants further consideration. In my view, authenticity is a highly elusive concept that is rarely well defined. For example, if what we mean by authenticity is the quest for unbridled self-expression, then we open ourselves to an enormous and sometimes grotesque therapeutic range (Schneider, 1985). Everything from ill-timed to catastrophic disclosures has been justified by such a range, and there are few, if any, guide maps to steer the unwary. On the other hand, if authenticity is defined contextually rather than individually, then many aforementioned pitfalls can be avoided. The reason for this is that authenticity attuned to context (vs. therapeutic whim) sensitizes the facilitator to the client's capacity to receive his or her disclosure, and this receptivity, in turn, guides the facilitator. For me, disclosure that is capricious or haphazard is not honestly attuned to the potential barriers to such disclosure, such as the client's readiness to receive it, and is inauthentic therefore within that particular context. To sum, I view the EI therapist as authentic to the context of his or her relationship, rather than the content of his or her individuality (see contribution by Portnoy, Chapter 12). Within this context, the EI therapist discerns a wide range of therapeutic stances, each of which is called out by given relational demands, filtered through each therapist's unique relational style.

How to Discern Appropriate Liberation Conditions

Given the above, let us consider two key guideposts for the coordination of EI therapeutic modalities. The *client's desire and capacity for change* are the initial and ongoing discernment criteria for existential-integrative practice.[1] How does the therapist gauge this desire and capacity in the client? First, she needs to explore what it is the client *wants*. What are his short-term objectives and his long-term goals? Is he here to eliminate a particular symptom, such as a simple phobia? Or is he here to deal with complex personality issues, such as depression, anxiety, or hostility?

Next, the therapist needs to reflect on the client's *capacity* to liberate his life. Does he have the intellectual skills to sort through and grasp his predicament? Is he emotionally ready for intensive self-exploration? Does he have the ability to deliberate upon and pause over his struggle? To what extent is he delimited by cultural, financial, or geographical issues?

These lines of inquiry appear straightforward enough, but they are subtler (and more challenging) than they seem. How many clients, for example, present one set of issues upon intake only to alter their story three or four sessions later? Or how many clients state one concern (e.g., anger at a spouse) but imply another issue (e.g., damaged self-esteem)? As noted existential therapist James Bugental observed, one must do more than listen for words; one must hear the music behind those words (see also Reik, 1948). The EI therapist, similarly, must attune herself not only to clients' stated reasons, but also to their implied and evolving reasons for therapeutic engagement. To be sure, there are many potential pitfalls in this approach (such as misreading clients' interests). But there are even greater risks in refraining from such a course, risks ranging from shortchanging to prematurely aborting the therapeutic project (Bugental & Bracke, 1992).

Furthermore, there is a notable difference between a therapist who attunes to a client as a whole person (whose desire and capacity for change may or may not mirror his or her presenting disposition) and the "fix it" therapist who solely focuses on a client's symptoms. While the latter therapist may be viewed as more initially beneficial, there are instances in which this situation could (and often does) reverse itself: (1) if the client's deeper motives for seeking therapy are unacknowledged and (2) if the opportunity for deepening is unacknowledged.

Hence, the atmosphere that is created between therapist and client has a profound effect; not only does it impact clients' capacities for therapeutic change, but it also modulates their interest in, or even motivation for, such change.

In this context, I take issue with conventional therapeutic integrationists (e.g., Beutler & Clarkin, 1990) who base their practice decisions on overridingly statistical (and traditionally diagnostic) grounds. While it is true that depth therapists can make "unnecessarily complicated" judgments about clients, as Beutler and Clarkin suggested, it is also true that symptom-oriented therapists can make unwarrantedly facile and restricted therapeutic assessments (e.g., see discussions of this problem by May, 1983; Wolfe, 1992). The EI antidote for these equally undesirable alternatives is to cultivate what Rollo May (1992) calls "therapeutic wonder." *Therapeutic wonder* accepts the need for conventional, experimentally driven assessments, *but only in the context of kinesthetic and intuitive checks* against those assessments. This means that surface impressions about clients are taken seriously and get significant consideration when planning treatment. However — and this is where EI therapy can complement conventional integrationist approaches — supreme consideration is accorded to therapists' *lived* engagement with clients and to the latent possibilities therein.

For example, if a client presents with an ostensibly simple symptom, such as cowering before her boss, an EI therapist would (1) invite the client into a disarming field of presence, (2) assess the client's singleness of purpose toward her problem, (3) assess her capacity to therapeutically address this purpose, (4) begin opening experientially to the client's own experiential communication (e.g., lability, touchiness around other issues, and so on), and (5) stand ready to invite or gently challenge the client to deeper spheres of liberation.*

Most often, in my experience, this sequence of evaluative criteria helps therapists and clients to make substantive, relevant treatment decisions. Usually these decisions favor broad- rather than narrowband therapeutic conditions (e.g., psychodynamic and behavioral as opposed to behavioral techniques only) to achieve their intended effects. (This is not always the case, however, and integrative approaches become relatively superfluous at such times.)

On the pages to follow, accordingly, I will focus on the decision to use broadband approaches to therapy. My special emphasis, of course, will be on the existential core of those approaches — the being, or experiential, level — and the primary offerings of that domain. Before I turn to this level, however, it is necessary to examine the use of relatively nonexperiential (i.e., conscious/programmatic/verbal) modalities as they are understood within the EI framework.

The Offering of Nonexperiential Liberation

Part of the therapeutic liberator's task is to recognize when curtailments are called for — nonexperiential footholds along the toilsome journey within. These footholds (which are facilitated by physiological, behavioral, and cognitive treatment modalities) can serve a variety of purposes. They can contain clients' distress, elevate their motivation, and ready them for deeper self-contact. Let us look more closely at these purposes in a range of clinical situations.

Clients in Acute Crisis

When clients are emotionally overcome, when they are contemplating suicide, or when they are physically acting out, concrete, narrowband liberation modalities are often the optimal therapeutic choice. Interventions such as supportive reassurance, safety containment, behavioral contracting, meditative exercises, cognitive restructuring, and medication or hospitalization may

* It is extremely important, it seems to me, to be continually open to (and at appropriate times "test the water" for) new levels of depth in our contacts with clients. The fruit that such preparedness can yield — in even the least likely clinical circumstances — is perpetually astonishing to me.

be the most helpful immediate steps. Although these steps are transitional within the EI framework, they can provide timely and productive reprieves.

During Early Stages of Therapy

Another period during which nonexperiential footholds can be relevant is at the outset of treatment. Reframing confusing or fragmentary material, for example, can help beginning clients acquire the patience necessary to address that material. For example, the therapist might say, "Your father just died, you just graduated from college, and your girlfriend has abandoned you for another man. It's no wonder you're feeling rocky." Homework assignments such as simple breathing exercises or positive visualizations can provide a soothing margin of safety in anticipation of intensive self-confrontation. I have found that counting breaths (1 to 10 and back down again) and visualizing temporary "storage bins" for troubling issues can be especially useful at these early stages.

Frequently, cognitive-behavioral techniques can provide a fertile opening for more experientially oriented interventions. Suggesting habit changes for compulsive eaters, for example, can be readily followed up with experiential questions and concerns. These questions might include, "What feelings does it bring up for you to eliminate junk foods from your diet?" "In what way is that reward you give yourself dissatisfying?" "What kinds of feelings come up when you cannot follow the grocery route we designed?" Cognitive restructuring can also stimulate experiential inquiry. For example, the therapist might say, "You asked one person on one day if he might be interested in getting together with you. What makes it so hard for you to try again?" or "There you go again, portraying yourself as unredeemably evil. I wonder what comes up for you as you stay present to that feeling? Do any other images or sensations arise?" The failure of cognitive techniques can further stimulate experiential inquiries such as, "What's going on that you can no longer make positive statements toward yourself?" The therapist might also suggest: "Instead of attending to what is reasonable, let's look at what you want to do right now."

Fragile or Highly Suspicious Clients

It is best to use explicit, low-pressure questions and suggestions when dealing with clients with extremely low self-esteem and tendencies toward paranoia. The most important initial task with such clients is to draw upon the aforementioned modalities to build an alliance. For example, simple, manageable tasks — making a call to a friend, reframing a catastrophic thought, structuring the week's activities — can contribute to the comfort level and effectiveness of the relationship. Although progress is likely to be slow, this safety net can help fragile and suspicious clients to stabilize, and increasingly to tolerate exploration.

Simple exercises, such as counting breaths or concentrative attunement to inhaling and exhaling, can also help to ground fearful or overstimulated clients. I have also found progressive relaxation (or the tensing and relaxing of group muscles throughout the body) to be notably decompressing for stressed or even depressed clients who need to learn how to self-soothe. Mindfulness meditation can also be an invaluable to tool to help clients begin the process of trust building and letting go.

Intellectually or Culturally Unprepared Clients

When clients are intellectually or neurologically limited, or when their cultures discourage experiential contact, the most pertinent liberation conditions may be non- or semiexperiential. Such approaches as behavioral shaping, social modeling, and cognitive restructuring may make substantive headway with these clients.

The prospect of experiential deepening, on the other hand, should not be discounted. I have found with mentally retarded clients, for example, that — relative to the warmth, safety, and genuine disclosures between us — technical achievements, such as instilling good grooming habits, simply do not measure up.

Similarly, culturally distant clients can sometimes achieve intimacy in facilitative settings. It is important that the therapist be ready for such engagements — or informative about their availability. For example, I have had clients, often from Hispanic or Asian backgrounds, who prioritize the consciousness of the collective over the mentality of individualism. While such clients do not spurn their backgrounds, they are often in great conflict with them — particularly in our hyperindividualized, contemporary ethos. Given the significance of this situation, I do my utmost to respect such clients' traditional dispositions (e.g., needs for propriety, decorum, and practicality), while at the same time recognizing their yearnings to forge a unique path. This means standing ready to support both traditional needs for structure (e.g., formality, goal setting) and idiosyncratic needs for spontaneity, rebellion, and affective exploration. Through time, I find this approach to be a potent brew. Whereas in earlier therapeutic phases clients may tend to think in dichotomous terms about their heritages (e.g., as "all good" or "all bad"), I find that by the end phases they develop a significantly more nuanced perspective.

There is another group of clients who are intellectually or culturally disposed toward pragmatic, solution-focused therapy. These clients tend to be intelligent, verbal, and very no-nonsense in their approach to life. Yet again, one should not presume that such clients are "frozen" in their single-minded agenda — they are often, depending on the therapeutic field, amenable to a fuller encounter. I had one such client, "Fredrick," who specifically defined his concern as "social phobia." Fredrick explicitly sought therapy to resolve his anxiety as a waiter. After taking a basic psychiatric history of Fredrick, I discerned that the therapy could take a multitude of directions, but I also wanted to respect his need and readiness for these directions, and particularly his pragmatic bent. Accordingly, I worked with Fredrick to methodically develop an exposure paradigm that would incrementally address his anxiety; at the same time, however, I also maintained an availability to Fredrick to explore relevant psychodynamic issues (such as abandonment fears), as well as transient somatic reactions. After about three months, Fredrick and I achieved enough comfort to begin our exposure regimen. To set the stage, we set up a chair and table in my office to simulate the restaurant setting in which Fredrick experiences his most acute anxiety. Fredrick wore his restaurant attire and role-played an encounter with me, as if I was a real-life customer about to begin my meal. At the point of our encounter, however, I did not exclusively encourage Fredrick to pair relaxation exercises (diaphragmatic breathing) with increases in anxiety; I did encourage him to stay present to feelings, sensations, and images that arose at various stages over the course of his desensitization. Through this work, Fredrick became increasingly relaxed while going about his duties with me. But also, and equally significant, he came to more deeply understand and process his anxious reactions, both within and without the role-play. Although Fredrick attained what he sought and ended our work within a relatively brief time frame, I believe our experiential work augmented his success and had generalizing effects well beyond his specific complaint. (See Barry Wolfe's illustration in Chapter 10, for a complementary perspective.)

Now let us turn to the consideration of broader-band semiexperiential interventions within the EI framework. These include, but are not limited to, psychosexual and interpersonal approaches that, while possessing experiential elements, primarily situate those elements within verbal and historical domains.

The Offering of Semiexperiential Liberation

An experiential moment, it will be recalled, is characterized by immediate, kinesthetic, affect-laden, and profound or cosmic dimensions. While traditional psychosexual approaches, such as psychoanalysis, recognize these dimensions, they tend to do so peripherally (or, at best, reservedly). Emotion, for example, is subordinated to ego-dominated understanding in psychoanalytically oriented modalities. Although interpersonal approaches (e.g., self-psychology) accord a more central role to emotions, therapist-based explanations and historical references sometimes truncate this role.[2]

For these reasons, psychosexual and interpersonal therapeutic orientations can be called *semiexperiential*. They incorporate but often do not ground themselves on experiential dimensions. Despite their qualified status, however, semiexperiential treatment modalities can be both illuminating and pivotal for our purposes. Below, we consider the use of such modalities within the EI framework.

When Childhood Sexual Issues Emerge

When clients imply or refer specifically to childhood sexual concerns, traditional psychoanalytic techniques, such as free association, genetic clarification, and tie-in with the transference, can be of significant initial value (Freud, 1963). Beyond helping clients to understand and re-experience their sexual injuries, however, it is frequently beneficial to invite them into the ontological domains that are purported to underlie those injuries. I use the term *frequently* because some clients (due to either capacity or desire) intractably resist these ontological domains and they are therefore immaterial within the EI context. For those clients who accept the ontological challenge, however, a wide range of experiential modalities can be offered. Each of these modalities assists clients into the immediate, kinesthetic, affect-laden, and profound or cosmic dimensions of the (aforementioned) material. Discussions of childhood traumas, for example, can be followed up by "here and now" explorations of the sensations, images, and feelings unearthed in these discussions. Angry or hurtful reminiscences can be accompanied by role-plays or dialogues aimed at redressing those reminiscences. A hate-filled son, for example, can rehearse or role-play what he would like to say to his father. Drawing upon the same format, a sexually molested daughter can reassess (and perhaps even reverse) her original response to her assailant (Mahrer, 1983).

Transference interpretations can also be supplemented by here-and-now explorations. Attention to the client's *experience* of the interpretation, for example, can help the client verify its accuracy. For example, if the interpretation fails to kinesthetically resonate with the client, it may be incongruous and require further clarification. If the interpretation does resonate, on the other hand, it affords the client a chance to become aware of the affect that underlies and informs his reactions. Such questions as "What are you experiencing right now?" or "How does what I say *feel* to you?" can be effective postinterpretive material.

Finally, free association can also be complemented by experiential considerations. The awareness of affect and body sensations, for example, can amplify that which is presented verbally. Moreover, relevant (or *focused*) free associating may be more effective than nondirected, random free associating. In order to be experiential, concludes Bugental (1987), free association (or what he terms "concern-guided searching") must meet these conditions:

> (a) The patient must identify a life issue which he wishes to explore more deeply and fully and describe it to the therapist completely — and often, repeatedly; (b) The patient must be as deeply immersed as possible while carrying out this description . . . , (c) The patient must maintain an expectancy of discovery, a readiness to be surprised. (p. 167)

When Childhood Interpersonal Issues Emerge

When clients imply or refer specifically to early childhood relationship deficits (e.g., parental neglect or abuse), the self-psychological use of empathy, explanation, and "optimal frustration" may be in order (Kohut, 1977). Therapeutic empathy, for example, can help restore clients' dignity, encourage their self-explorations, and strengthen their capacities to trust; childhood-based explanations can help clients make sense of (and intellectually contain) their difficulties. Drawing upon both explanation and empathy, finally, optimal frustration embraces the living (internal and external) therapeutic relationship. There are four basic components to optimal frustration: (1) repeated and inevitable disruptions of the therapeutic bond (e.g., therapists' decisions to take vacations at certain periods), (2) clients' dysfunctional responses to those disruptions (e.g., rage, anxiety), (3) therapists' empathic and rejuvenating alternative responses to the disruptions (e.g., consistency of support, clarity of explanations), and (4) re-establishment of the therapeutic bond (restoration of the external relationship and reparation of the internal, "self-object" relationship) as a result of the above responses.

While these moderately experiential procedures have been shown to be of significant ameliorative value, several EI accompaniments may markedly enhance that value. For example, empathic bonding, which has overtones of passivity, can be complemented by empathic challenging, which has suggestions of activation, engagement, and mobilization. Such challenges can help clients experience their childhood recollections as well as report on them. In addition to sharing with clients that a given memory "may be very difficult for you," for example, therapists can pursue more experiential lines of inquiry, such as, "What are you experiencing in your body right now?" "What other images are associated with that sensation?" "What would you like to say to your mother if she were right here in the room with you?" Timed appropriately, these challenges can accelerate growth processes in between periods of optimal frustration and transference.

Once the optimal-frustration period begins, therapists can continue intensifying their experiential challenges. They can deepen the impact of transference explanations, for example, by exploring clients' experiential resonance to those explanations. The therapeutic sequence might go something like this:

Therapist (T): You're upset with me because I failed to hear how upsetting my vacation was for you.

Client (C): That's right. You don't have the greatest timing, do you?

T: Your father didn't have the greatest timing when he left you alone with your sick mother for all those months either, did he?

C: [*Winces — tears well up*]

T: [*Warmly, sympathetically*] That struck a chord, didn't it?
C: You could say that.

Let us break off here a moment and consider the critical juncture the therapist has reached. On the one hand, he could pursue his client's developmental history and reminiscences about feeling abandoned. On the other hand, he could go in a more experiential direction. For example, what would happen if the thrust of his inquiry were not so much geared to the *why* and more to the *what* of his client's experience? The possible results are exhibited as follows:

T: See if you can stay with that chord a moment, Joe. Where do you feel it in your body?
C: [*Points to his stomach*]
T: [*Touches his own stomach*] What's there, Joe? Slowly now, can you describe it?
C: It's like a big pit, a black hole from which nothing can escape.*
T: What else? Any other images?
C: There I am, this little white face in the midst of that hole. I feel lost, like on a vast, dark sea. I don't know what's happening to me, do you?
T: See if you can stay with it a little longer to find out.
C: I see a cold, black room now. There's a little pudgy kid in that room.
T: Could that kid be you?
C: Yeah, he does feel like me.
T: What are you, or he, doing now?
C: Not doing anything. I'm in a lonely corner of that room just staring, just staring and hurting. . . . [*Tears well up again*]
T: You're really in that hole now, Joe. See if you can stay with it a bit longer and see what happens.
C: [*Tears flow freely*]

In time, the client will be able to occupy his despair with less panic, and possibly even with a sense of hope.

When Safety and Containment Issues Become Relevant

When clients are fragile, or when depth exploration exceeds tolerable limits, semiexperiential treatment strategies can be just the right tonic. Emphasis on genetic (historical) explanations in particular can provide desperately needed structure in given situations. Sometimes the provision of such explanations can mean the difference between suicidal impulsiveness and liveable shame, or catastrophic anxiety and manageable fear. Clients with characterological

* The primordial tone of this response, as suggested previously in another context, is one of the surest signs of its depth.

dysfunctions (e.g., borderline personality) can be particularly well served in such contexts (Volkan, 1987).

The use of genetic explanations to quell or bind anxiety, on the other hand, should not be overdone within the EI paradigm. As soon as clients appear anchored enough by the explanatory framework, it is often helpful to follow up with gentle experiential observations or suggestions. In so doing, experiential and explanatory approaches can coexist dialectically with one another, bracing and enhancing each other's power. For example, a recent client of mine (who could be characterized as an ambulatory schizophrenic) has modestly benefited from historical discussions concerning his mother, but he has benefited equally, I believe, by frank here-and-now acknowledgments of affect, sometimes about his mother but just as often about me, society, a philosophy book, or a co-worker. We do not explain these affects on the basis of his mother; we do not try to apprehend them at these moments; we simply acknowledge them, linger over them a while, and let them be what they are. Remarks or questions like, "You're really turned on by these ideas," "You don't like something that we're doing here," or "What is it you want to say to that fellow who bothered you?" can be deeply self-revelatory and empowering. Too much explaining, on the other hand, can be distancing, deadening, and disempowering — for both client and therapist.

When Clients Are "Stuck" or Seemingly Unreachable

Semiexperiential explanatory frameworks can also be helpful with clients who are stuck or appear to be both nonexperientially and experientially unreachable. Such reflections seem to provide foundation-shaking clarity and life-renewing possibilities for some of these clients. With their motivation for treatment restored and their appetite for exploration sparked, such clients can often be experientially re-engaged.

The Offering of Experiential Liberation

Just as physical support is necessary for physiological treatments and interpersonal assistance is central to interpersonal modalities, ontological attention, or the presence to being, is imperative for experiential approaches.[3]

What do I mean by *ontological attention*? I mean attention that transcends words, contents, and measurable categories. I mean attention not to physical or interpersonal hurts per se, but to the kinesthetic-affective implications of those hurts — the hurts that are locked up in the body, imagination, fantasy life, and intuition. Finally, I mean attention not merely to one's physiological or environmental or sexual smallness/greatness, but to one's smallness/greatness before the general condition of life.

Beyond *repairing* ontological wounds, moreover, experiential facilitation encourages *encounter* with those wounds — opening them up, seeing what they are about, and discovering their future *implications*. It is in this sense that breakdown, from the experiential view, is potentially breakthrough, disability is potentially capability, and anxiety is potentially renewal. The poet Rainer Maria Rilke (1991) mused eloquently upon these matters:

> Were it possible for us to see further than our knowledge reaches . . . perhaps we would endure our sadnesses with greater confidence than our joys. For they are the moments when something new has entered us, something unknown. (p. 266)

Our task, then, is to help clients constructively endure, explore, and transform their inmost experiential hurts. Artfully offered, this enterprise leads to deep intra- and interpersonal reconnection, broadened capacities to choose, and a more suitable harness of priorities within which to live.

Let us turn now to the four basic stances of the experiential liberation condition: (1) presence, (2) invoking the actual, (3) vivifying and confronting resistance (or protections), and (4) the rediscovery of meaning and awe. Although these stances are often sequential (i.e., presence precedes invoking the actual, invoking the actual precedes vivifying and confronting resistance, and so on), they sometimes cooperate irregularly with one another, so that the rediscovery of meaning and awe may directly follow presence, or vivifying and confronting resistance may directly precede invoking the actual. The manifestation of these phase alterations is dependent on many factors (such as the rate of the client's progress), and each factor must be responded to accordingly. The stances may also be coordinated, as intimated earlier, with non- and semiexperiential approaches (within our framework), with a resultant deepening and enhancement of those approaches. Therapeutic presence, for example, can intensify and elucidate the entire client-therapist encounter, invoking the actual can deepen and extend rational restructuring, and the rediscovery of meaning and awe can animate intellectual insight, as we shall see. Taken together, these facilitative strands help clients clarify and apply the EI operating assumptions: *constriction* (making oneself small) and *expansion* (making oneself great) are key existential capacities; dread of either polarity promotes extreme or dysfunctional (constrictive or expansive) counterreactions to that polarity; and the engagement with or integration of the denied polarities fosters psychospiritual vitality. While clients may not grasp these assumptions intellectually (as well they probably should not), they can often grasp them intuitively, implicitly, and metaphorically — in the successful aftermath of therapy.

Presence: A Primary Nutrient

There is a moving story about the travails of the distinguished philosopher Martin Buber (1937/1970) that vividly illustrates the life-and-death significance of therapeutic presence. According to Maurice Friedman (1991), Buber was in the throes of mystical rapture when a curious caller appeared at his door. This caller — a relatively dour and anxious young man — had sought Buber's advice about whether to go to the front in World War I. However, Buber — due to his rhapsodic musings — failed to give the young man the attention he later realized he should have.

The situation ended tragically, according to Friedman, as the young man ended up not only fighting at the front, but also dying there, which left Buber aghast. From that day forward, according to Friedman, Buber recommitted himself to being genuinely attuned in relationships, and not merely prepared or available.

"Presence," Bugental (1987) notes with lucidity, "is a . . . quality of being in a situation or relationship in which one intends at a deep level to participate as fully as [one] is able" (p. 27). Such a quality, he goes on to suggest, facilitates attention, concern, aliveness, and exploration.

May (1981) conceives of presence in terms of the "pause," which "calls forth continuous, unrealized possibilities" (p. 164). "It is in the pause," he elaborates,

> that people learn to *listen to silence*. We can hear the infinite number of sounds we never hear at all — the unending hum and buzz of insects in a quiet summer field, a breeze blowing lightly through the golden hay, a thrush singing in the low bushes beyond the meadow. And we suddenly realize that this is *something* — the world of "silence" is populated by a myriad of creatures and a myriad of sounds. (p. 165)

European existentialists, finally, succinctly characterize presence as *dasein*, which means to "be there."

Fully "being there" with clients (and oneself) cannot be overestimated as a fundamental experiential task. There are at least three (and probably countless more) therapeutic by-products of this task: (1) the illumination of the construction of clients' (or therapists') experiential worlds — highlighting both the obstacles and promises of those worlds (e.g., their battles, desires, and capacities for change), (2) the creation of a sense of safety — or what Craig (1986) calls "sanctuary" — within which delicate problems can be confronted, and (3) the deepening of clients' (or therapists') capacities to constructively act upon their discoveries.

In short, *presence* is an attitude of palpable — immediate, kinesthetic, affective, and profound — *attention*, and it is the ground and eventual goal of experiential work.

Let us turn now to the engagement of presence to illuminate (or assess) clients' worlds — the initial phase of experiential work. One of the first problems therapists encounter at this stage is how to orient themselves in the above worlds. Presence requires such a degree of receptivity to clients' material that not long after one is immersed in it, one is dizzied by its abundance. Fortunately, experiential therapy (within the EI outlook) provides an organizing structure for this dazzlement, a way to harness its receptive power.[4]

Smallness-Greatness "Clustering": Keys to Experiential Work

One of the first areas I reflect upon — even before any words are exchanged — is, What is my client expressing in his body? I am particularly alert to the constrictive or expansive *cluster points*, or polarizations, evident in his body.[5] I am also attentive to such resonances in my own body as barometers of his kinesthetic disposition. To the extent that I can register these impressions, I am privy to useful hypotheses about my client's battle — how and why he shrinks or inflates himself and the degree to which he is invested in these stances. Although I initially "bracket" these speculations for future consideration, I am often struck by their anticipation of the future concerns of our work. Here is a sample of my meditations:

> What kind of world is this man trying to hold together? What kind of life design do his muscles, gestures, and breathing betray? Is he stiff and waxy or limber and fluid? Is he caved in and hunched over or stout and thrust forward? Does he curl up in a remote corner of the room or does he "plant himself in my face"? What does he bring up in my body? Does he make me feel light and buoyant or heavy and stuck? Do my stomach muscles tighten, or do my legs become jumpy? Do my eyes relax, or do they become "hard," guarded? What can I sense from what he wears? Is he frumpy and inconspicuous or loud and outrageous? What can be gleaned from his face? Is it tense and weather beaten or soft and innocent?

Each of these observations begins to coalesce with the others, cumulatively disclosing a world. Each is a sampling of the constrictive or expansive terror my client is experiencing — and the expansive or constrictive armaments he has mobilized in reaction to that terror (see Reich, 1949).

Concurrent with its power to reveal, I am also aware of the power of presence to contain or support experiential material. This support is communicated to my client in the process of my attending. To the degree that I can permit my own embodied responses, my client is also encouraged to respond bodily. To the degree that I can trust myself with my client, he is also inspired to trust. My body/field becomes a sanctuary at such times, intimating a range of silent sentiments: "I am here for you," "I will not waver," and "I take you seriously." "The provision of human sanctuary," Craig (1986) elucidates,

> is manifested in the therapist's attunement as an alert, abiding . . . presence which is both permissive and protecting. Though the particulars of this embodied therapeutic mood fluctuate with the particulars of the therapeutic circumstances, what does endure . . . is a palpable sense of aliveness, respect, and nonintrusiveness. (p. 26)

The engagement of presence, Craig (1986) adds,

> requires constant discipline; discipline in remaining open to all aspects of my experience with the patient; discipline in understanding the salient features of this experience; discipline in determining just what features of this experience hold the greatest promise for opening new possibilities in the patient's existence; discipline in deciding just how these promising possibilities may be framed and offered to the patient in behavior, language, and mood; and, above all, discipline in identifying and transcending all those personal needs, feelings, beliefs, and assumptions of my own which may be interfering with a fresh, virginal perception of and response to the other. (pp. 27–28)

As we can see, the discipline of presence requires a very wide assortment of abilities. Although one can technically develop the art (see the pertinent skill-building exercises in the appendices), there is no substitute for what one has learned or will learn about it through living one's life. To the degree that one can effectively draw upon this learning, one can dramatically prepare the therapeutic "soil." (See Schneider, 1992, on the link between therapists' personal maturity and their effectiveness.)

To summarize, presence is the vessel for experiential work. It holds while illuminating that which is palpably — immediately, kinesthetically, affectively, and profoundly — relevant *between* therapists and clients and *within* clients. Time, intuition, and attention to constrictive and expansive cluster points can help therapists optimize presence. (Note again that these cluster points are not to be taken too literally; they are guideposts that, when coupled with clinical knowledge, can alert therapists to the salient junctures of moment-to-moment interaction. See "Ways the Stances Utilize Constrictive-Expansive Dynamics" for elaboration on this matter.)

Next, we turn to one overarching issue: how to assist clients *into* that which is palpably relevant.

Invoking the Actual: Creatively Inspiring Presence

Recently, a colleague of mine (I'll call him "Bob") relayed a most captivating vignette. He was consulting with a group of business leaders about a rift that had broken out in the organization of one of the leaders (I'll call him "John"). The rift centered on John's decision to fire a disgruntled employee. Before John could explain the reasons for his strategy, however, a highly respected fellow executive ("Joanna") began to speak, and her tones were far from measured. She chided John for his presumptuousness, moralized to him about his lack of social conscience, and derided him for his austerity. When Bob urged her to suspend her judgment for a time, she abruptly turned on him and began to question his partiality and motives. This caused other members of the gathering to remind Joanna of the need for proper decorum. "Be reasonable," they called out, but Joanna refused to yield her ground. Flustered but not daunted, Bob paused, studied Joanna a moment, and uttered one simple sentiment, "I sense that you are deeply hurting right now, Joanna."

Almost instantaneously, my colleague reported, Joanna doubled over in pain. Thick tears began streaming down her face. "You're right," she cried out, "I am hurting — and it has little to do with this meeting." Bob found out later that what Joanna's pain had everything to do with was her abusive, alcoholic father. She had just returned from his funeral, Bob recalled, and she felt betrayed and abandoned by him yet one final time. This was the context for her fierce opposition to John and her exaggerated sympathy for his employee.

There were many ways in which Bob could have intervened with Joanna, and there were many alternative assumptions he could have made about her behavior. He could have assumed, for example, that he could reason with her, the way her associates tried to do. He could have tried to psychodynamically explain or interpret her remarks. Or he could have assumed that she had inside information and that she was justified in her reaction. Yet none of these efforts would have connected with Joanna because none of them would have addressed her experience.

When I asked Bob to articulate the basis for his particular intervention, he groped for the right words. "It was something about her intensity," he said, "something about the way she looked when she was speaking and the kinds of words she used when she was speaking. There was a discrepancy there."

What Bob saw, I believe, is what many sensitive therapists see and feel with tormented clients — the extravagances they experience (Binswanger, 1975). In Joanna's case, these extravagances grouped around the need to exhibit greatness, righteousness, and invulnerability. But they also — albeit more subtly — clustered around the fears beneath those displays — fears of smallness, impotence, and helplessness. Bob was able to empathically "hone in" on those fears, share them with Joanna, and spur her transformation in consciousness.

By speaking to people's immediate, energetic experience, or by encountering their "living" constrictive or expansive panic, therapists can mobilize extraordinary capacities for renewal. Dramatic as it was, Bob's performance is emblematic of one of the most important clinical innovations on the contemporary scene — "invoking the actual." "Words are just brief sounds," elaborates Wilson Van Dusen (1965), the man who wrote the landmark article on the topic. "Words and symbols are lifeless unless they choke up, frighten, bring tears or alert like the actually numinous. The actualities I speak of are all more or less visible and palpable" (p. 67).

It is hard to overstate the infusion of richness this conception brings to our engagements. From the vantage point of invoking the actual, for example, every therapeutic moment must be seized upon, every transaction amplified. There is no justification for long-term passivity; prolonged inertness is a signal of decay.

The creative challenge of invoking the actual, or relevant, is one of its most invigorating features. I am enticed, for example, by the prospect of reaching an intransigent client or of finding myriad routes to her depths. To me, this is what makes our work so awe filled and so exhilarating in its potential to surprise. Let us look closer now at the mode of invoking the actual, drawing from a variety of my and others' case examples.

The moment a therapist begins to speak to her client, invoking the actual, or relevant, can begin, and it can set the tone for the entire session. Suggestions such as, "Take a moment to settle in," or questions such as, "What's of concern to you?" "What really matters to you right now?" or "Where are you at today?" can help clients begin to center on their concerns. Simple follow-ups to these queries, such as, "Tell me more," "Can you give me an example?" or "Is there anything else you'd like to share?" can fruitfully deepen what has been initiated. (See "Enhancing Presence Through Focus and Topical Expansion" in the skill-building section.) Finally, suggesting to clients that they speak in the present tense, that they invoke the pronoun *I* when discussing themselves, and that they become more aware of their bodies can consolidate the aforementioned processes. (See Bugental, 1987, for an elaboration on these initial processes.)

At the same time that I try to help clients center themselves on their concerns, I also try to help them actively confront, or encounter, those concerns. For example, I might comment on my experience of them energetically: "It feels to me that you are tight right now"; "I hurt when I hear that recollection"; "I feel like I'm spinning — I wonder if you do, too?" Or I might note what I hear and see: "I notice that your fingers are tapping"; "Your voice breaks when you make that statement"; "It seemed hard for you to smile just then." Finally, I might try to underscore the client's experience: "How do you feel as you make that statement? See if you can linger on it a while." (Although such commentaries can be enormously productive at the right moments, it is important to monitor the client's readiness and ability to handle them. Fragile or paranoid clients, for example, may not have the tools.)

Clients' investments in smallness or greatness can also help me facilitate their encounters. When I observe a pattern of flamboyance, for example, I am watchful for an undercurrent of shyness, reticence, or self-deprecation that can be explored. When I perceive a clustering of hesitancy and reserve, conversely, I am mindful of the upheaval, rage, and explosiveness that may need to be plumbed. The degree and frequency of these investments, moreover, clue me in on the degree and frequency of future struggles.

Although some clients display consistent polarization patterns, many do not. Some, for example, oscillate between smallness and greatness while others fluctuate within a given cluster. Some are polarized one way at the beginning of treatment (or at the beginning of each session) and polarized another way at the end of that time period. Still others — and this probably accounts for the therapeutic majority — are polarized in different ways as they uncover deeper levels of their existential pain (see "Ways the Stances Utilize Constrictive-Expansive Dynamics" in the appendices following this chapter). Our task as therapists is to help our clients face their polarizations as they arise, and to artfully assist them in deepening those encounters. Eventually, although not invariably, clients will arrive at the experiential core of their constrictive or expansive dreads. To the degree that they can identify (or resonate to) this core, the therapeutic task will become clearer. If they cannot identify it, the therapist's task becomes hazier from the experiential position. This latter outcome is not bad, however; it merely indicates that either more uncovering needs to be done or the client has reached her threshold within the smallness-greatness continuum.

It is also important to be mindful of any ethnic or cultural predispositions along the smallness-greatness axis that may mislead or confound our assessments. To an American practitioner, for example, an Asian client may appear excessively invested in smallness (e.g., accommodation, deference, and so on). Yet that very same client — relative to her background — may not feel the least bit concerned about that aspect of her experience and may, in fact, view it with some pride. It is of vital importance, therefore, not only to know something about the cultural background of one's clients, but to clarify, to the degree possible, how the clients themselves view those backgrounds. Do they experience them as crippling or salutary, forced or natural? If we can attune ourselves to the client's standpoint, we will be in a stronger position to guide.

One last frequently asked question is: What does a therapist do once a client faces his or her dread? My answer is threefold: (1) try to stay present to that client, (2) try to trust that the client's pain (as with most things) will eventually transform, and (3) try to assist the client to acquire that trust. Almost invariably, in my experience, clients' anxieties do change, especially as they face them. Either they dissipate and give way to liberation (e.g., meaning creation), shift and become new anxieties or concerns, or overpower the client and engender his or her resistance. Yet each is an instance of change, and each can be dealt with accordingly.

Given these caveats, let us consider some of the most useful strategies for invoking the actual of which I am aware. These derive from both my own and others' existentially oriented practices.

Embodied Meditation

Recently I have found embodied meditation to be of value, particularly to clients invested in making themselves small. "Ruth," for example, was a repressed, fearful young woman in her mid-30s. She lived alone and spent much of her life worrying about what others thought of her. This concern was especially debilitating to her desire to be more playful, creative, and spiritual in her life. Her life had become a prison. Although we made some headway discussing her personal history in relation to these issues, she continued to describe herself as feeling chronically "heavy," "cramped up," and "blocked." One day I invited her to try something different. "I'd like to try a simple meditation exercise with you," I explained, "that may help you to make fuller contact with yourself. Would you like to give it a try?" Upon her consent, I requested that she sit in a comfortable position (hands to the side, legs uncrossed) and begin to pay attention to her breathing. Next, I suggested that she close her eyes. Although this is not mandatory, I explained to her, it seems to deepen one's participation in the exercise. "Now, as you attend to your breathing," I continued, "you may notice all kinds of extraneous thoughts, feelings, and sensations. Try not to get caught up in those other stimuli. Simply acknowledge them and return to your breathing. To the degree possible," I went on, "try to draw your breaths in slowly, really attending to them, and do the same for your expulsions of air. Let them out slowly, mindfully."

After providing a few minutes for her to center on her breathing, I suggested that, as she's ready, she gradually shift her attention to her body. Once she was able to do this, I suggested that she carefully attend to any tension areas in her body, any areas that seemed to stand out or call out to her, as if in need. She immediately was able to identify such an area — her stomach — and we were off and running.

Me: Can you describe, as fully and presently as possible, what it is you sense there, Ruth? What do you feel around your stomach area?

Ruth: I have an image of being bloated, gassy, and disturbed. It's like knives sticking into me.

Me: That's a pretty strong image.

Ruth: Well, part of it is that I'm having my period, but that's not the whole thing. I often feel like this.

Me: What else is there?

Ruth: I feel like it's messy down there, that it's bubbling and teeming with stuff. It's not all bad, though. It feels like it's part of me, part of what I am in my depths. At the same time, I also feel sealed off from these churnings. It's like I'm underneath them, looking up at them. It's like I'm unaffected by them.

Me: Do any images or associations come up around what you're feeling right now?

Ruth: Well, it's like I feel in a great deal of my life. I feel estranged, cut off. It's like I'm cut off from the wild and expressive part of myself, the aspiring part. [*Tears begin to form*]

Me: See if you can stay with that feeling, Ruth.

Ruth: It's like this very special room I used to have as a child. This was my room. It was a place where I could feel safe, where I wouldn't be trampled on or mangled. [*Long pause*]

Me: What's happening now, Ruth? Do you want to share?

Ruth: Well, I realize how much I miss that room, how much that room meant play and wonder and magic. But as I got older, I just couldn't get away to that room, and I couldn't bring it out or draw on it in my life. I began to feel cut off from it.

Me: It sounds like the way you feel cut off from your gassy, active stomach, like there's something alive in there, something of you, but you just can't seem to be with it.

Ruth: Yes! It's like so much in my life I've cut off. [*Yells*] I'm sick of it! I want to dive into it, embrace it, and let myself be, just let myself be a *quote* "mess" for a change! For a friggin' change!

Me: [*After a long pause*] What's happening now, Ruth?

Ruth: The seal has broken loose somewhat. I feel like I'm in there with the tumult. I'm with it or near it. It's OK. It's me.

Although this single meditation did not transform Ruth overnight, it did — she and I agreed — go a long way toward helping her to identify her fears, find ways to survive them, and see possibilities for rejuvenating her world. That such results are common in connection with guided meditation is illustrated by another client of mine, Bill, who suffered from similar — albeit more complex — strangulations of his life design.

Bill was a 40-year-old single white male with a well-paying job and a comfortable overall living arrangement. He jogged regularly, met periodically with a small circle of friends, and was fond of mystery novels. Although Bill was outwardly confident, competent, and even commanding at times, in his deepest being he was terrified of these very qualities. He was terrified of strength, power, and greatness in a wide array of forms. For example, he often isolated himself, denigrated his self-worth, and shunned opportunities for intimacy.

At the same time, it was not always clear just what Bill feared. His commanding and even condescending manner, for example, contradicted any dread of greatness and implied, instead, anxiety about belittlement, dismissal, and insubstantiality. His indulgence in food and alcohol, similarly, betrayed fears of emptiness and a desperation to fill that emptiness.

Bill's greatest suffering, on the other hand, clustered around his inability to reach out to people, to fully expose and express himself, and to trust that he could be looked upon as special. Although we had alluded to these problems in our dialogues, it was not until Bill faced them in the following guided meditation that he genuinely came to understand and redress them:

Me: [*After having prepared Bill as I did Ruth*] See if you can describe, as fully as possible, what it is you feel in your stomach area, Bill.

Bill: [*Rubs his stomach, as I respond in kind*] I feel like there's a huge mass there, a multilayered wall, or fortress. I'm aware of my obesity right now.

It's like a tremendous covering of pain. There is some pain in there. It's just not clear what it's about. [*His face exhibits frustration*]

Me: Slowly now, Bill, just see if you can keep describing what's there. Take your time.

Bill: Yeah, there is something there, beneath the fat. It's like a hunger, or better yet, a hollow feeling. . . .

Me: Something like what you feel when you overeat?

Bill: Yeah, exactly! It's that emptiness, and it hurts real bad. It's scary.

Me: Do you feel like you can stay in there with it?

Bill: [*Pauses to reflect*] Yes, I want to stay in there.

Me: Good.

Bill: I suddenly got this image of going with my mother to a gathering of our relatives. I was a little boy — maybe 7 years old.

Me: Bill, see if you can describe it in the present tense, as if you were living it now.

Bill: We arrive at the front door. The house is dark; the relatives are nondescript. The first thing I want to do is dart behind this couch. [*His voice begins to waver, and his face begins to flush red*] There is this raggedy old couch. I run behind it. I won't even say hello to anyone. I just make a beeline for that couch! I feel tight, real scared. [*He speaks more rapidly, intensively*]

Me: I'm with you, Bill. Go as far as you feel able.

Bill: I'm this little boy, this little boy who's scared.

Me: Scared of what, Bill. Can you associate?

Bill: Scared of showing himself, scared of hurting himself or of being hurt, scared of "coming out."

Me: What does it mean for you to come out?

Bill: I don't know. It's just so frightening. I feel lost, abandoned, exposed — yeah, that's it, exposed. It's as if everyone will see me in all my ugliness, all my perverseness. I'm like this big, oozing blob.

Me: So what does that mean for you? What are you afraid will happen if you step out from behind that couch?

Bill: I feel like they're gonna shrink back from me or humiliate me.

Me: Yeah, but what makes that so scary to you?

Bill: I just don't feel like I could handle it — being out there in front of them. It's like I would crack up or something, or go out of control. Maybe I'd show them that I was as crazy as they think I am. Oh, it hurts so much. [*Caresses himself*]

Me: It feels important to keep caressing yourself for a while, Bill. You've gone to a pretty harrowing place. Maybe you can just take some time to soothe that little boy the way you are now. Let him know how you sympathize with him.

This latter comment illustrates the principle of building up while you're "stripping the client down." It is essential, during the uncovering process, to help clients rest or gather their resources from time to time — to bolster their capacities for risk.

Bill began to experience some rather startling shifts within himself after sessions such as the aforementioned. First, he felt increasingly friendly, or comfortable, with himself. Although he continued to be alone quite a bit, he was no longer as burdened by or devaluing of that experience. He even began to enjoy being by himself, and this helped him to trust and enjoy being with others as well. He felt like a shadow or weight had been lifted from him and that he was freed up to participate more fully in his life. Second, he no longer felt as empty or as wanting as he had before. He still had the urge to overeat or drink on occasion, but the urges were much less frequent than they had been. It was as if the urgency had faded, he said. He couldn't quite articulate it, but he felt like something very significant had happened during our meditation sessions, something that no other aspect of our work had duplicated.

What, specifically, occurred? While neither Bill nor I could answer this question definitively, I would postulate the following: Bill — like many, if not most, therapy clients — possessed a multitiered experiential profile. At one level he balked at smallness, mustering all his efforts to project dominance, substantiality, and greatness. At another level, he was terrified of these latter qualities. He did everything to avoid "coming out," exposing himself, or challenging others. In turn, he made himself small, reticent, and withdrawn.

It was not until I invoked the actual with Bill — through *embodied* meditation — that we could more clearly differentiate his situation. His fears of smallness (of deprivation, of emptiness), for example, were apparent in his references to his weight, his stomach girth, and his need for protective fat. His fears of greatness, on the other hand, were apparent in his memory of hiding behind the couch and appeared to underlie his anxiety about smallness. Although Bill also may have felt deprived and empty behind that couch, his primary anxiety, it seemed to me, was the effort, risk, and boldness it would take to step out in front of the couch, and this was a metaphor for his life. By gradually learning to survive — not merely report on — his recollection, Bill was unburdened of its spell.

Experimentation

The idea of using therapy as a laboratory, a place to try things out with clients, is neither unique nor original. Cognitive therapies, for example, make abundant use of the concept, and so do such varying approaches as gestalt, psychodrama, and systematic desensitization (see Beck, 1976; Perls, 1969; Moreno, 1959; Wolpe, 1969). The distinguishing feature of the model I present here is that it combines these respective modalities and creatively synthesizes new ones.

In addition to role-play, rehearsal, and creative visualization, for example, I also find live demonstration to be of benefit. Sometimes I invite artistically inclined — but creatively blocked — clients to draw me or draw something in the room. The exercise seems facile at first, but it is often quite profound. One client, for example, rediscovered a long pent-up joy in the artistic process; another simply took pride in expressing herself deeply. One man showed me a 20-page play he had written. It was about an offensive therapist he had seen and was full of antitherapist invective. The play, however, was critical for my work with this man because it showed that he could trust me, despite whatever professional identification I might want to preserve.

The old adage that "you don't really know what something is like until you experience it" holds for the subtle as well as the obvious and overt. One of my clients, for example, felt a lump in her throat. I asked her to place her hand on that lump and instantly she was able to associate to the abandonment she had once felt as a child. Sometimes I invite clients to pause, stretch in certain ways, or walk around the room. A colleague of mine, John Cogswell (1993), uses what he calls *walking therapy* to invoke the actual. When one of his clients is having trouble articulating whom he desires to be, what kind of people hold him back in his life, or simply "where he's at" at any given moment, Cogswell invites him to embody that desire, person, or experience in his walk. Hence, for example, one client might walk the walk of her father in order to better understand his influence on her life. Another might imitate the way his boss walks in order to improve his understanding of her personality. Still another might walk the way he is feeling that day in order to experientially identify his problem. It is surprising, concludes Cogswell, how much insight clients acquire into themselves and others through walking — as much or more than that typically achieved through role-play, he contends.

The more spontaneous, creative, and absorbing a therapeutic experiment is, the more valuable it is. A client of mine invested in keeping herself small, for example, contemplated a radical change in her career. Although she had begun to talk more earnestly about this career change, and although she fantasized about how it could transform her life, she refrained from actually inquiring into the prospect. She was on the brink of making such an inquiry, she once confided in me, yet she could not quite go through with it. It was then that I offered her a challenge: "How would you like to make your inquiry right now, in the safety of this office? You can use the phone right here — I'll even leave while you make your call. Or, if you wish, I can be right here with you. Then we can look at what came up for you."

At that instant, the entire tenor of our session shifted. What was formerly a rather sober exercise suddenly turned animated. Struggling to respond, my client both laughed (embarrassedly) and grimaced. She also resented me, in part, for directly challenging her. Although she ultimately declined my invitation, it was the experience of being invited — not its acceptance or rejection

— that really seemed to matter. The experience enabled her to look as closely as she ever had at how much she wanted to take a risk in her life and at ways in which she impeded herself from taking that risk. The experience also helped her to reconsider me — the ostensibly warm and gentle listener. How could I put her on the spot like that, she pondered, and steer our relationship in such unpredictable directions?

Despite her misgivings, however, her newly acquired ambivalence toward me brought our relationship to an unprecedented level of frankness. She realized that I could no longer be relied upon to magically save her, that only she could ultimately save herself. Eventually, she was able to make that terrifying phone call and courageously emerge from her cocoon.

It is not so much the kind of experiment that matters, but its capacity to absorb, inspire, and enliven. When I suggest role-plays, for example, I am continually attentive to clients' body positions, breathing patterns, and vocal fluctuations. "How does it feel when you say that?" I might inquire. "What's going on in your body as you enact this encounter?"

Role-playing entails more than trying out new interpersonal relationships; it also entails trying out new relationships with one's imagination, energy, and spirit. For example, Rollo May (1969) often speaks about the need for "wishing" within the therapeutic context, and I am in wholehearted concurrence with his position. *Wishing*, May writes, "is the imaginative playing with the possibility of some act or state occurring" (p. 214). To the degree that one is unable to wish, he elaborates, one is unable to will — which "is the full-blown, matured form of wish" (p. 288). To the degree that one is unable to will, I would add, one is unable to fully be. In order to foster these capacities, accordingly, I frequently encourage clients to "let their imaginations go" or "throw their judgments aside" for a time. "Let's see what happens if you trace that thought or feeling out," I might suggest. "Play with it, embody it, describe it as if it were happening." I often invite clients who are dysfunctionally invested in their greatness, for example, to contemplate stillness, abstinence, or routine. "What might it be like," I'd query, "if you didn't get wild tonight or didn't 'show up' your peers?" "What fantasies do you have around being ordinary, plain, or slow? Can you tell me in the first person?" It is also helpful for some of these clients to trace out their manifest patterns of behavior — their inclinations to dominate others or to take on more than they can handle. Beyond helping them to look at the merely cognitive consequences of such dispositions, however, I am particularly attentive to the toll those dispositions take at the level of their affect and bodies. "See if you can envision yourself beating that fellow," I might inquire. "What kind of feelings, images, or fantasies come up for you?" or "Imagine yourself in that prison cell. What are you seeing? What does it feel like in your body?" or "See if you can envision involving yourself in all those activities we spoke about. What would such a scenario feel like in your stomach, chest, and throat?" I am constantly surprised at how potent such questions can be — even with characteristically externalizing clientele.

The more deeply one can describe one's wish or fantasy, the more one can immerse oneself in its possibilities. When I ask clients to visualize a scene, for example, I urge them to "paint," "taste," or fully "re-create" that scene. I asked one man who was envisioning a confrontation with his boss, "What does the setting feel like? How warm is it? What kinds of decorations are around you? How formal is your attire?" I asked a woman reconstructing her dream, "How does the sensation of flying feel in your body? Is it sensual, or is it scary? Do you feel heavy, or do you feel feathery and light?"

If clients are resistant to envisioning an entire scenario, I encourage them to experiment with portions of that scenario — I might ask the man mentioned above to imagine being in the same room with his boss rather than confronting her; I might suggest reading up on a job as opposed to calling for an interview; or I might ask an alcoholic to picture one day of abstinence rather than a lifetime. Tiny though they may seem, these increments have proven crucial in my experience because they can shift the momentum of treatment.

Experimenting Outside Therapy

While experimentation within the therapeutic setting is invaluable, experimentation outside therapy, in my opinion, is even more beneficial. This is because outside experimentation reinforces intratherapy work and implements that work in the most relevant setting — life.

Accordingly, I encourage clients to practice being present and aware, especially in problematic situations. "See if you can stay with the thoughts and feelings that come up," I tell them, "even for the briefest moment." I also encourage clients to sort through what's operating on them in stressful situations — what assumptions they make, how they approach or avoid certain things, and what inner voices they hear. Some clients have found it helpful to observe how readily they give their power away in given circumstances; others have been impressed by their passive-aggressive behavior. Virtually anything clients perceive from this standpoint can be revelatory.

The cultivation of what Zen adepts and others have termed the *inner witness* can also foster extratherapeutic presence (see Bugental, 1978). To nurture this skill, I encourage clients to commit 20 minutes of each week to undistracted self-observation. "As nonjudgmentally as possible," I suggest, "just watch the flow of your inner experiences, and neither try to categorize nor figure out those experiences." Although some clients have difficulty with this exercise, others benefit greatly simply from the time they have taken with themselves and the needs, fears, and desires that they have unveiled.

Challenging clients to experiment with or act out extratherapeutic tasks can be of equal benefit. "See what happens if you are honest with your friend," I told one of my image-conscious clients; "try refraining from one confection tonight," I urged one of my compulsively eating clients, "then look at what that was like for you." Finally, I proposed to a client who was concerned about having children to "try making contact with children, reflecting on your own childhood, and visiting the places and things that children value."

Experimenting with the actual gives clients new opportunities to live. Although they may not always seize these opportunities, they are invariably vibrant and edifying.

Therapist-Client Encounter

One of the paramount vehicles for invoking the actual is the therapeutic relationship. This relationship, or *encounter*, as it has come to be known in experiential circles, includes, but also transcends, the psychoanalytic notions of transference, remembering, and explaining (Phillips, 1980).

The therapeutic encounter has three basic features: (1) the real or present relationship between therapist and client, (2) the future and what can happen in the relationship (vs. strictly the past and what has happened in relationships), and (3) the acting out or experiencing, to the degree appropriate, of relational material. Let me pose some examples:

> I am sitting with a client who communicates to me that "things are going OK right now," that he is really quite "upbeat," and that he had "no problem" with our tension-filled session last week. Yet something about this man's presentation is askew. His mouth is turned down, his gestures are stiff, and his words ring hollow. I could let the man ramble on, I reflect, but the most relevant issue, the issue evident between us, would not get addressed. Accordingly, I encounter him: "I feel like there's something important happening between us right now, Pete, like you have something more to say to me than 'everything's all right.'"
>
> An aircraft engineer succinctly and precisely summarizes his childhood history. He notices that I yawn slightly and that my eyes glaze over as he is talking, but he continues on without pause. I interrupt: "I think we both notice that I'm drifting, Terry; I wonder if you're drifting, too? What is it that really matters about what you're telling me?"
>
> An enraged teenage boy has just been sent to a foster home. He stares at me in disdain. Charily, I address him: "I feel like you want to let me or someone have it, John. Is there something you'd like me to know?"
>
> A woman who feels chronically victimized by and unable to confront her ex-husband suddenly bursts out screaming: "That fucking asshole! He makes me so sick. I'd like to kick him where it goddamn counts. Men make me sick!" Then she demurs, "Present company excepted, of course." "No!" I reply. "Don't qualify yourself. You're on fire right now. Now, how can you translate that fire for your life?"

A client labeled *ambulatory schizophrenic* steps into my office. He is suspicious, disheveled, and "sharp as a tack." "This system is corrupt," he raves. "Look at you all — you professionals, with your smiling faces and your fancy beards. You're just here to pacify me, to make me say, 'That's good, doctor. You're right, doctor. You know what's best, doctor.' And behind your masks you're afraid of us, aren't you? Afraid something's going to rub off on you. Just look right now. You're conniving ways to quiet me, to turn me into your pet-boy." "You make some valid points, Daniel," I concede. "There are people who are afraid of you and who will try to mold you to fit their image. You're also right that I'm one of those people sometimes. I was, in fact, a little scared of you back then; even now, I'm both moved and unsettled by your view. But I'm also willing — if you are — to keep taking a look at these problems and to see if we can work them out."

A street-hardened Latino man wonders how I, a Caucasian professional, can relate to him. "I don't know," I respond. "I admit we come from very different worlds. On the other hand, I've also been wounded in my life — in my own ways, within my own cultural context. While these may not be the same as your wounds, they may help me connect with yours."

"I'll tell you up front," a court-mandated alcoholic once bragged to me, "I've manipulated every shrink I've had for 25 years, and nothing's different here, so far as I can see." "Well, maybe nothing is," I replied, "and maybe you can manipulate me for the next 25 years, too. But what will that mean for getting on with your life?"

"I'm horrified by the idea of looking foolish," one client told me as she flushed red with anxiety, "and I can't keep the presence of mind to work with it." "But you just were able to work with it," I responded, "as I surmise that you just now felt foolish!" She concurred.

Existential psychiatrist R. D. Laing (1985) tells of a perplexing seven-year-old girl he once worked with. For months before he met her, Laing said, she had been both mute and nonresponsive. At their first session together, he tried talking with the girl, but that did not engender any dialogue. Then he tried joking with her, but that, too, garnered negligible results. Finally, Laing gave up on his efforts and simply decided to be with her. He sat next to her on the floor and delicately put out his hands. Slowly, she, too, put out her hands and lightly made contact with his fingertips. Then Laing closed his eyes and began to engage in a kind of hand dance with the girl, wordlessly matching her movements. When the hour was up, Laing reported, the little girl's father asked her how the session went. "None of your business!" she is alleged to have declared, and from that day forward she spoke.

What are the implications of these vignettes? The first, I believe, centers on the significance of realness in the therapeutic encounter. How else can clients learn to be real with themselves if they cannot be real with their therapists — if they cannot come up against their therapists' love, irritation, recognition of the obvious, and openness to varying approaches? How else can therapists get to know their clients deeply unless some of that depth is shared? It's not that therapists need to "spill their guts" with clients, but they need to be accessible, capable of being known. Bugental has often spoken about feeling deeply known by his clients even when he has not exchanged any words with them. Laing, it is clear from the above, would concur with Bugental's observation.

The second implication of the vignettes is that it is the process — over and above isolated contents — that fosters intra- and interpersonal growth. My attention to my client's downturned mouth, Laing's suspension of his efforts to speak to his client, and my acknowledgment of ignorance about another client's culture all took our encounters to new levels of possibility. The engagement of content-focused strategies, on the other hand, would probably not have availed us of these opportunities.

Finally, our encounters enabled our clients to experience their smallness or greatness by means of interpersonal as well as personal channels. By accepting his client's muteness (or smallness), for example, Laing enabled his client to consider verbalization (greatness). By acknowledging my client's (great) capacity for manipulating, I freed him to explore smaller but more relevant matters, like his life. By directing the aircraft engineer to his mechanistic smallness, finally, I liberated him to consider his spontaneous aliveness, value, and greatness.

Vivifying and Confronting Resistance ("Protections")

The implicit question that runs through the entire experiential offering is as follows: "Are you (the client) *willing* to continue living as you do, in this moment, in this way?" or, to put it another way, "Which side of your battle will you choose to affirm, the side that immobilizes or the side that evolves?"

While invoking the actual mirrors back to clients how they are encountering their typical yet miserable life stances, vivifying and confronting resistance reflects back to clients how they block themselves from such encounter and revert to the old shell. Hence, when the invitation to meditate, experiment, or encounter is repeatedly declined by clients, then the delicate problem of resistance (or what I increasingly term protections) must be considered. Resistances are *blockages* to that which is palpably relevant (i.e., threatening, anxiety provoking).

Resistances are not to be taken lightly, from the experiential standpoint. To the contrary, they are viewed as vital methods of self-preservation (May, 1983, p. 28). Although such methods may at first seem crude, crippling, or even life denying, to most clients they are starkly preferable to the alternatives.

Clients invested in smallness, for example, may perceive their sole alternative to be chaos; conversely, clients invested in greatness may perceive their only option to be obliteration. With choices like these, it is no wonder clients sabotage their own growth.

Accordingly, I always try to be respectful of resistances, acknowledging both their life-giving (e.g., protective) and their life-taking (e.g., destructive) qualities. I also try to be cognizant of the problems of prematurely challenging clients' resistance, which can often end up exacerbating their conditions rather than alleviating them.

There are two additional points to bear in mind about the experiential approach to resistances. First, it may be overly intense for given clients. To the extent that this is the case, semi- or nonexperiential alternative approaches may be in order. Second, although experiential approaches to resistance are cultivated throughout the treatment process, they are particularly relied upon in the closing stages — when clients face the greatest pressure to change.

Now let us focus on two important experiential tools for handling resistances — therapeutic vivification and confrontation.

Vivifying Resistance

As has been suggested, there are many times when it is better to indirectly, rather than directly, confront resistance. This is so not only because direct confrontation can therapeutically backfire, but also because it can convey the wrong message to clients — that the power of transformation is possessed by the therapist. But from the experiential standpoint, this is a deception. For it is the client who must discover that power, and it is the client who must grapple with its consequences.

Vivifying resistance, accordingly, is one way to empower clients to transform. How does vivification proceed? By gradually and methodically "holding a mirror up" to clients — helping them to see the kinds of worlds they have constructed, the kinds of compromises they have made to maintain those worlds, and the degree of courage necessary to overcome their situations. While these means may seem simplistic at first — for what client would deny such knowledge about her world — they are eminently sensible to those who know how deeply one must plumb to risk the anxieties of growth. Put another way, vivification helps clients to supportively and productively "hit bottom" in their lives and then mobilizes their commitment to change. Now let us look at several ways we can nurture that mobilization and the rewards that attend it.

Verbal and Nonverbal Feedback These modalities are the most rudimentary forms of vivification. First, let us consider the verbal modality. There are two basic ways to provide verbal feedback: noting and tagging. Noting alerts clients to initial experiences of resistance; tagging acquaints them with those that follow. Some examples of noting are observations such as, "This issue seems really difficult for you" and "You appear to be distracted right now." Some examples of tagging are, "Whenever we discuss this topic, you seem to want to change it" and "There you go again, preferring to argue rather than face your life."

Because I am trying to alert rather than shock, I sometimes find it necessary to temper my appraisals. For example, I might say to a client just beginning therapy: "I wonder if I'm pushing too hard right now. Maybe you can begin again where you feel comfortable." I also try to acknowledge the potential fallibility of my feedback; this helps clients to direct themselves to the relevant issues. "My observation may have been off base here," I might remark. "I appreciate your correcting me." Or I might say, "I wonder if we could suspend my observation for a bit, see how it feels to us at a later time."

I find the use of nonverbal feedback to be particularly elucidating to clients. Whereas verbal feedback appears to animate predominantly conscious domains of clients' resistance, nonverbal feedback seems to clarify primarily subliminal barriers and domains. By mirroring a client's crossed arms, for example, I was able to help her see how unexpectedly guarded she had been about a particular topic; by echoing a client's sense of being "choked up," I was able to apprise him of his "suffocating" relationship. (See Bugental, 1987, for an elaboration of nonverbal feedback.)

Reviewing Old Territory Resistances sometimes seem like broken records to clients, endlessly duplicating a theme. While the vivification process can often amplify that sense of repetitiveness, it can also provide fresh opportunities to transcend it. I try to alert clients to these possibilities and to subtle changes in their patterns of defensiveness. For example, I might point out to an intellectualized client his sudden use of the pronoun *I* or direct a client who chronically suppresses her sadness to an abruptly formed teardrop.

Tracing Out and Enabling Helping clients to trace out the consequences of their resistances and enabling them to be resistant are two other ways to catalyze productive change. I have often found it helpful for clients invested in smallness, for example, to detail the dullness, routine, and oppressiveness that they foresee in their lives. I have found it equally useful for inflated clients to peer into their unsettling futures. While such strategies may acutely frustrate certain clients, they can also alert them to present opportunities, which can head off their nightmarish fantasies.

Ambivalent clients can also benefit from the strategy of tracing out. Experientially detailing the pros and cons of a situation or anticipating the meaning of remaining ambivalent has helped my clients to substantively reassess their predicaments.

One of the most interesting and ironic features of vivification is that when all else fails, just allowing the client to resist can be the most salient remedy (see Erickson, 1965; Frankl, 1965). When I worked with highly resistive (nonviolent) children, for example, I found that divesting of a given treatment plan was more effective, frequently, than pressing for a particular strategy (Schneider, 1990/1999). Highly resistive adult clients also respond favorably to such divestitures. When such clients are allowed to simply be their withdrawn, grandiose, or intractable selves, they will frequently begin to relinquish those dispositions. For example, I suggested to one intransigent client that she just "be that way" and that she could use her time as she wished. At first she agreed and diverted us to another topic. As time went on, however, it became clear that she felt uncomfortable with this arrangement. When I worked with her to stay present to that discomfort, she acknowledged how infuriated she had become with herself and how tired she had become of treating herself like an invalid. It was then that she recommitted to change.[6]

Vivifying or modeling desired behavior is another way to catalyze resistant clients. By forming an alliance with the part of a client that could be, the therapist can tacitly underscore who that client is; the contrast between the two can invigorate the client to transform. I once told a client who was about to give up on herself, for example, that I was not about to give up on her, and that I would form an alliance with the part of her that believed. Although little changed at first, she gradually realized how absurd her hopelessness had been. Rollo May (1991) has also frequently taken these kinds of stands with clients. "As long as I can be of help to you," he was fond of conveying, "I will work with you."

In his classic study of Mercedes, May (1972) exhibited yet another mode for vivifying desired behavior to stimulate transformation. Mercedes, May writes, was a repressed African American female who chronically suppressed her rage. No matter what he tried, May lamented, he could not bring her to stand up for herself and affirm the indignation to which she was entitled. While this state of affairs was a problem in their early relationship, it was not, as yet, a matter of urgency. When Mercedes became pregnant, however, the situation changed. "Every couple weeks," May writes, "she came in reporting that she had begun to bleed vaginally." This was especially true when she dreamed about being attacked by her mother (p. 86). The prospect of miscarrying, May surmised, was one way she could subconsciously avoid these attacks since, in her mind, her mother deeply resented her pregnancy. "Some rage had to be expressed," May declared, or "we were confronted with the likelihood of a spontaneous abortion" (p. 87).

In a determined but "not wholly conscious" move to expedite this expression, accordingly, May "decided to express [his] rage in place of hers" (p. 87). "Chiefly," May elaborates, "I attacked her mother with other figures thrown in from time to time. What did these blankety blank people mean by trying to kill her for having a baby," he exclaimed (p. 87).

How did May's diatribes affect Mercedes? She was able to experience them vicariously, May suggested, and rapidly express "her . . . anger at the attackers in the dreams" (p. 88). She was also able to carry her baby to term. By embodying Mercedes' fury, then, May tacitly enabled her to reassess her docility, and by showing her that one could survive such a reassessment, he deftly inspired her to reform.

"What she got from me," May concludes, "was not just the *permission* without condemnation to express her struggle to be; she got the prior *experience*, from someone in authority, of her own rights and her own being. . . . My giving vent to my rage was my living out my belief that she was a person with her own rights" (p. 90).

Confronting Resistance

Confrontation, for our purposes, is a direct and amplified form of vivification; instead of alerting clients to their self-destructive refuges, however, confrontation *alarms* clients about these refuges and, in lieu of nurturing transformation, presses for and demands such transformation.

Yet confrontation, within the experiential context, is not synonymous with dictation of therapeutic change. Where confrontation challenges, dictation coerces, demeans, and alienates most clients. There are three significant risks associated with dictation: (1) that the client will argue with and further resist the therapist, (2) that the client will give over her power to the therapist, or (3) that the client will be turned off and abandon the process altogether.

In order to minimize these risks, experiential confrontation must be rendered artfully, carefully, and with deep sensitivity to its effects. Use of the first person singular, for example, can minimize unwarranted overtones of accusation or punishment. The statements, "I believe you can do more" or "I don't buy what you're saying," serve to illustrate this contention. Posing confrontations in the form of questions or descriptions can also enhance their impact. "You're scared shitless," Bugental (1976, p. 16) reflected to his "hail-fellow-well-met" client Laurence, and this is precisely how his client felt. Following the lead of Rollo May (1969, p. 253), alternatively, I often challenge clients to differentiate between *can't* and *won't* at given junctures. "You mean you *won't* respond to that job offer," I suggested to a client invested in her inadequacy; "You mean you *won't* make time in your day for a lunch break," I remarked to another client invested in his invincibility.

It is sometimes useful, finally, to apprise clients of the difficulty of confronting their resistances, especially when those resistances are threatened with extinction. "A part of you is doing everything it can to keep you where you were," I tell clients in such circumstances. "The most you can do is to realize this and look at what it suggests." (See "Confronting Resistance" in the skill-building exercises.)

Rediscovering Meaning and Awe

As clients realize how imprisoning their choices and responses have been and how capable they are of transcending them, they develop new ways of standing in the world and new conceptions of who they will become. They develop a sense of "aha," or resonance, within themselves that clearly apprises them of their predicaments. They may say things like, "I never realized how profoundly I miss creativity in my life and how urgently I need to reclaim it" or "Now I see how so much of my life has been wasted on shame — and it's time I broke the cycle!" But it is not just this or that realization that emerges from resonant experiences; it is the *freedom* to possess such experiences that is the pivotal EI gain.

Freedom, then, is a whole new way to be — not just to do certain things — and it is a sense of the depth and profundity of life. It follows, moreover, that the more one can experience oneself in psychotherapy, the more one can connect with what deeply matters; it is precisely this connection — this full readiness for engagement — that gives experiences meaning. Or to put it in the terms of Rollo May (1969), experiential liberation cultivates more than insight, which is conceptual and schematic. It cultivates intentionality, which is one's total "orientation" toward a given value or direction (p. 232).

But again, intentionality is not just an orientation toward a specific value or direction. It is an orientation toward being itself; an orientation that apprises clients of their whole position in life, from their quailing smallness to their pulsating greatness, and from their ordinary, everyday experiences to their aspiring and even visionary reach.

I call this sensibility *awe*, the humility and wonder, thrill and anxiety, or full living that can emerge from optimal experiential liberation (Schneider, 2004). (Note that I do not mean *awe* in the colloquial sense of dread or humbleness before a great being or object; nor do I mean it in terms of the peak experience of a drug or a transient high — these are but trivializations of the fuller, more paradoxical sense of awe, as used in this text. [See Schneider, 2004, for an elaboration.])

Hence, there are two aspects of the rediscovery of meaning in experiential liberation: the aspect of a whole-bodied orientation (intentionality) toward specific life directions (e.g., a new job, relationship, or project), and the aspect of a whole-bodied orientation toward life itself — awe — as a result of the newfound resonance to specific life changes.

Consider, for example, my client "Sylvia." Sylvia was a 55-year-old widow whose presenting problem was a terror of being alone and a consequent denial of that feeling through compulsive eating. After three and a half years of therapy, Sylvia learned to be OK with herself — OK with her losses, OK with her fears and regrets, and even OK with her sporadic dating life. But she learned something more. She learned to be OK with, and indeed even enraptured by, the trees that lined her neighborhood, the daily chats with her neighbors, the strolls she took with her four-year-old niece, the dinners she arranged for friends, the yellow-tailed birds she spotted on her way to work, the cloud formations on storm-drenched days, her cat, her health, and her participation in a charitable organization. Sylvia no longer needed to mask her loneliness with food, because she no longer felt so alone: She now had *being* to accompany her.

In sum, Sylvia benefited from presence — she noticed more, felt more, and expressed more. Whereas formerly she was appalled by her vulnerabilities, now she was more accepting of them, more appreciative of their dimensionality.

The key to Sylvia's presence was *practice*. She had practice being crushed and she had practice becoming bold. She had practice becoming aware and she had practice going numb — all these were preparatory for Sylvia, as they seeded her reverence for life.

It is this inward preparation — intentionality — that gives experiences meaning (May, 1969). The chief question, of course, is, How do we, as therapists, help clients to consolidate these meanings — what tools or inspirations can we provide? The answer is, no tools or inspirations are needed other than those clients have already gleaned from our being present with them and from their discovering (*internalizing*) the ability to be present with themselves.

Yet it is of vital importance that we reinforce these developments, especially toward the close of therapy. For example, I often invite clients to explore their specific values toward the end of therapy, which values they hold dear and how they plan on implementing those values. I also find it helpful to reflect back to clients, not merely what they say, but what I hear them intending: "You seem to be excited about getting out there and doing what you felt you couldn't do all those years"; "I feel exuberance when you speak about marrying your fiancée, a sense that you are deeply ready to be involved"; "I sense that you no longer need to be the flashiest guy on the block, that you can now enjoy quiet moments at home"; "I don't get the sense of you walking on eggshells anymore — you no longer downplay your power"; or "You're not going to let physical handicaps handicap you mentally — this is the message that you have declared to me today."

Embodied Meaning as Exemplified by a Dream

It is not so much the *why* of a meaning that counts experientially, but the *what*: "*What* do you experience when you talk about breaking free of your father?" "*What* would you like to say to that sibling who has neglected you?" "*What* does your dream imply for your life?"

A client of mine recently dreamed that she was in her grandparents' house. It was old, dark, and decayed. "I slipped on something," my client recalled, "but then was able to get a foothold." By the end of the dream, my client found herself looking out into an ocean. "It was green, vast, and just beyond the house," she said.

Rather than inquiring about circumscribed content areas of this dream, such as its potential sexual or archetypal significance, I asked my client what it meant to *her* — here, now, as she was speaking about it. "Can you picture yourself in the house?" I asked. "What do you see there? What is it like to see your grandparents' things, to touch them? Do they remind you of anything you see or possess now? How about your experience of slipping and regaining a foothold — is that what's happening in your life? What is it like, finally, to survey the sea at the end of your dream? What kinds of thoughts, feelings, impressions come to mind when you contemplate the sea? How do they compare with what you experienced in the house?"

After spending some time reflecting on and discussing these issues with my client, I then invited her to ponder a series of suggestions: "I wonder if a part of you feels like the house — old and decaying — while another part feels like the sea — green and vast. This greenness and vastness, however, frightens you a bit — it's a bit disorienting — so you slip back into the old part of yourself — the safe but decaying house. Yet just as quickly, you are able to get a foothold again and face the sea. Might this not be what's going on in your life right now — your struggle to break free?"

That my hypothesis had validity was borne out by my client in a subsequent dream. "I dreamed about a sturdy, self-assured businesswoman," she announced. "This woman was modern, but she could also appreciate the past. I dreamed that she visited the house of her deceased grandmother. Now, however, this businesswoman owned the house — and she had rearranged it to her own specifications. In so doing, she had brought new life and taste to the house, but she had also preserved many of the things left over from her grandmother. As with me in my life right now, she had found new ways to arrange old things."

To sum up, meaning wells up from the depths. While we, as therapists, can do much to share, reflect, and invite clients into specified meanings, we cannot assign these meanings. Only clients can assume that responsibility. On the other hand, we can help clients to articulate their meaning cultivations and to consolidate them in actual practice.

Frequently, this means helping clients to clarify the role that smallness has played in their lives — the parts of themselves they refer to as infantile, bored, trapped, or desperately alone. It also means helping clients to clarify the antidotes to these conditions, the possibilities for assertion, sociability, play, creativity, and spiritual inspiration. Conversely, it also means helping clients to clarify the role that greatness has played in their lives — the aspects of themselves they perceive as insatiable, reckless, tyrannical, or indulgent — and the opportunities, by contrast, to contain those polarities.

To the degree we succeed in these efforts, clients will no longer experience smallness and greatness as panaceas, necessities — chemical or alcoholic answers — but the rich and complex potentialities to which we have alluded. They are then free to grapple with those potentialities, to design the lives they have envisioned.

One final note: To the degree that experientially based meaning has been achieved by clients, nonexperiential and semiexperiential levels of their functioning also tend to be enhanced. Acting as a feedback loop, meaning cultivation tends to renew physiological vigor, restore environmental adaptation, optimize cognitive appraisals, revive id-superego integrity, and regenerate attachment-separation elasticity (see Antonovsky, 1979; Bugental, 1976, 1987; Frankl, 1962; Kobasa, Maddi, & Puccetti, 1982; Reed, 1987; Yalom, 1980, for empirical support for such loops).

Furthermore, the sense of awe, as previously indicated, is almost invariably detectable in the cultivation of experienced-based meaning (Bugental, 1987; May, 1983). This sense enables clients to embrace larger and more comprehensive dimensions of themselves (and others) and may importantly benefit society as a whole (Buber, 1970; Bugental & Bracke, 1992; Merleau-Ponty, 1962; Schneider, 2004).

The basis for such holistic reorientations may be described as follows: The freer that people feel to experience themselves, the less panic they harbor; the less panic, the less urgency they feel to rearrange and hence dysfunctionally distort themselves. To the degree that people can draw upon this strength, the more fully they can perceive, experientially reflect, and respond.

To summarize, the experiential liberation condition emphasizes four stances: (1) *presence,* or the holding and illuminating of that which is palpably — immediately, kinesthetically, and affectively — relevant (between therapist and client and within the client); (2) *invoking the actual,* or the invitation to clients to occupy (stay present to) that which is palpably relevant; (3) *vivifying and confronting resistance,* or the amplification of how clients block potentially life-altering experiences; and (4) *rediscovery of meaning and awe,* or the values, meanings, and spiritual sensibilities that ensue from overcoming protective blocks.

As a final note, experiential liberation has a long and venerated history within existential psychology and philosophy. Two of the pioneers of this approach, Soren Kierkegaard and Paul Tillich, set forth the foundational principles. Kierkegaard, for example, foreshadowed the entire depth-experiential project with a passage from his little-known masterwork, *Concluding Unscientific Postscript*. In this analysis of the discovery of truth, Kierkegaard intimates all the basic building blocks of experiential liberation: Individual truth, Kierkegaard imparts, is "objective uncertainty, held fast, in the most personal, passionate experience. This is the truth, the highest truth attainable to the existing individual" (cited in Tillich, 1963). Although Kierkegaard's language is characteristically elliptical, his elucidation is deft. "Objective uncertainty" is the whole-bodied (i.e., "personal, passionate") presence to all the possible sides of a given dilemma (the obscurely private as well as the overtly public); and the "held fast in . . . personal, passionate experience" is the whole-bodied clarification, illumination, or decision that emerges from the whole-bodied presence. Kierkegaard's final point is that truth is ultimately unknowable, and that holistic immersion, presence, and discernment are the best we humans can attain. Almost line for line, Kierkegaard's proclamation echoes the aims and tenets of the experiential approach outlined in this section, and almost word for word, his message is contemporary.

Tillich (1967) presages a similar perspective with his notion of "listening love," which is a "listening to and looking at the concrete situation [of a given dilemma] in all its concreteness," including "the deepest motives of the other person" (p. 109). Listening love, Tillich elaborates, facilitates a holistic immersion and deliberation process; it leaves no stone unturned and no standpoint shunned on the path to a moral decision. Although no moral decision is without risk, Tillich concludes: "The more seriously one has considered all the factors involved . . . , the absolute as well as the relative factors, the more one can be sure that there is a power of acceptance in the depth of life" [and the depth of our lives, I might add] (p. 111) for the decision rendered. Hence, Tillich, like his predecessor Kierkegaard, advocated for a whole-bodied presence to the resolution of moral quandaries. Tillich termed this presence *listening love*, but he just as readily could have called it *experiential liberation* — the conditions for invoking, vivifying, and consolidating life's *more*.

Summary of the EI Model

In this chapter I have considered the following main points: The aim of existential-integrative therapy is to set clients free. Freedom can be understood as the capacity for choice within the natural and self-imposed limits of living; it can also be understood on six increasing and intertwining levels: (1) the physiological, (2) the environmental, (3) the cognitive, (4) the psychosexual, (5) the interpersonal, and (6) the experiential. Each of these levels is characterized by the capacities to constrict, expand, and center (or direct) oneself. Dread of either constriction or expansion promotes extreme and dysfunctional counterreactions to that dread, whereas confrontation with or integration of the polarities fosters renewal, meaning, and a larger sense of life. This sense can sometimes lead to the humility and wonder, thrill and vulnerability that constitute awe.

The basis for discerning liberation at each level is the client's desire and capacity for change. This desire and capacity are dependent on many factors, including the stage of therapy, the cultural disposition of the client, and the relational field within which client and therapist dwell. The desire and capacity for change also impact clients' battles — the aspect of clients that presses to emerge (break through) and the aspect that pulls to revert (withdraw to a former polarity). Nonexperiential liberation modalities address desires and capacities for change on physiological, environmental, and cognitive levels; semiexperiential modalities address them on psychosexual and interpersonal levels; and experiential modalities address them on the experiential (or being) level.

The ability to sense when and how one should move from one liberation modality to the next and the ability to detect and redress (e.g., vivify) polarizations as they arise constitute the art of this approach.

In the Appendices at the end of this section, I provide a series of summaries and skill-building exercises designed to animate the above discussion. These materials emphasize experiential learning and skill building, but they also outline non- and semiexperiential offerings that lead up to the experiential stage.

Notes

1. These criteria compare favorably with Prochaska, DiClemente, and Norcross's (1992) five transtheoretical stages of client change: (a) precontemplation, (b) contemplation, (c) preparation, (d) action, and (e) maintenance.
2. There is, of course, a degree of oversimplification in these statements about practitioners from respective orientations: Many are more existential than one might be led to believe. Indeed, recent research suggests that, in general, good therapists embody personable, affect-centered qualities and that from the client's point of view, these are the qualities that count (Bugental & Bracke, 1992; Lambert, Shapiro, & Bergin, 1986; Schneider, 1992).

   It is time, it would seem, to make the cultivation of such qualities central (rather than peripheral) to the formal education of clinicians.
3. Although my formulation of experiential modalities draws from and parallels those of such luminaries as Bugental (1978, 1987), Eugene Gendlin (1978), Alvin Mahrer (1986), Rollo May (1969, 1981), Frederick Perls (1969), and Irvin Yalom (1980), it is based on a modestly different set of practical and theoretical assumptions. (See Schneider, 1990/1999, 1993, for the relevant comparisons.)
4. I want to be clear that when I speak of structure here, I do not mean some kind of objective, or cookbook, formula. I mean a phenomenologically based metaphor that can help therapists *understand* what is going on in their clients and *redress* (or heal) what is going on in their clients based on that understanding. To be sure, some experiential therapists resist even metaphorical criteria for working with their clients because they see in such criteria an element of depersonalization. But to the extent that one views metaphors as subservient to the person about whom they are applied, one can counter this objectifying tendency. It is quite probable, moreover, that antimetaphorical therapists themselves use such criteria — albeit implicitly — to organize their own outlooks. Here I simply explicate some of those subliminal criteria.
5. Such underlying qualities are roughly equivalent to May's (1969) concept of intentionality, which we shall discuss.
6. While this turnaround may be explained on the basis of flooding and desensitization paradigms, I do not believe these are complete explanations. It was the condition whereby my client could fully experience rather than merely visualize her defensiveness that led her to substantively change.

References

Antonovsky, A. (1979) *Health, stress, & coping.* San Francisco: Jossey-Bass.

Beck, A. (1976). *Cognitive therapy and the emotional disorders.* New York: Signet.

Beutler, L., & Clarkin, J. (1990). *Systematic treatment selection: Toward targeted therapeutic interventions.* New York: Brunner/Mazel.

Binswanger, L. (1975). *Being in the world: Selected papers of Ludwig Binswanger* (J. Needleman, Trans.). New York: Basic Books.

Buber, M. (1970). *I and thou* (W. Kaufmann, Trans.). New York: Scribener. (Original work published 1937.)

Bugental, J. F. T. (1965). *The search for authenticity: an existential-analytic approach to psychotherapy.* New York: Holt, Rinehart, & Winston.

Bugental, J. F. T. (1976). *The search for existential identity: Patient-therapist dialogues in humanistic psychotherapy.* San Francisco: Jossey-Bass.

Bugental, J. F. T. (1978). *Psychotherapy and process: The fundamentals of an existential-humanistic approach.* Reading, MA: Addison-Wesley.

Bugental, J. F. T. (1987). *The art of the psychotherapist.* New York: Norton.

Bugental, J. F. T., & Bracke, P. (1992). The future of existential-humanistic psychotherapy. *Psychotherapy, 29*, 28–33.

Cogswell, J. (1993). Walking in your shoes: Toward integrating sense of self with sense of oneness. *Journal of Humanistic Psychology, 33*, 99–111.

Craig, P. E. (1986). Sanctuary and presence: An existential view of the therapist's contribution. *The Humanistic Psychologist, 14*, 22–28.

Erickson, M. (1965). The use of symptoms as an integral part of hypnotherapy. *American Journal of Clinical Hypnosis, 8*, 57–65.

Frankl, V. (1962). *Man's search for meaning: An introduction to logotherapy* (I. Lasch, Trans.). Boston: Beacon Press.

Frankl, V. (1965). *The doctor and the soul.* New York: Knopf.

Freud, S. (1963). *A general introduction to psychoanalysis* (J. Riviere, Trans.). New York: Pocket Books.

Friedman, M. (1991). *Encounter on the narrow ridge: A life of Martin Buber.* New York: Paragon House.

Gendlin, E. (1978). *Focusing.* New York: Bantam.

Kobasa, S., Maddi, S., & Puccetti, M. (1982). Personality and exercise as buffers in the stress-illness relationship. *Journal of Behavioral Medicine, 5*, 391–404.

Kohut, H. (1977). *The restoration of the self.* New York: International Universities Press.

Laing, R. D. (Speaker). (1985). *Theoretical and practical aspects of psychotherapy* (Cassette Recording L330-W1A). Phoenix, AZ: The Evolution of Psychotherapy Conference.

Lambert, M., Shapiro, D., & Bergin, A. (1986). The effectiveness of psychotherapy. In A. Bergin & S. Garfield (Eds.), *Handbook of psychotherapy and research* (pp. 157–212). New York: Wiley.

Mahrer, A. (1983). *Experiential psychotherapy: Basic practices.* New York: Brunner/Mazel.

Mahrer, A. (1986). *Therapeutic experiencing: The process of change.* New York: Norton.

May, R. (1969). *Love and will.* New York: Norton.

May, R. (1972). *Power and innocence: A search for the sources of violence.* New York: Norton.

May, R. (1981). *Freedom and destiny.* New York: Norton.

May, R. (1983). *The discovery of being: Writings in existential psychology.* New York: Norton.

May, R. (1991). *The cry for myth*. New York: Norton.

May, R. (1992). The loss of wonder. *Dialogues: Therapeutic applications of existential philosophy, 1*, 4–5.

Moreno, J. (1959). Psychodrama. In S. Arieti et al. (Eds.), *American handbook of psychiatry* (Vol. 2). New York: Basic Books.

Perls, F. (1969). *Gestalt therapy verbatim*. Moab, UT: Real People Press.

Phillips, J. (1980). Transference and encounter: The therapeutic relationship in psychoanalytic and existential therapy. *Review of Existential Psychiatry and Psychology, 17*, 135–152.

Prochaska, J., DiClemente, C., & Norcross, J. (1992). In search of how people change: Applications to addictive behaviors. *American Psychologist, 47*, 1102–1114.

Reed, P. (1987). Spirituality and well-being in terminally ill hospitalized adults. *Research in Nursing and Health, 10*, 335–344.

Reich, W. (1949). *Character analysis*. New York: Orgone Institute Press.

Rilke, R. M. (1991). Letters to a young poet. In M. Friedman (Ed.), *The worlds of existentialism: A critical reader* (pp. 266–270). Atlantic Highlands, NJ: Humanities Press.

Schneider, K. J. (1985). Clients' perceptions of the positive and negative characteristics of their therapists (Doctoral dissertation, Saybrook Institute, 1984). *Dissertation Abstracts International, 45*, 3345B.

Schneider, K. J. (1993). *Horror and the holy: Wisdom-teachings of the monster tale*. Chicago: Open Court.

Schneider, K. J. (1999). *The paradoxical self: Toward an understanding of our contradictory nature* (2nd ed.). Amherst, NY: Humanity Books. (Original work published 1990)

Schneider, K. J. (2004). *Rediscovery of awe: Splendor, mystery, and the fluid center of life*. St. Paul, MN: Paragon House.

Tillich, P. (Speaker). (1963). *Kierkegaard's existential theology* (Part 2). (CD Recording T577 123, Paul Tillich Compact Disk Collection). Richmond, VA: Union PSCE.

Tillich, P. (1967). *My search for absolutes*. New York: Simon & Schuster.

Van Dusen, W. (1965). Invoking the actual in psychotherapy. *Journal of Individual Psychology, 21*, 66–76.

Volkan, V. (1987). *Six steps in the treatment of borderline personality organization*. New York: Jason Aronson.

Wolfe, B. (1992). The integrative therapy of the anxiety disorders. In J. Norcross & M. Goldfried (Eds.), *Handbook of psychotherapy integration* (pp. 373–401). New York: Basic Books.

Wolpe, J. (1969). *The practice of behavior therapy*. New York: Pergamon.

Yalom, I. (1980). *Existential psychotherapy*. New York: Basic Books.

Appendix

Summary of the Four Stances of the Experiential Liberation Condition

Experiential liberation entails four stances (invitations): (1) presence, (2) invoking the actual, (3) vivifying and confronting resistance, and (4) rediscovering meaning and awe.*

I. *Presence* holds and illuminates that which is palpably (immediately, kinesthetically, affectively, and profoundly) relevant *between* therapists and clients and *within* clients. It is the ground and eventual goal of experiential work. Specifically, its goals are:
   A. To illuminate the client's experiential world, to understand that world by deep immersion in the preverbal/kinesthetic experience of the client, and to clarify the salient features of that world (such as the smallness-greatness/constrictive-expansive clusters) that anticipate future problems and directions of treatment. Presence can also alert the therapist to the client's desire and capacity for change, which in turn may point in more traditional therapeutic directions within the existential-integrative schema.
   B. To provide the sanctuary, containment, and safety within which deep immersion can take place.
   C. To deepen the client's capacity to constructively act on her discoveries.

II. *Invoking the actual* is inviting or encouraging the client into that which is palpably relevant. The goals of invoking the actual are to help the client clarify, stay present to, and encounter her concern; this work is facilitated by assisting the client to attend to the here and now, make *I* statements, and pay attention to the preverbal processes behind her words. It is also facilitated through the engagement of meditation and imagery, deep somatic immersion, role-play and rehearsal, interpersonal encounter, use of fantasy and dream material, and extra therapy experimentation to practice and apply experiential skills outside the clinical setting.

III. *Vivifying and confronting resistance* (*protections*) are ways of helping clients overcome blockages to that which is palpably relevant.

* These stances are often sequential, but depending on many factors, such as the client's pace, they sometimes operate irregularly with one another and should be dealt with accordingly.

Note: It is important that vivifying and confronting be used to empower the client, and not the therapist or outside authority, to overcome his resistances. This conforms to our belief that the lasting power for change resides in the client, not in the one who instructs or directs him.

The goals of vivifying and confronting resistance (protections) are:

A. To vivify, feed back, or "hold a mirror up" to moments where the client blocks or defeats himself, to acknowledge erroneous feedback when it is discovered and to suspend judgment about feedback when it is questionable, to mimic or physically mirror the client's resistance where appropriate, to empathically trace out implications of the client's resistance, to model or act out the consequences of overcoming the client's resistance (which can, paradoxically, mobilize the client to break out of his victimized stance), and to enable or encourage the client's resistance where appropriate (which can also, paradoxically, mobilize him); and

B. To empathically confront resistance (when other means fail) by intensifying the vivification (e.g., by helping to alarm the client about, not merely alert him to, the ways in which he blocks or defeats himself) and to use challenging questions or suggestions where appropriate to foster that sense of urgency (e.g., "Do you mean you *won't* when you say you *can't*?").

IV. *Rediscovering meaning and awe* emerges from maximal encounter with self (being). The goal of such rediscovery is:

A. To experientially realize, discern, and act on that which deeply matters about one's life.

Note: When engaged maximally, this stance often leads to heightened abilities to experience intimacy, altruism, and spirituality (e.g., awe).

Ways the Stances Utilize Constrictive-Expansive Dynamics

I. *Presence* stresses the question, *What* is palpably relevant *between* the therapist (T) and the client (C) and *within* C. That which is palpably relevant is often (though not necessarily) that which C denies, and that which C denies often clusters around constriction (smallness, fragility, dissolution) or expansion (greatness, audacity, explosiveness). While C may be ostensibly angry (*expanded*), for example, the palpably relevant issue may be sadness (*smallness*). On the other hand, C's anger may indeed be the relevant issue, and discrepancies (such as sadness) may be absent. T needs to give C time, therefore, to explore whether her polarity is the palpably relevant one or whether it is essentially defensive in quality — in which case signs of discrepancy and denial should begin to manifest themselves.

II. *Invoking the actual* stresses inviting or encouraging C into that which is palpably relevant. This is done by artfully feeding back or providing here-and-now opportunities for C to "occupy" that which is palpably relevant. T might comment to C, for example, that "A tear has just formed in your eye," "I feel a sudden heaviness in your manner," "I wonder if we could role-play that meeting with your boss — see what feelings come up now," or, "You're really steaming — how might that help you get on with your life?"

The constrictive-expansive continuum can also alert T to (or make her watchful for) palpable relevancies that are very remote from C's overt presentation. Sometimes, very selectively, it is useful to test the water with this kind of foresight. For example, James Bugental's (1976, p. 16) comment to his inflated client Laurence that "You're scared shitless!" and "Bob"'s comment to the ostensibly enraged "Joanna," "I sense that you are deeply hurting right now, Joanna"* were foundational in their impact and catalyzing of the liberation process.

The worst that can happen in such circumstances is that the client will resist the challenge (in which case the resistance must be worked with). But at least he or she gets a taste of it. (Working with him or her more gradually might have postponed this taste, and its momentum, correlatively to encounter it in future.)

Summary of EI Decision Points

Below is a summary of decision points suggested by the EI theoretical framework. These, too, can be role-played, or simply reflected upon, in the course of study.

1. The first and ongoing question is, What is this client's desire and capacity for constrictive/expansive change? (Use presence, intuition, empirical knowledge, and dialogue with the client to render this judgment.)
2. If the client is in acute crisis, in the early stages of therapy, fragile, suspicious, or intellectually unprepared, consider nonexperiential liberation modalities (behavioral, cognitive, or medical).
3. If the client emphasizes childhood sexuality or interpersonal issues, or if he is at an impasse with nonexperiential and experiential liberation modalities, consider semiexperiential liberation modalities (psychoanalysis, self-psychology).

* As suggested in this section, such interventions can reflect both invoking-the-actual (emergent) and amplifying-resistance (regressive) aspects of treatment.

4. If the client appears physically, cognitively, and emotionally ready, and if he accepts invitations to deepen any of the concerns or conditions above, consider experiential liberation modailities (presence, invoking the actual, vivifying and confronting resistance, and rediscoving meaning and awe).

Skill-Building Exercises: Suggestions for Instructors

The following skill-building exercises — to be facilitated by instructors — can help students personally understand experiential liberation and translate that understanding into practice. The exercises are divided into two sections: those that are personal and those that are clinical (applied). While the personal exercises may be engaged variably over a course of study, the clinical exercises should be engaged sequentially, in the order presented.*

I. Personal Exercises

Exercises That Challenge Students to Be Present, to Face Resistance, and to Rediscover Meaning and Awe

The "Who Am I" Exercise Have students write down 10 phrases that best describe who they are (e.g., "I am a worrier," "I am a student," etc.) and order them in terms of priority and centrality to themselves (e.g., 10 is least central, 1 is most central). Have students do this reflectively, but not labor over it.

Complete the exercise in 15 minutes.

Immediately following the above, and beginning with the least central description, proceed to have students cross out each description, right down to the first and most central, if possible. As they are crossing out each description, have them be as mindful as possible of how that particular deletion/relinquishment feels to them. What are its implications for their lives?

Complete the exercise in 15 minutes.

For the next half hour, discuss with students the implications of this exercise. What was it like (for those students willing to engage it)? Did it reveal anything new or surprising to them? What did it imply for prioritizing their lives and for rearranging or losing those priorities? Did they welcome their identity descriptions and loss-of-identity descriptions, or did they resist them? If they resisted them, how did they deal with the resistance? How present were they able to be during the exercise, and what did the exercise imply about the kind of constrictive or expansive life designs they have created? Finally, what did the exercise imply about the clinical work they do, or the kinds of crises their clients experience? (See Bugental, 1987, for an elaboration on this exercise.)

* Although these exercises are rudimentary, they can also be emotionally challenging. It is important, therefore, to prepare students for such challenges and to support them as required.

Encountering One's "Double" This exercise is modified from a workshop given by Bugental (November 1993). An extremely important theme in the psychology of literature (Rank, 1925/1971), the double (or what the Germans call *doppelganger*) is equally significant for clinicians. Essentially, the double is the suppressed side (or pole) of one's personality; it is the side that is denied. The aim of this exercise is to sensitize students to this phenomenon and its rich EI implications. The exercise proceeds as follows: Have students break up into triads. Request that the members of each triad greet each other as if they met at a party. Stress that students simply be themselves with one another and not try to play a particular role. After four minutes, ask that students reflect on these interactions, and note their verbal and preverbal experiences. Next, request that students try a role-play (to the degree they feel comfortable). Suggest that they role-play a side of themselves that they are intrigued about but generally suppress in everyday life. Recommend that they genuinely immerse themselves in this role and attune to their manner of engaging it. Give them four minutes for this segment. Next, ask students to write down their experience of role-playing their double: What did it feel like? How much did they resist it? How much did they feel liberated by it? What are its implications for their lives (e.g., costs, compromises, possibilities)? Stress that these observations do not have to be shared with others. Finally, bring the class back to its normal arrangement and open the floor to discussion. (Tie the discussion to the pertinent EI themes, such as integration of polarities, presence, resistance, and meaning creation.)

Writing One's Own Obituary Instruct students to write a one- or two-paragraph description of how they would like to be remembered after they die. Afterward, discuss what this exercise was like for them. What did it bring up as far as how they are currently living their lives? What impact might it have on how they will live their lives in the future? What does it say about time, aging, and death? What fears and priorities does it signal?

This exercise should take approximately a half hour and is best offered on the last day of the term. (See Bugental, 1973/1974, for an elaboration on this exercise.)

II. Clinical Exercises

Exercise That Cultivates Presence

Begin this class exercise with the progressive tension and relaxation of group muscles, from the forehead to the toes. Then try a simple meditative exercise, such as attending to breathing or body sensations. Next, have students pair up and sit across from one another in silence for one minute. Ask participants to attune to their partner's body positions, gestures, facial expressions, and other nonverbal signals. Underscore the freshness and uniqueness of these experiential worlds. Then have students attend to their own thoughts, feelings, and sensations in response to their partners' presentations. Afterward, have students record and discuss these respective experiences.

The time for this exercise is 20 to 30 minutes.

*Exercises Aimed at Invoking the Actual (or Palpably Relevant)**

Enhancing Presence Through Focus and Topical Expansion Have students form dyads. One partner plays the therapist (T), and the other partner plays the client (C). T begins by asking C, "What is of concern?" or "What really matters to you right now?" (It is important that C discuss a concern that he or she feels comfortable relating.) T observes C's response and only nods or says, "Tell me more." Afterward, the partners discuss their experiences in terms of presence to body sensations, affect, imagery, and other nonverbal signals. Partners then switch roles.

The time per role-play should be 10 minutes. Discussion follows.

Further Enhancing Presence Through Focus, Topical Expansion, and Feedback Have students form trios. One partner observes and records his perceptions of the students who play C and T. The observer should especially note T's ability to facilitate C's presence and immersion in her concern. T is to do this by gently encouraging C to stay with and expand on her feelings, by empathically paraphrasing what she says (repeating key phrases, slowing her down, mimicking or mirroring as appropriate), and having her concretely describe an example of her problem. Afterward, each party should describe what happened from his or her vantage point and — time permitting — switch roles.

Time per role-play should be 20 minutes.

Deepening Presence Have students form trios. The observer this time is to note interaction. In addition to the above skills, the therapist is to help the client stay with *I* statements and personal and relevant content. T is to begin tagging points where the client diverges from relevant material or intellectualizes. T should also begin to alert the client to body movements, vocal tones, and points where the dialogue becomes intense or charged, as well as discrepancies between content and affect. T should use discussion, dream work, role-play, rehearsal, and meditation, and should even suggest experiments for C to try outside of the session to help him deepen his self-encounter and begin to understand, in a live way, the basis for his concern. (This exercise is aimed at deepening C's self-contact and initial felt understanding of his concerns. The point should be stressed that insight is to emerge from deep immersion in the subjective and not from T's interpretation.) Discuss from each perspective and switch roles.

Time per role-play should be 20 minutes.

---

* It is best if instructors themselves role-play the exercises described from this point on, so as to provide students with an example.

The Therapeutic Encounter Have students form trios again. This exercise is aimed at helping students to use the relationship to facilitate self-exploration and integration. The first focus here is on the impact of T's empathy in facilitating C's self-immersion and awareness. The second focus is on not only T's attention to transference/countertransference issues but also current interpersonal responses and how they affect C's self-contact. The observer should watch how T alerts the client to and handles disappointments, irritations, pleasures, and so on within the role-play relationship and how these are worked through. Does T disclose too much, too little? Does she evoke C's affect productively? The idea is to be able to struggle somewhat but be sensitive to and steadfastly maintain contact with C. Discuss from each perspective and switch partners.

Time per role-play should be 20 minutes.

Exercises Designed to Vivify and Confront Resistance (or Protections)

Vivifying Resistance Again, set up trios. Here, C agrees to role-play a resistant client. Discuss the importance of being sensitive to resistances — how they are perceived as familiar and safer than alternative life designs despite their destructiveness. T focuses on noting and tagging all resistant behavior — changes in vocal tone, gestures, facial expression, emotional blocking, intellectualization, projection, divergence from the present or from the relationship with T, superficial contact, and so on. T should gently challenge C to weigh (in a felt way) alternative directions or pros and cons of the particular resistance. The idea of this exercise is not to force or eradicate resistances but to vivify them and to help C observe how these resistances cripple his world. Moreover, this vivification helps C move toward taking responsibility for and making a decision about that which holds him back. The therapist cannot really force this, nor should she. Discuss from each perspective and switch roles.

Time per role-play should be 20 minutes.

Confronting Resistance Form trios. This time, C will role-play *chronic* resistance. T will attempt to empathically, but firmly, jar C into consciousness of his resistance and his ability to overcome that resistance. She can do this through nonaccusatory, first-person suggestions (e.g., "I believe you can say more") or evocative descriptions (e.g., "You look terrorized right now"). Such confrontation can also be facilitated through challenges to distinguish between *can't* and *won't* and between *might* and *will*. (It is important to alert participants to their option to withdraw from this potentially intensive exercise at any time.) Discuss from each perspective and switch roles. (It is especially helpful to discuss the empathic quality of T's confrontation as well as C's response to that quality.)

Time per role-play should be 20 minutes.

Exercise Aimed at Synthesizing Previous Skills and the Rediscovery of Meaning and Awe

This exercise draws upon all previous skills to facilitate meaning creation and a productive life direction. Form trios. T should help C to (1) focus on and stay present to a relevant concern, (2) meditate on and experiment with that concern, (3) attend to the immediate relationship as appropriate, (4) vivify and work through resistance/protections, and (5) rediscover meaning (and potentially, awe) as a result of the working through.

Time per role-play should be 30 minutes.

References

Bugental, J. F. T. (1973/1974). Confronting the existential meaning of 'my death' through group exercises. *Interpersonal Development, 4,* 148–163.

Bugental, J. F. T. (1976). *The search for existential identity: Patient-therapist dialogues in humanistic psychotherapy.* San Francisco: Jossey-Bass.

Bugental, J. F. T. (1987). *The art of the psychotherapist.* New York: Norton.

Rank, O. (1971). *The double: A psychoanalytic study* (H. Tucker, Trans.). New York: New American Library. (Original work published 1925)

Part 3
Case Illustrations of the EI Model

The cases in the following chapters elucidate the practical utility of the preceding EI guidelines. Selection of the case material was based on four criteria: (1) its experiential-integrative focus, (2) its clarity and conciseness, (3) its depth and originality, and (4) its ethnic and diagnostic diversity.

A significant cross section of the existential-integrative therapeutic community has been mobilized to contribute to this section. For example, while a number of the authors are world-renowned authorities, others are authorities in their particular regions or communities; and while all of the authors are highly accomplished writers, a few present their case material here for the first (or nearly first) time. Furthermore, a number of the contributors are representatives of mainstream traditions in psychology, for example, cognitive-behaviorism, psychoanalysis, and psychiatry, while a number of others are direct representatives of the existential-humanistic tradition.

One final note: While the EI guidelines and themes, such as smallness-greatness, nonexperiential, and experiential, are notable in each vignette — and will be alluded to in chapter headnotes — they may not be referred to explicitly in each vignette. This is because of each contributor's unique slant on his or her material; it is also, as previously noted, due to the flexible nature of existentially oriented therapy in general. Therefore, it is enough if the EI guidelines spark a fruitful dialogue about the case material. Ultimately, however, the vignettes must speak for themselves.

5
EI Approaches to Multiculturalism

In the following chapter, the EI approach is elucidated by three multicultural case illustrations: an examination of Latino psychospirituality, a perspective on African American liberation, and a reflection on existentialism as personalism — a Native American perspective. In the first illustration, on Latino psychospirituality, Lillian Comas-Díaz focuses on what she terms *Latin American humanism*. This philosophy is a synthesis of historical, political, and cultural influences that have informed Dr. Comas-Díaz's existential-integrative approach to Latino clients. In featuring her work with Mariana, Dr. Comas-Díaz shows how a culturally sensitive therapist can combine ritual, dream work, and cognitive-behavioral exercises with vibrant presence to promote healing and inner restoration.

Nowhere is the perception of being hyperconstricted, of being dismissed and wiped away, more acute than in the African American community, where every day debasements and historical biases take an exasperating toll. In the next illustration, Donadrian L. Rice elucidates the case of Darrin, an African American trucking manager who, despite an initial involvement with therapy, began to experience an intensifying crisis of identity. Through a series of cognitive, behavioral, and supportive interventions, Dr. Rice helps Darrin not only to gain a foothold on his faltering life circumstances, but also to begin the process of self-reassessment. Through this self-reassessment, and an increased understanding of his sociocultural predicament, Darrin becomes amenable to the next step in his therapeutic evolution — the ability to respond. This ability, Rice shows, helps Darrin to assume responsibility not only for his difficulties, but also for his possibilities, and the choice, freedom, and renewal that attend.

In the next case, Royal Alsup illuminates a little-known existential perspective — the existentialism of personalism, which has its roots in both Native and African American folk traditions, as well as the dialogical Jewish philosophy of Martin Buber. In his case of a 15-year-old American Indian girl, Dr. Alsup shows how the convergence of political awareness, empathic resonance, and experiential storytelling assuaged lifelong grief. Not only was the grief acutely personal, but it was also cultural and indeed ancestral, and it led to dire flirtations with drugs. By drawing on his existentialism of personalism, Dr. Alsup combines the elements of activism, appreciation for ritual, and profound experiential engagement to facilitate a remarkable renewal.

Latino Psychospirituality

Lillian Comas-Díaz

Lillian Comas-Díaz, PhD, is the executive director of the Transcultural Mental Health Institute, a clinical professor at the George Washington University Department of Psychiatry and Behavioral Sciences, and a private practitioner in Washington, D.C. Dr. Comas-Díaz served as the 2006 president of the American Psychological Association (APA) division on Psychologists in Independent Practice and is the founding editor-in-chief of the APA Division 45 official journal, *Cultural Diversity and Ethnic Minority*. She currently serves as an associate editor of the *American Psychologist*.

Latin American humanism emerged as a response to historical and geopolitical forces. Centuries of colonization shaped Latinos's sense of self. To illustrate, the heritage of cultural imperialism, economic oppression, and political subjugation has profoundly affected Latinos's personal sense of autonomy and agency. Instead of individual agency, Latinos frequently espouse a contextual co-agency rooted in spirituality (Keller, 2002). Notwithstanding the contemporary political status of Latin American countries, the colonization ideology is manifested in the psychological mindset of many Latinos (Quiñones, 2007). However, Latinos tend to respond to oppression and oppose adversity with a spirit of creativity and vitality (Beezley & Ewell, 1987). Their history of asserting the vibrancy of their traditions unfolds a path for the creation of meaning.

The humanistic lineage of meaning making is a source of healing and liberation. It promotes an "ideological ethnicity," or a tendency to find life meaning by revisiting cultural beliefs and rituals (Harwood, 1981). When informed with cultural knowledge, an existential-emancipatory perspective can be an appropriate psychotherapeutic approach for Latinos. In this narrative I present Latino psychospirituality, a healing approach that integrates existential, liberating, and cultural dimensions into psychotherapy. Afterward, I discuss a clinical case illustrating the application of Latino psychospirituality.

Core Elements of Latino Psychospirituality

Latinos's collectivist orientation frames their propensity to contextualize, connect, and integrate (Ho, 1987). Their relational orientation forms their sense of self, grounding identity into family, ancestry, community, environment, and spirituality. Psychospirituality encourages the use of cultural beliefs and traditions to heal and to develop spiritual wisdom. Many Latinos learn spirituality through imitation, participation in rituals, and cultural osmosis (Comas-Díaz, 2006). Consequently, there is a plethora of spiritual allusions in Latino daily life (Koss-Chioino & Vargas, 1999). As a way of life, spirituality helps Latinos to deepen their sense of meaning and purpose (Muñoz & Mendelson, 2005; Tree, 2001). Psychospirituality embraces the belief that everything has a spirit. That is, humans, animals, plants, inanimate objects, and even the cosmos are considered to have a spiritual nature (De La Cancela & Zavala Martinez, 1983). Such spirits partake in people's lives and communicate through dreams, visions, intuitions, and other supernatural means. Additionally, Latino psychospirituality addresses ontological wounds, whereby the therapist focuses on the awareness that transcends words, contents, and measurable categories (see Schneider & May, 1995; and Part 2, this volume). In the section to follow, I will discuss the core elements of Latino psychospirituality. They are contextualism, *sabiduría*, *mestizaje*, and magical realism.

Contextualism Most people process information according to their degree of context relatedness or their relationship between self and other. Collectivistic Latinos tend to be embedded in their circumstances, whereby their perceptions, judgments, and behaviors are guided by the connection to context. In other words, Latinos endorse contextualism (see also the case study by Stolorow in Chapter 12). A theory of behavior that promotes the tendency to describe the self and others, contextualism uses more contextual references and fewer dispositional references (Choi, Nisbett, & Norenzayan, 1999). Thus, collectivistic Latinos are inclined to be more context-bound than individualistic persons, who tend to be context-free. Contextualism promulgates a combined locus of control where the context determines which locus of control will prevail (Comas-Díaz, 2006). Along these lines, many Latinos believe important things happen in life outside of their control (De Rios, 2001; Falicov, 1998). This conviction is not an external locus of control, but a cosmic locus of control. Consequently, sociocentric Latinos align their personal/relational agency with divine or cosmic will (Coelho, 2003). In this regard, contextualism recognizes the decisive influence of factors outside of individuals' power in life.

Sabiduría *Sabiduría*, or wisdom, states that healing and spiritual development are interconnected (Ruiz, 1997). An existential and mystical knowledge, *sabiduría* enables people to live life with meaning. Therefore, *sabiduría* teaches that illness offers an opening for integration and personal growth. In this regard, sociocentric Latinos view life as an instructive experience where they learn and teach existential lessons. *Sabiduría* involves the perception of life setbacks as opportunities for growth and self-improvement (Ruiz, 1997). Health and wellness entail a balance of body, mind, and spirit. *Sabiduría*, the reward for living life with meaning and purpose, exemplifies wholeness, connectedness, and evolvement (Coelho, 2003). Hence, *sabiduría* honors the ancient knowledge of cultural traditions while promoting consciousness and enlightenment. As an illustration, *dichos* psychology is based on achieving *sabiduría*. Drawing from Spanish proverbs or sayings, *dichos* psychology captures folk wisdom and addresses the problems and dilemmas of life (Aviera, 1996; Comas-Díaz, 2006; Zuñiga, 1991, 1992).

Mestizaje Latinos comprise an ethnic rainbow. They are mestizos, the offspring of the fusion of diverse races to create a new species (Ramirez, 1998). *Mestizaje* requires a dialectical cultural adaptation while remaining grounded in cultural roots. In other words, *mestizaje* entails a syncretism that promotes identity reformulation. *La Raza cósmica*, or *La Raza*, is a widespread term used among many Mexican Americans to denote the Latino racial syncretism that promotes civilization (Vasconselos, 1997). For instance, the Latino worldview is a product of the syncretism of different orientations, including, but not limited to, European Christianity, Native American animism, and African spirituality. An iconic illustration of *mestizaje* is the Lady of Guadalupe, the patroness of the Americans. *La Morenita* (the little Mexican Black Madonna) represents the syncretism of the Mexican goddess Tonantzin and the White Spanish *Virgin de la Guadalupe* (Castillo, 1996). A classic example of syncretism, *mestizaje* promotes a pan-relational worldview and involves ancestral, sacred, and cosmic affiliations in the healing encounter.

Magical Realism Research has documented that Latinos tend to use more fantasy, magical thinking, and dissociation than their Anglo and African American counterparts (Pole, Best, Metzler, & Marmar, 2005). Magical realism may explain these findings. Magical realism involves the interpenetration of reality with fantasy (Maduro & Martinez, 1974). An alteration of reality mediated by spiritual intensity (Zamora & Faris, 1995), magical realism is an attitude toward reality expressed through cultural forms involving a belief in the supernatural. Magical realism has its roots in Latino indigenous beliefs. For instance, the Toltec philosophy states that we are in a continuous dreamlike state where reality communes with imagination and magic (Ruiz, 1997). Magic realism is translated into daily life through the permeability of boundaries. For instance, *familismo* allows nonbiological individuals, such as godparents, *compadres/comadres* (co-parents), and friends, to become family members. These permeable boundaries extend beyond death (Shapiro, 1994). Magical realism not only infuses life with fantasy, but also blends objective and subjective realities. In summary, magical realism is a manifestation of interconnectedness or the belief that the self is intertwined with the other.

The following case vignette illustrates the application of Latino psychospirituality.

Mariana: An Artist at Life

"I'm here because my friends begged me to see a psychologist," "Mariana" said as soon as she entered my office. A mixed-race Latina, Mariana stated that she got into an argument with an African American policewoman. Mariana's neighbors called the police because the music in her apartment was too loud. "It was my 30th birthday," Mariana explained. However, she acknowledged having an anger management problem ("I almost got arrested"), and thus agreed to give therapy a second chance. "I had couch time before," she said, referring to her previous treatment. "I would like to try something closer to my culture." Upon exploration, Mariana revealed that she was interested in holistic and spiritual approaches. "I grew up Catholic, but I'm a spiritual tossed salad now," Mariana explained, adding that she endorsed a syncretistic Christianity and a goddess-oriented and indigenous spirituality.

We began with relaxation techniques. Afterward, I taught her the centering technique developed by Jose Silva (Silva & Miele, 1977). This relaxation/meditation method has a Latino spiritual foundation. Working within this approach facilitated the emergence of a therapeutic alliance. As a result, Mariana felt more comfortable in controlling her angry outbursts. Subsequently, I explored substance use/abuse and she reported that she smoked marijuana and drank alcohol occasionally. "*No por mucho madrugar se amanece mas temprano*," Mariana responded with this *dicho*, stating that you do not need to start early to accomplish a task. Although Mariana recognized that she drank too much during parties, she saw nothing wrong with smoking pot. Instead of confronting her at that point, I decided to cement our relationship by conducting a cultural genogram (Hardy & Laszloffy, 1995).

The cultural genogram revealed that Mariana was an only child of a Black Colombian mother and a Mexican Colombian father. Both parents were educators. Mariana spent her first 14 years in Colombia before moving to the United States. The genogram revealed that she was named after her mother's twin sister. Mariana reported being very close to her aunt, who was also her *madrina*, or godmother. Mariana's childhood was punctuated by a tragedy. The Colombian guerrillas kidnapped her aunt for a year, until "Maria," Mariana's mother, gathered the ransom. The guerrillas kidnapped people at random, regardless of social class, to instill terror in the population. According to the newspapers, Maria and the guerrillas made the exchange, but when Mariana reached her sister, she was shot in the back and fell dead in Maria's arms. "Not only did I lose my aunt, but also my mother, who became emotionally absent," Mariana said without emotion.

Entresueño Mariana reported that she suffered from nightmares that she could not recall. I offered suggestions such as self-induction statements to remember her dreams, recording her dreams in the middle of the night, keeping a notebook by her night table, and others. I called this approach *entresueño* (in between dreams or a lucid dreaming) to denote a meditative state of not being asleep or awakened. The *entresueño* seemed to work, as Mariana began to remember her dreams, in particular, a recurrent one. She saw *La Llorona* chasing her. *La Llorona*, or *La Malinche*, is a Mexican icon based on Hernán Cortés's indigenous lover and translator who helped him to conquer Mexico. After bearing the conquistador two mestizo sons, La Malinche killed them. She committed murder to prevent Cortés from taking their sons to Spain. La Llororna is called "the crying one" because she cries in her search for her murdered sons. We discussed the dream from a psychodynamic perspective. Additionally, I suggested guided imagery to explore its cultural meaning. After helping Mariana to relax, I guided her through the healing light exercise. This exercise, borrowed from yoga, is part of the "eye movement desensitization and reprocessing" protocol (Shapiro, 1995). I asked Mariana to visualize a cup and place it six inches above the crown of the head. Then, I instructed her to imagine a ray of light in a color that she associated with healing. She identified golden yellow with healing. The goal was to have the healing light enter Mariana's crown and flow throughout her body, cleansing and healing. I suggested to Mariana that she accompany the light at points in her body that coincide with the chakras or energy centers (Brennan, 1988; Fox, 1999; Myss, 1996). Mariana discovered an obstruction in her belly and she began to cry. "What's happening?" I asked. "I feel something here." "Shine your healing light into your pelvis. What do you see?" "My unborn child."

Using a method developed by physician and Latino healer Marcelo Urban (personal communication, November 25, 2000), I asked Mariana to identify her emotion. "Guilt," she replied, "I killed my baby." After completing breathing exercises Mariana moved her guilt throughout her body into the earth. Afterward, we reprocessed her feelings and Mariana changed the negative cognitions into positive ones. "What do you need to do?" Mariana replied, "To continue cleansing," as she invited her healing light into her pubic area. "My daughter is golden now." She concluded the exercise with affirmations of love.

We discussed Mariana's guided imagery during the next therapy session. She revealed that she had repressed the traumatic abortion. Mariana reported that she got pregnant at 15 by "Jose," her boyfriend. "She was a love child and I called her Amada (loved one)," Mariana emphasized. "My parents ordered me to stop seeing Jose." Mariana started to cry, "I had an abortion." After a while she said, "That was my *quinceañera* party," sarcastically referring to the sweet 15 Latino coming-of-age milestone. She expressed rage at her parents, especially toward her mother. "I envisioned Aunt, who was childless, raising my daughter Amada," she added. We explored Mariana's feelings about her role in the abortion. "I need to forgive myself," she concluded. To facilitate this process, I suggested a meditation exercise where the person places the right palm on several chakras and enunciates statements of forgiveness and compassion (Marriot, 2004). Mariana completed the exercise and wept at each station of forgiveness: "I can start forgiving myself." During this meditation, Mariana saw Tlazoltotl, the Toltec goddess of carnal love and desire. In her aspect as Tlaelcuani, the goddess forgives sexual transgressions (Cisneros, 2001). Mariana decided to confess to the goddess as part of her forgiveness ritual. "I am at peace at night. My nightmares turned into *entresueños*."

Arpillera After her family's tragedy, Mariana developed body aches that had no physical basis. She connected them to her *madrina*'s murder, her subsequent move to the United States, and her abortion. "Can you help me?" Once more, I suggested a mind-body exercise. The method, adapted from several sources (Kleinman, 1988; L. Mehl-Medrona, personal communication, August 10, 2006), involved a series of questions to the self:

Q: Who are you?
A: I'm Mariana.
Q: Where did you come from?
A: I have always been here.
Q: Why are you here?
A: I don't need to be here anymore. Mariana needs to let me go.
Q: Can you explain yourself?
A: I don't need to.
Q: Where are you going?
A: Into the light.
Q: What aspect of Mariana are you?
A: I'm her *madrina*.
Q: What do you need in order to go into the light?
A: I will let Mariana know in a dream.

Latino psychospirituality teaches that the dead continue their relationship with the living though dreams, visions, visitations, or the intercession of folk healers (Council of National Psychological Associations, 2003; Shapiro, 1994). For instance, spirits of the dead may appear in dreams and visions to provide solutions to problems and to convey messages. We discussed Mariana's experience from this perspective. Mariana stated that the spirit of her aunt had always been with her since she died. I asked Mariana if she could give herself permission to receive her aunt's message in a dream. At our next appointment Mariana reported a dream: Her mother and aunt were sitting next to each other sharing a blood transfusion. "They looked just like Frida Khalo's painting of herself as twins joined by a vein."

Q: Can you bring that dream here?
A: They are in my heart.
Q: What do you need to do?
A: Cut the blood supply.
Q: What is happening?
A: I am cauterizing my mother's wound — and mine.

Facilitated by permeable boundaries, Mariana "inherited" her mother's complicated bereavement. She became empowered to sever the connection and let go of her *madrina*. Mariana engaged in several spiritual rituals to help her *madrina* go into the light. Soon after the completion of the rituals, Mariana reported that her physical aches had been reduced significantly. However, Mariana expressed fear of dying without living her life. "I have ignored my calling," Mariana indicated during a therapy session. An attractive mixed-race Latina, Mariana worked as an architect. "Looking exotic is a double-edged sword," she said referring to her being a woman in a male-dominated workplace. "I need to understand what makes my heart sing." As Toksoz Karasu (2003) recommended, the therapist helps the client commune with her spiritual nature in order to heal. Therefore, I invited Mariana to meet her inner guide. A person, animal, object, ancestor, religious/historical person, or other figure, the inner guide is a wise and compassionate source that advises the person. The inner guide exploration has been described as uncovering the "eternal internal" by centering down where peace, power, and serenity reside within every person (Kelly, 1941). Health practitioners have used the inner guide or advisor technique for healing (Rossman, 2000). As an illustration, Carl Simonton, Stephanie Matthews-Simonton, and James Creighton (1978) taught cancer patients to communicate with their inner guide through visualization or mental imagery for healing advice. Similarly, psychotherapists have used the inner-guide technique. For instance, Marsha Linehan (1993) integrated the "wise mind" into her cognitive-behavioral treatment approach. I followed Deena Metzger's (1992) and Martin Rossman's (2000) suggestions for the inner-guide meditation.

T: Where is your guide?
C: In my heart.
T: Go there and let me know what you see.
C: Archangel Gabriel.
T: Is he communicating with you?
C: *She* is saying not to be afraid.
T: How are you feeling?
C: Encouraged. [*tears stream from Mariana's eyes*] Gabriel is asking me to tell my story.
T: What do you want to do?
C: An *arpillera*.

Mariana suddenly remembered: "Gabriel came to me when Madrina was killed. She announced that Madrina was in peace." After this revelation, we continued working on Mariana's anger and depression. She stopped drinking alcohol and using marijuana ("I was medicating my fear, but now I'm wiser," she said). On November 2, Day of the Dead, Mariana completed an *arpillera*

(Latino folk tapestry). The weaving told the story of her *madrina's* murder and her mother's depression. The top of the *arpillera* depicted Archangel Gabriel welcoming Mariana's *madrina* into heaven. As part of working through, Mariana asked for a chakra-balancing exercise. When we reached her heart chakra I asked, "How have you not let yourself be who you are?" "Being afraid of love," she said.

Mariana enrolled in courses on spirituality and healing. She continued working on opening her heart, as she put it. She learned to trust her inner guidance and to embrace a receptive attitude. She joined a women's spirituality group and earned a leadership position in the assembly. During our last therapy session, Mariana reported that she had a vision. Ix Chel, the Mayan patroness of weaving, told her to teach others to weave their *arpilleras*. *Arpilleras* have a cultural, political, and spiritual significance. They are detailed, hand-sewn, three-dimensional, textile pictures that illustrate the stories of oppressed Latinos (Ginaturco & Turtle, 2000). *Arpilleras* represent Latino resistance, resilience, and transformation. To illustrate, Chilean women weaved their trauma stories of political repression and torture into these beautiful folk expressions (Agosin, 1996). To weave an *arpillera* is healing, liberating, creative, and spiritually uplifting. *Arpilleras* tell stories of all aspects in life (Ginaturco & Turtle, 2000) and sublimate suffering into conscious art. Moreover, they symbolize the creative expression in composing one's life (Comas-Díaz, 2006).

"Therapy helped me to become an artist at life," Mariana said as she showed me her latest *arpillera*. The tapestry depicted a woman weaving an *arpillera*. A circle of women surrounded her. Among the women were Maria, her twin sister Mariana, and Gabriel holding Amada in her arms.

Of Love and Other Demons I used Latino psychospirituality in working with Mariana. This orientation combined existential, liberating, and cultural dimensions into psychotherapy. Mariana's cultural beliefs became a foundation for her transformation. She recovered, reconciled, and reformulated her identity. With the help of magical realism, *entresueños*, *dichos*, and cultural traditions, Mariana transformed herself from a sufferer into an artist at life. She sublimated her adversity into creativity with the help of her vibrant cultural traditions. Mariana's healing journey is not unique. In working with Latino clients, psychotherapists can become more culturally competent by endorsing an existential-integrative approach combined with psychospirituality.

Six months after our last session, I received a package in the mail. It contained a book, *Of Love and Other Demons*, by Colombian Nobel Laureate Gabriel García Márquez. Inside the book a note read, "Thanks for witnessing in my search for love. Mariana: Daughter of Maria, niece of Mariana, sister of Gabriel and mother of Amada."

References

Agosin, M. (1996). *Tapestries of hope, threads of love: The arpillera movement in Chile, 1974–1994*. Albuquerque: University of New Mexico Press.

Aviera, A. (1996). "Dichos" therapy group: A therapeutic use of Spanish language proverbs with hospitalized Spanish-speaking psychiatric patients. *Cultural Diversity and Mental Health, 2*, 73–87.

Beezley, W. H., & Ewell, J. (Eds.). (1987). *The human tradition in Latin America: The twentieth century*. Wilmington, DE: Scholarly Resources.

Brennan, B. A. (1988). *Hands of light: A guide to healing through the human energy field*. New York: Bantam Books.

Castillo, A. (Ed.). (1996). *Goddess of the Americas/La Diosa de las Américas: Writings on the Virgin of Guadalupe*. New York: Riverhead Books.

Choi, I., Nisbett, R. E., & Norenzayan, A. (1999). Causal attribution across cultures: Variations and universality. *Psychological Bulletin, 125*, 47–63.

Cisneros, S. (2001). Guadalupe the sex goddess. In M. Sewell (Ed.), *Resurrecting grace: Remembering Catholic Childhoods* (pp. 158–164). Boston: Beacon Press.

Coelho, P. (2003). *El peregrino* [The pilgrim]. Mexico City: Grijalbo.

Comas-Díaz, L. (2006). Latino healing: The integration of ethnic psychology into psychotherapy. *Psychotherapy. Theory, Research, Practice & Training, 43* (4), 436–453.

Council of National Psychological Associations. (2003, November). *Psychological treatment of ethnic minority populations*. Washington, DC: The Association of Black Psychologists.

De La Cancela, V., & Zavala Martinez, I. (1983). An analysis of culturalism in Latino mental health: Folk medicine as a case in point. *Hispanic Journal of Behavioral Sciences, 5*, 251–274.

De Rios, M. D. (2001). *Brief psychotherapy with the Latino immigrant cliient*. New York: Harworth Press.

Falicov, C. J. (1998). *Latino families in therapy: A guide to multicultural practice*. New York: Guilford.

Fox, M. (1999). *Sins of the spirit, blessings of the flesh: Lessons for transforming evil in soul and society*. New York: Three Rivers Press.

Ginaturco, P., & Turtle, T. (2000). *In her hands: Craftwomen changing the world*. New York: Penguin Press.

Hardy, K. V., & Laszloffy, T. (1995). The cultural genogram: Key to training culturally competent family therapists. *Journal of Marital and Family Therapy, 21*, 227–237.

Harwood, A. (1981). *Ethnicity and medical care*. Cambridge, MA: Harvard University.

Ho, M. H. (1987). *Family therapy with ethnic minorities*. Newbury Park, CA: Sage.

Karasu, T. B. (2003). *The art of serenity: The path to a joyful life in the best and worst of times*. New York: Simon & Schuster.

Keller, H. (2002). Culture and development: Developmental pathways to individualism and interrelatedness. In W. J. Lonner, D. L. Dinnel, S. A. Hayes, & D. N. Sattler (Eds.), *Online readings in psychology and culture* (Unit 11, Chap. 1). Bellingham, WA: Center for Cross-Cultural Research, Western Washington University. Retrieved from http://www.wwu.edu/~culture.

Kelly, T. K. (1941). *A testament of devotion*. San Francisco: Harper Collins.

Kleinman, A. (1988). *Rethinking psychiatry: From cultural category to personal experience*. New York: Free Press.

Koss-Chioino, J. D., & Vargas, L. A. (1999). *Working with Latino youth: Culture, development and context*. San Francisco: Jossey-Bass.

Linehan, M. M. (1993). *Cognitive-behavioral treatment of borderline personality disorder*. New York: Guilford Press.

Maduro, R. J., & Martinez, C. F. (1974, October). Latino dream analysis: Opportunity for confrontation. *Social Casework*, 461–469.

Marriott, S. (2004). *Total meditation*. San Diego: Thunder Bay Press.

Metzger, D. (1992). *Writing for your life: A guide and companion to the inner worlds*. San Francisco: Harper Collins.

Muñoz, R. F., & Mendelson, T. (2005). Toward evidence-based interventions for diverse populations: The San Francisco General Hospital Prevention and Treatment Manuals. *Journal of Clinical and Consulting Psychology, 73*, 790–799.

Myss, C. (1996). *Anatomy of the spirit: The seven stages of power and healing*. New York: Three Rivers Press.

Pole, N., Best, S. R., Metzler, T., & Marmar, C. R. (2005). Why are Hispanics at greater risk for PTSD? *Cultural Diversity and Ethnic Minority Psychology, 11*, 144–161.

Quiñones, M. E. (2007). Bridging the gap. In J. C. Muran (Ed.), *Dialogues on difference: Studies of diversity in the therapeutic relationship* (pp. 153–167). Washington, DC: American Psychological Association.

Ramirez, M. (1998). *Multicultural/multiracial psychology: Mestizo perspectives in personality and mental health*. Northvale, NJ: Jason Aronson.

Rossman, M. L. (2000). *Guided imagery for self-healing: An essential resource for anyone seeking wellness* (2nd ed.). Tiburon, CA: H. J. Kramer.

Ruiz, M. (1997). *The four agreements: A Toltec wisdom book*. San Rafael, CA: Amber-Allen Publishing.

Schneider, K. J., & May, R. (1995). *The psychology of existence: An integrative, clinical perspective*. New York, McGraw-Hill.

Shapiro, E. R. (1994). *Grief as a family process: A developmental approach to clinical practice*. New York, Guilford.

Shapiro, F. (1995). *Eye movement desensitization and reprocessing: Basic principles, protocols, and procedures*. New York: Guilford.

Silva, J., & Miele, P. (1977). *The Silva mind control method: The revolutionary program by the founder of the world's most famous mind control course*. New York: Pocket Books.

Simonton, O. C., Matthews-Simonton, S., & Creighton, J. (1978). *Getting well again: A step-by-step, self-help guide to overcoming cancer for patients and their families*. New York: Bantam Books.

Tree, I. (2001). *Sliced iguana: Travels in Mexico*. New York: Penguin Books.

Vasconcelos, J. (1997). *The cosmic race: A bilingual edition* (D. T. Jaén, Trans.). Baltimore: Johns Hopkins University.

Zamora, L. P., & Faris, W. B. (Eds.). (1995). *Magical realism*. Durham: North Carolina University Press.

Zuñiga, M. E. (1991). "Dichos" as metaphorical tools for resistant Latino clients. *Psychotherapy, 28*, 480–483.

Zuñiga, M. E. (1992). Using metaphors in therapy: *Dichos* and Latino clients. *Social Work, 37*, 55–60.

An African American Perspective: The Case of Darrin

Donadrian L. Rice

Donadrian L. Rice, PhD, is professor and chair of the department of psychology at the University of West Georgia in Carrollton. A graduate of Saybrook Graduate School in San Francisco, Dr. Rice also received training from R. D. Laing at the Philadelphia Association Clinic in London and is a licensed psychotherapist.

The purpose of this contribution is to introduce the reader to an appreciation and application of existential psychotherapy for the African American population. More importantly, I suggest that existentialist concepts such as freedom, being, meaning, identity, choice, and responsibility are relevant to situations faced by African Americans today. While it is true that these concepts have import for other groups as well, I find them to be particularly pertinent to African Americans, considering their unique historical experience in the United States.

In treating this topic, the question may be raised whether African Americans are subject to psychological principles that are fundamentally different from those of any other group. In response, I submit that there is no evidence in the clinical literature to suggest that African Americans function differently psychologically. However, as Vontress and Epp (2001) point out, the therapist should consider whether the methods for assessment and diagnosis that one would use for the majority population are appropriate for the minority members of that particular culture. Studies of sociodemographic variables as they relate to mental illness have found little or no support for the notion that racial minority groups in the United States have more mental illness than do whites (Cockerham, 1985). Yet, while the above findings may be true, the real question of therapeutic relevance for African Americans must be addressed.

What makes the experiences of African Americans unique from those of other minority groups and other oppressed groups is the historical fact of slavery and its aftermath. And because of slavery, many African Americans carry residual feelings of resentment and mistrust toward European Americans (Vontress and Epp, 2001, p. 378). While other groups have suffered discrimination, mistreatment, and isolation from mainstream America, they were never considered to be outside of the human family. Various groups — such as the Chinese, Italians, Irish, Germans, European Jews, and others — can all tell stories of struggles in the face of opposition in the early days of the formation of this country. Except perhaps for Native Americans, who have endured a different kind of hardship, all of the above-mentioned groups have been able to assimilate into American society and find social as well as personal freedom.

The uniqueness of the African American experience in a historical context is found in the fact that this is the only minority group to have been systematically stripped of country, culture, language, family, personal identity, and humanness. As William Grier and Price Cobbs (1969) stated:

> The black experience in this country has been of a different kind. It began with slavery and with a rupture of continuity and an annihilation of the past. Even now each generation grows up alone. Many individual blacks feel a desperate aloneness not readily explained . . . non-black groups pass on proud traditions . . . while the black man stands in solitude. (pp. 22–23)

This statement by two prominent African American psychiatrists makes explicit the uniqueness of the African American experience and how it is situated in a historical context. When Grier and Cobbs speak of a "rupture of continuity and an annihilation of the past," I would add that this has resulted in a rupture in the continuity of being for African Americans. One's sense of identity, existence, freedom, and responsibility is inextricably bound up in one's awareness of the past. Not awareness of the past for awareness' sake, but awareness in order to incorporate the past into a meaningful present. Many African Americans suffer alienation largely because the present is meaningless in light of their past.

Psychological theories and therapeutic techniques that focus solely on internal dynamics and behavioral deficits stemming from early childhood experiences in the family make an assumption that may not be valid for most African Americans. The Caribbean-French-born psychiatrist Frantz Fanon (1967) suggested that while many cases of mental disturbance can be traced to the family environment, the opposite of that process seems to emerge in people of African descent. As he states, "A normal Negro child, having grown up within a normal family, will become abnormal on the slightest contact with the white world" (p. 143).

Now, beyond meeting basic needs, the primary function of any family in any society is to ensure the transmission of the operating rules of that society. If we assume that in the "normal" African American home the parents are culture bearers of the social system, what, then, can Fanon mean by such a statement? First, Fanon recognizes the significance of the sociohistorical context in which people of African descent find themselves in European and American societies. Second, and perhaps more importantly, he recognizes the ontological (*being*) obstacles that are necessary for eventual transcendence.

In an attempt to elucidate the psychological impact of European colonization on African nations, Fanon writes,

> In the *Weltanschauung* of a colonized people there is an impurity, a flaw that outlaws any ontological explanation. Someone may object that this

> is the case with every individual, but such an objection merely conceals a basic problem. Ontology — once it is finally admitted as leaving existence by the wayside — does not permit us to understand the being of the black man. To be black, he must be black in relation to the white man. (Fanon, 1967, pp. 109–110)

Fanon goes on to explain that while it may seem that being white must also be in relation to being black, he rejects this proposition as false. In Fanon's view, a black person is ontologically inert in the eyes of a white person. One cannot define the being of another when one is essentially powerless. This powerlessness is rooted in the social fabric. Therefore, a person or group repeatedly treated as a fringe member of the human family and stripped of autonomy will react in a certain way, only to be seen by mental health experts as further evidence of their maladjustment. From the perspective of existential-integrative psychology, the black person in this situation can be characterized as "suspended between freedom and limitation," where the expression of freedom is limited in this case by powerlessness and social restraints (Schneider and May, 1995, p. 6).

Vontress and Epp (2001) illustrate the effects of powerlessness and social restraints experienced by African Americans in the following way:

> Regardless of the conditions under which people live, they must still adjust to the fact that they are humans. . . . African-Americans are, first of all culturally alike because they are members of the human species . . . they share biologically dictated behaviors of all members of the human group . . . they are forced to adjust to the same climatic conditions as are other Americans . . . as members of the national culture, they take on the behavior, attitudes, values, of Americans in general . . . they are influenced by the culture in the region in which they live. Thus, Marcus, a native of rural Alabama, is apt to betray his roots by the manner of speech peculiar to that region. Fifth, because of Marcus's African ancestry, European-Americans are apt to react to him as if he were inferior, a fact that leaves psychological scars on him and on members of his group. (p. 372)

This unique experience of powerlessness and ontological inertness presents a challenge for the therapist encountering the African American client. The tendency of therapists to see the problems of African Americans or anyone for that matter solely in terms of genetics, intrapsychic disturbance, or behavioral maladjustment highlights the need for the kind of understanding provided by an existentially based therapy. The existentialist approach helps to explain Fanon's belief that a normal African American child growing up in a normal home will become abnormal upon the slightest contact with the white world. This "abnormality" is predicated on the rupture in the continuity of being that has been imposed by a sociohistorical context. As Kirk Schneider and Rollo May (1995, p. 6) point out, "dread of freedom or limitation . . . due to past trauma promotes dysfunctional or extreme counter-reactions" between the polarities of freedom and limitation. Hence, questions of being, meaning, freedom, identity, choice, and responsibility emerge as essential themes in the therapeutic process.

Psychotherapists and other mental health professionals treating African Americans must give consideration to the sociohistorical context that may contribute to the client's symptoms. I do not intend this statement to mean that one ignores biochemical imbalances, intrapsychic disturbances, and environmental influences. African Americans are subject to the same psychological and biological factors promoting mental illness or mental health as are other groups. However, it is imperative that the therapist distinguish between a disturbed individual and a disturbed society — a disturbed society being one that wittingly or unwittingly erects barriers to personal freedom for any of its members.

In an article addressing the aftermath of the Rodney King verdict, Johnson (1992) states,

> There remains a system of white privilege in America. There has never been and there is not now a "level playing field." We are twice oppressed. First, by the external forces, stigmas and racial devaluation which is the historical inheritance of America. But more importantly, by our internal oppressors — those images which we in the African-American community hold of ourselves. (p. 6)

Those images we hold of ourselves as ontologically inert, socially restricted, and powerless are the result of the sociohistorical fact of oppression. The images have been internalized and sustained by a residual of negative attitudes directed toward African Americans and transmitted intergenerationally. There is evidence that this psychological internalization can have both positive and negative consequences on neurological functioning (Wexler, 2006). For this reason, issues of freedom, power, being, and responsibility must be addressed in a therapeutic context. For the African American, this is essential. It is essential because, as May (1981) states,

> We choose our way of responding to other people who make up the context in which our freedom develops. The paradox that one can be free only as one is responsible is central at every point in freedom. But the converse is just as true: one can be responsible only as one is free. . . . You have to have some sense that your decisions genuinely matter to take responsibility for them. (p. 64)

The job of the existentially oriented therapist is, as May puts it, "to help the patient discover, establish, and use his or her freedom" (p. 64). By integrating the polarities of freedom and limitation, the existentially oriented therapist encourages a more "invigorating life-design" that offers more choices (Schneider & May, 1995, p. 6). In other words, the therapist enables the client to achieve a meaningful life. In the current vernacular, we might say that the therapist *empowers* the client. This empowerment should not be confused with its simplistic use as found in many self-help books, but is the existential sense of coming to realize one's freedom and responsibility, regardless of the circumstances.

Actualizing this awareness of personal responsibility and the freedom to choose in the client is part and parcel of existential psychotherapy. Problems of being, meaning, freedom, responsibility, and their manifest symptomatology (i.e., anxiety, depression, fear, doubt) can only be explored in a context in which the experience of the person is understood as essential to the therapeutic process.

Up to this point, I have tried to develop a general framework for understanding the experiences of the African American client. In doing so, I have implied a certain prerequisite I believe to be pertinent to existential therapists, that is, an awareness and sensitivity to the effects of social, political, and historical events on the client. This does not mean that the therapist must immerse herself in the intricacies of these areas before treating a client, but being aware of the sociohistorical context helps to establish a framework for understanding the client's present experiences. Certainly a therapist treating a client who experienced the atrocities committed in Rwanda or the government-sanctioned starvation and genocide of thousands of people in war-torn Sudan would take into account the devastating impact of such experiences. The existential therapist of any ethnic origin should demonstrate social and cultural competence, or perhaps what Vontress and Epp (2001) refer to as "cultural intuition," which they describe as the "immediate knowledge, sensation, and rapport that counselors often experience when they relate to clients from their own cultures" (p. 377).

The Case of Darrin

"Darrin," a 32-year-old African American male, was referred to me by a mental health facility, which reported that, in their judgment, Darrin could benefit from having "a black therapist." During my initial interview with Darrin, he appeared to be both anxious and depressed. He also showed physical signs of weight loss and sleep deprivation.

Darrin's original contact with the mental health clinic had been made through his company's employee assistance program, which he had consulted because of feelings of depression and an inability to get "a good night's sleep." As part of his treatment at the mental health clinic, he was given a prescription for a sleeping agent and weekly therapy sessions.

His therapist's report to me indicated that Darrin had had no previous emotional problems and there was an improvement in both his state of depression and his ability to sleep after the sessions started. The report attributed his emotional state to overwork and suggested that he take time away from work and rest. However, after a two-week rest period, his symptoms returned, coupled with a breakdown in rapport between Darrin and his therapist. After three more weeks of sessions with Darrin, the therapist, who was white, decided that a black therapist might have more success with him.

I asked Darrin to tell me about himself and the events that had brought him to this point in his life. He was open and spoke in a very deliberate manner. He described his early childhood as normal for a child growing up in the 1960s. He is the oldest of four siblings, and both parents were present in the home when he was growing up. His father worked full time as an electrician for a construction company and often found part-time work wiring homes on weekends. His mother worked as a food services coordinator for a school district. He described his parents as warm and loving but, at the same time, strict in discipline. He elaborated that as children, they were constantly told that they should strive toward a better life than they had then. He said that he had always found this a curious statement because he felt he had a good life already.

While he described his early life as normal and enjoyable, he noted that he began experiencing feelings of despair upon entering junior high school. His entrance into junior high was significant in that he was required by his parents to attend what was then a predominantly white school. This particular school district was experimenting with a voluntary desegregation plan, which translated into black children volunteering to attend predominantly white schools and white children remaining where they were. Darrin's parents decided it would be advantageous for him to attend the white school because they perceived it as better than the black school. In actuality, there was a measure of truth to this perception because of the disparity in funding.

At any rate, Darrin marked this event as a turning point in his up-to-then uneventful life. Throughout his years in junior high and high school, he was told relentlessly by his parents how he had to prove himself and be a better student than the white students. Furthermore, he was told that he always had to be on his "best behavior" because his teachers and fellow students would judge his race based on his behavior. This resulted in his feeling that he "could never be himself."

Upon graduating from high school, Darrin received a partial scholarship to attend college. He completed two years and then decided not to continue. After a year of desperate searching, he finally landed a job at a trucking firm. His decision greatly displeased his parents, who, at this point, thought he was "throwing his life away." Within five years, he had risen through the ranks to become a district manager in charge of large portions of the Southeast. After three years in this position, his symptoms began to emerge. They began with a general, nonspecific feeling of disinterest in his work and progressed to alternating moments of anxiety and depression.

He also revealed that at this time he was greatly in debt, resulting in frequent letters and phone calls from collection agencies. He described himself as having "expensive taste," which, in his case, included a late-model luxury car, a lavishly appointed condominium, and designer clothes. Furthermore, he expressed the belief that the people whom he managed did not respect him; he was considered incompetent and was only in his position because he was black. He voiced resentment toward his creditors, his fellow employees, his family, and himself. He summed up his situation as not being able to please anyone and, at the same time, trying to do and be what everyone wanted him to do and be.

Existentially, Darrin's feelings of anxiety and depression can be understood as resulting from an interruption in the continuity of his being. The dread of physiologically expansive feelings of hyperresponsibility usurped his sense of identity, meaning, freedom, and personal power when his parents defined his position in life and how he was expected to be in the presence of others. In the vernacular of the existential-integrative model, while Darrin's physical feelings of hyperresponsibility represent the expansive end of the polarity, his sense of being-in-the-world had become constrictive: His experience of his options were limited by what he perceived as external forces.

However, we must keep in mind that the actions of Darrin's parents should be framed in a sociohistorical context. For a black to achieve success in the white world, he or she had to be better than what would normally be expected for that position. Jackie Robinson had to be a better baseball player; Wilma Randolph had to be a superior runner; even in the fictional *Guess Who's Coming to Dinner*, Sidney Poitier's character had to have the prestigious career of college professor in order to make it palatable for him to be engaged to marry a white woman. Darrin's parents were conforming to a sociohistorical situation that dictated a prescription for the behavior of any African American who wanted to gain a minimum of acceptance in the white world. Therefore, acting from their own experiences of feeling the need to constrict their "true sense of self" in order to expand the "prescribed self," their dysfunctional expansive-constrictive polarity was internalized by Darrin. For Darrin, it was not a simple matter of being black but, rather, his "blackness" in relation to the "whiteness" of others. This is an experience that African Americans limited to their own social milieu do not have. But at the moment when contact is made with the broader society, the reality of being black takes on a different meaning. Darrin's definition of himself had been replaced by one that allowed him no ontological resistance.

My initial work with Darrin began with my efforts to quell the tide of telephone calls and letters from his creditors. I informed them that Darrin was under my care and that arrangements were being made to satisfy his debts. With the cooperation of the creditors, much of Darrin's primary anxiety symptoms — which were associated with threats of repossession, foreclosure, and general financial ruin — dissipated. He reported that he felt less anxious and was sleeping better. Realizing, however, that keeping his creditors at bay was only a temporary measure for alleviating his problems, I knew that additional therapeutic intervention was necessary to effect a more productive change in this aspect of his behavior.

It would be well to pause and take note that existential therapy can involve a variety of specific techniques, not only for different clients, but also for the same client at different times. Schneider and May (1995, p. 145) point out that "the client's desire and capacity for change are the initial, and foremost, existential-integrative selection criteria." For Darrin's immediate problem (i.e., his spending habits and creditors), I found behavioral intervention, coupled with rational restructuring, to be most effective (Ellis, 1962; Goldfried & Davison, 1976; Meichenbaum, 1977).

Some of the overt changes in his behavior included establishing a budget that included regular disbursements to his creditors and selling off some of his more financially cumbersome possessions. At the same time, cognitive or rational restructuring was used to help him internalize his behavior at an intellectual and feeling level. Learning to respond differently to a situation in which he had previously felt powerless and constricted represented for him a new freedom in this area of his life. My role as an existential therapist is to help the client establish his or her freedom (see May, 1981). For the therapist to understand this role is pre-eminently existential.

Commensurate with freedom is *responsibility*, the ability to respond. While, in one sense, responsibility sets limits on freedom, as May (1981) has pointed out, choices are expanded when responsibility is viewed as the ability to respond (Emery & Campbell, 1986). The cognitive-behavioral techniques served as a tool to help Darrin expand his awareness of his existential choices. Realizing that he could respond to his situation in a manner that empowered him helped him to eliminate the disabling aspect of his anxiety. It should be made clear that the cognitive-behavioral techniques were not seen as an all-encompassing theoretical position but, rather, as a strategy of liberation to help Darrin accomplish what he wanted to accomplish for himself.

Psychodynamically speaking, Darrin's free-spending patterns could be seen as resulting from a kind of pre-oedipal overgratification. This is an issue that perhaps should not be overlooked and could provide important understandings for the insight-oriented therapist. However, resorting to internal dynamics exclusively can only serve to further comfort and enhance the client's victim status. The essential questions of being, meaning, freedom, and responsibility cannot be addressed in this context. Furthermore, there is little room for understanding the sociohistorical context.

A particular psychodynamic position I found to be relevant in the development of my composite understanding of Darrin was Alfred Adler's theory of the inferiority-superiority complex (Ansbacher & Ansbacher, 1956). Stated briefly, it says that every person moves toward a chosen goal and is therefore moving from a feeling of relative inferiority to a feeling of superiority, which includes wanting to be a worthy human being. Darrin's attempt to move from inferior feelings of non-self-worth, powerlessness, meaninglessness, and lack of freedom to superior feelings of self-worth, power, meaningfulness, and freedom could be summed up according to Adler's psychology of the individual. From this perspective, Darrin's feelings and behavior were obviously "neurotic."

However, to stop the analysis here would overlook an essential point. For Adler, these complexes arise within the individual, a point I am not disputing. But for Darrin as an African American, feelings of inferiority do not stem from the imagined "organ" inferiority or "birth order" inferiority of which Adler speaks, but rather from an inferiority that is rooted in a sociohistorical context that has been internalized. Since before the establishment of this country as a sovereign nation, the African American has been considered an inferior being.

The fact that Darrin did not perceive himself as an active force, capable of directing his own life and bringing possibilities into existence, has historical significance that extends beyond the family and environment. While I believe this to be a crucial point, I do not want to suggest that Darrin, or any other African American, is historically "fixated." I mean only that the therapist should expand the walls of his or her theoretical orientation in order to grasp the fullness of the client's existential situation.

After helping Darrin gain some measure of control over his financial problems, the more important work of helping him to realize his own part in the actualization of his self-worth and sense of power began. Basically, this is a task for each person, to be decided by each person, because the therapist cannot decide for the client how this sense of self-worth and power is to come into being. However, the therapist can facilitate this awareness through a careful prioritizing of the client's concerns.

Darrin's first concern was his dissatisfaction with the direction his life had taken. From his point of view, he had done everything to make amends for the disappointment he caused his parents when he dropped out of college. His second concern was that while he was considered extremely competent on his job and commanded the respect of his peers, he felt ridiculed and belittled by them. Consequently, all his efforts to meet expectations and to please everyone only resulted in feelings of not being himself.

To offset his negative summation of himself, I asked Darrin to make a list of what he considered to be his strengths. Surprisingly, despite his despondency, he was able to list quite a few. Some of his strengths included good interpersonal skills, intelligence, persistence, and loyalty. He saw himself as being able to handle adversity constructively most of the time and capable of feeling deep empathy toward others. I then asked him to focus on how each one of the strengths he listed had played a role in some of the choices he had made in life.

This exercise brought him to the realization that his decision to drop out of college was based on his desire to assert his freedom and move beyond the environmental, familial, and social restraints that dictated his existence at the time. I pointed out that it was precisely those strengths that had allowed him to succeed in the socioeconomic realm on his own terms without the benefit of a college degree. He was able to see how, even in his present job, his strengths had been the source of his progress.

What this exercise accomplished was a reframing (see Dilts, Grinder, Bandler, & Delozier, 1980) of the meaning Darrin had attached to his choices. Once he began to view his choices from a different vantage point, I introduced the issue of responsibility — the responsibility that places limits on freedom (May, 1981) — and the ability to respond that expands the choices one can make (Schneider and May, 1995). I asked Darrin to reflect on what he considered to be the major transformative choices in his life and to state how he had accepted or not accepted responsibility for each of those choices. At the same time, I asked him how he could respond to any of the difficulties in his present situation in a manner that would empower him.

These questions served as a catalyst to help Darrin understand not only his existential freedom, but his responsibility in exercising that freedom. Incidentally, the above exercise can be used in any therapeutic orientation, but the very nature of the questions is existential. The exercise gave Darrin a chance to experience himself as an entity separate from his environment, with the capacity to respond upon his own initiative rather than merely reacting.

Finally, I addressed with Darrin the overriding issue of racism and its concomitant effects (i.e., feelings of inferiority, self-doubt, lack of self-worth, and so on). The specific experiences he noted — the beliefs that he had to be better than whites in order to be accepted as an equal or that any progress he made in his career was due to his race rather than his abilities — both have an element of truth when viewed in a sociohistorical context. To invalidate this experience with substitute psychospeak explanations (i.e., inferiority complex, paranoia, and so on) would only serve to "mystify" (Laing, 1967) and do further violence (Laing & Cooper, 1971) to the experience. In other words, it was important for Darrin to understand the sociohistorical precedence for the present attitudes he felt victim to. Whether his experience was valid in an objective sense is irrelevant. It is irrelevant because the sociohistorical context already provides for the possibility of the pervasiveness of these racist attitudes. However, it was equally important for Darrin to realize his own responsibility in exercising his freedom to transcend the negative confines of the sociohistorical context. What Darrin was to confront ultimately was not the inferiority and self-doubt imposed from without, but inferiority that emerges from within when the choice is made to constrict not only responsibility, but also the ability to respond.

For Darrin, the veil of inferiority and self-doubt was lifted when he began experiencing himself as a person apart from his race, that is, as one who is free to choose, to act, and to be. While race can be a source of identity, that which is invalid racial-cultural heritage (i.e., nonbeing, inferiority) and that which is valid immediate experience (i.e., freedom, meaning, being) are reconciled in an existential encounter that encompasses the sociohistorical context. To dismiss the influence of either the past or present social context would be delusional. However, freedom comes with the awareness that one's personal and collective history does not determine present choice, but rather acknowledges the past in order that one may fruitfully move beyond it to facilitate the cycle of freedom (Fanon, 1967).

Darrin's journey toward liberation and freedom began with his recognition that the choices he made in the past could be made meaningful in the present when he acknowledged his responsibility for those choices. Moreover, personal acknowledgment of his ability to respond opened him up to heretofore unrecognized potentialities.

In closing, I want to make the point that the racial/ethnic heritage of the therapist is unimportant. What is important is that the therapist be grounded in a broad education that offers him or her the necessary sensitivity to the sociohistorical influences on the client. An existential framework can lend invaluable perspective to that understanding.

References

Ansbacher, H., & Ansbacher, R. (1956). *The individual psychology of Alfred Adler: A systematic presentation in selections from his writings.* New York: Basic Books.

Cockerham, W. C. (1985). Sociology and psychiatry. In H. I. Kaplin & B. Sadock (Eds.), *Comprehensive textbook of psychiatry IV.* Baltimore: Williams and Wilkins.

Dilts, R., Grinder, J., Bandler, R., & Delozier, J. (1980). *Neurolinguistic programming: The study of the structure of subjective experience.* Cupertino, CA: Meta Publications.

Ellis, A. (1962). *Reason and emotion in psychotherapy.* New York: Lyle Stuart.

Emery, G., & Campbell, J. (1986). *Rapid relief from emotional distress.* New York: Rawson Associates.

Fanon, F. (1967). *Black skin, white masks.* (C. L. Markman, Trans.) New York: Grove Press.

Goldfried, M. R., & Davison, G. C. (1976). *Clinical behavior therapy.* New York: Holt, Rinehart and Winston.

Grier, W., & Cobbs, P. (1969). *Black rage.* New York: Bantam Books.

Johnson, J. (1992). D.C. counselors speak out on King verdict and its underlying problems. *The Advocate, 16*, 6–7.

Laing, R. D. (1967). *The politics of experience.* New York: Pantheon Books.

Laing, R. D., & Cooper, D. G. (1971). *Reason and violence.* New York: Vintage.

May, R. (1981). *Freedom and destiny.* New York: Norton.

Meichenbaum, D. (1977). *Cognitive-behavior modification.* New York: Plenum.

Schneider, K. J., & May, R. (1995). *The psychology of existence: An integrative, clinical perspective.* New York: McGraw-Hill.
Vontress, C. E., & Epp, L. R. (2001). Existential cross-cultural counseling: When hearts and cultures share. In K. Schneider, J. Bugental, & J. Pierson (Eds.), *The handbook of humanistic psychology: Leading edges in theory, research and practice.* Thousand Oaks, CA: Sage.
Wexler, B. (2006). *Brain and culture: Neurobiology, ideology, and social change.* Cambridge, MA: MIT Press.

Existentialism of Personalism: A Native American Perspective

Royal Alsup

Royal Alsup, PhD, is a therapist and director of the new Humanistic Psychology Program at Sonoma State University. A co-director of the Transpersonal and Existential Psychotherapy Center in Arcada, CA, he has over 35 years of experience living with, advocating for, and counseling culturally diverse clients in northern California. His special area of interest is the social consciousness of mental health professionals.

Existentialism of personalism sees the human personality as sacred and punctuates both inner and outer life as sacred. An "I and Thou" encounter with the Supreme Personality of the Creator takes place through dialogical meeting in the three aspects of human life: (1) interpersonal relationships; (2) the physical, natural world; and (3) inner psychic phenomenology. Existentialism of personalism embraces interconnected attitudes of aesthetic, sacred consciousness with social, political awareness. Transpersonal and existential realities are captured in the sacred and profane events of life. The ecstasy and numinous awesomeness of an I-and-Thou encounter with the Supreme Personality can be experienced in any time and in any place and through any object, person, or event. It is not limited to an inner, individualistic mysticality, nor is it particular to community worship and ceremony. The personal relationship with the Supreme Personality creates a sense of being and becoming that is spontaneous and goes on ceaselessly in a constant dialogue with self, other, and nature. It is contained in form and is experienced in existential, concrete, everyday lived life.

Flora Jones, Wintu medicine woman, speaks about the spirits like they are living personalities in a partnership of existence with human beings. Witness the following statement, quoted by Knudtson (1975):

> This is what the spirit tells me — get my people together. . . . Whoever has sacred places must wake them up, the same as I am doing here — to keep my old world within my heart and with the spiritual. For them to help me and for me to help my people. (p. 14)

The personalism expressed by Flora Jones is the basis of most African American and American Indian traditions. Both of these traditions have a dual theme of Being-in-the-World and Being-beyond-the-World. The Supreme Personality is experienced as an integrated intelligence and love that is expressed through the archetypes of mythologies, rituals, worship, dreams, and visions.

The archetypal spirituality of the meeting in the Between confirms that the Supreme Personality lies within the human personality and in the meeting as the Ground of Being. The Supreme Personality, as a living personality, offers love, knowledge, mystery, gift giving, and sharing in relationship with the human person. The I-and-Thou encounter brings to awareness constellations of fascination and fear, destiny and freedom, death and life, anxiety and joy, interest and surprise, love and shame, and guilt and excitement.

Existentialism of personalism came out of my practice and theory in a circle of understanding and interpretation through dialogue with American Indians and African Americans. Alex Haley, in his book *Roots* (1976), describes how the father of Kunta Kinte presented his infant son to the universe. He writes, "Carrying little Kunta in his strong arms, he walked to the edge of the village, lifted his baby up with his face to the heavens, and said softly, … Behold — the only thing greater than yourself" (p. 13). Haley is showing that the living universe is the father/mother of Kunta Kinte and that the child's personality is sacred. In the Navajo tradition, the man who holds his infant up to Father Sun and says, "Father Sun, this is your child" (J. Rivers & J. Norton, personal communication, June 1, 1992), is expressing that the universe is personal and loving. The Navajo infant is a direct descendant of the living universe, and therefore, its personality is sacred. African American and American Indian traditions demonstrate a continual dialogue between the human personality and the Supreme Personality that reveals the sacred and the profane as not separated but forming an interconnected metaphysical reality that is remythologized in every I-and-Thou meeting.

American Indian ceremonies emphasize the sacredness of the human personality. The Hupa Boat Dance ritual creates sacred space for a mysticism that revitalizes the community and makes the tribal members feel special in the perceptions of the Creator. This is a spirituality in which the tribal members know they are recognized by the Creator. The Boat Dance honors the dead and helps their spirits to make the crossing into the Great Mystery. It is also a ritual for reminding the living that they are sacred and that every individual is important in this communitarian worldview. The archetypal sounds from the dance and the archetypal experiences of the observer/participants allow this serious ontological enactment of death to become an experience of beauty.

The following case is presented to demonstrate effective psychotherapy based on existentialism of personalism and its use with American Indian clients. Mental health professionals working with American Indian clients need to practice indwelling, which brings about the joining of the therapist and client in a cultural context and makes diagnosis and treatment culturally appropriate. Indwelling requires the professional to go to gatherings and ceremonies, such as the Boat Dance, attend funerals of tribal members, do home-visit psychotherapy with immediate and extended families, and work with the Indian shamans. Therapists also need to practice communicative social action, which is the use of cultural knowledge to educate and inform county-, state-, and federal-agency workers about cultural values and attitudes concerning aspects of life such as death, silence, limitedness, and freedom in their professional treatment of American Indian clients.

The case example is typical of ones involving American Indians, especially if there has been a death in the family. Although the death is not to be talked about, the cultural tradition provides that the death experience for the person and the survivors be settled in ritual and ceremony. In cases pertaining to American Indian youth, there is often involvement in the juvenile justice system. A non-Indian therapist who is not familiar with the American Indian cultural stricture against talking about the deceased may make assumptions in court reports that the adolescent Indian client is not cooperating with treatment. For example, the youth may not disclose that his or her recent substance abuse problems arose as a result of the emotional trauma surrounding a death, and the therapist unfamiliar with the culture will label the nondisclosing, nonverbal Indian youth *untreatable*. Often in such a case, the district attorney will recommend that the youth be placed in a residential treatment facility or in the state's youth prison. These placements are usually far from the youth's home, separating him or her from the healing, cultural matrix of family, tribe, landscape, and shaman. This separation further aggravates the grief process and, for most American Indian youth, superimposes posttraumatic stress symptoms upon the death and grief trauma.

The psychology and worldview of the American Indian holds that it is in the silent solitude of the mind and heart, along with the ceremonial way, that one understands one's limitations and freedom. When an American Indian youth is pressured by the dominant culture's mental health professionals to speak about a death in the family, he or she becomes painfully caught in a clash of cultural values. The cultural conflict over how to process the experience of death brings about feelings of dread, despair, anxiety, isolation, and limitedness. American Indian cultural norms prescribe that one can only speak with respect for the dead, and it is better not to speak at all than to risk drawing the spirit of the deceased back into the world. The therapist's ignorance of the importance of silence, words, rituals, and ancestors disrupts the dialogical healing process in the meeting of client and therapist. The tribal tradition is a stronger determinant of what the youth will share with the psychotherapist than is the court's intimidation.

The Case of an American Indian Girl

This case study concerns a 15-year-old American Indian girl who resisted treatment of substance abuse that was a symptom of unresolved grief from the loss of a family member. She had been to approximately five culturally insensitive therapists to whom the juvenile justice system had referred her. The reports from the therapists consistently labeled her as *silent* and *resistant* and concluded that she could not benefit from treatment and therefore that incarceration in a youth prison was the only solution.

Session 1 The American Indian girl entered the therapy session saying that she had seen me at a tribal ceremony and funeral and that she trusted me. Then she fell into silence for about 10 minutes. I then told her a coyote-buffalo story that deals with tradition and one's role and function in tradition. In traditional Indian stories, coyote-buffalo are seen as both transpersonal and existential, and the stories teach moral development that balances the sacred and the profane. The coyote-buffalo story became a touchstone of reality for her to relate to instead of to the therapist. The story took her out of her silence, made her feel cared for, and brought about excitement and inspiration that helped her relate her own personal story to the mythic tale. At my suggestion, she used art materials with enthusiasm to make a collage to express herself symbolically.

By projecting her intimate feelings and the caring of her tribal traditions onto the symbols of the collage, she was able to integrate cognitively and affectively her tribal moral tradition as it was expressed in the story. The storytelling made her aware that the choices she was making had been taking her away from her "path of life," causing her to be psychologically and spiritually out of balance. She used alcohol and drugs to mask the pain of her feelings of disharmony, discomfort, and suffering.

Through the storytelling and art making, she had an experience of her personal mythology and how it was unfolding in the greater tribal mythology. She saw her personal life story reflected in the character who is both ordinary and divine (coyote) in struggle with the wholly transpersonal, the Great Spirit (buffalo). The cognitive and affective domains of learning and moral development were both evoked and brought to self-awareness through the coyote-buffalo story.

Session 7 In this session, I gave the Indian girl an assignment to do a collage of how she saw her tribe and what the tribe represented in her life. As she worked, her tribal story unfolded and she expressed the feelings of safety, security, belonging, and love that she received from the experience of being known by the Creator. Being known by the Creator allowed a unity of consciousness and a peak experience for her in the concrete making of the collage. Her collage showed a landscape symbolizing her tribal land within certain boundaries. The symbols of rituals, the landscape, and the Creator expressed that these touchstones of reality talked to her personally to reassure her of her Indianness within the sacred cathedral of her tribal land. The symbols in her collage brought about a psychological transformation of her attitude from one of depression, constriction, and limitedness to one of joyfulness, expansiveness, and freedom.

By the end of this session, the girl was more self-affirmed and seemed to have more of a sense of how she fit within the boundaries of her daily life because she felt more centered. She started talking about how she had been losing her sense of being and her sense of identity. Now she could see her limitedness within this mythological world, but she was also inspired and excited about claiming her freedom by not feeling driven to conform to the non-Indian youth at her high school. Now she saw that following her tribal ways and the morals of living nonindulgently would help free her from her addiction to methamphetamines. It gave her an experience of how the limitations of her Indian traditions also provided her meaning, purpose, and freedom.

Session 12 At this session, I suggested she do a collage about her family and the role or function her family members played in the tribal community. I also told her another coyote story. In this one, the coyote reverses all the destruction caused by the loggers' greed. All the trees are returned to the forest by blue-shirted logger-shamans, who put the trees back in the ground, reattach the boughs and limbs, and thus re-establish all the natural habitats of the animals. American Indian stories unite consciousness with the unconscious, thereby giving the Indian a deep sense of direction and purpose. The structure that gives meaning in this psychological process is what existentialists call *intentionality* (May, 1969).

The girl enthusiastically started a new collage that showed her family members, who were loggers as well as dance people. Members of her family traditionally brought their dance regalia and dancers to help with the tribal renewal ceremony that puts the earth back in balance. This artistic moment was literally a renewal of her personality in that it gave her a real sense of her identity as an Indian person. The affective awareness of her family as loggers who were also dance people working for the earth's balance made her feel a deep I-and-Thou meeting with me. This dialogical presence was the true healing event because it made her feel her connectedness to a therapist who was truly interested in her family mythology and her tribal community. She felt proud of belonging to her family and tribe, and her sense of freedom sparkled through her joy and excitement.

There were several more sessions in which the girl further strengthened her sense of Indian identity. She started living according to her traditions, and the pride she took in her family's role in the tribal community as dancers and regalia makers helped her to abstain from using drugs. In a year, she was released from probation and became an honor student. Her new, stronger sense of identity as a tribal member helped her to confront the isolation that resulted when she lost her substance-abusing friends, and this gave her a context of greater freedom and potential.

The death and grief issues were addressed in psychotherapy through the indirect, symbolic processes of storytelling, art making, and dreamwork that honored her need for silence and her sense of being. During therapy, she had a dream that reassured her that her family member had survived the journey from ordinary life to the spirit land. The dream relieved her depression and her grief and put her back on her tribal path of life.

Conclusion

The mental health professional needs to be alert to the following for the healing dialogue to be created in the Between with American Indian clients:

1. A mythological worldview that is based in the concrete, existential events of daily life and reflects a personalism of the transpersonal and immanent Creator
2. The sacredness of all human personality
3. The social existence of the Supreme Personality, who addresses the American Indian through various touchstones of reality — ritual, story, song, myth, dreams, visions, regalia, and the landscape that is more global than regional
4. The independence, uniqueness, and wholeness of the American Indian client in response to the address from the Supreme Personality
5. The individuation process of the American Indian that helps maintain and develop a "we" psychology and brings about individuation through participation in community
6. The importance of confirming American Indians' identity or sense of being, their tribal family, and their personal mythology as these unfold in the I-and-Thou moment within the therapeutic setting
7. The need to practice indwelling by attending ceremonies, visiting families, working with tribal healers, and engaging in communicative social action

The existential psychotherapist who uses storytelling, art making, and dreamwork facilitates the creative pause as it is described by Rollo May (1981):

> The pause is the essence of creativity, let alone of originality and spontaneity. One cannot avail oneself of the richness of preconsciousness or unconsciousness unless one can let oneself periodically relax, be relieved of tension. It is then that the person lets the silences speak. (p. 176)

Finally, it is ontologically necessary in psychotherapy with American Indian clients to draw upon silence, or the creative pause, and to use tribal symbol systems through storytelling and art making. Silence in the therapeutic milieu creates an environment where the internal conflict of opposites — death and life, meaninglessness and meaning, limitedness and freedom — can be creatively resolved. Silence allows the symbols to emerge and to integrate the troubled psyche. Through the use of tribal symbols in the therapy session, the therapist witnesses and confirms the integrity of the Indian persona. In this manner, an I-and-Thou meeting is created, bringing about the client's confrontation with his or her freedom. This shift in attitude brings about the existential healing.

References

Haley, A. (1976). *Roots.* New York: Doubleday.
Knudtson, P. N. (1975, May). Flora, Shaman of the Wintu. *Natural History,* 6–18.
May, R. (1969). *Love and will: A search for the sources of violence.* New York: Norton.
May, R. (1981). *Freedom and destiny.* New York: Norton.

6
EI Perspectives on Gender, Power, and Sexuality

Perhaps it is because of its paternal lineage, or perhaps it is because too few are exposed to its philosophy — whichever the case, existential therapy is rarely connected with feminist analyses of gender, power, and sexuality. This is unfortunate. As the case studies to follow attest, feminist understanding of women's (and men's) conflicts with gender, power, and sexuality is intimately connected with existential themes. Among these themes are not only freedom, limitation, constriction, expansion, anxiety, and responsibility, but also, and equally important, courage, presence, and encounter. In the first study Laura Brown anatomizes the power (which is intimately connected to freedom) that underlies meaning making. In her therapeutic work with "Emma," Dr. Brown provides essential conditions for empowerment through presence, an egalitarian relationship, and modeling. From there, she helps Emma to embody her power in relationships, from her relationship with Dr. Brown, to her relationship with lovers, leaders, and society. Although there are stumbles along the way, Dr. Brown helps Emma to realize her core priorities, which include her identification as a lesbian woman, her search for a substantive partnership, and her pursuit (in spite of her Christian upbringing) of a Jewish spirituality.

In a parallel but robustly unique account, Joan Monheit elucidates the case of "Marcia," a 28-year-old bipolar client who struggled with her lesbianism. Although the focus of Monheit's study is gay identity, the case of Marcia evokes key existential issues. Among these are Marcia's struggle to break free of her religious and spiritual heritage (unlike Emma, in Brown's study, Marcia fought against her Jewish moorings); her fear of being abandoned by her family for being gay; her struggle to assert herself and become more visible in the world; and her battle to integrate sexual, cultural, and spiritual dimensions of herself. Drawing on both practical and experiential resources, Monheit helped Marcia to gain a foothold on her bipolar condition, her financial dependency, her skewed relationships with loved ones, and, finally, her debilitated approaches to herself. Through a live and embodied connection, and after four arduous years, Monheit helped Marcia reclaim the parts of herself that she had denied — her gayness, her religiosity, and her right to live, even as that living differed with those around her. There are few higher gifts.

In the final study of this chapter, Ilene Serlin explores the dynamic interplay between existential issues of freedom and limitation (or Dionysian and Apollonian yearnings), confrontation with mortality, and solitude versus community, in the lives of her single-women clients. By comparing and contrasting the struggles of the poet Anne Sexton with those of her featured client "Maria," Serlin richly animates a female existential view. Specifically, Serlin shows how debilitating oppositions between the sexual and spiritual and the wild and ladylike can be fruitfully encountered and transformed. Drawing on her dream and symbolic life, authentic encounter, and experiential immersion, Dr. Serlin supports Maria on the integrative path. This is a path with which many people (let alone single women) struggle, but too few have the opportunity to see through. In this light, Dr. Serlin models a challenge — to both her clients and profession.

Feminist Therapy as a Meaning-Making Practice: Where There Is No Power, Where Is the Meaning?

Laura S. Brown

Laura S. Brown, PhD, is a feminist psychotherapist who has been practicing in Seattle since 1979. She has written extensively on feminist therapy theory, ethics, and practice, including the award-winning book *Subversive Dialogues: Theory in Feminist Therapy.* Her work has focused on psychotherapy with survivors of complex trauma.

Feminist therapy is a theory of therapy grounded in feminist political analysis of issues of gender, power, and social location as they manifest in human lives and human distress. Born of the feminist movement of the late 1960s and early 1970s, this model began as a protest against the oppressive dynamics of psychotherapy as practiced at that time, dynamics in which women's cultural subjugation was reinforced in the therapy office by the pathologizing of normative experiences and the reification of rigid binary gender roles as norms for mental health (Brown, 1994).

Because feminism is concerned with how patriarchal cultures oppress people, feminist therapy has always been interested in ways in which people experience power and powerlessness stemming from experiences of oppression, marginalization, silencing, and stigma. The initial interest of this field was in the ways in which sex and gender shaped those experiences, although feminist therapy's analysis has since expanded to include oppression and disempowerment arising from the range of social locations such as culture, social class, ethnicity, sexuality, spirituality, disability, colonization, and stigma. As humans are seen to have intersecting and multiple identities (Root, 2000), each of which may become foreground at different junctures of an individual's life, feminist therapists attend to the shifting meanings given to those various identities by the social context, as well as the meanings that the person gives to those identities. Empowerment and meaning making are central concerns of feminist practice.

Viktor Frankl (1963) famously wrote of how some of the most disempowered people in history, the Jewish inmates of Auschwitz, found meaning in the midst of the utter meaninglessness of the death camps, saying,

> We who lived in concentration camps can remember the people who walked through the huts comforting others, giving away their last piece of bread. They may have been few in number, but they offer sufficient proof that everything can be taken from a person but one thing: the last of the human freedoms — to choose one's attitude in any given set of circumstances, to choose one's own way.

Reading these words from the standpoint of feminist therapy, it is possible to interpret that a component of what was meaning making for these individuals, who made the existential choice to act as humans rather than otherwise, was the capacity to be powerful. That is, in making a choice — in choosing to connect, to nurture others, to have their own pre-imprisonment values inform their actions rather than being controlled and defined entirely by the horror around them and the absence of humanity attributed to them by their Nazi captors — Frankl's fellow inmates found power in the most powerless of places. They rejected internalized oppression in the midst of profound and lethal external oppression and, as such, were more powerful on this important dimension and existentially more free than those guarding and killing them.

Empowerment, a core dynamic in feminist practice, can thus be seen as a value deeply congruent with any meaning-making process, and powerlessness as a barrier to full-on engagement with the existential psychodynamics with which life presents us all (Yalom, 1980). Although not every feminist therapist will center on or foreground issues of power and powerlessness as existential dilemmas, it is my belief that such dilemmas are inextricably interwoven into the enterprise of feminist therapy. The development of feminist consciousness, that is, the awareness that one's oppression is not one's fault, but rather reflective of cultural norms, and that the tools for liberation may lie in some large part in one's own hands, is a goal of every feminist therapy session (Brown, 1994). Such a consciousness may be seen as a way of describing existential aliveness and awareness with careful attention to the political realities of the social context. Just as existential psychotherapists have noted that full contact with life's realities may lead to healthy distress (Yalom, 1980), so feminist-therapy theory argues that a fully alive, empowered person will feel distress about the unfair, unjust, and oppressive realities of life (Brown, 1994) and will come to understand how they are part of a larger cultural milieu that both acts upon them and can be acted upon.

Feminist therapy construes power not simply as control over resources, human and material, which is the usual manner in which power is construed in dominant culture. This concept is seen as limited in its reflection of dominant culture values, restricting power to the privileged few. Instead, feminist therapy is also concerned with powers available to all humans, irrespective of whether they have access to power over others. A powerful person knows what she or he thinks and is able to think critically about her or his own thoughts and those of others. Powerful people know what they feel as they are feeling it and can use their feelings as a useful source of information. They are not numb; their current feelings are about current, not past or possible future, experience; and they are able to soothe themselves and contain their feelings in ways that are not harmful to themselves or others. Powerful people are able to have effective impact on others and are able to be flexible and influential without regular negative consequences. Powerful people are in contact with their bodies and able to accept those bodies as they are rather than be focused on making the body or some part of it larger or smaller, and powerful people do not intentionally engage in behaviors that hurt the body. Powerful people are able to know their sexual desires and act on them in ways that lead to pleasurable outcomes consistent with their values without unusual difficulties. Powerful people have systems of meaning making that assist them in responding to the existential challenges of life and that give them a sense of comfort and well-being.

All of these ways of being powerful can only be evoked by encountering our clients as whole humans, a biopsychosocial-existential/spiritual framework. Empowering the people with whom we work as feminist therapists to be fully alive and develop an awareness that they are not the problem, but do hold the solutions in their hands, is what I have described as "subverting patriarchy" (Brown, 1994) as it is represented in the minds and hearts of humans in distress. I have been given permission by one woman, with whom I have worked on and off for more than two decades, to tell some of her story here as a means of illustrating feminist therapy as a meaning-making practice. It is a story of the long, careful process of empowerment, of how one woman became seen and known by me, her therapist, and by herself.

By the time you read this, "Emma" (as I am calling her here) will have read and commented on this vignette. Her perspectives on her experiences of meaning making will have met mine and been integrated into this work. Thus, although I cannot call her by her own name here, she has contributed her feedback. Her words are directly present, and importantly, she has always been the primary author of her meaning-making narrative in her therapy work with me. Feminist therapy establishes a collaborative, egalitarian relationship in which both parties are seen as expert, bringing important skills to the table. As a therapist I can create the context in which empowerment and meaning making can occur; the people with whom I work are themselves the ones who identify what it is that creates meaning for them, and the paths they must take on that journey. I invite people to be aware, to know, to see and hear themselves differently than they have previously done; I subvert and deconstruct the problematic realities that have informed them. Only the clients have the power to enact that subversive process and to decide how it will be embodied and enacted.

The Case of Emma

Emma is a European American woman in her late 50s. A middle child and only daughter, she grew up in a rural Midwestern community on the family farm. Her family culture was one of fear and numbness; no overtly physically or sexually abusive acts were ever perpetrated on her, but the family's fundamental religious faith terrified her as a small child. Church services were replete with images of hell and its fires, and messages about the ease with which any person could fall into them; her faith was an emotionally abusive experience. Expressions of warm emotion and physical closeness were absent in her family culture, aside from the caring behaviors of one family elder to whom Emma was close in her early childhood. Because fear was the one emotion present and evoked in her family, fear is what has informed Emma's life for many years. Many of her decisions have been founded in fear; freeing herself from fear so that she can know her desires and choose how and whether to express them has been a central theme of the work we have done together.

Emma knew from when she was quite young that she was attracted to other girls, a desire that she realized was not only forbidden, but also one of the sins that would consign her to the fires of hell forever. Desire, however, is a powerful thing; she and her high school sweetheart, posing as only good friends and roommates, did what many young lesbians of her age cohort did: They refugeed to Seattle, a large city far from home where no one knew them. But even there fear ruled her. While she was safe to no longer go to church and thus stopped the trauma of being subjected weekly to threats of hell, the terror of being seen, known, and punished in secular society for being lesbian was pervasive. And in that era she was right: Although by the time she first came to meet with me in 1983 Seattle had begun to become the queer-affirmative, welcoming city with protective laws on its books that it is today, when Emma arrived there a decade earlier the police were still raiding lesbian bars and throwing women into jail for simply having a beer in the presence of other women. She and her partner were isolated; they knew, and did not want to know, other lesbians, because to be known was to be at risk. In Maslovian terms, Emma's life was concerned with basic safety issues; meaning making was the furthest thing from her mind. She was simply relieved that she was no longer going to church, although also terrified that her home-town preacher had been right and that her falling away from faith meant a ruinous end. So her internalized oppression, developed from an early age, disempowered her and led her to a cautious, narrow life.

Emma found a job and did very well even though she had little formal education past high school. She was promoted through her company's ranks and became a respected and well-regarded employee. To her co-workers, she was a woman with no home life. She lived with her "roommate," and then by herself with her beloved cat when the roommate moved back to the Midwest. As was true for many lesbian relationships of that era, isolation had taken a toll; the couple had no support, no place where they could turn to process the normal challenges and struggles of intimacy, no models of how two women could build a life together. Secrecy and solitude drove wedges. For Emma, the meaning of life was work and coming home to Bubba the cat. On the surface, where she was visible, her life appeared shallow and devoid of meaning making.

Yet she yearned for meaning. She read voraciously in the literature of metaphysics, Eastern religions, and philosophy. Just as her desire for women could not be squelched by the homophobia and bias of her social environment, neither could her desire for meaning making be snuffed out by the terrorizing tropes of the faith of her childhood. She was fearful that by reading this material she was adding to her term in hell, but her powerful need to make sense of life drove her forward.

Emma first called me for an appointment in 1980. We met once, and then she went away. I had been in practice only a short time and was beginning to be known as a psychologist who was openly lesbian. When we talked about this later, after she returned to work with me in an ongoing way a year or so later, we speculated that perhaps she needed to be able to see this strange creature, the psychologist (i.e., respectable person) who was also open about being lesbian (a forbidden and dangerous stance to take in Emma's realities). She also needed me to see her; prior to our encounter she was known as a lesbian by women with whom she was involved and their small, carefully guarded social circles, which were open by invitation only to carefully vetted others. But to be in public, so to speak, in my office, even though it is a confidential setting, was a first and frightening step for her. Someone saw her as herself, Emma, a lesbian, and she saw herself reflected back. As she said in her comments on this section,

> The early sessions were testing and seeing if you would reject me, as it felt society had done. It was sort of . . . well, if I reveal who I really am, will I be rejected? I never was. The bond of trust that was developed was crucial to the work. I came to know I could tell you my deepest fears and not be rejected. That there was one person who would listen unconditionally. Knowing it was safe was essential because it hadn't been safe on the outside. (Emma, personal communication, August 2006)

Although the experience of embodiment is not often represented by being seen, it is my belief that the phenomenon of mutual gaze is one of the primary — and thus most powerful — ways in which humans come to know that we exist. Gaze between infant and caregiver is an early component of the attachment process. The infant sees herself or himself being seen by the caregiver, and so begins to know that she or he exists. When the gaze is loving and benign, the infant experiences herself or himself as lovable and good. To be invisible in her desires, as Emma had been for her entire life, except in circumstances that conspired with the dominant culture to label those desires dangerous and criminal, had had a profound negative effect on Emma. She saw herself as needing invisibility for safety, because she knew with utter and certain faith that the gaze of others, in particular heterosexual others, would be shaming, rejecting, and punitive. By making herself invisible she had done what feminist therapists identify as resisting patriarchy (Brown, 1994); no one could punish her for being lesbian if no one could see a lesbian where she stood. She could live her life, but her resistance had a price, part of which led her into therapy.

Although much of our early work together focused on such topics as relationship struggles with her then-partner and some specific phobias that were affecting her life, on reflection back over more than two decades we can both see that an important part of our work together was the embodiment of the loving and benign gaze in our relationship, and the presence of a powerful and empowering lesbian directing that gaze to her. I like Emma very much; she is decent, caring, and hardworking, kind to others, a *mensch* to use the Yiddish term that I shared with her early in therapy. I also respect her for what she has accomplished. Initially, much of the empowerment that occurred in our work together was about her beginning to see herself reflected in that way, and to slowly begin to transform her internalized oppression at the level of basic self-worth. She also was able to look at me and see *lesbian* configured very differently, as a relatively content person who was publicly known for her sexual orientation and appeared to be neither struck by lightning nor shunned by society.

A phenomenon that has persisted as a theme in our work is Emma's internalized homophobia, which is a common source of disempowerment for lesbian, gay, and bisexual (LGB) people. Internalized homophobia can be defined as the manner in which negative societal views of homosexuality and LGB persons become part of an LGB individual's self-constructs. Internalized homophobia is deeply disempowering in multiple and complex ways; an LGB person may not overtly hate herself or himself for being queer (a term currently in use by sexual minority communities to describe ourselves), but may evidence it in subtle ways, such as devaluation of overtly queer persons (as an example of this, see the many personals ads for same-sex partners specifying that the person should "look straight" to be acceptable), undermining the value of same-sex relationships by having expectations of infidelity or impermanency, or avoiding associating with known LGB people for fear of being perceived oneself to be queer. Internalized homophobia also presents itself at a number of important meaning-making junctures. LGB persons struggle with whether they are humans of worth in the eyes of a divine being. They may restrict their career choices, forgo parenting, or soothe the pain with drugs, alcohol, or compulsive sexual acting out. In numerous ways, internalized homophobia drains energy, self-knowledge, and thus power from LGB people.

Emma restricted herself in many ways because of her fears. At work she was afraid to be more successful than she already was; if she became seen as a competitor, she reasoned, her peers would seek to uncover "dirt" about her — in other words, the fact of her lesbianism. She was afraid that if she asserted her desires in her relationship that she would be rejected, as her then-partner was older, more educated, and more sophisticated than she, thus representing someone to whom she was supposed to defer. If rejected, she despaired of meeting someone else, since their social circle was tightly closed and comprised only of carefully vetted lesbian couples. That her partner was relationally challenged and so damaged by her own internalized homophobia that she was incapable of valuing Emma was invisible at first to Emma; she expected to be devalued and, due to her internalized homophobia, she expected her relationship to be full of difficulty and eventually unrewarding.

Empowerment, increased range of personal choice, and decreased fear all developed in the context of the overt topics under discussion. Emma continued to be fearful about many things much of the time, but in small corners of her life her fears ceased to rule her. Our work at this level took a number of years in which we did the dance of two steps forward, three to the side; Emma would gather the courage to become more visible, and then have to rest in this newly exposed place, face the fears engendered by that new location, and learn to breathe deeply into the reality that she was being seen and not harmed. The power of her internalized oppression was great; the potent mixture of fire-and-brimstone hate-based religion and cultural homophobia had affected her at the cellular level of her psyche. The detoxification process was a painstaking one for us. In our initial years together, I frequently made missteps, not appreciating the depth of the disempowerment from which she suffered. Fortunately, our relationship was based in the feminist principle of egalitarianism, and Emma had learned that she could tell me to back off of my bright ideas about what to do. In that process of challenging an alleged authority (the person in the room with the psychology degree), she also had the embodied relational experience of knowing that such a challenge could be not only survived, but also delighted in.

I cannot recall precisely when Emma began to circle cautiously around the topic of organized religion. I do know that by the time she broached that very radioactive topic she had established a new relationship. She had also found a different job and had had a brief experience on the board of a small lesbian community organization where she had been able to see herself in a leadership role. She had begun to know and meet other lesbians, see and be seen by them. Her homophobia continued to guide her; she feared that her co-workers would encounter her in the company of her new acquaintances. She had come out to her parents on a visit they made to Seattle; to her surprise, their response, although less than enthusiastic, was not the wholesale rejection and condemnation that she had expected. My hunch is that it was this semiadequate experience of being seen by her parents as not condemned that allowed her to touch the radioactive territory of faith and a divine being.

For as she began to feel more personally powerful and less driven by fear in other corners of her life, Emma became less and less willing to accept what she was coming to realize had been a lie — the lie that she was hated by G-d* because of her desires. I have previously commented that this lie, which is a common experience for LGB persons, functions as a kind of endemic betrayal trauma (Brown, 2003). I believe this to have been the case for Emma; she experienced betrayal and fear, and for many years had acted like a trauma survivor, avoiding anything that reminded her of the trauma. But her increasing sense of personal power made it more difficult for her to leave this area of her life deadened. As I had earlier mentioned, she was insatiably curious about the meaning of life, seeking, via the safety of books, answers to the questions of what her presence in the world was for.

Consequently, the second half of our work together, leading up to the present time, has been about Emma's journey toward a safe place of meaning making. By safety I do not mean avoidance of distress; rather, in order to move forward beyond more core Masolvian needs, Emma needed to know that wherever she might go in the interpersonal realm to pursue this dangerous and important journey she would face no unnecessary dangers because of her lesbianism. Zimberoff (2005) has proposed a feminist reformulation of the famous pyramid of needs, adding the spiritual/meaning-making component to the tip of the structure. She notes that individuals do not move in a linear fashion up the pyramid, and she argues that activism, altruism, political activity, and creativity might be seen as empowerment-language manifestations of the self-actualization component of the hierarchy as originally envisioned. She also notes, as do I, that freedom from oppression is necessary for persons to be able to make movement toward empowerment in the material and existential realms.

Indeed, for Emma, as for many lesbian, gay, bisexual, and transgender (LGBT) people (O'Neill & Ritter, 1992), any contact with religion was distressing. Even apparently benign, queer-affirming churches with openly lesbian, gay, or bisexual clergy triggered the trauma of her earlier abuse by punitive

* Editor's note: The expression "G-d" stands for "God."

religion. In our work, as we explored what about the experience was so deeply triggering and disempowering, she was finally able to identify that any and all Christian images and symbols, even reinvented as the loving expression of the divine, felt dangerous to her. The name and face of Jesus Christ had been the identity of her oppressor, of the one who hated her for being who she was.

And so Emma took a giant leap. During one of her tentative stabs at exposure therapy for her religious trauma, she attended a local new-age church. One Sunday a rabbi came to speak. She came to therapy that next week reporting that she had felt drawn to him and to what he had to say. But how could she possibly attend a synagogue? Would she not, among Jews, be once again negatively visible — this time as not a member of the group, not eligible to be there?

These questions were complicated, and yet made approachable, by my identity. Emma had known for many years that I am a Jew. I take off from my practice on the Jewish holidays, and my speech is interlaced with Yiddishisms learned from my grandmothers. Emma was worried that I would feel her to be presumptuous. The balance of power in our relationship, which was always precarious, tipped in my favor; as the "real Jew" in the room, as well as the therapist, Emma was ceding to me her authority to follow her desires in Rabbi Wolf's direction.

At this point let me note that there is nothing disguised here about Emma's faith journey. I thought long and hard about whether to make her choice more neutral and less visible so as to better universalize her story. Yet the relational space between us created by my supporting her exploration of Jewishness, and our collaboration in the process of empowering her to do so, would ring much less authentically if the reality of which faith we were talking about were stripped out of this story.

I shared with Emma a story I had learned while attending Hebrew school as an adolescent. My teacher had told us that a Jew had a *Yiddishe Neshama*, a Jewish soul, and that this soul, not anything else, was what made one a Jew. Sometimes, she said, a *Yiddishe Neshama* ends up being born into a family that is not Jewish; so the person carrying that soul often suffers and feels alienated from the faith in which they are raised. Perhaps, I suggested to Emma, she was an example of what my teacher had told me? Was she willing to risk knowing if that were true? I asked her. I offered her the story as an invitation to listen to her desires, to empower her in what was feeling, at a deeply embodied level, like the right path, even though it was frightening.

Emma went to synagogue. There she found resonance with her heart's deepest meanings. Rabbi Wolf was a student of Jewish mysticism, which assigns vibrational frequencies to letters of the Hebrew alphabet and integrates meditative practice into worship. Emma found herself literally vibrating, at one with the chanting of the word *Shalom*, the Hebrew term for peace. As the sounds of the chant rang through her body, she tentatively allowed herself to know that she might be someplace safe, someplace where she would be seen with loving and compassionate eyes, someplace where she could find an image of a divine being who did not hate her. She found herself returning for the continuing embodied experience of peace, acceptance, and divinity.

This is not to say that Emma did not have, and does not continue to have, struggles with her meaning-making journey into Jewish life. Her internalized homophobia surfaced strongly again with this new, strange group of people. It took her several years to carefully observe how members of her congregation treated other queer people who came there to worship; once again, she cycled through Zimberoff's reinvention of Maslow's hierarchy, needing to establish safety in this new, strange, but tempting place. She allowed herself to become an integral part of synagogue activities. She used Torah and Kabbalah study classes as means of deepening her capacity for critical thinking and expanding the safe space in which her spiritual development was emerging. She would come to our sessions excited and frightened, finding her power, her voice, and her vision, fighting with her fear that told her that she would be punished for knowing her desires and making meaning of her life. But she has persisted. She now struggles with whether to come out to her family as a budding Jew and whether to formally undergo conversion, and is beginning to decide that she is perhaps the one who knows how and if she is a Jew — that the power to put her public identity together with her soul might be in her hands.

What has been astonishing to see occurring parallel to Emma's movement into a meaning-making system that enlarges, rather than shrinks, her horizons is how she has also moved in other parts of her life. I see her being less and less run by fear, and more by her marvelous curiosity. She has begun to consider that heterosexual people are not her enemy, and to take back from a few individual straight folk the power she gave them to make her invisible and worthless. She can get mad at me and tell me off; our power is far more balanced today than ever it was.

So one might wonder how any of this is a story of feminist therapy. As I have earlier noted, feminist therapy is an epistemic system, not a technique. At each point in the process of feminist therapy, I as the therapist am continuously searching for ways to empower the people with whom I work, to invite them to be aware of and develop their multitudinous forms of personal power. When Emma came into my office in the early 1980s she had little such power; today she is increasingly a powerful woman, one who knows what she feels, how she thinks, and where the location of her meaning-making process is situated. She is not always sure of her value; her internalized homophobia retains its power to stop her in her tracks at times, but she remains in struggle with it. Our work has been feminist therapy because of the continued emphasis on the development of feminist consciousness, and Emma's empowerment as a woman, a lesbian, and a human searching for meaning.

"In the beginning there is creation," says the first line of the Bible. In the beginning there is also power, power that creates structure, meaning, aliveness out of *tohu vavohu*, chaos and formlessness. So, too, in feminist therapy: In the beginning we search for sources of power within our clients, power that allows them to create aliveness and energy from the void and numbness of oppression and disempowerment.

References

Brown, L. S. (1994). *Subversive dialogues: Theory in feminist therapy.* New York: Basic Books.

Brown, L. S. (2003). Sexuality, lies, and loss: Lesbian, gay, and bisexual perspectives on trauma. *Journal of Trauma Practice, 2*, 55–68.

Frankl, V. (1963). *Man's search for meaning: An introduction to logotherapy* (I. Lasch, Trans.). New York: Washington Square Press.

O'Neill, C. W., & Ritter, K. Y. (1992). *Coming out within: The stages of spiritual awakening for lesbians and gay men.* San Francisco: Harper.

Root, M. P. P. (2000). Rethinking racial identity development: An ecological framework. In P. Spickard & J. Burroughs (Eds.), *We are a people: Narrative in the construction and deconstruction of ethnic identity.* Philadelphia: Temple University Press.

Yalom, I. D. (1980). *Existential psychotherapy.* New York: Basic Books.

Zimberoff, A. (2005). *Integrating Prochaska's stages of change with a feminist reformulation of Abraham Maslow's pyramid of needs.* Unpublished manuscript.

A Lesbian and Gay Perspective: The Case of Marcia

Joan Monheit

Joan A. Monheit, LCSW, is a psychotherapist and consultant in private practice in Berkeley, CA, and has trained extensively with James Bugental. Along with working with individuals and couples, she leads Writing Through Grief and Healing Through Writing groups and workshops. She is an award-winning poet and a national presenter on the use of writing as a therapeutic process, and she has been a clinical director of Pacific Center for Human Growth, an adjunct faculty member at JFK University, and a social worker with Hospice of Marin.

A primary concern of existential psychotherapy is the relationship among freedom, limitation, and choice. For lesbians and gay men, the choice is not in being lesbian or gay; that is a given. Rather, the choice is either to embody one's affectional and erotic desires and allow for all the possibilities of who one is or to limit oneself by imitating the perceived norms of the culture, thereby constricting expression of not only one's sexuality, but many other aspects of the self as well.

Inherent in this concern is the issue of self-acceptance: the freedom to express oneself fully in relation to self, others, and the world. This very human struggle is intensified for lesbians and gay men because of both *homophobia* (the fear or dislike of lesbians and gays by others) and *internalized homophobia* (self-hatred). Lesbians and gay men must daily answer the question: With whom can I be myself? The dangers are real. Physical safety, economic security, and acceptance by others are all threatened. And hiding one aspect of the self affects other dimensions of the self, such as self-esteem, creativity, and the ability to love.

Even for those who appear to be comfortable with being gay, the issue goes deeper. One of my clients, whom I will call "Gary," was "out" as a gay man. He wore gay buttons, did not hesitate to tell others that he was gay, held strong political beliefs, and displayed a good intellectual understanding of being gay. Gary's parents and siblings knew he was gay, although no one would talk about it with him. It especially saddened and angered him that he could not talk with his mother about his life, which included his relationships with his friends and his activities. As he said to me at one session, "I can't just change the subject; this *is* my life."

While Gary appeared to be comfortable with himself as a gay man, he was not. After the breakup with his first lover, Gary stopped being sexual for over six years, adopting one strategy used by lesbians and gay men: "It's OK to be gay as long as I'm not sexual." But since he could not be sexual, he was unable to fully embody who he was as a gay man; nor, for that matter, could he express his full humanness.

Therapeutic work concerning the freedom to express oneself and therapeutic work touching on lesbian and gay identity issues are mutually reinforcing. As clients gain a greater sense of self and possibilities, they also learn to accept themselves as lesbian or gay; as they learn to accept themselves as lesbian or gay, they become increasingly more able to express all of who they are and to experience a widening sense of possibilities.

The Case of Marcia

The interweaving of the concerns of freedom, limitation, choice, and sexual identity is illustrated in greater depth in my work with a client I will call "Marcia." While there are differences between lesbians and gay men, not the least of which is gender, the basic issues are the same.

Marcia was a 28-year-old Jewish woman referred to me by another lesbian client. "I'm very unhappy and need help from you," she said to me with tears in her eyes the first time we met. We worked together for four years.

Marcia was in a secret sexual relationship with a married but separated woman, a relationship she ended shortly after we began therapy. Marcia was fighting constantly with her mother, who lived in the area and with whom she had almost daily phone contact. She experienced herself as highly critical and judgmental, which she said created much conflict in all her relationships. She also described herself as "very needy."

Since early childhood, Marcia had a skin condition that flared up under stress. Ten years previously, while away for her first year of college and during her first serious relationship with a young man, Marcia had a psychotic break and was hospitalized. She was diagnosed as bipolar and had been on lithium since.

Marcia was the eldest of three children and the only girl. Her family was religiously observant and identified strongly with Jewish culture. She was expected to date and marry within the Jewish religion. No one in her family knew of her sexual relationships with women. In fact, Marcia hid the existence of all of her intimate relationships from her family, including an on-again, off-again four-year relationship she had with a non-Jewish man. Marcia's fear was so great that she worried about her mother calling her early one morning, finding her not at home, and surmising that she had spent the night with a lover. Marcia's psoriasis flare-ups were an expression of this fantasy, a genuine physical expression of her extreme difficulty in maintaining separate boundaries between herself and her family.

The two areas of her life on which Marcia wanted to focus in her therapy were her sexuality and her relationships. Though she acknowledged her emotional and sexual attraction to women, she could barely use the *L* word, *lesbian*. Although she wanted to explore being a lesbian and her attraction to women, for almost two years we could barely touch the topic. When we did, she would change the subject.

Marcia's experience had taught her that she had very few options in life: She had to be a good, attentive daughter or her behavior might, literally, kill her parents. Because of her belief that she had no choice, she rebelled the only way she could, by keeping her life secret and having loud, angry fights with her mother, fights that would end with both of them in tears.

A significant aspect of our work was Marcia's learning how to make contact with her subjective self. I would encourage Marcia to sit or lie on the couch quietly and make contact with her body and then with any thoughts or emotions relating to her inner life. She was so used to focusing "out there," onto others, imaging stories about people's lives, that she did not know how to pay attention to herself. She focused on me, as well, wondering what kind of car I drove, did I have a partner, what I did when I was not in the office working.

Our sessions would often look like this: Marcia walks into my office, sits on the couch, and asks how my weekend was. We explore her need to check in with me this way, or I give a brief answer, or we simply acknowledge this ritual and then I ask her to lie on the couch or sit with her eyes closed and see where she is. It is easiest for her to focus on physical sensations, so we begin there. Face, neck, chest, belly — suddenly, she jumps out of this process and asks me if I had seen a show last night on television. I ask her to return to herself, her sensations in her body, then emotions. Periodically, she interrupts her going inward, then, gently, I continue guiding her focus back to herself. The combination of her learning to "stop and check in with yourself," as I would say to her, and my listening to her and letting her know that she was acceptable was instrumental in her coming to accept herself and her sexuality.

I wondered how I could help Marcia to have a clearer sense of herself, to distinguish her needs from other people's needs of her, particularly her parents' needs. Could I help her act from a sense of herself instead of either trying to appease her parents or reacting against them? Could I enable her to find out who she was as a sexual being?

First, we looked at two symbols of her freedom and her developing sense of identity: being responsible for her own money and her own health. To this end, we talked about Marcia opening her own checking account. Up to this point she had only a joint account with her parents, an account into which her parents would sometimes deposit money. Ostensibly, her parents' rationale, she thought, was to make sure they could keep track of her spending, in case she had another manic episode. We talked about her fears of being financially independent, what it would mean for her to be in charge of her own finances. Soon she opened a new checking account for herself and stopped receiving money from her parents, relying, instead, on the income she earned herself.

Next, we looked at the second symbol of her freedom: being responsible for her own health. Marcia had told me that she wanted to begin to decrease her lithium and see if she could eventually get off it entirely. Not only was Marcia's physician uncle monitoring her lithium levels and supplying her with the lithium, but she was also going to the same doctor, a friend of the family's, that she had been seeing since childhood.

First, I made a referral for her to see a psychiatrist, who made an evaluation and began a very gradual process of decreasing her lithium. Marcia began buying her own lithium and had the psychiatrist, rather than her uncle, monitor her periodic blood tests. Second, Marcia chose a woman physician to oversee her general health needs, one whose medical philosophy included a holistic approach more in keeping with Marcia's own beliefs about health care.

Marcia felt some anxiety when she began exploring the areas of managing her money and her health, but eventually she was able to make these two significant transitions fairly easily. Her actions enabled her to have primary experiences in being responsible for herself, which reinforced her sense of freedom to express who she truly was.

Weaving in and out of our sessions was the theme of her sexuality. For over two years, Marcia was celibate, choosing to focus on building nonsexual, though increasingly intimate, relationships with other women. Being celibate also enabled her to establish a deeper relationship with and reliance on herself and gave her time to gently dance with the *L* issue. It was important that she take all the time she needed to explore her sexuality and the meaning of being a lesbian.

As Marcia began to embody a sense of herself, she began to become more involved in social activities with women in general and lesbians in particular.

She tentatively started to date women. As our work progressed, she became aware of her need to integrate an identity of herself as a lesbian and also as a Jew. She began to attend religious services at a lesbian and gay synagogue and joined a Jewish women's spiritual group. Earlier in our work, Marcia could not have involved herself in these activities, but now it was important to her to decrease her isolation and receive support and acceptance from people similar to her.

A year and a half into our psychotherapy, Marcia and I had our first pivotal conflict. Just as, without awareness, she had reacted against her parents instead of choosing her own way, Marcia stopped being the "good" client and began to reject my facilitation of her work in our sessions. Whereas she had long been trying to do what I suggested in order to explore her concerns, she would now sit straight up on the couch and, as she had done at the beginning, talk about other people. When I pointed that out, she would say, "What good is therapy anyway? I'm spending too much money. Maybe I should just stop." Marcia was trying, in the only way she knew how, to assert herself. And so, staying with her subjective experience, we began to talk about that.

"Marcia," I said, "what do *you* want to do right now?"

"Nothing," she said stubbornly.

"You sound so young. How old do you feel?"

"Seven," she replied. "I'm not going to do what you want me to do!"

"You don't have to. You get to do whatever you want. You can be here, you can leave, you can talk or not. It's all up to you."

Sometimes I would ask her about feeling seven years old and protecting herself. "How do you feel, insisting that you won't do what I suggest?" As we explored this, I was able to point out that by saying only "no" to me, like she had with her family, she was acting, once again, from a set of limited possibilities on how to assert herself. I suggested that she might *want* to be quiet, check in with herself, and see what she was aware of — even if that was what I was suggesting that she do. She could make the choice for herself. Perhaps there were more meaningful ways in which she could now assert herself.

"I'm not your mother, and you're not really seven anymore, even if you feel that way," I said to her. By Marcia's being able to see and experience her process of reacting by saying "no" to me, instead of acting from within herself, she became aware of how she limited herself and, therefore, began to feel a true sense of choice in how she responded.

During our third year of work, Marcia became sexually involved with a close woman friend. While this relationship was mutually supportive, the other woman was basically heterosexual. This seemed to reflect Marcia's own ambivalence regarding her lesbian sexuality. Although the relationship was brief, Marcia was able to use her new self-awareness to explore many crucial issues. She could identify her own fears, or internalized homophobia. What would her parents think if they knew? (Total panic!) How would the rest of the world treat her? What would it be like to give up being in an "acceptable" relationship? How was it to make love with another woman? How did she feel touching and being touched?

During this relationship Marcia did come out to one of her brothers, and despite her fears, his reaction was quite supportive. Then came a family crisis: Marcia's brother reported to her that their mother had deduced the fact that Marcia and another woman had been lovers. Marcia became frightened and was not able to talk directly to either parent about her lesbianism, nor did they initiate a dialogue with her. It was crucial that Marcia choose for herself when and how to tell her parents. In therapy, she decided that she was not yet ready to have that conversation.

At the end of our third year of work came our next major conflict, which, though extremely difficult for both of us, was crucial in helping Marcia understand that she could have a serious disagreement with someone, be angry, stay instead of leave, and actually work out the conflict. One session, Marcia told me that the local health club, the YMCA, was offering a membership special and that she was going to join. I had been encouraging her to exercise more, so that she could also support herself through being more fully in her body. She knew that I had been a long-standing member of the health club myself. I grew concerned, realizing that being at the same gym might create difficulty in our working together. How would it be for us to run into each other while working out or in the locker room? How would she be able to focus on herself if I was there? We took a couple of weeks exploring these questions, and she finally decided she would not join this particular gym. Then she went on a month-long vacation. During the first session upon her return, after telling me about her travels, Marcia said, "Joan, I decided I still really want to join the Y, and if you don't want me to, then maybe I should just stop therapy!"

"Marcia," I said, "I know this is really scary for you to talk about, and I really appreciate your telling me. I don't think you'll have to quit therapy over this. Let's hang in here together and see how we can deal with this situation. Are you willing?"

Session after session she would come in, angry and scared, and we would discuss the problem. I was certain that I was right that we should not be at the same gym, yet neither of us knew how to solve the problem. "Marcia, we're in the soup. I don't know how we'll solve this, but I know that what we're doing is really significant," I said. "That we can both stay here and talk, and even be angry together, is important. You don't have to leave. You can stay and tell me what you think. I trust our relationship."

Finally, we did work out a compromise, which entailed setting up certain hours when each of us could go to the gym so that we would not run into each other. I know there were other possible solutions to the problem — I could have changed gyms, for example — but what was important was that we were able to stay together in a place of disagreement and uncertainty and work it out. Our grappling with this conflict further reinforced Marcia's experience that she could express herself and her needs and still stay in relationship with someone, a freedom she had not trusted before.

We were gradually coming to the final phase of our therapy, termination. Marcia took a job for five weeks at a resort in Idaho, where she spent much of her nonworking time alone, reading, writing letters, bike riding, and generally enjoying her solitude, a new experience for her. At the end of the five weeks, she went to a weeklong women's festival in Michigan. Here, Marcia was with many other lesbians and experienced herself as attractive and well liked. She became sexually involved with a woman who lived on the opposite coast. This time, the woman was a lesbian. Over several months, the two women became more and more intimate, through visits, letters, and many hours of phone calls. When they decided to live together, Marcia chose to move to where her new partner lived.

Marcia and I set the date of our last session for three months in the future. Given a supportive relationship that satisfied her both sexually and emotionally, one in which she could feel positive about her lesbian identity, Marcia was now ready to come out to her parents.

Marcia and her mother were able to spend time together, disagreeing, but not having the destructive fights that had been such an old pattern. They had a few family therapy sessions, and Marcia even brought her new partner to her parents' home for dinner during one of her visits.

We ended therapy acknowledging all the difficult work Marcia had done to bring her to this point in her life at 32. She was establishing an adult relationship with her family and forming a positive and mutually supportive relationship with a woman. She now had greater ability to control her psoriasis. As Marcia developed the freedom to express herself, she began to feel more secure with her lesbian identity, and as she experienced more fully what it meant to be a lesbian, she became more content and accepting of herself. In Marcia's therapeutic work, the dynamic interaction of freedom, limitation, and choice provided a context within which Marcia could discover and experience her ability to respond to her own nature and to make decisions that expressed her sense of self.

Women and the Midlife Crisis: The Anne Sexton Complex

Ilene Serlin

Ilene Serlin, PhD, ADTR, is a licensed psychologist in private practice in San Francisco and a registered dance/movement therapist. She is a fellow of the American Psychological Association and past president of the Humanistic Psychology division of the APA. She has studied Gestalt, existential, and archetypal psychology with Laura Perls and James Hillman, and has taught at Saybrook Graduate School, the University of California at Los Angeles, the C. G. Jung Institute in Zurich, and Lesley University. Her writings include *Humanistic Psychology* and *Women: A Critical-Historical Perspective and Laura Perls and Gestalt Therapy: Her Life and Values.*

"Maria" walked in one day crying, "My mother died when she was 45 years old, my stepmother did not live past 45, Anne Sexton committed suicide when she was 45, and I, being 45, am afraid that I will not make my 46th birthday." That week, Maria took an overdose of sleeping pills.

What was the mystery of her identification with Anne Sexton? How was Maria part of a tradition of women, from Anne Sexton to Sylvia Plath to Marilyn Monroe, who identified with a tragic heroine whose creativity led to death? These women wrestled with the ultimate existential concerns of freedom and limitation, but in a way that was unique to their particular roles as women. The aim of this commentary is to discuss how existential psychotherapy can be relevant to this group of women, by outlining the course of treatment with one individual woman.

Most single women over 40 remember the recent popular article claiming that their chances of marrying were dismal. They may also remember Anne Sexton's suicide in the 1970s. Together, these events point to an existential dread locked into their psyches: "What will become of me? Will I be alone? What gives my life meaning and value?"

This section looks at these questions through a case history. It raises questions usually hidden from public discourse: the use of alcohol, self-medication, and suicide in single women over 40 and their attraction to the romanticism of darkness as a demon lover. Finally, it explores an existential-integrative approach that addresses fundamental issues of *mortality, freedom, solitude,* and *commitment.*

Many of the talented women I have worked with, most of whom had not had children, balanced the needs for autonomy with the needs for relationship, felt vulnerable, and faced aging alone. Their creativity was not in the service of work and consciousness, but in the service of the unconscious; they immersed themselves in journal writing, doomed love affairs, and dreams. Like many women generally, they knew how to swoon, and their form of surrender was sexual, mystical, and ecstatic. Darkness exerted a strong pull and death a romantic fascination. Death was often envisioned as a dark or ghostly lover. The 1992 film version of *Dracula* (directed by Francis Ford Coppola) speaks of the archetypal combination of death, blood, and bliss. Instead of denying death, as is so common in our culture, these women experience death as a morbid fascination, an obsession, an addiction — in fact, as an escape from living. Finally, in defining themselves as women-selves in a repressive society, these women often experience being misunderstood, with conflicts between sexuality and spirituality, between images of whore and virgin, between being wild and being ladylike. Their difficulty in freeing themselves from creative blocks, from death, and from constricted sexuality seems to be related to their difficulty in separating from their mothers and standing alone.

The more I became concerned with these issues, the more I felt that women needed alternative role models to these romantic, tragic heroines. Can women be creative, alone, separate, loving, and still thrive? What would it take, therapeutically, to help them? And what can we learn about this complex in women, the conjunction of creativity, spirituality, sexuality, and darkness, so that other women can be helped?

In an obituary for Anne Sexton, the poet Denise Levertov wrote, "We who are alive must make clear, as she could not, the distinction between creativity and self-destruction. The tendency to confuse the two has claimed too many victims" (Quoted in Middlebrook, 1991, p. 397).

I call the pattern of romanticizing and identifying creativity with self-destruction and death the *Anne Sexton complex*. How women might have this complex yet still live and balance their finite ordinary lives with their expansive selves is the subject of this commentary. This investigation will take the form of the case history of one woman, whom I will present, phenomenologically, using her own words. I will review the major themes of her life and connect them with the themes of Anne Sexton's life. Finally, I will draw some conclusions about how the Anne Sexton complex is a particular way of living out fundamental existential themes for some women, and how an existential-integrative approach to therapy can help them find a more constructive ending to their stories.

The Case of Maria

When Maria came for her first session, I was impressed with her grace and intelligence. She was petite, her blond hair was pulled back, and she was artfully dressed and groomed. She spoke about her life with clarity and insight and seemed serious about helping herself in therapy.

Born in the Southwest, she had three sisters, a stepbrother, and a stepsister. Maria described her mother as "like Anne Sexton. She never really wanted children and was restless," playing out the role of the 1950s conventional American housewife. Maria's mother and sisters, she said, "were all dependent women, not able to stand on their own feet, not able to make a stand for themselves." Her mother died when Maria was 19, and her father left at the same time. Sent to live with an uncle, Maria had recurring images of being an orphan. At age 30 or 31 she was raped, and she said that life never came back together for her after that. She went to live with her sister in an attempt "to find family" but found that it did not work. Instead, she came to Boston, where she had been trying to create a new life for the past year and a half. She worked in a corporate office with mostly men, still had not made any friends, and was very lonely.

Freedom While acknowledging that she had managed to break away from the role her mother had played out, Maria was still not enjoying her freedom. Ironically, she imagined that housewives envied her independence and fantasized that she was spending her time partying and being romanced. Instead, she worked hard and came home to an empty apartment, where lovely objects were tastefully arranged. Nothing messed up her life, no one interrupted, and she had everything just as she wanted. What was missing? Other people, mess, life, and a meaningful focus. When I asked her how she was using her creativity, she said she had no outlets. She called herself a "closet artist" and knew that she had to "dig down" and find out what her life's calling was supposed to be. She was becoming increasingly isolated. She said sadly that she was "getting scared. I work all day and cry all night, and life is getting out of control." Drinking was an effort for her to find "spirits," or courage to connect and create. Her freedom was a "false freedom," she said, since she actually stayed in her apartment all weekend. The poignant picture I received was of a beautiful woman torn between a fearful independence and a need for connection. These pulls were illustrated in her dreams.

Dreams

Ghostly Lover The first dream Maria told me about was a powerful one for her; her high school boyfriend Dennis appeared, saying, "Call me." She and Dennis were the "first" for each other and seemed destined for marriage. They then both married others and lost touch (until recently, when they became available to each other again). He married someone "safe," said Maria. "I had too much passion." He stayed with Maria as a fantasy, but she felt that she already lived more in fantasy than in reality. She said, "I've never really been on the earth. [I'm] ethereal — [and] never owned property." The theme of being attached to fantasy — to what has been called the Ghostly Lover, and of therefore not having lived life fully haunted Maria and was a continuing theme of our work.

The Sacrifice of the Witch She then told me of another significant dream:

> A man and a woman are traveling together. He is from a Latin American country. She carries with her a little creature — it might be a bird. It seems small and fits in between her hands. They enter a forest and come upon a community of people living in the forest. To honor the man, they take the woman and tie her to a cross. They set the cross on fire, and she is burned to death.

Maria explained that, upon awakening, she kept trying to make it come out better, to convince herself that the woman did not die, but she reasoned that she had to have died. She could not have survived the burning cross.

Maria called this her first *sacrifice dream*. Her associations were that she gave an animal, her symbolic self, to the man before she herself was sacrificed. She did have a black cat and felt close to animals, and she said, "Women were burned at the stake for living alone and talking to animals." This meant to Maria that they were close to their instincts. She elaborated, "I always said I'd be burned as a witch. I am a threat, but to whom? To the established order because I've always been self-sufficient." Her early memories were of being called "the single type," taking care of herself and living alone. When I asked her what quality she might have that threatened others, she cried, saying, "I'm out of touch with my power. I have no idea what it might be." Despite this, Maria described herself as very competent at work, sometimes threatening to others, with a strong intuitive sense of their dynamics. She longed to use this capacity constructively, to be a healer, but she did not know how. Tearful, she described the sacrifice dream as being about her blocks in transformation, her ability to find the inherent power in a dangerous or pathological situation.

Virgin/Whore In another dream, Maria was drinking and dressed like a gypsy. Images of the whore came up as Maria described how her mother wanted her to be wholesome and ladylike and disapproved of her being a dancer. Maria was fascinated with the image of the whore, danced topless once, and had a friendship with a woman who was a prostitute.

As she described this image to me, I was struck with Maria's blond beauty. She was always dressed in white. She said she was called *Madonna* at work, and she was afraid of the whore image. Maria had been raped, and she was afraid after the rape that people would accuse her of inviting it. She tried not to "look as if she were inviting trouble," and she was afraid that her past would create problems in her relationships with men. As she talked, she normally sat in a composed and ladylike way. Yet when she laughed, and when she drank, a whole different, bawdy, and life-affirming side emerged. She had a wonderful sense of humor, which she credits with having saved her in the past.

Sleeping Beauty For the last 13 years, Maria had been celibate. She felt that she had to purify herself, to let something die so that she would be ready for something new.

Just before her suicide attempt, Maria had a dream of crashing cars. She was surrounded by "paramedics and a woman in white [her therapist] was standing over me. . . . I asked the woman whether I would live or die. I know now that it was my unconscious breaking through, ready for a big change."

When Maria took the sleeping pills, she had been drinking. She later described the sensation while drinking as one of drifting off. Pills, for her, intensified the speed of the drifting, until the point where she blacked out. Later, Maria discovered a journal entry she had scrawled during that time. It included the telephone number of her Ghostly Lover. She remembers or reconstructs that she was dreaming about him. She describes the feeling as being "in another grip . . . like another force had given over. I was compelled . . . and fearless in it, too. I was willing to go." Going into a state of suspended animation while in perfect physical condition and awakening to the Ghostly Lover is like the story of Sleeping Beauty. Death, oblivion, dreams, and the Ghostly Lover are all intertwined.

Ironically, Maria awoke from her swoon to see real paramedics in white standing over her. They took her to the hospital. Among the few possessions she packed to take with her was the biography of Anne Sexton, which she continued to read while in the hospital. As in *The Portrait of Dorian Gray*, life paralleled art, and art paralleled life.

Transformation After this incident, Maria entered a treatment center, while continuing to see me for individual psychotherapy. The use of therapy groups was a key adjunct to our existential-integrative path. The following is an account of Maria's treatment and what contributed to her recovery.

In the hospital, Maria asked me if it were possible to reverse the trend. I said, "Yes, if you're willing to give birth to yourself over and over again, to rediscover your innocence." I asked whom I was to her, and she said, "The figure in the dream of whom I asked, 'Will I live or die?'" Apparently I was a nurturing mother figure to Maria, one who would either lend her strength as she weighed life and death or foster her strength to create her own life.

Later she said that the figure in the dream that held her small animal, or her "self," made her feel safe. I also made her feel safe.

> You validated me . . . carried me along until I could do it for myself . . . because it's a long journey back [*Laughs*]. Something got set in motion . . . the idea of risk. I remember writing in my journal, "Be willing to risk your own life — even death itself." I've gained something, but only because I was willing to lose it, lose my life. It reminds me of the New Testament scripture: "He who shall lose his life shall find it."

Her dreams and her lover were two-edged, about freedom and limitation and how to integrate them in life. Being willing to risk her own life, like the image of sacrifice in her dream, allowed Maria to really choose life later.

Groups were an important part of the treatment center and Maria discovered that she liked living with people: "What turned it around was having people around. I've not been alone since." An existential-integrative approach combined the most important aspects of individual, group, and community therapy. Maria enjoyed attention from the men and began to experience herself more clearly as a woman. She began to consider calling "Dennis" (the

Ghostly Lover with whom she had actual contact recently) and to end her relationship with him, sensing that she needed to do this in order to be available for a real man and to live in a committed relationship.

She understood that it had been only eight months since her contact with Dennis, but since then she had lost 20 pounds and gone into a deep depression. Thinking of his message in her previously mentioned dream as a "call," we talked of all the times in life when one might hear a call to the forbidden, to mystery and danger. For Maria, the call was to the underworld, and Dennis was an imaginary guide: "He played a part in my hitting bottom." Her task, however, was not to remain in the underworld but to disintegrate and reintegrate into real life, community, and creativity.

When I asked her what changed for her, she said, "It took a near-death experience to give me life. It was like being reborn, starting from scratch." When I asked what it felt like to have life come back, she said,

> It feels rather amazing . . . wonderful . . . just to feel. I didn't know I was cut off from my feelings. Now I know. The only access was through my dreams. I feel younger. I was getting ready to grow old and die. I'd been doing that for a long time. There was no sex in my life, I was like a little old lady.

At this point, she expressed a willingness to "dare to connect. Instead of reading about it, I'd rather be out experiencing freedom. . . . I've not been able to watch TV since last April. Life is more interesting than watching TV."

Later that month, Maria came dressed in gold, with gold earrings and a suntan. Expressing a new interest in diet and health, she noticed the transition from lunar to solar imagery. She said, "You know my love affair with cats. This is a night world calling, related to moons and cats, to the unconscious and dreams." Her new solar energy related her to the day world, to sunshine and the overt.

Thinking back over her journey, Maria felt that it was all leading somewhere hopeful. "I marvel a lot these days at the turn my life has taken. Something got rolling, and I couldn't have planned it." Her tone of voice expressed a new innocence. She said,

> It feels like a rebirth. I feel like a child struggling to express myself, my brain wiped clean, having to relearn. I've given a lot of thought to the long period of celibacy — I think it was a really healthy thing. An opportunity to get to know myself, my own body, and myself as a woman.

The Heroine's Journey: Death and Rebirth Soon after leaving the treatment center, Maria had a dream about "messy sex." She was ready to "mess up" her "pretty apartment" with another person and give up some of her carefully managed control. She thought of herself as "completing a cycle . . . coming back to myself. My hair is long and blond again. I feel alive."

The next month, she met a man and moved in with him and his 16-year-old son. He was of Mediterranean descent; he and his children were dark, but his former wife was blond. Themes of dark and light were coming together.

The choice of being with him came out of her newfound courage. She said it was like her choice of whether to live or to die. It was a leap of faith. "You have to be able to go around the corner to see what is there. I knew it was risky. But I chose to live."

Maria described another change in terms of her need for freedom. She said, "I've always been independent and free. Now I don't want to be so free. I'm really happy, comfortable, letting him be the boss. I don't need my own car." Maria was trying to find a balance between the dependent-housewife stereotype, which she was fleeing, and a freedom that left her isolated. She was finding her way to a mutually determined interdependence, which meant negotiating long hours over household tasks and objects. Maria admitted enjoying this process: "I've never had an opportunity to care for people, to clean, someone else to shop for." I noticed that there was a certain pride in her use of the word *us*. As she put it, "I knew the meaning of life was in relationship, but I didn't know how to get a relationship. I also wasn't able to go on alone." Here Maria was expressing a new balance between needs for work and needs for nurturance, a balance especially difficult for many women (Bateson, 1989, p. 240; Gilligan, 1982, pp. 62–63).

When I asked her about the similarities and differences between her story and Anne Sexton's, she said,

> I am like Anne Sexton in that we both have a strong identification with our mothers. Anne Sexton also has similarities with my mother. My mother was a woman caught, or trapped, in the politics of the 1950s, not allowed to express herself in any domain other than in the context of home and family. Like many women in the 1950s, Anne Sexton sold cosmetics out of her home for awhile — the same brand of cosmetics my mother sold. I have come to understand that I have lived my mother's unlived life.

In both Maria's and Anne Sexton's families, Maria said,

> . . . the basic bond was between the women. Men were observers. Coming to Boston was an attempt to break away. I was always attempting to have my own life. Even my sisters were controlling me. [There was] too much enmeshment in the maternal womb. My own mother died when I was 19. I was literally thrown out into the world. I still needed a lot, was still a baby. I stayed in that little girl neediness. It's time to grow up and have a life. I'm still an adolescent. Staying virginal was a way of staying

attached to my mother and pleasing her. But I'm older than her now. She died just 28 days before her 46th birthday.

Like Anne, Maria had always experienced a strong pull downward: "Something drew me down, and I couldn't stop it. There really was a sense of going down." When Maria returned to her sister's house, she was aware of seeking a feminine environment, one closer to the earth and feminine values. However, there the death pull "began to get very strong, to pull me. Both of my sisters also have a struggle. My older sister didn't think I'd live past 46." There was the thought that "one of us will succeed in killing ourselves . . . almost like a curse." About their similarities in age, Maria observed, "It is perhaps a symbolic age, to cross the threshold that midlife presents to us and to meet the challenges that growing older represents." On the other hand, unlike Anne Sexton, Maria had a strong sense of being close to her father. Their drinking bonded them, and she once noted in a journal that she was "daddy's girl."

Maria's effort to break away from her home and individuate herself parallels the hero's journey. The hero must confront challenges, learn to be alone, overcome darkness, and bring his newfound wisdom back to his home and community. Missing are comparable stories for the heroine's journey, which could have provided a road map or sense of hope for Maria. Therefore, as a feminist therapist I empowered her to see her road as a heroine's journey so that she could take responsibility for her life. She said,

> While I was in the middle of it, I didn't understand all those dreams. I felt that everything that happened was absolutely necessary. You know how some people say, "You got me on the rebound"? I say, "You got me on the rebirth."
>
> What is it that saved me? I don't know. Maybe Anne and the other women having died saved me, in that I was able to examine their lives and learn from their lives. I tried to understand why they died, perhaps so that I wouldn't have to follow them. But I had lost hope, and it has been asked how I got it back. It came back gradually. I think I entrusted my "self" to others while I worked on the problem, while hope grew again. Others carried me while I was relearning who I am. Because today I am not who or what I was. The old self is lost to me — it has been sacrificed. I am in the process of reinventing my life. But I had to lose it in order to find it. I, of course, didn't know that this was what was happening. I know about it only in retrospect. The question has been asked, How does one decide whether to live or die? I decided to die. Maybe you have to decide to die before you can decide to live. I still decide daily. We take time before going to sleep at night to say what we are grateful for that day. I sometimes now say that I am grateful for my life. That is a big thing to say, and I feel it.

She then had a dream about a house burning down to ashes. However, in the dream was an image of a "phoenix rising from the ashes." What was burning?

> All my preconceptions of security. I tried to move back to my home state — to my sister's house — so that her family would be my family, but that blew up. There is nothing left to hold onto. It is the *Alchemical Negrito*, a blackening, getting to the essence. The suicide attempt (and depression leading up to it) was the beginning of the return. All the parts, in ritual sacrifices, sacrificed over and over, until the sacrifice was complete.

It is now time to "get to the essence of the spark of life, to find my own voice, my own spirituality." In a new dream, she "was choosing a bird for a pet." She said there were

> lots of white birds. A yellow bird, peering down, asking to be picked. Expectant attitude. A spiritual dream. The bird is the soul. White birds are a purity of soul. A yellow bird is some sort of divine being. So many white birds, just one yellow one. Actually, I want to buy a yellow canary, a bird that sings. Brings beauty again.

Maria and her lover share a sense of spirituality. They say grace together before meals and "gratefuls" before bed. It is "good to share that," she says. She experiences "a sense of calm, serenity, grace." They have been talking about marriage. It's "very scary," she says, but they are "creating rituals together." Helping each other with the "soul losses" they experienced. She had tried "feminist, spiritual" paths alone and now needs to do her soul and spirit work with another person. She notices, "People romanticize being a little bit crazy. I think I used to. I'm much more concerned with daily life now, being real. I don't think the purpose of life is to be happy, just to live it." When she is scared, Maria recognizes that she thinks of Dennis and takes refuge in fantasy, but then she says, she "can tell the difference between a fantasy and everyday life."

I mostly listened to Maria, providing a sense of a maternal safe space and supporting her to see this stage as a journey to find her own voice and respect her own decisions. We used artwork and dreams to discover the archetypal and symbolic patterns in her unconscious (Harding, 1975). A developmental approach helped her come to terms with her relationship with her own mother and create her own self as a woman. A narrative and feminist approach informed our collaboration and sense of sisterhood and solidarity (Heilbrun, 1988); after her suicide attempt, I visited her in the hospital. She kept a journal and dream notebook, and writing became a form of therapy for her. In her capacity as a powerful woman, Maria confronted the basic existential themes of freedom, aloneness, death, and meaning. Maria's journey went through stages of death and rebirth, bringing in a spiritual perspective. At times we literally practiced meditation and breathing techniques to help her quiet her anxiety and feel centered.

Recently, Maria came in reporting that the relationship was stable and a source of comfort for both of them. She had just survived her 46th birthday. Maria had had a dream in which she remembered one line: "You will not live beyond the 9s." Upon reflection, she understood that 45 was 5 × 9 and that 4 + 5 = 9. The number 9 was also symbolic of pregnancy, the period of gestation before something comes to fruition. She called her period of celibacy and hibernation her period of *dormancy*: "like I just went to sleep, turned it all off, Sleeping Beauty, a butterfly in a cocoon." She now had "so much willingness to comingle, to share our lives. I was attracted to men who were wrong. I just made the decision to stop. The change was imperceptible, unconscious. If I had intended to do it, I couldn't have." When I asked her what difference it made that she understood her journey in these terms, she said, "Some people have a need to study metapsychiatry, spirituality. I think I'm one. My sisters are not. I've been on this quest, the need to know, to understand." Commenting on the descent necessary for her rebirth, she said, "Other people don't really descend. Perhaps what was different was that the beginning of my journey was a conscious choice to make the quest. Without the descent and sacrifice, no change would have occurred. I had to kill part of myself." The image of an animal with its foot in a trap came up, an animal that had to gnaw off its foot in order to survive. Maria said,

> I think what makes my work with the unconscious different is that for the most part my trusting the unconscious has its basis in awareness and spirituality. If you trust the unconscious and are one with it, you are unconscious and act from this unconsciousness. But if you trust the unconscious and are aware, as a witness, [of] its workings in your life and in your dreams and respectful of its power to both create and to destroy, you stand apart from it and are not identical with it. I think the difference is between a conscious descent and an unconscious one.

By descending thoroughly, by being celibate and mostly containing the psychic process in journals rather than acting it out self-destructively (as did Anne Sexton), Maria was able to find the path to ascend.

Maria just finished reading Anne Sexton's biography by Diane Middlebrook. At the end of the reading, she felt "really sad" but also found "something sweet, something reclaiming" in it.

In summary, what were her similarities to Anne Sexton? Both were fascinated by death and darkness and both were very close to their mothers and the other women in the family, but this very attachment condemned them to live out the women's unfinished business. Both rebelled against the conventional role of housewife, experiencing a split between a heightened sexuality and ladylike behavior, images of the whore and the madonna, and needs for freedom and security. Both exhibited strong intuitive abilities, uncanny powers, healing abilities, and felt close to images of the witch. Both turned and returned to spirituality as salvation, looking for grace and redemption. Both were hungry for spirit, but spirit impregnated with the matter of the tribe, of culture, and the body. And both were heroines without adequate role models and with incomplete journeys of return.

Maria said she was different from Sexton in that she was less obsessed with suicide and closer to her father. She also wanted to be married, to care for another person, and to be interdependent.

Let us now turn to Diane Middlebrook's biography of Anne Sexton to see how Anne Sexton's life exemplified the heroine's journey as a descent (Perera, 1981).

Anne Sexton

Anne Sexton, the first publicly described "confessional poet," died in 1974 at the age of 45. She came from a conventional middle-class background and worked as a fashion model but went on to win professorships, international recognition, and a Pulitzer Prize.

Although Sexton tried to live a conventional life, she understood that "one can't build little white picket fences to keep nightmares out." The combination of a puritanical New England climate and a feverish sexuality ran through her family, causing eruptions and conflict. Maria, too, experienced a conflict between conventional values and heightened, almost hysterical sexuality, with a lack of a healthy sensual outlet.

The eruption of repressed and intense sexuality took the form, as it did in Maria's dreams, of witch imagery. Sexton wrote:

> I have gone out, a possessed witch,
> haunting the black air, braver at night;
> dreaming evil, I have done my hitch
> over the plain houses, light by light:
> lonely thing, twelve-fingered, out of mind.
> A woman like that is not a woman, quite.
> I have been her kind. (Middlebrook, 1991, p. 114)

In Sexton's poems, the housewife becomes an adulteress and witch while the poet is a magic maker. These are all a consequence of breaking out of the conventional woman's role. The witch image, however, is polarized into good witch and bad witch. Like Maria, Sexton had good-witch energy; she was empathic, intuitive, and had ways of "knowing." The bad witch was destructive, hysterical, and selfish. Given the double bind of convention and impulse, breakdown could be seen as a logical response.

> The mental hospital [is] a metaphorical space in which to articulate the crazy-making pressures of middle-class life, particularly for women.

> The home, the mental hospital, the body: these are woman's places in the social order that apportions different roles to the sexes; and woman herself is the very scene of mutilation. (Middlebrook, 1991, p. 274)

Sexton and Maria were both strongly connected, through their bodies, to the women in their families. They both came from conventional American families with strong ideas about what constituted "proper, ladylike behavior." Both rebelled and, in different ways, refused to be domestic. The rage they felt was partially expressed in a pull toward independence but primarily in killing off parts of themselves. Both experienced a strong split between their little girl, madonna, and virgin sides and their whore and vamp sexuality. The frustrated combination of sexuality, knowing, power, and anger came together in the image of the witch. They were both very attached to their mothers and searched for a form of feminine spirituality that would embody nurturance and grace. Both were beautiful and needed beauty in their lives but preferred to die as Sleeping Beauty rather than risk imperfection. Both sought to balance freedom and security, meaning and emptiness, loneliness and relationship. Both saw death as warm arms, as a release from the struggle of living.

Maria's Escape

How did Maria escape death? What can we learn from her heroine's journey and descent into the underworld that might help other suicidal women? First we will look at her case in terms of existential-integrative theory and follow this with a description, in her own words, of the major turning points of her psychotherapeutic journey.

Existential Theory This case can be understood in terms of four major existential theorists. The first is Irvin Yalom (1980), who describes the confrontation with death as one of the primary existential challenges. Certainly Maria faced death, both symbolically and in reality. Her fundamental challenge was whether she would choose to live.

As her therapist, I understood that she needed to look at death directly if she was going to re-experience her will to live. So I supported her in discussing her thoughts about death and surviving the suicide attempt. She literally weighed her values in life and described her decision-making process. I didn't try to make her feel better or happier, but used my presence to "hold" her so that she could feel and face her strong emotions. Ironically, facing death can bring the courage to live and to create. Existential psychoanalyst Rollo May (1975) notes: "By the creative act . . . , we *are* able to reach beyond our own death. This is why creativity is so important, and why we need to confront the problem of the *relationship between creativity and death*" (p. 20). Therapeutically, I supported Maria's reconnection to her art, even if it meant painting with black colors.

Although Maria has the aesthetic sensibilities of an artist, she had devoted her artistic vision to her inner world and fantasy and now needed to turn it outward to create a real life in relationship with others. Here the therapeutic work was relational and focused on helping her with issues of relatedness and intimacy.

May states that the role of the artist is to express the general conditions of the culture through symbol, and the courage of the artist is the greatest kind of courage. Insofar as both Maria and Anne Sexton embody artistic sensibilities struggling to create life through symbol and the imagination, they demonstrate the existential task of creating in the face of death. If they create themselves and their own lives, however, it may be asked what self they are creating. Maria explored her repertoire of selves through artwork and writing and found a balanced center.

An object-relations approach informed our understanding of how Maria's family taught her to identify with a false self, and how eager she was to find her more authentic self. Making a therapeutic alliance with this healthy part enabled her to shed some of her masks. Humanistic psychologist James Bugental (1987) stresses the importance of authenticity and subjectivity in the creation of a self in the world:

> Our subjectivity is our true home, our natural state, and our necessary place of refuge and renewal. It is the font of creativity, the stage for imagination, the drafting table for planning, and the ultimate heart of our fears and hopes, our sorrows and satisfactions. (p. 4)

Finally, the confrontation between life and death, the courage to create in the face of death, and the authenticity of a subjective self can be understood in terms of paradox. May comments that "genuine joy and creativity come out of paradox" (Schneider, 1999, p. 7). In Kirk Schneider's (1999) paradoxical model, the human psyche is described as a continuum of constrictive and expansive possibilities. The dread of constriction and expansion promotes dysfunctional extremism or polarization, whereas confrontation with or integration of the poles promotes optimal living (p. 27). Insofar as Maria and Sexton oscillated between the poles of expansion out into life and withdrawal into depression and a fantasy world (light and dark imagery, sexuality and spirituality), these extremes can be understood as resting on a continuum, with the therapeutic task being to name and integrate the poles.

However, the *solitary* journey toward independence emphasized by most existential theorists may be modeled after the heroic journey toward consciousness. The pull toward unconsciousness and the need for nurturance and interdependence as part of a woman's journey may not be adequately described by conventional existential theory. This case raises the question of the role of relationship and caring within the context of existential theory.

The Psychotherapeutic Journey What helped Maria face her darkness, integrate opposites, descend, and find renewal? What about this journey is unique to women?

First I provided Maria with an installation of hope. This was done by framing her experience as a journey where she could come through with increased spiritual and psychological wholeness and making a therapeutic alliance with the healthy and creative parts of her. I then invited her to *stay present* to her pain, her distortions, and the denied and projected parts of herself. In keeping with the experiential emphasis in EI therapy, she was encouraged to be *embodied*, and to allow her authenticity to emerge. As the therapist, I stayed present to my own familiarity with Maria's issues and felt my way into her pain. Although I did not disclose any of the facts of my own life, I nevertheless let the emotional resonance of my empathy and presence speak for itself nonverbally. When her pain became too great, we contained it with humor and with her writing. Presence was a critical part of the sessions, as I listened to her silence, to her presence (*dasein*), and gave her my immediate, kinesthetic, and profound attention. I trusted my own bodily response to the way she made me feel, including my tears, and the desire to hold her hand when she was in the deepest part of her suicidal depression. I had a sense of *invoking the actual* when I attempted to help Maria feel the experiential component of her symbolic material. Only later in the sessions did Maria let me know that as she had felt that something very dark lay ahead, she was looking for a therapist who could contain and accompany her. We both sensed this desire and allowed it to emerge in the sessions. All I might need to do in the sessions would be to comment simply, "Why the tears?" thus opening the way for her disclosures. Once she was able to express her emotions, Maria could let me see not only her expansive, independent, and capable side, but also the small side — the little girl who needed to be held and contained. We named the parts of herself that emerged and helped her to accept and integrate them. To contain her, I used the reality of the therapist-client encounter to help her express difficult material, to experience trust in a relationship, and to connect our work to the future potential of our relationship. Finally, I used an *aesthetic perspective* that enabled her to see her life as a composition, to bring her extremes into a more integrated whole, and to *create in the face of the void*.

An essential part of Maria's healing was to see her individual story in a larger cultural perspective. The balance between nurturance and work, *solitude* and *relatedness*, and the themes of sacrifice, *home* and *homelessness*, and the closeness between *death* and *rebirth* are especially close to the psyche and psychotherapy of women. Sacrifice was the basis of the early primordial fertility rites and was a necessary part of the spring rebirth. Feeling sacrificed to the dominant patriarchal culture and experiencing the plight of homelessness through the dispossession of an archetypal place in the world brings women together in a bond of empathy and shared humanity. This bond can also unite a female client and female therapist in an empathy of an intense, preverbal sisterhood. When asked what made the therapeutic contribution, Maria chose to describe her experience of therapeutic empathy in terms of how Enki created two servant-mourner figures who "groaned with" the goddess Erishkigal in sympathy (Perera, 1981, pp. 69–71). To "groan with" implies a way of being with a client that does not distance but noncognitively "feels with" her experience and allows her to descend into the underworld, transform the pain into image and symbol, and re-emerge with strength. This process entails what I have elsewhere termed *kinaesthetic resonance* (Serlin & Stern, 1998).

As we worked, I followed and stayed with Maria in her progress and changing imagery. I asked her what she saw in the images. The first series of images had to do with feeling the void, "clearing the underbrush," or clearing the space for change to happen. It is important here for the therapist not to impose her own interpretation on these images, but instead using a client-centered approach to support the meaning that the specific image has for the client (Serlin, 1977; Serlin, 1992). Maria understood the images to mean that she needed to let go of her sexuality, her car, vestiges of her old life, and illusions that her sisters could provide a home for her and that her Ghostly Lover could provide a relationship. Once she saw a path through the images, it was much easier for her to implement this path in her real life (e.g., breaking off the relationship with her Demon Lover).

The second set of images had to do with her descent. These had to do with her experiencing her aloneness, her nakedness and vulnerability; tracking the images in her dreams and journals; and experiencing her images of fire, darkness, crosses, and sacrifice. During this period, Maria focused on her readiness to create her own life and to meet another person without any baggage or encumbrances from her past. When she did meet a man, she was free and ready to move into a relationship with clear intentions of creating a stable home and place for herself. At this point, we drew images of her ideal home, from specifics of the kitchen table to those of her very new role of stepmother.

Her third set of images had to do with rebirth, light, and interdependence. Staying with Maria's process meant trusting the logic of her psyche and helping her to put her images and experiences into the context of a meaningful story.

This existential-integrative approach to her work included holding and containing, use of presence, a narrative reframing to enable hope and the possibility of a future, dreamwork, meditation and breathwork, and relational and attachment theory to face the basic existential challenges of the human condition.

Summary

Maria's own words provide the most vivid summary:

> I am only beginning to understand the relationship between Ilene and myself. If it had just been the benefit [of being with] just anyone, it wouldn't have made a difference who I was talking to. But I had tried to talk to several people, and basically I was faced with [a] total lack of understanding, either not wanting to understand what I was talking about because it was too personal and painful or unable to understand because it was too foreign to their experience.... In any event, the world offered me nothing of care or concern for my experience or my feelings. It was unable and unprepared to give me anything to help me in my suffering. I just suffered, and by asking them to listen, and getting no response, my suffering was increased.
>
> So not anyone will do. With Ilene, she did listen, but I think also she did more. She was a witness to my suffering; she felt what I was feeling and felt for me. She didn't intervene or try to change my feelings or thoughts. She allowed me to process my dreams and my experiences as they arose.
>
> There are moments when I have nothing to say, and we just sit in the quiet. These moments can be so comfortable — time almost seems to stop. It is difficult to put the experience into words. Once I referred to it as a "holy moment" — such peace and quiet and closeness. Just letting the moment be.
>
> Sometimes I have just sat quietly weeping, and Ilene is just there.
>
> I have always known, somehow, that she sincerely cares — perhaps seeing tears in her eyes while I was telling a dream or my feelings. I was even concerned when I was in the middle of a suicide attempt to mention in my "note" that her bill should be paid. This work requires, I believe, a degree of selflessness. I am very grateful to Ilene.
>
> Her witnessing of my suffering has made a difference. Just being seen and heard by another. And her listening and sharing in my deep mourning. I remember sitting and telling her of some experience or dream and watching her eyes fill with tears. It had an impact on me. I still remember the sense of that moment. My suffering moved another. She had no agenda of her own. Not trying to change me, or teach me, or show me. She just listened and quietly mourned with me.
>
> The ability to listen is a rare quality, born of love. The ability to sit in silence is even more rare — a holy moment when two sit as one. The feeling has no need for explanation — indeed cannot be explained. It is a wordless experience that occurs in the silence.
>
> Once a week, for an hour, I was listened to.

References

Bateson, M. (1989). *Composing a life*. New York: Atlantic Monthly.

Bugental, J. F. T. (1987). *The art of the psychotherapist*. New York: Norton.

Gilligan, C. (1982). *In a different voice*. Cambridge: Harvard University Press.

Harding, M. (1975). *The way of all women*. New York: Harper & Row.

Heilbrun, C. (1988). *Writing a woman's life*. New York: Ballantine Books.

May, R. (1975). *The courage to create*. New York: Bantam.

Middlebrook, D. (1991). *Anne Sexton*. Boston: Houghton Mifflin.

Perera, S. (1981). *Descent to the goddess: A way of initiation for women*. Toronto: Inner City Books.

Schneider, K. J. (1999). *The paradoxical self: Toward an understanding of our contradictory nature*. Amherst, NY: Humanity Books.

Serlin, I. (1977). Portrait of Karen: A gestalt-phenomenological approach to movement therapy. *Journal of Contemporary Psychotherapy, 8*, 145–152.

Serlin, I. (1992). Tribute to Laura Perls. *Journal of Humanistic Psychology, 32(3)*, 57–66.

Serlin, I. A., & Stern, E. M. (1998). The dialogue of movement: An interview/conversation. In K. Hays (Ed.), *Integrating exercise, sports, movement and mind* (pp. 47–52). New York: The Haworth Press.

Yalom, I. (1980). *Existential psychotherapy*. New York: Basic Books.

7
Innovations in Short-Term EI Practices

In this alternative chapter, pioneering existential therapist James Bugental stretches the proverbial envelope with his sketches for a short-term existential approach. While this proposal may seem at odds with the common understanding of existential-integrative approaches, this is not necessarily the case. To the extent that existential approaches are understood as attitudes, atmospheres, and life encounters, they are not inconsistent with brief or even momentary interpersonal engagements. R. D. Laing, for example (as discussed in Part 2), was legendary for his one-session encounters, and, as we shall see with both Dr. Bugental and Dr. John Galvin in the illustrations to follow, short-term approaches can provide a taste or a start toward long-term reawakening. As Bugental emphasizes, however, short-term existential therapy is rarely a substitute for its long-term, holistic counterpart, and beginning movements can rarely be equated with consolidated shifts. In this light, Bugental and Galvin's proposals must be viewed in the pragmatic and sometimes spontaneous contexts in which they are initiated, and not overrated. As Galvin so eloquently frames it, short-term existential therapy at its best emulates the encounters of "two road-weary travelers, meeting by the fire in the corner of a dimly lit inn. . . . In the morning, these travelers will part but each will feel more prepared for the journey that remains."

Preliminary Sketches for a Short-Term Existential-Humanistic Therapy

James F. T. Bugental

James Bugental, PhD, is a founding father of the existential psychotherapy movement in the United States. Along with Rollo May and Irvin Yalom, Dr. Bugental has provided the foundational concepts of existential-humanistic therapy to the emerging generation of existential-humanistic practitioners throughout the United States. He is a world-renowned author of such books as *The Art of the Psychotherapist*, *Psychotherapy Isn't What You Think*, and *The Search for Authenticity*, along with numerous other publications. Bugental is professor emeritus at Saybrook Graduate School.

Editor's Note: The article to follow is a response to the need among many therapists to work within strict funding and time parameters. Although Dr. Bugental was ambivalent about these requirements, the following was his attempt to redress them. Therefore, the short-term existential strategy to follow is not intended to replace more commonly effective formulations, but to complement them, where appropriate, with substantive, client-empowering attitudes — attitudes that can enhance posttherapy transformation.

Intention Parameters

In sketching a shorter-term regime for psychotherapy, I have been guided by three principles:

1. Emphasize the autonomy of the person who is the client; that is, insist that the change agency is the client's own self-discovery rather than the insight, power, or manipulations of the therapist.
2. Demonstrate to the client the power of the natural *searching process** and help the client learn to continue to use this power in her or his posttherapy living.
3. Avoid building habits or expectancies that would be countertherapeutic if and when the client undertook further and deeper therapeutic work.

Phase-Structured Procedure

Short-term work requires a clearly (and usually explicitly) defined and limited focus of effort (*goal of treatment*), and thus a more overt structure to maintain maximum gain from limited opportunity.

This structure is best grasped when it is organized into the phases detailed below. It is not intended that each of these phases occupy an interview. The pace of moving through them will vary with each client-therapist pairing. Generally, however, these phases need to follow the sequence described here.

First Phase: Assessment The following questions should be asked:

1. Is the presenting problem such that it can be isolated to some extent and made explicit or objective?
2. Is the client's urgency (pain, anxiety, other distress) such that the client can still detach sufficient ego function to sustain the apparently indirect approach?
3. Can the ego function to support intensive searching; that is, can the client's observing ego make a truly therapeutic alliance?

* For an elaboration on the searching process, see J. Bugental, *Psychotherapy and Process* (Reading, MA: Addison-Wesley, 1978).

If the answer to one or more of these questions is negative, that condition must be addressed before moving to the next phase. If each answer is favorable, the next phase may be started.

Second Phase: Identifying the Concern Encourage the client to present his or her concern in the most succinct form.

Seek to shape the issue into as explicit or objective a form as is valid. This is a delicate operation in which the therapist's intent to shape the issue must not be allowed to introduce an artifactual distortion of the client's actual concern.

Contract to work with the client toward greater understanding and some resolution of the issue. The contract needs to be as explicit as is realistic and may well be reduced to written form as an aid to maintaining its focusing effect.

Third Phase: Teaching the Searching Process The client is instructed in how to engage in the searching process by:

1. Getting centered (present)
2. Mobilizing concern (the identified issue plus the emotional energy attached to it)*
3. Learning the significance of resistances and of not working them through (i.e., shorter-term, less deep, or lasting changes are explained)
4. Beginning the search

Fourth Phase: Identifying Resistances As the searching goes forward and resistances are encountered, the therapist teaches their significance as cues to what is conflicted.

The client is encouraged to take note of these occasions and then to return to the search. *Again, this is a key point of difference from long-term therapy: There is no working through of resistances. As a consequence, changes are apt to be more shallow and possibly less lasting.*

It is essential that the client recognize the difference; otherwise, he or she may not appreciate the limits of short-term work and may mistake them for limits of all therapy.

Fifth Phase: The Therapeutic Work From the beginning and regularly the therapist needs to bring to the client's attention in a meaningful way the two crucial parameters of the work:

---

* Mobilizing the concern is similar to what was previously described in ths volume (Part 2) as "invoking the actual." See also Bugental's elaboration in *The Art of the Psychotherapist* (New York: Norton, 1987, pp. 207–212).

1. This is a time-limited effort; that limit needs to be recognized and not ignored.
2. This is work directed toward the identified concern. Other issues will repeatedly appear, but they must not displace the central and contracted concern.

It is important and often difficult to keep this focus on the contracted concern. By the very nature of the searching process, that concern will be redefined and reidentified more than once.

The sensitivity and skill of the therapist are tested here, for the work can easily degenerate in a seeming randomness (which might be valuable in longer-term work) with a resulting inadequate therapeutic impact when the allotted time is exhausted.

Another hazard is that an overly literal and zealous rigidity about the focus on the explicit concern can similarly lead to so superficial an inquiry as to be impotent therapeutically.

Sixth Phase: Termination Handling the time parameter is an important part of the therapeutic process itself. If a fixed number of sessions has initially been agreed upon — as is usually desirable — then that limit must be observed. Of course, a new contract can be negotiated if both parties agree to it, but the original plan should not be casually dismissed. Clients need to recognize the aborting of the work as arbitrary and something they may want to address. Similarly, clients may gain from the confrontation with their finitude that this ending demonstrates and the way it reflects the limit to life itself.

As the last session of the contracted time occurs, it is desirable to call on the client to assess what has been accomplished and what remains to be done (akin to the meaning-discovery phase noted in Part 2). Concurrently, some attention may be given to the client's having begun to incorporate the searching process into his or her extra-therapy living.

While clients and therapists may negotiate a follow-up contract to continue the work, there is a potential countertherapeutic pitfall to be avoided: A series of short-term therapeutic efforts is not the equivalent of long-term psychotherapy. The effort to insist on one limited engagement after another is a major resistance to commitment to one's life, disguising a deeper sense of genuine need.

Brief Encounters with Chinese Clients: The Case of Peter

John Galvin

John Galvin, PhD, is a licensed psychologist, management consultant, and fellow of the University of Hong Kong Business School. A graduate of Saybrook Institute in San Francisco, he has over 30 years of therapeutic experience in the Asian community.

Throughout the ages, writers have found the journey a powerful metaphor for reflecting on and describing life's experiences. Homer's Ulysses journeyed back from Troy; Chaucer's pilgrims traveled from inn to inn; Mark Twain's Huck Finn rafted down the Mississippi; and Herman Melville's Ishmael set sail with Captain Ahab and the crew of the Pequod.

An event common to all these travel books is the encounter of the hero and some stranger or some strange event. As the encounter unfolds, we find the traveler risking a genuine confrontation with some aspect of the human condition or in some way revealing his or her deepest thoughts and feelings.

Existential therapists develop an affinity for these moments of encounter. They are the points in the therapeutic journey where healing takes place, if healing is possible. They are the moments when choices are made and when choices are required. They are the moments when life is affirmed, despite all the forces that negate it. These encounters are the moments when consciousness affirms or denies what the will desires and when the client begins to take a hand in creating himself or herself.

As an existential therapist, I see myself as a traveler journeying through life prepared for these encounters. The existential literature highlights the importance of the existential encounter, and my experience as a therapist frequently confirms that it is extremely important.

Much of the therapist's training is directed at developing the knowledge and skills required to make the most of these encounters. The therapist learns to recognize the client's often vague, indirect invitation to encounter, to understand and overcome the barriers the client raises in order to avoid encounter, to listen and understand and not interfere in the unfolding of the client's experience. But most fundamental is the therapist's commitment to be genuinely available to share in these moments of encounter.

Even when dealing with psychotic patients, I have learned not to rule out the possibility of encounter. The presence, the authenticity, the respect, and the humility that invite encounter may even pierce the veil of psychosis. When working with psychotic patients, I maintain the same attitude I maintain with other clients. I knock politely at their hospital doors and ask if I can come in. I listen attentively to their psychotic conversations and, as best I can, allow myself to be moved emotionally.

On several occasions, I have been astonished to discover that an encounter did take place. One Chinese youth whom I had evaluated when he was admitted to the hospital in the midst of a severe psychotic episode remembered me most vividly when, months later, we met by chance in a busy vegetable market. He told me how he had felt frightened and alone at the time we met and that I had given him a sense of hope.

Existential encounters, as they are called in the literature of psychotherapy, can happen at almost any time. Some come in the context of therapy, and others come on the occasion of some brief, chance meeting.

Over the years, my work with the Chinese has led me to particularly value the power and importance of brief, sudden existential encounters. Unlike Americans, who have come to appreciate the professional role of the therapist and commonly engage in extended periods of psychotherapy, the Chinese are not likely to seek help from a therapist. What I have come to appreciate are the short, often one-time, encounters with these people. They are usually people with whom I have already established a relationship through some other activity. Despite the brevity of the encounter, much of what I recognize as therapeutic takes place.

The Case of Peter

One such encounter took place after a presentation I gave on loneliness and the new immigrant. As the audience dispersed, "Peter," a young Chinese man who had recently immigrated to the United States from Southeast Asia, approached me and started a conversation. Initially, he asked some theoretical question. We sat down together in one corner of the room. As the room emptied, I asked Peter if he had ever experienced loneliness when he first immigrated to the United States. His response was immediate, without thought: "No, I didn't!" His denial was intense. An experienced therapist develops a sixth sense for self-deception, those lies directed at oneself and designed to protect. Peter's denial, artificial in its intensity, actually suggested to me that he wanted to talk about an experience of loneliness. I prepared myself for a quick reversal. I gave him my full attention, kept silent, and waited.

A brief silence followed Peter's denial. When he sat back in his chair, his body stiffened, his breathing stopped, and his expression went blank. Then, just as suddenly, life came back into him. He sat forward and said, "Yes, I did experience loneliness."

I replied, "Please, tell me about it."

Peter wanted to speak, to open up. This was a critical moment. My attitude, my words could slam the door shut as quickly as it had opened. The process of socialization makes judges of us all. The therapist must learn to remove the judicial robes and stop being the gatekeeper who only allows the appropriate and logical to enter consciousness. Presence and empathy are the keys that open the door to encounter.

The choice to continue was his. I communicated, more by my attitude than verbally, that I was ready to listen and understand. He was free to talk or not.

An individual's life is a rich tapestry of experiences. Some of the threads that make up this tapestry we weave with our own hands, and some, the hands of fate weave for us.

Peter's narrative began.

He was born Chinese in the Vietnamese city, Saigon. He belonged to a community of migrant Chinese who had left their own lands seeking opportunities in a foreign culture. In Vietnam, they chose to maintain their Chinese identity, and the Vietnamese chose to view them as foreigners.

At the end of the Vietnam War, North Vietnamese troops occupied Saigon. These "liberators" forced many Chinese, mostly traders and business executives, to leave Vietnam. The contingencies of life had ended their comfortable middle-class lifestyle and scattered Peter's family among three countries. Several brothers went to Canada, his oldest brother and his parents went to Great Britain, and Peter and his sister went to the United States.

Peter explained that he was the youngest in a large family. As he grew up, he enjoyed the companionship of his father, who, older and retired, had time to appreciate the joys of nurturing a young son.

Peter's father made a powerful impression upon him. He gave Peter a sense of security in a turbulent world, and though he was the youngest and least experienced of the children, Peter's sense of self-esteem was enhanced by his father's attention.

As I listened, I understood that Peter's father was a central figure in his world, Peter's primary source of meaning, of self-esteem, of security — what existential therapists call the *existential ground* that supports one's psychological existence.

As a refugee, Peter was separated from his father, but the bond remained strong. Peter's father wrote letters, and there were occasional telephone conversations. Frequent talk of a future reunion of the entire family gave Peter hope and a goal.

In life, our strengths can easily become our weaknesses. The bond between Peter and his father fostered psychological vitality, but if broken, it might leave him shattered, thrown into a crisis. This happened one cold English day.

While walking the streets of London, his father slipped on a piece of ice and fell. His head injury was fatal. He never regained consciousness, and doctors pronounced him dead upon arrival at a London hospital.

An ill-placed step and a life ends. There was no time for last good-byes, no slow unraveling of the bonds that gave Peter security, and no time to develop a more mature sense of independence. His father was dead, and Peter faced the world alone, an unwilling master of his fate.

"I felt a deep sense of loneliness. Memories of my father and our experiences together filled my waking hours and haunted my dreams. I wanted to see my father but knew I would never see him again."

During our encounter, Peter relived the loneliness and depression that had followed his father's death. I encouraged and supported him by reflecting back to him his feelings and the meanings he expressed by stating, for example:

"You knew he was gone forever but couldn't accept it."

"He departed so suddenly."

"You felt so isolated when you were unable to attend his funeral in London."

"He made you feel important."

Peter's longing for his father and the undeniable fact of his absence reminded me of a line of poetry: "We long for what has been and desire what is not." (For a moment, I, too, felt a longing for what had been and for what was not, a longing for my younger brother, who had died.) I directed my awareness back to Peter, who explained: "I worked during the day and went to school at night, but it all seemed meaningless. I got up in the morning, dressed, went to work, attended school. I didn't speak with people unless they spoke to me. I couldn't start a conversation. I didn't want to talk to anyone. After school, I went home to sit alone in my room. I turned off all the lights and sat curled in a chair. I sat there for hours until I fell asleep, exhausted."

Alone in his room, shrouded in darkness, he brooded. He clung to the memories of his father. While these memories caused him pain, they offered comfort as well. Human experience is paradoxical. We can entertain both joy and sorrow simultaneously, and one can evoke the other.

The darkness of Peter's room represented how he experienced his present life. All the people and the things around him had fallen away. Only he was left, alone with the memories of his father and, gradually, alone with less and less will to live.

Peter felt himself like a man clinging to the jagged edge of a rock, legs and body dangling precariously, while below him loomed a vast and empty pit. He was tired, alone, and in pain. The only thing that kept him from letting go were those brief moments when a memory of his father gave him a sense of value.

I commented: "Death would be an escape from the pain."

Peter looked at me. I suddenly felt as if I were in that dark room with him. He said, "I knew this couldn't go on. I had to do something, end it all."

"To be or not to be" — like Hamlet, Peter struggled with indecision, unable to choose either life or death. How long this struggle lasted, he found it difficult to say. Three weeks, four weeks . . .?

"I lost all sense of time," he said. "Each day was the same. I can only remember sitting in the darkness, paralyzed, unable to do anything."

Then, one evening, a memory of something his father once said tipped the balance. "I remembered my father saying, 'Life is full of opportunities, but you must grasp them and work hard for success.'"

These were simple words of advice from a retired Chinese business executive to his youngest son. However, in Peter's dark cave of depression, these words echoed in his memory. The insight was simple: He had to make a choice, and it was his choice. To live or to die? It was up to him.

Peter's paralysis of will ended.

It is difficult to describe in words the depth of feeling that accompanied this narrative. Peter's face reflected, in its quick changes, the moods that filled him as he struggled with his choice. At one moment he argued for the meaninglessness of it all and, in a voice full of rancor, described the burden of pain that life offers the weary in place of a helping hand. Then, the next moment, he countered this mood with happy memories of family and friends. It was not an objective debate, but a deeply personal struggle. I felt as if Peter had grabbed me by my arm and hustled me onto a roller coaster. A slow, reflective ride up toward hope, then a horrific rush of air as we careened downward into anxiety, then banked sharply right, then left, and up once again.

The intensity of this encounter left a lasting impression on me. Not all meetings are so vigorous. Some are calm, gentle, as pleasant as a summer breeze under a clear, star-filled sky. Others are full of anguish and struggle, with a sense of helplessness threatening — like finding oneself caught in an undertow, with the fingers of death pulling one down.

As therapists, our own fears and anxieties limit our work. Our own inner paradoxes, our undigested memories, our compromises with life, pull us back from encounter. For me, it was the death of a younger brother, the sorrow that still remained, the courage I needed to continue living my own life with a heightened sense of mortality. During moments of encounter, I have often wondered at the dexterity of conscious awareness, how it jumps between my experiences and the experiences of others.

At some point Peter made a choice for life; his conscious intellect served to provide the rationale. His father would want him to go forward, to make something of himself. It was his duty to live and to remember his father. He recalled many things his father had said and wove into the tapestry of his life, a philosophy of hope and purpose. He would finish his studies; he would do something for other people; he would make his father proud.

I asked, "What did this experience mean to you?"

He sat thoughtfully for several moments, then responded, "People need to make choices in life. We need other people, but sometimes we need to stand alone. I learned I needed to grow up. I was too dependent upon my family." He made it sound so simple and so obvious.

I was curious and perhaps somewhat selfish. I asked what, if anything, did it mean to him to have shared these experiences with me.

He responded, "I never talked to anyone about what happened. I feel I understand it all a bit better now. I never thought it through like this. I felt I relived it all, but with more self-awareness. In some way I feel happy, proud, and I am more aware of my strength."

The encounter ended there. He said good-bye. I think I saw him twice briefly after that, and it has been years since this encounter took place. This and similar experiences have left me with vivid memories, and I find my own life strangely enriched by them.

A conventional perspective perceives existential psychotherapy as an intensive, long-term process. As such, few would judge the interaction between Peter and myself as a form of existential therapy.

I have never been inclined to limit psychotherapy to the formal setting of a psychologist's office. Throughout the years, I have worked primarily with disadvantaged and troubled teens, the mentally ill, ethnic minorities in the United States, as well as the less-affluent Chinese population of Hong Kong. Intensive, long-term psychotherapy requires a great outlay of money, not to mention a cultural milieu that encourages and supports this form of therapy. For the most part, these were lacking among the people I have served.

Even though the conditions that might support a psychological practice of intensive existential psychotherapy were lacking, I regularly encountered people who were struggling with issues that commonly surface during existential psychotherapy: accepting responsibility for one's life, integrating a growing sense of one's individuality with the powerful demands of a communalist culture, facing the anxieties of choice, accepting limitations, having the courage to create, searching for meaning, confronting life's paradoxes.

Professionals whose formal practice of psychotherapy overlaps with other mental health and social work activities may find many people engaging them in brief, intensive interactions that have the potential for significant existential liberation.

Over the years, I have developed four guidelines that I attempt to follow when I sense a person is inviting me to engage in an existential encounter. Perhaps others may find these guidelines helpful:

1. Never underestimate the willingness of people to open their hearts and minds during these brief encounters. Many people have an intuitive understanding of existential themes. They may not have read the literature or attended courses, and they may not belong to an ethnic and social group known to be psychology minded, but they have in some way departed the safe havens of conventional society and undertaken the path of existential liberation.
2. Focus on a particular life situation, a concrete, specific event in a person's life. Avoid an intellectual discussion. The genius of the existential perspective lies in its appreciation for the *existential moment*, an intense conscious engagement with a salient, specific, concrete life event. As the story goes, a person asked a chess master, "What is the best move in chess?" Of course this question cannot be answered in any absolute sense, so the master replied that the best move at any

given time depends on the ability of the person and the specific context of the game. A person who is confronted with a choice, with the paradoxical pull of two equally valid concerns — community and individuality, limitations and possibility, or any other significant existential issue — begins to find liberation by being more immersed in the experience itself. There is no absolute answer. How a person thinks, feels, and acts depends upon her abilities and the context as she understands it.

3. An ability to hear, understand, and reflect back the explicit and implicit feelings and meanings that a person is expressing is crucial to evoking an existential moment. I continue to be amazed at how rapidly a conversation moves to a deeper level when one listens for feelings and meanings.
4. Accept and understand a person's defenses, his or her reluctance to express certain feelings and to confront certain issues. It is easy to feel pressured by the lack of time and to try to push the person forward. An existential therapist engaged in long-term, intensive psychotherapy greatly appreciates the importance of working through the client's defenses. This principle applies even when one is seeing a person only once. Often it is by helping a person face certain defenses that one makes a contribution. Various forms of brief psychotherapy are increasingly popular, and the therapist is inclined to play a very active and directive role in order to achieve results within the limited time available. In my view, during these existential encounters the therapist can accomplish more by doing less.

Let me end with the image of two road-weary travelers meeting by the fire in the corner of a dimly lit inn that gives temporary shelter to life's wandering pilgrims. In the morning these travelers will part, but each will feel better prepared for the journey that still remains. For me, this simple image says much about what it means to be an existential therapist.

8
EI Mediation of Addiction: Alcoholism

Traditionally, substance abuse has been treated nonexperientially — either medically, behaviorally, or cognitively. Experiential modalities, when they were used, were considered both questionable and gratuitous. Yet substance abusers notoriously fail in traditional treatment, and core issues remain festering.

In this chapter, Barbara Ballinger, Robert Matano, and Adrianne Amantea show that there is a key place for experiential liberation stances in the treatment of substance abusers. Properly timed and offered experiential stances minister to the preverbal-kinesthetic bases for the abuse and catalyze alternatives for change.

The client in this study seems hyperconstricted. He's dependent on his parents, unable to find meaningful work, and discouraged about his relationships. His alcoholism appears to be a mask for this desolation, both elevating and — at requisite times — quelling his moods. By allowing herself to be fully present to "Charles," the therapist helped him to become present in return, to deeply center himself; and by mirroring his struggle back to him, the therapist reminds Charles of his fuller self.

By the end of their session, Charles feels "lighter," "uplifted," and markedly less "burdened." He has gone into his hell, as Rollo May would say, and emerged with more authority. While he will eventually need to actualize this authority, as the authors indicate, we must not underestimate what he has already done. Specifically, he has already laid the groundwork for such actualization by widening the latitude of his consciousness. He has become more of an occupant, less of a prisoner of himself, and he has engaged his expansive and constrictive dreads soberly, thereby increasing his chances for transforming them soberly.

A Perspective on Alcoholism: The Case of Charles

Barbara Ballinger, Robert A. Matano, and Adrianne C. Amantea

Barbara Ballinger, MD, received her medical degree from the University of South Carolina School of Medicine. After an internship in family practice, she completed a residency in psychiatry at Stanford University School of Medicine, where she was also a Linda Pollen fellow in the lab of David Spiegel. She also studied and was influenced by Irvin Yalom, James Bugental, and John Ruark. Currently, she is in private practice in Menlo Park and is assistant professor of psychiatry at Stanford University. Dr. Ballinger notes, "In my clinical work I strive to maintain compassion, foster mindfulness, and to revise my paradigm of health as new information requires."

Robert A. Matano, PhD, is a psychologist in private practice in Oakland, CA, and is an assistant professor, emeritus, of psychiatry and behavioral sciences in the Department of Psychiatry at Stanford University. He served as director of the Alcohol and Drug Treatment Center at Stanford for over 15 years.

Adrianne C. Amantea, PhD, has a private practice in San Diego. She specializes in treating children/adolescents and adults who suffer from depression and anxiety. She worked with individuals who were drug and alcohol dependent at Stanford's Alcohol and Drug Treatment Center. She lives with her husband, James, and her daughter, Sophia.

The excessive consumption of alcohol is a major source of serious medical, social, and economic problems in the United States. It is the third leading cause of preventable death (Mokdad, Marks, Stroup, & Gerberding, 2004). A 2001 analysis estimated deaths attributed to alcohol at 75,766, with a staggering 2.3 million potential years of life lost; that is approximately 30 years of potential life lost per alcohol-attributed death. The most common chronic cause of death is alcoholic liver disease, with motor vehicle crashes the leading acute cause (U.S. Department of Health and Human Services, 2004).

Alcohol affects virtually every organ in the body. In addition to the liver, it is associated with disease in the gastrointestinal tract, heart, pancreas, and brain, any of which may cause chronic disability. When exposure is in utero, it can cause mental retardation. It complicates other psychiatric illnesses and is associated with greater use of nicotine (Li, Hewitt, & Grant, 2004; Grant, Stinson, et al., 2004). Though medical costs were high at $18.9 billion, it was lost productivity from alcohol-induced morbidity, at $87.6 billion, that was the single greatest category of alcohol-related costs in 1998. Total alcohol-related cost estimates were $184.6 billion (Harwood, 2000).

Males are more at risk than females for both abuse and dependence (Grant, Dawson, et al., 2004). The risk over time has been found to be slightly higher for lower-income and less-educated males (Vaillant, 1996). Young adults are especially likely to binge drink and drink heavily (Substance Abuse and Mental Health Services Administration, 2006), often leading to tragic consequences (Hingson, Heeren, Zakocs, Kopstein, & Wechsler, 2005), such as accidents, assaults, suicide, violence, and crime. The greatest percent of change in alcohol-related lost economic productivity since 1992 has been the increase due to incarcerated persons (Harwood, 2000). Thirty-two percent of drivers aged 16 to 20 who died in traffic crashes in 2003 had measurable alcohol in their blood, and 51% of drivers aged 21 to 24 who died tested positive for alcohol (National Highway Traffic Safety Administration, 2004).

Alcohol is widely consumed in the United States; 61% of adults were current drinkers in 2003 (National Center for Health Statistics, 2005). Alcohol abuse and dependence are present in 4.65% and 3.81%, respectively, of the population (Grant, Dawson, et al., 2004).

While the quantification of the impact of alcohol abuse is invaluable in our understanding, as clinicians we ultimately approach our patients and clients in terms of their suffering and compromise to agency. Because of distortion in a person's ability to be aware and responsive in the present moment, both introspective honesty and interpersonal intimacy are inevitably compromised. We propose that an approach that fosters mindfulness offers recovering drinkers a powerful tool for inner integrity and attention to meaningfulness.

The Biopsychosocial Perspective

The dominant model for the study of alcoholism in the United States today is described by the term *biopsychosocial*. It encompasses the study of genetic, neurobiological, psychological, sociocultural, and behavioral factors associated with alcoholism. In previous decades, researchers speculated on distinct clinical subtypes (Cloninger, 1987), with an implicit assumption that alcoholism is always multifactorial (Gilligan, Reich, & Cloninger, 1987). Currently, the cutting edge in alcohol research is in the influence of genes, environment, and the interplay between the two (Bachtell, Wang, & Freeman 1999; Hill, 2000; Schuckit, 1998). The paradigm for exploring the factors that cause alcohol abuse — the biopsychosocial perspective — is less useful in explaining the *experience* of alcohol abuse (its meaning to the alcoholic) or in addressing such concepts as responsibility. Existential psychotherapy, on the other hand, focuses on just such areas of inquiry. It is based on belief in the abuser's responsibility (and privilege) to define the meaning of not just his alcoholism, but of his life itself. When used in concert with an informed biopsychosocial understanding, and based on the therapist's competence and compassion, it adds not just another dimension, but a more profound one, to alcohol treatment.

Alcoholism Treatment

In the United States, more than 700,000 people are treated for alcohol abuse on any given day (National Institute on Alcohol Abuse and Alcoholism [NIAAA], 2000). Fuller discusses an overview of various treatment modalities currently in use and their effectiveness. The major behavioral approaches include cognitive-behavioral therapy, motivational enhancement therapy, and Alcoholics

Anonymous (AA) or related 12-step programs. Pharmacotherapy may supplement such efforts (Fuller, 1999).

The number and variety of treatments reflect our incomplete understanding of the multiple factors influencing alcoholism and the lack of consensual outcome criteria for successful treatment, as well as the personal preferences of clinicians. Over the last 10 years, however, evidence-based treatment has become increasingly influential. In the latest edition of his book *Drug and Alcohol Abuse*, Marc Alan Schuckit (2006) offers a comprehensive update (mostly post-2000) of the diagnosis and treatment of alcoholism. The long-term maintenance of gains made in treatment remains a challenge for virtually every recovering alcoholic, with life context and coping skills requiring continual effort and attention.

Probably significant in such coping difficulties is the pervasive use of denial among alcoholics. A biopsychological explanation of this phenomenon is that alcoholics are compromised in their ability to perceive or interpret internal cues due to a predisposition to labile regulation of arousal (Tarter, Alterman, & Edwards, 1983). As a result, they learn to avoid attending to their own internal states. They seek distraction from their confusing emotions and can become estranged from their own subjective lives.

Existential Psychotherapy and Alcoholism Treatment

The Concept of Being In existential psychotherapy, the entire focus of attention is on subjective and intersubjective experience. Put alternatively, it is concerned with the individual's being in the world, a condition shared by us all in that we must each experience it uniquely. The concept of being requires awareness, in the deepest possible sense, of one's unique presence in the present as it becomes the future. Therefore, it can only be approached through one's own immediate experience. It requires a willingness to encounter, to engage with one's full attention, in the present moment, one's layers of pretense and diversion. We each construct a veil of distracting irritations and pleasures, of mental busywork, designed to protect us from awareness of our deepest existential concerns: death, isolation, responsibility, and how we are to find meaning in our lives. Continuous awareness of such profound problems of existence would cause us terrible anxiety. Our diversions, if they are effective — that is, flexible and mature — allow us to go about our daily lives relatively unencumbered.

Alcoholism and Being To remain disengaged from the awareness described above, however, to refuse ever to "think deeply not about the way one came to be the way one is, but that one is" (Yalom, 1980, p. 11) is to live a constrained and fragile psychological life in which the deep self is cloistered from awareness. The alcoholic does live just such a tenuous life, chronically estranged from the deep self; in the long run, addiction, rigid and suffused with denial as it is, is not an effective defense against existential anxiety.

In existential psychotherapy, we presume that if one wants to experience the full dimensions of what it means to exist, the depth of one's being in the world, one must access the deep self and allow it expression to the relatively outer self, and thence to the interpersonal relationship, if desired. Generally, such access can only be maintained reliably through disciplined pursuit, just as diligence is required to sustain mastery of the violin or the stamina of the runner. Certainly therapists must be willing to forge these paths in their own mental lives if they are to have any hope of helping others who feel unable to do so. Alcoholics, with their avoidance of uncomfortable emotion, are usually skeptical of the value of tolerating sustained discomfort.

Alcoholism and Existential Awareness: Chemical Armor and a False Future

The chronic warding off of existential awareness is often experienced as an illusion that one is in control of one's life. This is a common attitude among alcoholics. Since their drinking provides a particularly predictable subjective experience, they become particularly sensitized to the discomfort of unpredictable events. In addition, as suggested earlier, people who become alcoholics may have unusually labile arousal regulation, and hence be especially uncomfortable in the face of change.

Alcoholics know that by drinking, they can give themselves the comfort and reassurance of a known future and superimpose it like camouflage over the unknown that actually lies ahead. The fact that this chemical future is false because it is contained within the illusory reality of their addiction may eventually become troublesome. But until it does, drinking serves as a rigid and powerful chemical armor against an unappealing option — living life as it is.

The Decision to Seek Treatment

Occasionally in life, we experience what Irvin Yalom (1980) calls *boundary situations*, situations in which our usual defenses fail in the face of some severe stressor and we become flooded with anxiety, more aware than usual of our existential vulnerability. Alcoholics who seek treatment are often motivated by such experiences, particularly ones that remind them of their mortality. Their physicians, for example, may have told them, for the first or tenth time, that they are killing themselves. Or they may have had a brief glimpse of the denied deep self buried beneath their chemical armor. In any case, they decide to change.

The Case of Charles

"Charles" is a 30-year-old man who recently resumed outpatient treatment for a 15-year history of alcohol abuse and dependence. He first sought treatment two years ago after he was seriously injured in a car accident in which the intoxicated driver, his friend, was killed. Charles states that he can still clearly remember his shock and outrage at his friend's death and the stark realization that struck him "like an ice pick in my chest" that it could just as easily have been him who died. Death, he said, had "never seemed personal" before.

In direct response to this event, according to the patient, he entered and successfully completed a 30-day inpatient alcohol treatment program. Though he had been in and out of various alcohol programs since he was a teenager, mostly under parental pressure, he describes this program as his first real commitment to stopping drinking.

He has been generally successful at not drinking for the two years since, except for an occasional "one or two beers." He has attended AA meetings religiously and found them helpful. He has, however, continued to have a conflictual and dependent relationship with his parents, has been unable to define meaningful work for himself or sustain a satisfying relationship, and has been finding the temptation to drink increasingly irresistible over the last several months, to the point that he feels his sobriety "is beginning to crumble" for the first time since his inpatient treatment. These are the concerns being addressed in treatment.

Earlier we mentioned the tendency for the alcoholic to use denial diffusely as a defense. We associated this with a habitual tendency to avoid focusing on his own internal states or emotions. We also discussed the concept of encounter as crucial in existential psychotherapy. As it seems likely that the alcoholic patient, with his pattern of immediate retreat in the face of emotional discomfort, will find it difficult to sustain an attitude of encounter, we reiterate how essential it is that the therapist remain stalwart in its pursuit. This is to in no way suggest that she should limit her empathy or sensitivity to the patient's limits but, rather, model for him tolerance of emotional discomfort as implicit to a process of self-discovery. Such tolerance is particularly important for the alcoholic because it is a capacity that is essential to his maintaining sobriety.

The therapist should also give the patient her full attention — intellectually, emotionally, and intuitively — so that he will experience her presence as fully as possible. Again, this is in part modeling to enhance his experience of the present moment. An example of this process follows:*

* Editor's note: The existential approach illuminated here may not be appropriate for certain alcoholic clients, for example, some in early stages of recovery. Yet, as the authors imply, it may be more appropriate than is generally assumed.

Therapist (T): Charles, what do you want from your parents?

Patient (P): [*Long pause. Moves around in his chair and then settles down with his elbow on the table and his head pressed against his hand. Looks down with a confused expression. His leg is shaking.*]

T: I notice your leg is shaking.

P: [*Laughs*] Yes. [*Still looking down*]

T: I wonder where you are right now.

P: Well, last session I was really angry with my parents, and I felt constricted. [*Puts his hand up to his heart*]

T: Where in your body do you feel your anger?

P: In my chest. [*Takes a deep breath*]

T: How did that feel?

P: It felt like I was blowing out some steam.

T: Your voice cracked when you made that statement.

P: Yes, well . . . [*Pause*] I guess the feelings of my anger go from my heart up to my throat.

T: Can you envision being in the same room with your parents?

P: Oh, yeah.

T: Can you do that now?

P: [*Closes his eyes*] It's uncomfortable. I feel like I'm being watched closely and judged, like they don't trust me. [*Opens his eyes. Seems stiff*]

T: Try, if you can, to stay with the feelings that come up.

P: OK. [*Closes his eyes again*] My body feels rigid just visualizing them. I'm at their house attending my sister's birthday party. I really don't want to be there, and my parents are asking me to stay for dinner.

T: How do you feel?

P: Pulled, frustrated, I feel like exploding. [*Pauses*]

T: Stay with that sensation.

P: I can feel my face turn red, and my arms feel like the blood is rapidly pumping through them. I want to yell at both my parents and tell them I'm sick of them pulling at me. [*Talking loud*] I want acceptance from them for who I am and not for who they want me to be. [*Silence. Breathing heavily. His upper body and head are wavering from side to side. His hands are in fists and are on the arms of the chair. His eyes are still closed, and his jaw is clenched*]

T: This issue is clearly very difficult for you.

P: [*Eyes are still closed*] Yes, it is. [*Sounds angry*]

T: What's happening for you right now?

P: I think I need to come down from this anger.

T: I wonder if I was pushing you too hard.

P: No, no. [*Smiles, seemingly embarrassed*]

T: What are you thinking?

P: Well, now I feel lighter somehow, like I couldn't lift anything heavy right now. Kind of a feeling of being immobilized.

T: Are there any other images or thoughts that you can attribute to these feelings?

P: Probably experiencing the anger in here. I guess just thinking about what I want from my parents brings these feelings out.

T: How are you feeling now?

P: I feel uplifted.

T: Can you describe what that feels like?

P: Just that there's more lightness, really, I don't feel so burdened. It helps to get in touch with how my body reacts to what I'm thinking. I guess using alcohol kept me from feeling anything. I can't explain it.

T: Actually, you've explained it very clearly.

Note that the work the patient is doing is focused heavily on tolerating and communicating his internal states. He does not appear to be ready to encounter issues such as his own responsibility for his relationship with his parents, which, from an existential psychotherapy perspective, will eventually have to be addressed. Even though there is little reference to alcohol in this vignette, the experience of sustaining uncomfortable emotion and finding that he can get through it is directly relevant to the process of recovery, as was discussed earlier.

Summary

Alcoholism is a pervasive problem in the United States today. The biopsychosocial perspective underlies our current approach to understanding and treating alcoholism. While effective in studying populations, this approach does not address the alcoholic's subjective experience or such qualitative issues as meaning and responsibility. Existential psychotherapy, with its focus on immediate, subjective experience, personal meaning, and other concerns related to the fact of existence, can augment other approaches to alcoholism treatment. The attitude of encounter, central to existential psychotherapy, is particularly relevant for helping the alcoholic break the typical cycle of denial and avoidance, and therefore is directly useful in the patient's recovery.

References

Bachtell, R. K., Wang, Y.-M., & Freeman, P. (1999). Alcohol drinking produces brain-region selective changes in expression of inducible transport factors. *Brain Research*, *847*, 157–165.

Cloninger, C. (1987). Neurogenetic adaptive mechanisms in alcoholism. *Science*, *336*, 410–416.

Fuller, R. K., & Hiller-Sturmhöfel, S. (1999). Alcoholism treatment in the United States: An overview. *Alcohol Research & Health*, *23* (2), 69–77.

Gilligan, S., Reich, T., & Cloninger, C. (1987). Etiologic heterogeneity in alcoholism. *Genetic Epidemiology*, *4*, 395–414.

Grant, B. F., Dawson, D. A., Stinson, F. S., Chou, S. P., Dufour, M. C., & Pickering, R. P. (2004). The 12-month prevalence and trends in DSM-IV alcohol abuse and dependence: United States, 1991–1992 and 2001–2002. *Drug and Alcohol Dependence, 74*, 223–234.

Grant, B. F., Stinson, F. S., Dawson, D. A., Chou, S. P., Ruan, W. J., & Pickering, R. P. (2004). Co-occurrence of 12-month alcohol and drug use disorders and personality disorders in the U.S.: Results from the National Epidemiological Survey on Alcohol and Related Conditions. *Archives of General Psychiatry, 61*, 361–368.

Harwood, H. (2000). *Updating estimates for the economic costs of alcohol abuse in the United States*. Report prepared by The Lewin Group for the National Institute on Alcohol Abuse and Alcoholism, National Institutes of Health, Department of Health and Human Services. NIH Publication 98-4327. Rockville, MD: National Institutes of Health.

Hill, S. Y. (2000). Biological phenotypes associated with individuals at high risk for developing alcohol-related disorders: Part 1. *Addiction Biology, 5*, 5–22.

Hingson, R., Heeren, T., Zakocs, R., Kopstein, A., & Wechsler, H. (2005). Magnitude of alcohol-related mortality and morbidity among U.S. college students ages 18–24: Changes from 1998 to 2001. *Annual Review of Public Health, 26*, 259–279.

Li, T. K., Hewitt, B., & Grant, B. F. (2004). Alcohol use disorders and mood disorders: A National Institute on Alcohol Abuse and Alcoholism Perspective. *Biological Psychiatry, 56*, 718–720.

Mokdad, A., Marks, J., Stroup, D., & Gerberding, J. (2004). Actual causes of death in the United States, 2000. *Journal of the American Medical Association, 291*, 1238–1245.

National Center for Health Statistics. (2005). *Health, United States, 2005*. Hyattsville, MD: U.S. Centers for Disease Control and Prevention.

National Highway Traffic Safety Administration. (2004). *Traffic safety facts 2003 annual report: Early edition*. Washington, DC: U.S. Department of Transportation.

National Institute on Alcohol Abuse and Alcoholism. (2000). *Tenth special report to the U.S. Congress on alcohol and health*. Washington, DC: U.S. Department of Health and Human Services.

Schuckit, M. A. (1998). Biological, psychological and environmental predictors of the alcoholism risk: A longitudinal study. *Journal for the Study of Alcohol, 59*, 485–494.

Schuckit, M. A. (2006). *Drug and alcohol abuse: A clinical guide to diagnosis and treatment*. New York: Springer.

Substance Abuse and Mental Health Services Administration. (2006). *Results from the 2004 National Survey on Drug Use and Health: National findings*. Retrieved from http://www.oas.samhsa.gov/NSDUH/2k4NSDUH/2k4results/2k4results.htm#fig7.3.

Tarter, R., Alterman, A., & Edwards, K. (1983). Alcoholic denial: A biopsychologic interpretation. *Journal of Studies on Alcohol, 45*, 214–218.

U.S. Department of Health and Human Services. (2004). Alcohol-attributable deaths and years of potential life lost: United States, 2001. *Morbidity and Mortality Weekly Report, 53*, 866–870.

Vaillant, G. E. (1996). A long-term follow-up of male alcohol abuse. *Archives of General Psychiatry, 53*, 243–249.

Yalom, I. (1980). *Existential psychotherapy*. New York: Basic Books.

9
Spiritual and Religious Issues From an EI Perspective

EI therapy addresses entangled lives, and sometimes these lives are entangled by religiosity. In the case to follow, Louis Hoffman shows how the particular entanglement of fundamentalist Christianity can be addressed by EI therapeutic principles. While some would question the relevance of an existentially oriented approach to a traditionally religious client, Dr. Hoffman illustrates that, with a few modifications, such an approach can be supremely relevant, and not appreciably different from equivalent work with secular clientele. As with secular clientele, the question for the religious client is to what degree is he polarized (compulsive about, overidentified with) his debilitating issue, and how best to help him become conscious of this polarization, so that he can forge new choices and new realizations about the direction of his life. In his work with "Kevin," Dr. Hoffman shows convincingly that a religious and culturally sensitive existential-integrative approach helps disentangle lives — first, by empathizing with the position of those lives; second, by mirroring the battle lines that are posed by those lives; and third, by facilitating direct immersion in the turning points of those lives, thereby methodically expanding consciousness (or in the case of Kevin, the God image).

An EI Approach to Working with Religious and Spiritual Clients

Louis Hoffman

Louis Hoffman, PhD, is a faculty member at the Colorado School of Professional Psychology and also maintains a private practice in Colorado Springs, Colorado. His interests include religious and spiritual issues in psychotherapy, existential and depth psychotherapy, diversity issues, and philosophical issues in clinical psychology. Co-editor of *Spirituality and Psychological Health*, Dr. Hoffman has also authored numerous book chapters, journal articles, and conference papers.

Religious and spiritual issues in psychotherapy, long relegated to the profession's margins, are now being propelled to the forefront of psychological thought. Currently viewed as a form of diversity for which therapists should receive training, books dealing with religion and spirituality abound in the current psychological literature (Cox, Ervin-Cox, & Hoffman, 2005; Richards & Bergin, 2005; Schneider, 2004; Sperry & Shafranske, 2005). However, many therapists have not received adequate training to deal with these issues.

This narrative explores an existential-integrative approach to working with religious and spiritual clients. When integrating psychological theories, it is imperative not to introduce concepts or approaches inconsistent with the theoretical base upon which the therapist draws. Using existential theory and practice as a foundation, this study integrates contemporary psychoanalytic theory along with experiential techniques that draw from Gestalt theory.

Theoretical Issues

Existential Perspectives on Religion and Spirituality Existential philosophers, theologians, and psychologists have engaged with religious and spiritual issues since the inception of existential thought, often traced to the writings of Søren Kierkegaard in the mid-19th century (Kierkegaard, 1843/1985). Similar to their disposition toward psychotherapy, existential writers' relationship with religion has been tenuous. Many existential thinkers, such as Jean-Paul Sartre and Friedrich Nietzsche, have been skeptical toward religion. Nietzsche, in particular, was critical of the more common types of religion in his time, which he viewed as blindly faithful to the views of the church (Kaufmann, 1975). He did not, however, view all religion as problematic. Even though he proclaimed himself an atheist, Nietzsche believed religion, when inclusive of a self-critical component, is beneficial to many individuals. Other existential thinkers, such as Sartre, were much more doubtful about the maintenance of any religious belief (Kaufmann, 1975; Sartre, 1943/1984).

Still other existential writers, such as Kierkegaard (1843/1985), Martin Buber (1937/1970), and Paul Tillich (1952), took a more favorable view of religion. Even these writers, however, voiced concerns about the same uncritical belief or blind faith to which Nietzsche alluded. Tillich is probably the best known advocate of existential approaches to theology and religion. Consistent in existential approaches to religion is an emphasis on subjectivity. Faith, belief, or religious practice is personal and subjective if it is to be healthy. When religious practice and belief is reduced to a blind allegiance to a religious group or acceptance of religious doctrines, it is not authentic and often not conducive with psychological health.

Tillich, in *The Courage to Be* (1952) and *The Dynamics of Faith* (1957/2001), emphasizes that faith, or healthy spirituality, is not easily attained. Healthy spirituality must incorporate an encounter with existential issues (Hoffman, 2005). When religious belief is used as a defense to avoid authentically encountering existential issues such as death, freedom, responsibility, isolation, and meaning, it is counterproductive. However, religious practice can facilitate a healthy facing and working through of such existential issues. This understanding forms a primary assumption of the integrative approach espoused here. In achieving healthy religious belief, many spiritual wounds, psychological distortions (i.e., transference and projection issues regarding God or Ultimate Reality), and systemic issues with the religious community must be addressed.

Buber (1937/1970), in his *I and Thou*, provides a good basis for the relational component of existential thought as it applies to the religious context. In this contribution, Buber distinguishes between I-*It* and I-*Thou* relationships. I-It relationships are characterized by treatment of the other as an object, whereas I-Thou relationships demonstrate a deeper, more authentic engagement with the other. According to Buber, these characterizations can also be applied to the manner in which individuals relate to God. For example, many religious individuals relate to God as a distant, impersonal object, while others relate in a manner that reflects an intimate, vulnerable modality. Existential thought emphasizes the importance of genuine experience and authentic engagement in various areas of life, including religious life.

A final existential theme with implications for the current discussion is the role of the unknown. Elsewhere, I (Hoffman, 2005), have built upon the work of Tillich (1952, 1957/2001) and Ernest Becker (1973, 1975), to emphasize the importance of being able to contend with the unknowns in healthy, spiritual experience. Many religious individuals prefer to focus on reified, concrete conceptions of religion that are constricting. This often leads to oppressive and domineering forms of religion with little room for Kirk Schneider's (2004) conception of awe. Healthy religion, conversely, maintains recognition for limitations in knowing along with other personal limitations in the religious realm.

Religious Experience From a psychological perspective, religious experience can be conceptualized in a variety of ways. Broadly defined, religious experience pertains to the behavioral, physical, cognitive, and emotional experience flowing from a real or perceived relationship with a transcendent being or reality. This definition is sufficiently diluted to be inclusive of many types of religious experience and interpretations. The breadth of the definition is encompassing of everything from the experience of glossolalia (speaking in tongues) within the Christian charismatic traditions to Schneider's (2004) religiously neutral — but spiritually central — focus on awe and mystery.

One example of religious experience pertinent to this chapter is the God image. Theory regarding the God image can be traced as far back as Ludwig Feuerbach (1841/1989) and Sigmund Freud (1927/1961, 1938/1950); however, the theory and terminology were formalized in the writing of Ana-Maria Rizzuto (1979) and Lawrence (1997). The God image refers to an individual's emotional and relational experience of God. Lawrence (1997) differentiated the God image from the God concept, or one's cognitive or theological understanding of God. Both the God image and God concept are psychological constructs that are not dependent upon the actual reality of God.

Early research on the God image indicated that it is largely formed on the basis of an individual's experience of his or her parents (Brokaw & Edwards, 1994; Hoffman, Jones, Williams, & Dillard, 2004; Tisdale et al., 1997). However, other research suggests additional factors, such as how the God concept, culture, and gender influence how a person experiences God, particularly at the level of affect (Hoffman et al., 2004). It is worth noting that the early research emphasizing parental influence on the God image is largely consistent with traditional psychodynamic interpretations of transference as applied to God. The later research, suggestive of a more complex process, is more consistent with existential reinterpretations of the transference process.

Classical psychoanalytic approaches to transference emphasize the historical component of transference, occasionally focusing exclusively on parental influence. In contemporary psychoanalysis, the focus remains on parental relationships as the primary basis of transference; however, it allows for a broader contextualization in which contemporary relationships are also expressed in a transference dynamic (Mitchell, 1988; Stark, 1999). For example, while the basis for all transference reactions begins with parental relationships, contemporary psychoanalysis often maintains that other relationships, such as spouses and other important figures, mediate and contribute to transference reactions. In classical psychoanalysis, the influence of current relationships is downplayed, if considered at all. Existential theory advocates for an even more complex transference process that is not bound to the historical. These theorists allow for a genuine encounter between therapist and client and consideration of the implications of future possibilities (see Chapter 10 of this volume). I would add to this that existential theory allows for greater conceptualization of how intrapersonal wrestling with existential issues can be projected into relational processes. For example, Becker (1973) proposed that Freud's inability to resolve his death issues largely created his rigid, authoritarian, and destructive relational processes with many of his followers.

If this understanding is applied to the God image, the various components influencing this form of religious experience can be seen. As previously noted, it is emphasized in classical psychoanalysis that early caregiver relationships play a role in the God image. In accordance with contemporary psychoanalysis, other important relationships must also be considered. When an existential approach is incorporated, other intrapsychic processes, including the major existential themes, must be considered. For example, the existential givens of death, finitude, and freedom interact with the relational transference process through heightening, diminishing, or altering the emotional experience.

Working With Religious Experience Existential theory emphasizes the importance of awareness (centering), choice (freedom), experience (immediacy), and relationship (encounter) in the healing and growth processes. Each of these has important implications for working with religious clients, which will be briefly addressed here and demonstrated in a case illustration.

Many religious individuals engage in religious practices in an automatic, ritualistic manner grounded in authoritarian teaching. While even this form of religion has psychological benefits for some individuals, it also builds an impersonal, rote approach to religion. Existential-integrative therapy seeks to increase clients' ownership of their religious and spiritual beliefs through the promotion of self-exploration of these beliefs, their origins, and their consequences. As clients become more aware of their beliefs, they also become more aware of the need to take ownership and responsibility for those beliefs. This is often a difficult process because it involves letting go of the security associated with the uncritical religious belief. Frequently, this in turn leads to an increase in anxiety, a heightening of resistance, and an antipathy toward the therapist. Therapists must be cautious in not imposing a direction upon clients during this process, particularly if a client chooses to retreat to a safer, more concrete religious grounding at times. Instead, the therapist must create a space within which the client feels safe to explore his or her beliefs. If clients feel the therapist does not respect or desires to eradicate their beliefs, they will not feel safe in exploring them.

The distinction between the God image and God concept suggests the God concept is developed more cognitively while the God image is derived more from experience. Given this, the God concept is more likely to be impacted by the cognitive portions of therapy; however, the God image is resistant to cognitive interventions. The provision of experiential opportunities is essential for a more holistic, complete healing. Various process interventions and techniques, including invoking the actual, imagery, guided meditation, and Gestalt practices, such as utilization of the empty chair with God, can be effective in bridging experiential components into the therapy.

The Case of Kevin

Initial Session "Kevin" had been a consumer of therapy for several years when he first arrived in my office, referred from his therapist, who was retiring. He had a strong sense of how therapy should proceed from a few years of group work (a divorce recovery group) and two individual therapists. For about five years he had not known life without therapy and could not imagine being deprived of his weekly visits.

A 48-year-old Caucasian male, Kevin initially presented to "Dr. Rosen," who referred Kevin to me after several months of therapy, with the goal of working through the pain related to his marriage and divorce. While his primary focus was to continue working on the goals he began to address with Dr. Rosen, he expanded his focus during his previous therapy and now wanted to include gaining insight into what he contributed to the problems in the marriage and divorce to avoid repeating these patterns. In the initial sessions, we reframed this issue into more existential language that emphasized deepening his understanding of his choices, responsibility, and avoidance patterns.

In our first session, it quickly became apparent that Kevin was testing me. He was a devoutly religious man whose church made him profoundly aware of the "dangers of therapy." Toward the end of the session came the moment of truth as he inquired about my religious background: "I know you must be a good therapist, or Dr. Rosen would not have referred me to you. He said you were a good fit for my concerns, which I'm guessing means you are a Christian." The intenseness of Kevin's eyes told me that this seemingly passive comment was a very important test if I was to gain his trust. I offered a version of my standard response, which partially avoided the implicit question, through identifying myself as a therapist who specialized in working with religious and spiritual issues in therapy.

Not surprisingly, the intensity did not fade and Kevin persisted: "What church do you attend?" Living in small communities much of my professional career, I have learned that answering a question like this is dangerous. My preference is to be pretty honest and open about most questions clients ask me; however, I am much more cautious in the opening sessions in order to avoid shifting the focus of therapy on me. Questions of religious affiliation are loaded questions. While I may consider myself a Christian, many within the Christian community, which may include the client, would disagree with this appraisal. Sharing a specific religious affiliation adds another set of issues. Stereotypes of a religious group or, in this case, a denominational affiliation often bring misconceptions. These can create situations in which the client feels less free to talk about his or her spiritual concerns. On the other hand, avoiding these questions can create a sense of suspicion that is reinforced by the client's religious group. The art of dealing with these situations involves creating a way to assure the client that his or her beliefs will be respected without offering information making it more difficult for the client to freely discuss his or her spiritual beliefs and concerns. My beginning standard statement, that I specialize in religious and spiritual issues in therapy, offers a starting point; however, it rarely is enough to alleviate the fears of religious clients who are skeptical of psychotherapy. These fears must be alleviated through a more personal process.

In responding to Kevin's question, I created a bridge from my standard statement to a more personal discussion of his concerns: "I generally don't share what church I attend, but recognize this is an important question for you. You have some concerns about me that are valid and I would like to know more about that." The intensity in Kevin's eyes decreased as he began to share his story. He began with his spiritual wounds. Kevin grew up in a very strict religious environment where correct behavior and correct beliefs were harshly enforced. As Kevin grew older, the rigidity relaxed, at least on the surface, but religion remained very important. When Kevin was 21, he married a very domineering, religious woman. She knew scriptures well and often used them to control the relationship. Whenever Kevin disagreed with "Sherry," his wife, she responded with scripture. When she knew their minister agreed with her, she often suggested they go to their minister to have him mediate. Later, Kevin found out that this was only suggested after conversations with the minister where Sherry was assured she was right.

Kevin remained in this relationship, often the subject of severe emotional and religious abuse, for many years. Sherry frequently withheld affection and attention when Kevin was not acting in accordance with her expectations. If he were to challenge this, she used scripture, statements from their pastor, or other religious sayings to attack and belittle him. Even when Kevin knew Sherry was taking these sayings and statements out of context, he did not know how to respond and felt wounded by her forcefulness.

When their children graduated and went off to college, Kevin began therapy for the first time. The therapist was a "Christian counselor" he was referred to by his church. He attended for 15 sessions, the maximum allowed by the therapist, and grew in confidence during this time. Sherry was very upset about Kevin's new independence and became more emotionally abusive. Kevin decided to temporarily separate from his wife, not intending to divorce her. Sherry was enraged. She enlisted many people from her church in confronting Kevin's "sins." He received visits from their pastor and several elders in the church, encouraging him to repent and return to his wife. He returned to see the counselor he attended previously, who also encouraged him to repent and work things out with his wife. As things continued to get worse, Sherry filed for divorce claiming she was entitled to a divorce because Kevin was unrepentant of his sins. Following the divorce, Kevin attended several different churches in the same denomination. None of them allowed him to participate in the church rituals because of the divorce. Deeply wounded, Kevin began searching for other churches until finding one that was supportive of his divorced status while retaining his core beliefs. Kevin quickly became involved in this church.

Kevin's first concern was that I would not be respectful of his faith or encourage him to abandon his beliefs. He had known people who had this experience previously and was warned about therapy for this reason much of his life. Though Kevin did not express a second concern, his story did. The story about Kevin's experience with the Christian counselor pointed toward a fear that I may judge Kevin for his divorce. As I remained empathetic to Kevin's story, his fear faded away. At the end of the session, a brief discourse solidified his trust.

Therapist (T): Your faith is very important to you and helped sustain you through some very painful experiences.

Client (C):[*Tears welling up*] Yes, I couldn't have made it this far without my faith.

T: I want you to know that I appreciate that faith and am thankful you have it.

C: [*Smiles, quickly letting out a breath while relaxing his shoulders*] Thank you. I knew if Dr. Rosen recommended you, you were okay. But I needed to hear that.

T: The importance of faith in your life makes it important to me, too. I think it will be an important part of the therapy process.

The first session is critical in working with religious clients. If they are not assured their faith will be respected, they often will not return. If a safe place is not created to talk about faith, then clients may leave this aspect of themselves out of the therapy, which limits the healing process. By showing respect for their faith and inviting them to bring spirituality into the therapy room, a space is created for a more holistic approach to therapy.

First Phase of Therapy Kevin rarely missed a session as therapy progressed. He reported looking forward to therapy as one of the highlights of the week. For Kevin, the therapy relationship felt very intimate and close, yet I felt a distance. In previous relationships, the individuals Kevin felt closest to were often people he admired. The intimacy he felt was often not shared by them. While he recognized this, he still felt closer to them than to individuals, such as his ex-wife, with whom he spent more time and shared more of his life.

This pattern fit with Kevin's religious beliefs. It was very easy for him to perceive a close relationship with God, because God was similar to other idealized relationships. It was also evident that Kevin's perceptions of his relationships and his religion were much different than my own. In my view, the God Kevin spoke about seemed very distant, uninvolved, and strict. However, Kevin described God as very loving and close. I viewed Kevin's approach to religion as very strict, rigid, and rule-bound, while Kevin viewed himself as very open religiously. Part of this was due to our different vantage points. Kevin came from a very conservative church and gradually moved to a less conservative church. While I, too, grew up with a conservative Christian background, I had migrated to a place that most would identify as the liberal or progressive fringe of Christianity. Because of this similarity in our spiritual origins, I remained very alert to watching for signs that I may be encouraging Kevin toward a spiritual path similar to my own.

Early on, it became evident that I was an idealized figure to Kevin and he was invested in keeping me idealized. There were several times where I made small slips in therapy, such as being late to an appointment, which appeared to upset Kevin. However, when I attempted to explore this with Kevin, he very quickly denied any negative feelings. These conversations were generally followed with Kevin spending much of the session talking about how much therapy was helping him. During the same period of therapy, Kevin approached God in a similar manner. When things were not going as Kevin hoped in his life, particularly his spiritual life, I would encourage Kevin to explore any feelings about God. Kevin could not acknowledge any negative feelings or frustration about God, even when it seemed apparent to me that he was, at the least, disappointed God was not doing more to rescue him from his situation. His answers were always very quick and firm that everything with God was really good.

The similarities in his way of relating to me and to God were evident. I conceptualized these as being connected to feelings of security. Through his idealizing of me, as his therapist, and God, he attained a type of security, particularly against the unknowns. In the past, when Kevin went through phases of being convinced that God was rejecting him or was ambivalent toward him, Kevin became suicidal. When the idealized God was in question, the pain seemed overbearing, especially when the belief in a better life after death appeared in question (i.e., he was afraid of being condemned to hell because of his perception of being rejected by God). Because Kevin discussed a recent suicidal ideation in the first session, I wanted to leave these idealizations intact until Kevin established some other forms of security in his life. This became the focus of much the first 12 to 15 weeks of therapy.

A second reason for allowing these idealizations temporarily to remain was connected with Kevin's previous relationships. He had a fear that if conflict emerged, things would revert to his earlier relational patterns or I would drop him as a client. Recognizing Kevin's need to develop relationships that were healthy, including a healthy amount of conflict, was important. I did not want to encourage the idealization, facilitating his dependence upon this pattern; however, at the same time, I did not want to prematurely challenge his idealization. I intentionally allowed the idealization to continue until he developed other forms of support and a stronger therapeutic alliance.

Second Phase of Therapy Several factors symbolized the transition to the second, more productive phase of therapy. Kevin's discussion of suicide ended and he talked more about the future. During the period when the suicidal ideation decreased, he reported that knowing he had a scheduled appointment helped him manage his suicidal ideation. The more established he became in the therapy relationship, the more he was able to take this security into the world outside the consulting room. Allowing Kevin to talk freely about his religious beliefs and being empathetic to his life situations strengthened the therapeutic alliance and his trust in me. I also recognized a difference in the way Kevin talked about his relationships outside of therapy, which represented a more positive approach to relating to others.

The real transition occurred when we had our first "fight." Kevin arrived in session with his forehead so tight that his eyebrows almost seemed joined as one. He spewed out, "Am I the type of person who would take my emotions out on others and create physical pain to avoid things?" The previous week Kevin informed me that he was going to a specialist about his headaches. The doctor rather bluntly told him that his headaches were due to dealing with stress poorly. Kevin, who rarely in his life lost his temper, felt enraged and loudly disagreed with the doctor's diagnosis. After this appointment, he returned to work. His boss, who had given him permission to leave work, asked about how it went. As Kevin told him what happened, his boss responded saying, "Kevin, anyone wound up as tight as you is bound to have an ulcer or a headache or something." Kevin, feeling very upset and rejected, kept it to himself this time.

Recognizing the importance of my answer, I immediately felt torn. Though I make it a policy to be honest with my clients, I felt a strong urge to lie in this instance. Partially, I wondered if this was too early to give the answer that I knew would lead to a tense session. I decided to push forward. I explained as sensitively as possible that his tendency to suppress and avoid emotions, which we had discussed previously, can lead to somatic symptoms. Kevin sat silent, noticeably angry. I attempted to explore his feelings toward what I said and he denied having any feelings. This time, I confronted his answer, stating he appeared angry. He insisted he was not upset and spent most of the rest of the session berating the medical doctor and his boss (i.e., berating me). The anger in this session was the most emotion I had seen out of Kevin.

Half expecting Kevin to cancel the next week, I was very pleased when he arrived on time. He sat down, tears already welling up, and told me that he was very angry at me last week because he felt I "didn't believe in [him] and was judging" him. This led to a very powerful session in which Kevin started exploring and sharing his feelings for the first time. I expected this would bring new opportunities to discuss spiritual issues, but felt it would first be necessary to finish working through the relational issues that were initiated by the honest discussion from the previous week. In a sense, the therapy relationship provided the model for his spiritual relationships. By working through his conflict with me, Kevin became more open to reconsidering his conflict with God.

In earlier weeks in therapy, I attempted to use a variety of imagery techniques to assist Kevin in exploring his experience of God. Typically, I would facilitate some relaxation processes and then have Kevin focus on any emotional sensations or what he was feeling in his body. Then I began encouraging Kevin to explore aspects of his life and how he imagined God would respond. Kevin quickly provided superficial and defensive answers. After working through this conflict, I attempted a similar process utilizing a more experiential piece. Once he was relaxed and focused on his bodily experience, I asked him to close his eyes and imagine a picture of God. I had him closely examine God's face, clothing, and posture. Then, reminding Kevin to closely pay attention to God, I said, "Imagine God was not aware of anything about you until today. You meet God for the first time." I could see a pleasant expression on Kevin's face. "Now God becomes aware of the many things you've discussed in therapy . . . your divorce, your conflict with your previous churches . . ."

Kevin's eyes filled with tears. Upon seeing the emotion, I allowed Kevin to stay there for a few moments and then encouraged him to return his focus to us. In similar exercises previously, he described God with a sympathetic response, even though I had occasionally noticed a twitch in his face when describing certain issues. This time, however, Kevin perceived that God furrowed his eyebrows, much the way Kevin often does. Kevin was very surprised by this reaction. This was the first time Kevin acknowledged any negative feelings toward God. Much of the rest of the session was spent processing this experience and what it meant.

Over the next several weeks, Kevin began to open up more about his frustrations with God, his church, and other aspects of his religious beliefs. After a while he stopped attending church. At first this concerned me, as I feared therapy unintentionally eradicated Kevin's faith. However, his anger at God gave me hope. If he abandoned belief altogether, he would not be so angry at God. As therapy persisted, he was able to re-evaluate many of his beliefs and his relationship with God. After a while, he reported feeling that he knew and understood much less of God, but felt much closer to Him (Kevin continued to perceive God as a male). Kevin had become more comfortable with the unknowns despite limited direct attention to this topic. This insight was one of the most freeing aspects of his therapy journey. It created freedom for him to explore his faith and beliefs without fear of losing his relationship with God. He returned to church finding it much more fulfilling despite agreeing with much less of what he heard.

Conclusion of Therapy Kevin worked through many other issues in therapy, not all of which were related to his religious beliefs. Over time, Kevin was able to identify how other existential issues impacted his thoughts about God. He became increasingly curious about how his belief system developed over time. As he thought back through his spiritual development, he could see how it was often based upon fear. Fear drove his religion: fear of death, fear of himself (or, in his words, his "proclivity toward sin"), and fear of being alone. His religious beliefs protected him from the anxiety and fear related to these issues. Unhealthy religion often serves as a defense against the existential realities, while healthy spirituality assists in engaging with them on a deeper level. Over time, Kevin was able to move from using religion as a defense to using it as an aid in engaging existential issues on a deeper level. As this occurred, I moved from psychoanalytic exploration of his defenses to experiential encounter with those defenses.

Many of the existential issues were addressed through implementing other experiential processes in addition to the imagery. Imagery worked very well for Kevin, especially following the experience noted above. I began frequently utilizing imagery with many experiential approaches, including the empty chair technique. We began with Kevin closing his eyes across from the empty chair and then describing God in as much detail as he could. His initial descriptions of God frequently changed through the therapy process. Early on, his descriptions were very similar to typical depictions of Jesus with neutral and constricted facial expressions. As therapy progressed, various depictions of God were described and God became much freer in his expressions. Interestingly, during the early restrictive depictions of God, Kevin frequently would become irate with God for how much religion controlled and restricted his life. As God became freer in his facial expressions, Kevin became freer in his own life. He was more authentic in his relationships, more open to experiencing and sharing his feelings, and more open to new relationships with people with whom he previously would not associate because of religious differences. He even began dating a woman he would not date previously — despite his interest — because she belonged to a very different church.

By the end of therapy, Kevin had undergone many significant changes pertaining to the existential issues. His anxiety decreased as his fears of eternal death, judgment, and the unknowns faded. As he also worked through his fears about God, he became much freer with his emotions. This allowed for more authentic engagement in his spiritual life as well as with others. His feelings of isolation decreased as his relationships became more intimate and meaningful. Shortly after Kevin ended therapy, I received a note in the mail letting me know of his engagement to the woman he had been dating. For Kevin, this was the final measure of success with all he worked through while in therapy.

Discussion and Implications

The integrative approaches used in this case shifted as the therapy progressed. Early portions of the therapy utilized existential-humanistic approaches to relationship building along with contemporary psychoanalytic techniques to help Kevin develop insight, particularly around how his early relationships impacted current relationships and his religious experience. As Kevin's defenses decreased, I transitioned to primarily experiential and Gestalt approaches, which are consistent with existential therapy.

In his discussion of the importance of myth in personal meaning systems, Rollo May (1991) defines myths not as false, but as that which cannot be proven to be true. In accordance with this understanding, all religion is myth. This does not mean that religion is an illusion, as Freud would say, or a delusion, as Sartre would say. Rather, it places religion in the realm of belief, not fact. Religion, when understood as a myth, provides a powerful meaning system. It acknowledges the limitations of religion without relegating it as false or pathological. Religion, when overly structured and rigid, often serves as a defense against the existential issues and authentic religious or spiritual belief. In this conception, it is not religion per se that is healthy or unhealthy, but the way a person is religious.

For Kevin, religion had been a defense that did not allow for authentic engagement with God or others. As he was able to work through the defensive aspects of his religious belief, he was freed to approach it more authentically. In addressing religion as a defense, James Bugental's (1987, 1999) emphasis on working with the defenses informed my approach. Whereas a psychoanalytic approach is more apt to confront the defense, I chose to work with it, recognizing it as necessary and healthy for Kevin's stage of therapeutic readiness. As the therapy relationship deepened and engendered more trust, the rigidity of Kevin's defensiveness lessened and I transitioned into more experiential approaches. This was not an easy process. As Kevin went through this growth process, he encountered a period of spiritual dryness. Prayer and other religious rituals lost all meaning. He stopped going to church, reading the Bible, and engaging in religious activities. Despite an apparent loss of faith, conceptualizing this process in the context of St. John of the Cross's idea of the dark night of the soul provided an alternative perspective.

Gerald May (2004) describes the dark night of the soul as a period of spiritual dryness. Further, it is characterized by a loss of interest in the traditional rituals and activities, such as prayer. It is not a loss of faith, but part of a transformation to a different type of faith that is less dependent on the traditions that were important during earlier phases of spiritual development. While not all people experience a dark night, Kevin's experience elucidates this process very well.

In closing, it is important for therapists who utilize this approach to have familiarity with religious and spiritual issues in therapy in addition to existential therapy. For those therapists with the appropriate background, existential-integrative therapy provides a powerful antidote for the religiously compromised client.

References

Becker, E. (1973). *The denial of death.* New York: Free Press.

Becker, E. (1975). *Escape from evil.* New York: Free Press.

Brokaw, B. F., & Edwards, K. J. (1994). The relationship of God image to level of object relations development. *Journal of Psychology and Theology, 22,* 352–371.

Buber, M. (1970). *I and thou* (W. Kaufmann, Trans.). New York: Simon & Schuster. (Original work published 1937)

Bugental, J. F. T. (1987). *The art of the psychotherapist.* New York: Norton.

Bugental, J. F. T. (1999). *Psychotherapy isn't what you think: Bringing the psychotherapeutic engagement into the living moment.* Phoenix, AZ: Zeig, Tucker & Theisen.

Cox, R. H., Ervin-Cox, B., & Hoffman, L. (Eds.). (2005). *Spirituality and psychological health.* Colorado Springs: Colorado School of Professional Psychology Press.

Feuerbach, L. (1989). *The essence of Christianity* (G. Eliot, Trans.). Amherst, NY: Prometheus. (Original work published 1841)

Freud, S. (1950). *Moses and monotheism* (K. Jones, Trans.). New York: Alfred A. Knoff. (Original work published 1938)

Freud, S. (1961). *The future of an illusion* (J. Strachey, Trans.). New York: Norton & Company. (Original work published 1927)

Hoffman, L. (2005). A developmental perspective on the God image. In R. H. Cox, B. Ervin-Cox, & L. Hoffman (Eds.), *Spirituality and psychological health* (pp. 129–149). Colorado Springs: Colorado School of Professional Psychology Press.

Hoffman, L., Hoffman, J., Dillard, K., Clark, J., Acoba, R., Williams, F., & Jones, T. T. (2005, April). *Cultural diversity and the God image: Examining cultural differences in the experience of God.* Paper presented at the Christian Association for Psychological Studies International Conference, Dallas, TX.

Hoffman, L., Jones, T. T., Williams, F., & Dillard, K. S. (2004, March). *The God image, the God concept, and attachment.* Paper presented at the Christian Association for Psychological Studies International Conference, St. Petersburg, FL.

Kaufmann, W. A. (1975). *Nietzsche: Philosophy, saint, anti-christ* (4th ed.). Princeton, NJ: Princeton University Press.

Kierkegaard, S. (1985). *Fear and trembling* (A. Hannay, Trans.). New York: Penguin. (Original work published 1843)

Lawrence, R. T. (1997). Measuring the image of God: The God image inventory and the God image scales. *Journal of Psychology and Theology, 25*, 214–226.

May, G. G. (2004). *The dark night of the soul: A psychiatrist explores the connection between darkness and spiritual growth.* San Francisco: Harper.

May, R. (1991). *The cry for myth.* New York: Norton.

Mitchell, S. A. (1988). *Relational concepts in psychoanalysis: An integration.* Cambridge, MA: Harvard University Press.

Richards, P. S., & Bergin, A. E. (2005). *A spiritual strategy for counseling and psychotherapy* (2nd ed.). Washington, DC: American Psychological Association.

Rizzuto, A. -M. (1979). *The birth of the living God: A psychoanalytic study.* Chicago: University of Chicago Press.

Sartre, J. -P. (1984). *Being and nothingness* (H. E. Barnes, Trans.). New York: Washington Square Press. (Original work published 1943)

Schneider, K. J. (2004). *Rediscovery of awe: Splendor, mystery, and the fluid center of life.* St. Paul, MN: Paragon House.

Sperry, L., & Shafranske, E. (Eds.). (2005). *Spiritually oriented psychotherapy.* Washington, DC: American Psychological Association.

Stark, M. (1999). *Modes of therapeutic interaction.* Northvale, NJ: Jason Aronson.

Tillich, P. (1952). *The courage to be.* New Haven, CT: Yale University Press.

Tillich, P. (2001). *The dynamics of faith.* (1st Perennial classics ed.) New York: Perennial. (Original work published 1957)

Tisdale, T. C., Key, T. L., Edwards, K. J., Brokaw, B. F., Kemperman, S. R., & Cloud, H. (1997). Impact of God image and personal adjustment, and correlations of the God image to personal adjustment and object relations development. *Journal of Psychology and Theology, 5*, 227–239.

10
Cognitive-Behavioral Innovations of EI Practice

Recently, cognitive-behavioral therapy has been undergoing a remarkable transition. Spearheading this shift are two cognitive-behavioral innovators who are impacting the national therapeutic landscape — Barry Wolfe and Steven Hayes. Dr. Wolfe is a leading member of the psychotherapy integrationist movement as well as former head of the Psychosocial Treatment Research Program at the National Institute of Mental Health, and Dr. Hayes is a highly prolific originator of a new cognitive-behavioral paradigm. This paradigm (Acceptance and Commitment Therapy [ACT]) was recently featured in *Time* magazine (February 13, 2006) as an emerging alternative to standard cognitive-behavioral practice. In the cases below, Wolfe and Hayes demonstrate how their innovative frameworks not only coincide with existential-integrative practices, but draw heavily from an existential-humanistic philosophical base. For example, Dr. Wolfe opens his illustration of anxiety disorders with an urgent appeal for an existentially based understanding of anxiety. This understanding in his view both supplements and bolsters standard cognitive-behavioral practice. He goes on to describe several of literally hundreds of examples where clients benefited from existentially oriented expansions of cognitive-behavioral interventions. In his featured case of "Leonardo," Wolfe shows how obsessive-compulsive disorder can be understood from the perspective of death anxiety, and how experiential confrontation coupled with cognitive-behavioral exercises transformed Leonardo's world.

Dr. Hayes, in collaboration with Kara Bunting, elucidates his ACT perspective with a thorough two-pronged approach. First the authors present a methodical and illuminating case study that illustrates the ACT model as well as related EI formulations. The case features "Ben," a married man who becomes intractably obsessed over his wife's fidelity. In a clear and holistic fashion, the authors show how language, identity, and experience become fused and defused, and how ACT stances along with EI principles help to disentangle Ben from his crippling lot. Following the case, the authors present a remarkable commentary on the nature, history, and potential for rapprochement between ACT and existential-humanistic therapy. In particular, they discuss how ACT formulations echo core EI tenets elucidated in this volume, and the hope thereby of an expanded cognitive-behavioral/existential collaboration.

Existential Issues in Anxiety Disorders and Their Treatment

Barry E. Wolfe

Barry E. Wolfe, PhD, is president of the Center for Training in Psychotherapy Integration, which develops training programs in integrative models of psychotherapy. He is the author of *Understanding and Treating Anxiety Disorders: An Integrative Approach to Healing the Wounded Self*, published in 2005 by the APA.

My clinical experience over the past 30 years with several hundred patients suffering with anxiety disorders has led me to two broad conclusions. The first is that anxiety disorders are typically generated by failed efforts to confront and solve a finite number of unavoidable existential dilemmas that every human being will experience. The second conclusion is that these disorders can be comprehensively and durably treated by an integrative psychotherapy that begins with symptom alleviation and then proceeds to emotion-focused work on the patient's specific existential crises.

In this illustration, I will describe a number of the specific existential dilemmas that these patients have struggled with and that appear to be at the root of their anxiety disorder. This is not a comprehensive list but rather one that captures the dilemmas of the vast majority of anxiety disorder patients that I have treated. I will then present a brief description of my integrative perspective on anxiety disorders that includes an etiological theory of their nature, development, and maintenance and a model of integrative psychotherapy. The illustration will conclude with a case history that animates the clinical strategy and specific techniques employed in this integrative psychotherapy.

Existential Crises as the Bedrock of Anxiety Disorders

It is not immediately obvious that the various manifestations of anxiety are all based in existential dilemmas. Nothing in the literature or the mainstream treatments would suggest this possibility. In applying the mainstream cognitive-behavior therapy for anxiety symptoms, however, it became apparent that not too far below the surface of a patient's more typical focal awareness lie a number of feared catastrophes that result in a bout of terrifying panic. As the behavioral technique interoceptive exposure* was eventually shaped into an intensive focusing exercise on the somatic indicators of anxiety, it became patently clear that these feared catastrophes represented the provenance of an anxiety disorder. The ultimate feared catastrophes turned out to invariably involve an existential crisis. More specifically, the anxiety and panic associ-

* *Interoceptive exposure* refers to a systematic program of asking a patient to focus his or her attention on frightening bodily sensations until they no longer make the patient anxious.

ated with any given anxiety disorder appear to result from the patient's inability to confront a specific existential crisis.

One patient suffering from panic disorder, for example, discovered through the above-mentioned focusing technique that his panic symptoms were rooted in his terror associated with growing old. Employing the same technique, a patient suffering from obsessive-compulsive disorder discovered that he lived in terror lest his intrusive violent thoughts would result in causing harm to a loved one. Another patient's public speaking phobia was traced to the individual's inability to tolerate humiliation and failure. Yet, it is an ontological given that we all grow old, hurt the ones we love, and fail and humiliate ourselves sometime in our lives. In addition to the above-mentioned fears, the overwhelming ontological givens have included:

1. Difficulty in accepting one's mortality
2. Difficulty in accepting the inevitability of loss
3. Difficulty in accepting personal responsibility for one's thoughts, feelings, and actions
4. Difficulty in tolerating painful affects
5. Difficulty in "facing the void"
6. Difficulty in accepting that a significant aspect of life's meaning may have been destroyed
7. The conflict over whether to trust or distrust loved ones and people in general
8. The fear of committing one's life to another human being
9. The conflict between being free and having emotional security
10. The conflict over whether to authentically express our feelings or stifle them in the quest for approval or in order to maintain the security of a highly valued relationship

Because of space limitations, we will consider in detail only half of these.

Fear of Death The fear of dying is the most common root fear in anxiety disorders that I have encountered in my clinical work. This fear is not restricted to a specific anxiety disorder. Rather, it is one that has been the source of panic in patients with obsessive-compulsive disorder (OCD), generalized anxiety disorder (GAD), panic disorder with or without agoraphobia, and specific phobias (Wolfe, 2005b). Much of the time, this fear remains outside of our focal awareness. It usually surfaces into our conscious awareness whenever we have a close brush with death or when a loved one dies. The awareness of one's mortality is typically a frightening experience. Such an event has been referred to as a *memento mori*. This ancient Latin phrase, freely translated, means "Remember you will die," and it was typically spoken by a servant to a parading Roman general who was being feted for his military triumphs.

A *memento mori* is an experience that shreds one's defense of invincibility, leaving one vulnerable to the painful awareness of one's pending nonexistence (Yalom, 1980). The anxiety and panic associated with a *memento mori* functions as a kind of protest, an unwillingness to face this painful ontological given. Once we fully allow the realization of our eventual death, this awareness may be accompanied by intense feelings of despair, humiliation, helplessness, or rage (Wolfe, 2005b). One patient, for example, with a severe bridge phobia, contacted his despair over the thought of his death through imagery work. Associated with his fear of bridges was the presentiment that he would hurl himself over the bridge once he reached the top of its height. I asked him to imagine doing just that, hurling himself over the bridge. As he saw himself plummeting to his death, he began to cry despairing tears because he felt totally incapable of living a satisfactory life. At that moment, he contacted his belief that he would die before he had lived (Wolfe, 2005b). This insight pointed us toward a two-pronged integrative psychotherapy involving both exposure-based therapy to help him confront his fear of crossing bridges and a more traditional exploratory psychotherapy to help him identify and modify the blocks to his creating a satisfying life.

Fear of Loss A second major fear that appears to underlie many cases of anxiety disorder is the fear of loss. Eventually, we lose everything in life, including life itself. People go through their lives, however, fearing the loss of loved ones, careers, physical prowess, and, at a less concrete level, we fear the loss of illusions, expectations, and dreams (Viorst, 1986). Early in my career, I treated a 19-year-old college sophomore whose entire life and identity had been built around the dream of becoming a concert pianist. When his professors informed him that he lacked the requisite talent to ever achieve his dream, he first went into a series of panic attacks, progressed to feelings of emptiness and despair, and eventually began the painful task of constructing alternatives for his young life. This is a pattern I have seen very often with patients suffering from anxiety disorders. They move from experiencing anxiety and panic attacks, to confronting their feared "catastrophes" and experiencing the accompanying feelings, to constructing new alternatives and options in their lives.

Often a combination of losses can trigger panic attacks leading to panic disorder. A 50-year-old physician began having panic attacks after his oldest son went off to college. At the same time, he began incurring physical injuries during athletic competitions. Our imagery work revealed that the former event let him know that his idyllic life was changing, while his injuries marked the beginning descent of his physical prowess. Once he could allow himself to face these losses, he moved into a period of despair and depression. He had to mourn those very real losses. From there he was able to shift his focus to the life he had left. This shift in perspective was aided by a telling metaphor. He said, "I am always trying to stop time and I can't." As his feelings of frustration and powerlessness clearly emerged, I imagined him on the big clock on Westminster Abbey trying to hold back the movement of the minute hand. I invited him to share that image. He felt the impossibility of his efforts. I then asked him to climb onto the minute hand and "ride time." For some inexplicable reason, this metaphor caught hold of his imagination and he began to shift his focus to improving his current life. He and his wife began to take long-promised trips together. He had a younger son who was a baseball fanatic and the two of them bonded over the sport. He made some adjustments in his medical work. Together, all of these adjustments pulled him out of his despair. Over the past decade, he has improved in every facet of his life.

Freedom versus Security Many anxiety patients simultaneously fear freedom and security while intensely desiring both. This is particularly true of patients who have been diagnosed with agoraphobia. Although freedom is sought because agoraphobic patients cannot stand to be told what to do, they also find freedom terrifying because of its isolation and lack of ready support. Søren Kierkegaard (1844/1944) spoke of the "dizziness of freedom." For individuals suffering from agoraphobia, that is no mere metaphor, but rather a feature of the panic attacks they experience when they confront their own freedom. For agoraphobic individuals, the freedom they fear has many variations. They fear (1) having to make their own decisions, (2) the absence of support, and (3) the feelings of isolation that arise when they are alone and free. Security, however, brings up other terrors: the fear of being controlled, beholden to others, trapped and unable to choose for themselves. When they are alone, they seek company, and when they are with others, they seek to escape too much togetherness. They fear both autonomy and commitment, and there is no gray area in between.

A previously housebound agoraphobic patient had a 60-mile zone of safety by the time he began therapy with me. Beyond that distance, he would experience panic attacks. He wished to extend his range so that he could vacation at one of the nearby ocean beaches. The exposure-based symptom-focused phase of the treatment did just that by gradually extending the distance he traveled from home. The depth-oriented phase of treatment uncovered several of the early experiences that had influenced his fear of confinement and fear of being alone. He had been briefly incarcerated for drunk driving, which left him howling in terror because he was trapped and helpless. On the other hand, he once motorcycled into the Alaskan wilderness for several weeks. The experience of isolation eventually resulted in panic attacks and a profound sense of his insignificance, which he found unbearable. He could not bear to look up into a night sky because the experience would leave him with an unbearable awareness of his inconsequentiality. The remediation of these root fears involved encounters with a number of other ontological givens: (1)

accepting that he was a separate consciousness; (2) enhancing his capacity to accept responsibility for his actions, thoughts, and feelings; (3) extending his capacity to think beyond black-and-white categories; (4) exploring the value of commitment to tasks, values, and people; (5) tolerating the experience of painful emotions; and (6) exploring the possibility of constructing a life that includes some freedom and some security.

Fear of Painful Feelings One characteristic common to all patients with anxiety disorders is an intense fear of painful emotions. These emotions include rage, helplessness, humiliation, and despair. These emotions are so painful and difficult to experience that patients have developed a number of protective screens against experiencing them. Yet it seems to be an ontological given that everyone experiences all of these painful emotions sometime in their lives. Anxiety and panic symptoms appear to serve as a major protective screen against contacting these searing emotions (Wolfe, 2005b). These feelings can be accessed if a patient allows himself or herself to focus intensively on the bodily sensations of anxiety or on the feared object or situation.

The above-mentioned patient with obsessive-compulsive disorder, for example, was constantly plagued by the obsessional thought that he was going to smash his girlfriend in the face. This thought produced such anxiety that he engaged in numerous rituals to "cancel" the thought and thereby reduce his anxiety. After focusing intensively for several minutes on this thought and its corresponding image, he began to experience intense despair and humiliation. These feelings were associated with the core belief that he was a loser and was therefore destined to be alone for the rest of his life. Apart from the loneliness that this feared state of affairs would bring, my patient was more concerned about how others would view his inability to maintain a romantic relationship with a woman. The humiliation and despair were so painful that he would do virtually anything to bring an end to these feelings. Once he was able to experience these painful feelings, we began to work on his perspective about life and relationships.

Fear of Commitment The final existential issue prominent in anxiety disorders that I wish to mention is the fear of commitment. This fear dovetails with the difficulty that these patients have in trusting people. A surprising number of patients whom I have treated feel that their early caretakers have betrayed them (Wolfe, 1989, 1992). These early experiences shaped an attitude of distrust that often played an integral role in undermining later relationships, romantic and otherwise. These patients tend to develop self-protective interpersonal strategies that often elicit the very responses from others that they fear (Wachtel, 1997; Wolfe, 2005b). Commitment, therefore, carries connotations of being trapped, controlled, dominated, or just of having chosen badly.

One patient who meets criteria for generalized anxiety disorder, for example, has demonstrated the same pattern in several serial romantic relationships. He very quickly falls in love with a young woman in whom he has imbued all of the qualities of the perfect mate. Over time, each woman becomes human to him. As she does so, his anxiety begins to increase. The more flaws she inevitably shows, the greater the anxiety until he is regularly having panic attacks whenever he is with her. The constant fog of anxiety now obliterates the good qualities that she actually possesses and leaves him convinced that he has made a mistake. He will grant in each case that the woman continues to love him and treat him very well most of the time. But when she reveals her foibles, he begins to doubt the entire relationship and makes plans to end it. He constantly catastrophically cogitates that he is making a mistake. Therapy focused on helping him understand the source of his idealization of women, his fear of making a mistake, education about the nature of committed relationships, and the necessity to learn better ways of communicating — and resolving conflicts — with his partner.

Fear of the Rigors and Realities of Everyday Living This is the category under which all the other fears comfortably fall. This perspective suggests that a person with an anxiety disorder perceives himself as a person who cannot cope with — and therefore needs protection from — the rigors and realities of everyday living. Anxious individuals create indirect strategies for coping with the unavoidable realities of life, but these strategies keep them from facing these realities head on. As I have suggested elsewhere, "Such strategies range from behavioral avoidance to cognitive ritual and emotional constriction, and they usually produce unintended interpersonal consequences that have the paradoxical effect of reinforcing the patient's painful core beliefs about the self" (Wolfe, 2005b, p. 122).

An Integrative Etiological Model of Anxiety Disorders

The psychotherapy integration movement arose as a response to the limitations that practicing therapists, psychotherapy theorists, and researchers found in the so-called pure-form psychotherapies. Yet it was equally clear that each psychotherapy perspective has much to teach us. Over the course of three decades, the psychotherapy integration movement has matured into one of the major developments in the field of psychotherapy (Norcross, 2005).

Only recently have efforts been devoted to developing integrative psychotherapies for specific classes of mental, behavioral, and emotional disorders. Over the past two decades, I have been developing an *integrative perspective* on anxiety disorders. By integrative perspective, I mean two separate but interrelated models: an integrative etiological theory and an integrative psychotherapy for anxiety disorders. Each model represents a synthesis of the existing perspectives on anxiety disorders, including psychodynamic, behavioral, cognitive-behavioral, humanistic-experiential, and biomedical perspectives.

The etiological model attempts to describe the nature, development, and maintenance of anxiety disorders. The guiding premise of this model is that anxiety disorders are based in patients' chronic struggle with their subjective experience. The experience of severe anxiety in selected situations gives rise to *conscious* anticipations of impending catastrophe, which at an implicit level reflect a fear of exposing unbearably painful views of the self. When patients confront these "self-wounds," they experience such overwhelming affects as humiliation, rage, helplessness, and despair. Thus, anxiety disorders appear to possess a conscious layer and an implicit layer in terms of what the anxiety symptoms mean to the individual.

The external and internal cues that produce anxiety arise from one's perception of relationships between certain life experiences and intense fear. That is, certain experiences are perceived as self-endangering. The cues themselves often function as a kind of abbreviated shorthand for the painful memory that exists beyond the individual's conscious awareness. Thus, for example, an agoraphobic patient's fear of losing control is signaled by a feeling of lightheadedness, which was the same feeling she had when she panicked at the sight of physically disabled people years before.

Self-wounds result from the interaction of damaging life experiences and the cognitive and emotional strategies designed to protect individuals from their feared catastrophes. These strategies, however, keep the person from facing his or her fears and self-wounds head-on. The contexts in which self-wounds develop usually entail some existential dilemma that cannot be faced. The self-wounds and the contexts in which they develop make it extremely difficult for individuals to confront similar existential dilemmas in the future. One very successful gentleman was reared under the tutelage and dominance of his overcontrolling mother, who would tolerate no backtalk. He implicitly learned that speaking his mind would result in retaliation or abandonment. Now, whenever a woman he is interested in criticizes him, he becomes extremely anxious, feels trapped, and may well experience a panic attack. He has never been able to sustain a romantic relationship because of his anxiety.

In response to the initial anxiety, patients typically engage in cogitating about being anxious (i.e., self-preoccupation), avoiding the fear-inducing objects and situations, or engaging in negative interpersonal cycles. These strategies result in the temporary reduction of anxiety and the reinforcement of the patient's underlying maladaptive self-beliefs. Psychological defenses in this model serve as self-defeating efforts to protect one's image of the self (see Wolfe, 2005a).

All painful views of the self suggest a perception and experience of self as one who cannot cope with the rigors and realities of everyday living. Since these realities are ontological givens, anxious individuals must create indirect coping strategies that protect them from intolerable affective states while at the same time keep them from facing these unavoidable realities head-on. Below is an illustration of how the model analyzes a specific anxiety disorder.

A Self-Wound Model of Social Phobia

The specific self-wounds associated with social phobia tend to involve core self-perceptions as socially inadequate, unlovable, or unworthy (Wolfe, 2005b). These wounds often derive from frequent shaming messages received from the person's family of origin or his or her expanded social environment. The individual internalizes these toxic opinions, which result in a generalized view of self as defective or inferior. Social situations and public speaking opportunities produce the experience of self-endangerment. The self-endangerment experience is the intense anxiety or panic that "protects" the individual from having to experience the excruciatingly painful feeling of inadequacy. The extreme humiliation that a person feels when faced with his or her sense of inadequacy is unbearable and is thus avoided by experiencing instead the often more painful panic attack. These self-wounds lead to the individual's failure to manage necessary social and public interactions.

Self-endangerment leads to a shift of attention to a preoccupation with one's social — or in this case — public speaking limitations and with imagined rejecting reactions of a hostile or disdaining audience. This self-preoccupation, or what I call *obsessive cogitation*, about the potential catastrophic meaning of one's immediate anxiety is the first major maintaining factor in public speaking phobia. Self-preoccupation results in the awareness of a discrepancy between the experience of the way one is versus the way one ought to be. The experienced gap between the actual self and the idealized standard produces anxiety or pain (Higgins, 1987).

A second major maintenance process is avoidance. Social phobics will avoid speaking opportunities and social engagements. Avoidance leads to a short-term reduction of anxiety, but it reinforces the underlying self-wounds and therefore the social phobia.

A third maintaining factor is the interpersonal strategy of impression management, which is basically to present oneself in such a way as to manipulate a positive impression from others. When a positive impression is communicated to the anxious individual, he or she experiences a temporary reduction of anxiety because the individual does not have to face the feared negative self-belief or self-image. This reassurance is only temporary, however, because the anxious individual knows at some level that he or she is not being authentic. Because the other person has been fooled, his or her credibility as an accurate judge of the anxious individual has been undermined. Anxious people therefore have great difficulty in believing positive feedback proffered by others. Finally, because of these above-mentioned strategies, the self-wounds remain unhealed, resulting in the continuation of the social phobia.

An Integrative Psychotherapy for Anxiety Disorders

The integrative psychotherapy, most simply put, combines a symptom-focused treatment with a later effort to identify and modify the behavioral, cognitive, and emotional strategies that prevent the patient from confronting his or her specific existential dilemmas. The final step in the treatment is a supportive and process-directive experiential therapy that helps the patient to face, process, and ultimately solve his or her existential crisis.

The symptom-focused treatment typically comes first because it is often necessary to teach patients anxiety-management skills before they are willing to do the necessary but painful work of confronting and coping with specific existential issues in their lives. As the research evidence indicates, it is possible to provide patients with effective tools to manage out-of-control anxiety and materially improve their lives (Barlow, 2001). At the same time, it is clear that these pure-form therapies typically do not engage the existential dilemmas (at least not with any consistent success) that appear to drive the symptoms of a DSM-IV (APA's *Diagnostic Statistical Manual of Mental Disorders*, fourth edition)–diagnosed anxiety disorder (Wolfe, 2005b). The following case demonstrates a typical unfolding of the treatment sequence.

Case Example: The Fear of Death Underlying a Patient's Obsessive-Compulsive Disorder

"Leonardo" is a 50-year-old actuarial scientist who is plagued by the thought that because of mistakes he made in the past, his life has been prematurely shortened. The stimuli that trigger the thought and the severe anxiety include asbestos, fiberglass, cigarettes, and pesticides. If he is exposed to any one of these stimuli, a complex thought chain follows: Cigarettes remind him of the fact that he smoked as a young man. Although he stopped smoking 25 years ago, he believes that his earlier mistake dooms him to a shortened life. He believes he will develop lung cancer and die. Even though the probabilities are low, he will be one of the unlucky ones, he believes, because his character is flawed by frequent selfish and sexual thoughts.

Each stimulus reminds him of an earlier association with it in which he mistakenly allowed him or his loved ones to be dangerously exposed. Asbestos, as another example, reminds him of when he remodeled his house many years ago and may have dangerously exposed himself. The probability of a dangerous exposure is always infinitesimal. To reduce his anxiety, Leonardo consults the Internet and absorbs all of the available information of the risk that each triggering stimulus poses for contracting lung cancer. Since in every case, the probabilities are very small, his anxiety is temporarily reduced until the next time he is triggered by one of the above-mentioned stimuli.

Leonardo grew up in Milan, Italy, the son of a university professor and a schoolteacher. After graduating from the University of Milan, he came to the

United States to do graduate work in statistics at Harvard University. He was very fond of his parents, but they were somewhat reserved emotionally, particularly his father. His father died at the age of 67 after a stroke. His mother, who had smoked for decades and did not stop smoking until the age of 62, died of lung cancer when she was 85 years old. In fact, it was her death that coincided with the onset of Leonardo's severe anxiety and obsessive-compulsive symptoms. Leonardo made no connection between the contiguous events of his mother's death and the onset of his OCD symptoms.

The Symptom Alleviation Phase of Psychotherapy A basic assumption underlying my integrative psychotherapy is that patients with anxiety disorders need to develop some ways of managing their anxiety before they can address the underlying existential crisis. For Leonardo, the symptom cycle progressed as follows: Exposure to the feared stimulus led to obsessional thoughts about his being doomed because of his prior inadvertent mistakes. The obsessional thoughts led him to engage in a thought-neutralizing ritual, jumping on the Internet and absorbing as much information as possible. This ritual temporarily reduced his anxiety until his next exposure to a triggering stimulus, which initiated the next OCD cycle. This symptom pattern seemed to be a perfect fit for the behavioral treatment of choice for OCD: exposure plus response prevention (EX/RP) (Foa & Franklin, 2001). We began by employing a self-initiated version of EX/RP. This procedure involved having Leonardo purposely expose himself to the various triggering stimuli by imagining, for example, smoking cigarettes or being exposed to asbestos. He was instructed to simultaneously avoid consulting the Internet for information about the probabilities of contracting lung cancer.

Later, when he became aware that accepting his mortality was the existential crisis underlying his obsessive-compulsive symptoms, he learned to short-circuit his anxiety by acknowledging each time that he is triggered by one of his typical stimuli because he is really struggling with accepting his mortality. This helped him learn how to bypass the obsessional thinking and the Internet information-gathering ritual. He was able to make good use of the strategy for undercutting the OCD process. After three months' work, he was mostly able to stay off the Internet and to use the diaphragmatic breathing that I had previously taught him to reduce the anxiety that occurred when he imagined being exposed to his triggers.

The Depth-Oriented Phase of Therapy Once he felt he had some control over his anxiety, we agreed to move to the next phase of treatment, the depth-oriented phase, during which we attempted to elicit and heal the underlying self-wounds and resolve his existential crisis (Wolfe, 2005b). Leonardo was asked to focus all of his attention on his obsessional thought — that his inadvertent past mistakes have foreshortened his life and he was therefore doomed to die in the very near future. This focusing technique clarified for Leonardo a number of critically relevant issues. First, it was determined that his root fear was the fear of his own death, a prospect that befuddled — as much as it terrified — him. Second, the fear of dying was associated with an entire network of catastrophic thoughts that linked his making egregious errors earlier in his life with his imagined premature death or the death of his loved ones. Third, he was thoroughly convinced that he would necessarily pay for his mistakes with his life because he harbors sexual and selfish thoughts. Fourth, he noticed the parallel between his association of prior mistakes with premature death and the moral paradigm of his religious upbringing, which can be summed up by the New Testament metaphor "the wages of sin is death." Finally, because his scientific training made it difficult for him to believe in an afterlife, he had to confront the unbearable thought that the end of this life meant the termination of his existence forever. His mother's death had been a *memento mori* that brought him deeply in touch with his own mortality. Feelings of despair accompanied his awareness of the inevitability of the end of his existence. The OCD symptoms can be seen as an effort to stave off that awareness and the associated painful feelings.

The therapeutic work now shifted to a basic existential task that we all eventually must face, to help Leonardo make his peace with his mortality so that he can live the rest of his life with greater passion and less fear. From an existential and phenomenological perspective, meditation on one's eventual death is a precondition for achieving meaning and freedom from fear in everyday life (Yalom, 1980).

With these assumptions as a guiding paradigm, we spent a great number of the following sessions talking about and encountering the anxiety of his eventual death from every possible angle. I asked him to imagine his death and the funeral that followed. The point of these exposure-like discussions was to help him face the issues that he had been fending off: (1) He will die, (2) he does not know when he will die or the causes of his death, and (3) he cannot know the contribution of his past choices to bringing about his eventual demise. This work continued for at least a year, as his mind kept rejecting the idea of his death. Eventually, but very slowly, he began to emotionally accept his mortality.

Once he had made significant progress toward accepting his eventual death, I attempted to draw his attention to his unresolved religious beliefs. The cast of his thinking seemed to follow the worldview of the Catholic religion, with its emphasis on sin, retribution, and redemption. There were, however, many precepts that he could not accept, most particularly the concept of an afterlife. I asked him to revisit these issues with a priest of his choosing or at least to engage in some thought about his core convictions regarding the meaning of life.

Another facet of this work was to challenge his belief that he was a bad person. This core self-belief was maintained by his conviction that thinking a "bad" thought was the same as acting it out. This *thought-action fusion* is a common element in most individuals who suffer from OCD (Shafran, Thordarson, & Rachman, 1996). Consequently, for Leonardo, imagining sexual interactions with a woman who was not his wife was akin to committing adultery. I asked him to imagine a stone fortress that separated his thoughts from his actions. Within the confines of the fortress, he was allowed to think whatever thoughts he desired so long as he did not venture beyond the wall to act them out. Leonardo made good use of this metaphoric image in helping him normalize his thoughts while retaining appropriate limits on his behavior. This exercise became more effective as he allowed himself to accept his eventual death.

The exposure paradigm changed over time. Instead of having him focus on his eventual death, he focused on the possibility that he had made mistakes that affected how long he may live. He had to acknowledge that as a possibility, as remote as it might be, and live the rest of his life in the best way possible. Another major focus of the work was on the fact that he had smoked as a young man even though he knew it was not good for him. He worked very hard to accept the fact that he had indeed made a mistake. Because he was cognizant of his very high intelligence, he found this task humiliating and had to work through many self-recriminations for the "unintelligent" and potentially lethal risks that he took.

The final phase of this work involved a focus on the rest of his life. There were two tasks that we worked on: (1) helping him to enjoy his current life and (2) planning for his retirement, which was to happen within the next two years. Enjoying his current life was made problematic by the highly stressful nature of his job. And it had become clear that his periodic anxiety attacks, which were triggered by specific substances (e.g., asbestos, cigarettes, fiber glass particles), were perfectly correlated with a significant increase in his level of stress at work. The challenge was for Leonardo to make sure that he includes in his life tasks activities and people that he truly enjoys, and to teach him how to stay in the present so that he could enjoy his life. The second task was for him to generate possible postretirement activities and to explore the level of interest that he has in each.

At present, Leonardo has made good progress on all fronts. He now possesses tools to short-circuit anxiety when it arises and it arises much less frequently. The latter fact is due to the good work he has done to emotionally accept his eventual death. He continues to work on the reorganization of his belief system about life and death. Finally, he has also improved in his ability to stay in the moment and experience his life more fully. And he continues to test out the viability of specific postretirement volunteer and paid activities.

Summary

The severity that anxiety disorders sometimes reach can disguise the fact that their roots seem to lie in the interaction of a person with a damaged perspective on their self struggling with an existential crisis. It is very easy to get lost in the symptoms, strategies of avoidance, and the very real pain that people with anxiety suffer, and not observe or empathically know the ontological givens with which they are struggling. Because of that pain and the sense of being overwhelmed that the symptoms of an anxiety disorder can produce, it is important to address these first in treatment. Such symptom-focused treatment is necessary but not sufficient. Later, the self-wounds and the existential issues can be elucidated and successfully managed.

References

American Psychological Association. (1994). *Diagnostic and statistical manual of mental disorders* (4th ed.). Washington, DC: Author.

Barlow, D. H. (2001). *Anxiety and its disorders: The nature and treatment of anxiety and panic* (2nd ed.). New York: Guilford Press.

Foa, E. B., & Franklin, M. E. (2001). Obsessive-compulsive disorder. In D. H. Barlow (Ed.), *Clinical handbook of psychological disorders* (3rd ed., pp. 209–263). New York: Guilford Press.

Higgins, E. T. (1987). Self-discrepancy: A theory relating self and affect. *Psychological Review, 94*, 319–340.

Kierkegaard, S. (1944). *The concept of dread* (W. Lowrie, Trans.). Princeton, NJ: Princeton University Press. (Original work published 1844)

Norcross, J. C. (2005). A primer on psychotherapy integration. In J. C. Norcross & M. R. Goldfried (Eds.), *Handbook of psychotherapy integration* (2nd ed., pp. 3–23). New York: Oxford University Press.

Shafran, R., Thordarson, D. S., & Rachman, S. (1996). Thought-action fusion in obsessive-compulsive disorder. *Journal of Anxiety Disorders, 5*, 379–391.

Viorst, J. (1986). *Necessary losses*. New York: Ballantine Books.

Wachtel, P. L. (1997). *Psychoanalysis, behavior therapy, and the relational world*. Washington, DC: American Psychological Association.

Wolfe, B. E. (1989). Phobias, panic and psychotherapy integration. *Journal of Integrative and Eclectic Psychotherapy, 8*, 264–276.

Wolfe, B. E. (1992). Self-experiencing and the integrative treatment of the anxiety disorders. *Journal of Psychotherapy Integration, 2*, 29–43.

Wolfe, B. E. (2005a). Integrative psychotherapy of the anxiety disorders. In J. C. Norcross & M. R. Goldfried (Eds.), *Handbook of psychotherapy integration* (2nd ed., pp. 263–280). New York: Oxford University Press.

Wolfe, B. E. (2005b). *Understanding and treating anxiety disorders: An integrative approach to healing the wounded self.* Washington, DC: American Psychological Association.

Yalom, I. (1980). *Existential psychotherapy*. New York: Basic Books.

Language and Meaning: Acceptance and Commitment Therapy and the EI Model

Kara Bunting and Steven C. Hayes

Kara Bunting, MA, is a clinical doctoral candidate at the University of Nevada, Reno. Her research interests and publications are in the area of human language processes and acceptance and commitment therapy.

Steven C. Hayes, PhD, is Nevada Foundation professor in the Department of Psychology at the University of Nevada. An author of 27 books and 360 scientific articles, during his career he has focused on an analysis of the nature of human language and cognition and the application of this to the understandin\g and alleviation of human suffering.

Behavior therapy and, even more so, clinical behavior analysis might be the last place one would look to find modern expressions of some of the core ideas of humanistic thought. Nevertheless, over the last 20 years a post-Skinnerian tradition has emerged within behavior analysis that builds a bridge between humanism/existentialism and behaviorism. It was not a bridge specifically built to connect these lines of thought, which may make its existence all the more notable. Rather, acceptance and commitment therapy (ACT [said as a single word, not as initials]; Hayes, Strosahl, & Wilson, 1999) and the analysis of language and cognition on which it is based, relational frame theory (RFT; Hayes, Barnes-Holmes, & Roche, 2001), is an exploration and extension of a certain type of functional behavioral thinking. What has resulted is an end product that overlaps in many ways with the core values and considerations of integrative experiential approaches.

We will explore this connection in a somewhat odd way. Normally in a chapter of this kind, a model would be described, underlying philosophy explored, and connections made. When that process seemed complete, a case might be described and related to these issues. The potential for misunderstanding between experiential and behavioral perspectives is so great, however, that it seems counterproductive to begin with conceptual issues. Every term is fraught with difficulty. Even very basic terms that have relatively clear meaning need to be explained, because, as part of a larger system of thought, they mean something different than might be supposed: behavior, empirical, science — the list is both long and basic. It is made worse by the fact that ACT/RFT researchers and clinicians deliberately use multiple language systems, such as the language of freedom in their clinical work and the language of determinism in their scientific work, because they take a pragmatic view of language and are not being functionally inconsistent when they use inconsistent terms to accomplish different ends.

In this contribution, we will begin with a case. We will describe what we do, using terms that avoid jargon or can be quickly defined as we go. Then we will describe more theoretically what we are trying to do, and finally we will connect this work to the existential-integrative framework represented in this volume.

An ACT Case

"Ben" presented in therapy complaining of serious distress related to his relationship with his wife. Ben reported that the arguments had escalated to the point where he felt he might want a divorce, but he stated he loved his wife and wanted to be in the relationship. Ben related that he saw the chief problem as his jealousy. Ben's wife often traveled without him for her job and that was when problems began. Ben reported increasing worries that she would get involved with another man, although he did not think she had ever been unfaithful. Ben's anxiety was not the only problem; Ben had also begun trying to reassure himself by investigating his wife's activities. Ben had begun to take time off of work to return to his house to check that she was not home with another man or to go through her things without her knowledge. Ben called as often as a dozen times throughout the day to see where she was and with whom. If she left the house for a few hours to run errands, Ben would inquire where she had been so he could determine if she had been absent for more time than he thought her errands would take. If she returned from her travels with a new article of jewelry, he questioned her about its origins and would want to see the receipt. When he was unable to procure adequate evidence of her innocence, he would accuse her of having an affair.

Ben's wife had first responded by reassuring and arguing with Ben with little success. She then began to conceal any information she thought might worry him, which resulted in Ben becoming even more suspicious when he discovered her behavior. Eventually she became angry with Ben for not trusting her and withdrew from him. Ben reported he and his wife went through periods where they rarely spoke because they were both avoiding the possibility of his jealous reactions. Ben reported he knew his behavior was irrational and was ruining his marriage, but he felt he could not stop. Ben no longer enjoyed any part of his marriage, he was so consumed by looking for signs of his wife's infidelity. Ben's worries were also interfering with his concentration and hurting his performance at his job, and his supervisor was becoming irritated by all the time Ben took off work. Ben reported his attempts to reassure himself that his worries were unfounded and his efforts to stop thinking suspicious thoughts were mostly fruitless; he felt his anxieties had only increased with time. Ben could not see a way out of his anxiety and was considering divorcing his wife and had begun looking for an apartment for himself.

Conceptualization From an ACT perspective, the client's behavior with respect to his unwanted private events (his jealous and anxious thoughts and feelings) had trapped him into a struggle that was consuming more and more of his vitality and was stripping his life of values and meaning. When Ben became anxious about his wife being unfaithful, he attempted to suppress his worries, which only created additional anxiety due to the self-amplifying processes of experiential avoidance and thought suppression. Ben would have a jealous thought, then worry that he might not be able to get rid of that thought, then worry that he would behave in a jealous manner to control his anxiety and push his wife further away, all of which created more anxiety, which then was interpreted as fear related to his wife — and the entire process would repeat. As he dealt with this anxiety by engaging in overt behaviors to control his feelings, such as tracking his wife's activities, he was creating distance in his relationship and moving away from contact with valued parts of his life, including meaningful time with his wife. This decrease in intimacy with his wife in turn was accompanied by even more feelings of insecurity.

The therapist began by asking Ben to look at the effectiveness of his efforts to deal with his feelings of jealousy. Ben admitted that far from helping matters, his behavior seemed to be making things much worse, at least in the long run. Ben could temporarily reassure himself by finding out what his wife was doing, for example, but this had consequences in terms of their relationship and a few hours later he would be worried again.

The therapist noted in early sessions that Ben had difficulty telling the therapist about his jealous thoughts and behavior as well as his positive emotions around his relationship with his wife. Ben looked away from the therapist and became tearful when he spoke of his concern that his wife might want another lover. He would often stumble through his words or pause mid-sentence for several seconds. Ben revealed that he had not told anyone else about the difficulties he had been having, although he had several close friends. Ben did his best to hide the extent of his worries from his wife as well; he reported she was unaware that he had been leaving his job specifically to check on her activities. He reported that they did not talk about his behavior except when they were arguing.

ACT Processes in Ben's Case

Acceptance ACT emphasizes the acceptance of present-moment experiences, including thoughts and feelings. Through their efforts to avoid or change these inevitable feelings, human beings decrease their behavioral freedom and may, as in the case of Ben, engage in experiential avoidance or control strategies that generate even more unwanted private experience. For instance, Ben was at times avoiding asking his wife about her day when they were together for fear that something she said would worry him or trigger a jealous reaction. As a result, Ben and his wife were talking less and less and he was feeling even less secure in their relationship. ACT teaches acceptance of private events as what they are. For Ben this meant accepting jealous feelings and thoughts about his wife's fidelity. ACT holds that thoughts do not have to be believed or disbelieved but merely experienced. For Ben, acceptance did not mean accepting the reality of his wife's infidelity, necessarily, just accepting that he had thoughts and feelings about her being unfaithful. The therapist worked to help Ben just to notice his thoughts and feelings mindfully and allow them to occur without trying to change them or argue with them. Part of this process for Ben was also actually learning to feel his anxiety in a somatic sense, noticing things like physical agitation or increased heart rate and focusing on them rather than trying to push them away.

Acceptance in the therapeutic relationship was also important in Ben's case. The therapist hypothesized in early sessions that Ben was ashamed of his feelings of jealousy and might expect the therapist to have judgmental reactions to his feelings and behavior. The therapist responded to the client's reports about his thoughts and behavior in an accepting manner without trying to reason with the client about his thoughts or behavior or to convince him to change, as he had been doing to himself. The therapist hypothesized it was important she not be alarmed or excessively concerned by his reports or behave in a way that suggested it was urgent for him to change, since this might affirm his worries that his jealousy was unacceptable, which would only increase a self-amplifying struggle. The therapist also helped Ben observe how he was behaving around his difficult thoughts and feelings in the relationship with the therapist, including his tendencies to look away when he felt emotional. Ben was able to notice he was looking away to avoid unwanted feelings. The therapist eventually encouraged him to try looking at her as he talked about difficult private events, as well as to work on noticing and accepting the thoughts and feelings this generated.

At first Ben reported this was difficult, but eventually Ben was surprised to find he noticed not only feelings of shame, but also positive feelings around the intimacy this authentic expression created. As therapy continued, Ben was able to take a more curious and accepting stance toward his thoughts and feelings rather than viewing them as problems to be solved. Ben began to notice more feelings of love for his wife and observe how these feelings often related to his jealous feelings. Ben eventually began to communicate more openly and directly with his wife about his feelings of both jealousy and love. Ben's wife responded to these communications in a way that deepened the intimacy of their relationship, and later in therapy Ben was surprised to find himself having far fewer of the jealous feelings he had learned to accept.

Defusion Acceptance is enabled by a context of cognitive defusion, in which thoughts are experienced as a process rather than as facts or products that are literally true or false. Thoughts often occur for human beings as reality, rather than words about reality. ACT exercises and teaching are targeted to create a context of cognitive defusion, where experiences like thoughts and feelings are labeled as *thoughts* and *feelings*, treated not as literal reality but as private events to be experienced that do not necessarily require any response (including avoidance or control). In the context of defusion, for example, Ben's thought "my wife could be at home with another man" could be noticed as just a thought ("I'm having a thought that my wife could be cheating on me") rather than as a literal reality prompting Ben to leave work to see if she was at home with another man. ACT encourages the awareness of thoughts through exercises that physicalize thoughts, emphasize their language nature, and treat them more playfully. Through increasing awareness of thoughts and undermining their literal quality, ACT aims to reduce their believability and thus increase the flexibility of the individual to behave with respect to his immediate environment.

For Ben, defusion work created a fundamental shift in the way he was relating to his worries about his wife. As Ben recognized his jealous thoughts as thoughts, he found it easier to not let them determine his behavior, thus increasing his sense of choice. In addition to allowing for more flexible behavior, cognitive defusion may help individuals to relax efforts to control private events. Ben also reported feeling less overwhelmed by his internal events when he accepted his thoughts rather than debating their reality within himself.

The therapist enhanced the work around defusion exercises in therapy by modeling defusion within herself and supporting a context of defusion in the therapeutic relationship. Modeling defusion included behavior like occasionally labeling thoughts as *thoughts* regardless of positive or negative content (beginning statements with "I'm having the thought that"), thus illustrating that defusion is not about avoiding negative thought content by labeling thoughts. Modeling defusion also involved the therapist not taking her thoughts too seriously, such as by smiling and saying, "I'm having the thought that I'm a terrible therapist," and moving on after a memory error.

Defusion also requires the therapist not to get too invested in the rightness or wrongness of clients' thoughts, which requires the therapist accepting her own feelings and thoughts around the thoughts the client discloses and not convincing or arguing with the client. In Ben's case, this at times required a delicate balance when he made statements suggesting he had decided to leave the wife he loved because his predicament was hopeless. The therapist needed to model both acceptance and defusion by responding with statements like, "It sounds like right now you are thinking that leaving is the only solution," and redirecting the client toward noticing the precipitating thoughts and feelings by following up with questions like, "Did some difficult thoughts and feelings come up today that led into this feeling of hopelessness?" Noticing and accepting thoughts and feelings within the client and within herself allows the therapist to recognize the client is sharing a thought about giving up and feelings of hopelessness distinct from the reality of the client actually giving up on therapy. Responding in an accepting and defused manner also requires the therapist noticing and accepting difficult thoughts around the possibility of the client actually leaving therapy, such as what the therapist might be doing wrong. If the therapist cannot react from an accepting and defused place because of a desire to control thoughts and feelings, the result will be a restriction in behavioral range that could result in less therapeutic responding.

Transcendent Sense of Self In the current Western cultural context, it is common to relate to oneself through content notions of self. These concepts of self are often focused on verbal descriptions and self-evaluations (I am a good/bad husband; I am a jealous person). These evaluative notions of self can give way to fused self-concepts that limit behavioral flexibility. ACT exercises promote the experience of a more transcendent sense of self, known in ACT as *self-as-context*. By *self-as-context* we mean the experience of a continuity of consciousness — the self as a perspective from which private events like thoughts (such as the evaluations previously iterated) and feelings are experienced. This profound sense of self seems similar to what existential psychologists refer to as an *I-am experience* or a *pure experience of being* (see Part 2).

Self-as-context defines the self as the arena in which thoughts and feelings occur, rather than the realm in which thoughts and feelings define the self. Since thoughts and feelings do not define who one is in this notion of self, awareness of thoughts and feelings is easier without attachment to what thoughts and feelings are. One of the goals of acceptance and cognitive defusion is the ability to be connected with immediate experience rather than language about experience. In the case of Ben, the therapist used the metaphor of a chessboard to explain self-as-context. In this metaphor the board represented this transcendent sense of self, and the pieces were Ben's thoughts. The black pieces represented Ben's unwanted thoughts, like, "My wife will leave me," whereas the white pieces represented the thoughts he used to try to reassure himself, like, "I'm a supportive husband." The metaphor illustrates the battle that is often going on with the client's thoughts, but also the nature of the self, as the board merely contains the pieces without any proclivity to have the battle go a certain way. ACT also uses experiential exercises to promote this sense of self in clients. Experiential exercises may focus on having clients notice changing feelings or bodily sensations, for example, and then note a consistent sense of consciousness that is present even as these experiences change.

Contact with the Present Moment ACT emphasizes presence to the moment and descriptive verbal observation of that experience, rather than verbal evaluations. This focus on description and immediate experience is very similar to mindfulness and meditation practice. From a present, descriptive standpoint, one can have private experience that is more in contact with the immediate world than the world of verbal evaluations or verbally constructed futures and pasts. From this perspective, one can appreciate experiences as they occur and respond more flexibly to the immediate environment.

For Ben, present moment work often involved "staying with" his emotional experience rather than trying to divert from it. When Ben began to touch on difficult feelings, or even warm feelings for his wife or the therapist, he would often change topics or begin talking quickly. The therapist would gently observe this process with Ben and try to bring him back to the feelings that were coming up for him in the moment and encourage him to observe and describe what he noticed around remaining present with that immediate experience. The therapist's presence with Ben was also important to this process. At one point early in the therapy Ben responded to it by becoming agitated and asking the therapist to stop looking at him. The therapist questioned him about his response, and Ben eventually reported feeling that the therapist's presence evoked emotion in him. Later in therapy Ben related the elucidation of this process in therapy to increased ability to be present with emotional communication to his wife.

Values ACT works to enhance psychological and behavioral flexibility in service of what individuals would aspire to pursue if their attention was not focused on avoiding private experiences. In other words, ACT aims to free up individuals to choose lives that are shaped by values rather than fear. ACT considers values to be verbally defined qualities of actions that are directions for life rather than goals to be met. Values are seen as guides for acting in ways individuals subjectively evaluate as reinforcing in everyday life. The space of behavioral flexibility created by other ACT processes allows values to be freely chosen ("I'd really like to be a loving and inspiring partner"), rather than dominated by fused verbal content ("I should value being a reliable provider"). Within the defused and accepting context that ACT processes support, value issues often emerge organically as therapy progresses. The work of the therapist can involve noting these values, but may also involve ACT exercises directing clients to better refine these values and separate them from fused verbal content.

Ben's initial report was that he was interested in therapy to get rid of his experiences of anxiety and jealousy. From the perspective of fusion and emotional avoidance, clients commonly will state that what they want out of therapy is the elimination of some part of their experience. From the standpoint of the ACT processes of acceptance, defusion, presence, and a transcendent sense of self, however, choice is possible. Ben later identified that what he really wanted out of therapy was not to lose his relationship with his wife. As ACT work progressed, this desire evolved into a real value — Ben began to find ways he valued being his wife's partner and to report more fulfillment and meaning in that relationship. Ben even began to extend some of his values around partnership with his wife to other relationships in his life, including those with his co-workers and family.

Committed Action ACT addresses the execution of valued actions through exercises focused on committed action. Committed action involves identifying barriers (such as difficult private events) as well as specific goals that are in the service of chosen values. Once values have been defined, the other ACT processes can be used to address psychological barriers that individuals see as problems in behaving with respect to those values. Ben set goals around improving the quality of his relationship with his wife at first, and later set more specific goals with respect to co-workers and family. Ben also began to look at what kept him from achieving these goals. For Ben, barriers to his values with respect to relationships often arose around difficult emotions. Ben often found himself behaving in ways that were not in service of the values he had chosen in therapy when he felt hurt, angry, or vulnerable.

At one point in time, the therapist was unable to see Ben for two different weeks in one month. When the therapist returned, Ben began the next session saying he felt he had completed the work he wanted to do in therapy and was ready to terminate. The therapist was surprised because Ben had expressed feeling that his work in therapy was continuing to enhance his relationship with his wife and seemed to be appreciating progress with ACT processes and relationships. When the therapist asked Ben about his reasons for ending, Ben cited his decreased jealousy but talked quickly and looked away from the therapist frequently, as he had earlier in therapy. When the therapist observed Ben's physical behavior and asked if this could in any way relate to her absences, Ben became tearful. As much as Ben had been seriously considering leaving a wife he loved because of difficult and vulnerable feelings in the relationship, Ben's emotional reaction to the therapist's absence led Ben to want to distance himself from the therapeutic relationship he was finding beneficial. Ben was able to relate these emotional barriers to the therapy with conflicts he had in other close relationships and, as a result, worked on noticing these barriers in the relationship with the therapist. By acting with respect to values and using ACT processes to identify barriers in the manner in which Ben did, larger and larger behavioral patterns of values-based action can be built. The client can also continue to apply these processes outside of therapy in service of a more valued, fully engaged, and behaviorally flexible life.

Case Outcome At the conclusion of therapy, Ben reported feeling his relationship with his wife was better than it had ever been. Ben and his wife were able to have conversations that Ben said he had previously avoided because of his own difficulties with experiencing emotional vulnerability. Ben reported that he actually felt more loved by his wife, both because of their greater intimacy and because of the development of their relationship in other areas. Ben reported having experiences of appreciation for his wife that he had never known prior to therapy. Ben admitted still feeling jealous or anxious about his wife's activities at times, but he no longer checked on her activities when he had these feelings. Ben reported he and his wife were also able to joke about some of his jealous reactions, an outcome he could never have imagined at the beginning of therapy. Ben reported feeling his relationships with co-workers and family had improved as he became more able to notice and discuss his feelings rather than be ruled by them. At the end of therapy, Ben stated, "It's not just that things are better — it's that I'm experiencing them better."

Humanism and Behaviorism

We have not attempted to describe this case in a fashion that deliberately connects the dots between a behavioral and experiential approach. Rather, we have described the case more or less in straightforward terms. It should be obvious, however, that the approach described overlaps in important ways with experiential approaches. It is our intention that this case be the grounds for a brief conversation about the nature of contemporary contextualistic behaviorism and its connection with humanistic psychology.

Although some humanistic psychologists (e.g., Schneider & May, 1995, this volume; Maslow, 1971) advocated exchange rather than an oppositional relationship between humanistic and behavioristic psychologies, there has been surprisingly little integration of these schools of thought. Most practicing therapists would probably acknowledge their mutual influence, but intellectual leaders in these traditions point to the seemingly deep philosophical and methodological divides. Like a dialogue between representatives of different political parties, often the differences themselves are characterized in mutually biased ways that make meaningful connections difficult. Roy José DeCarvalho points to the process: "Phenomenological and existential psychologists have deemed the positivist idea of experimental psychology to be philosophically immature. In return, experimental psychologists have considered . . . [phenomenological and existential psychologists'] study of consciousness and subjectivity as the pursuit of an illusion" (1991, p. 3). In addition to the differences in philosophy, differences at the level of investigative method are also stark. For example, qualitative and descriptive phenomenological methods and experimental research methods seem to exist in an almost orthogonal reality, with limited contact between them (Moss, 1999). This gulf has resulted in the sense on the part of many therapists that a choice must be made between addressing fundamental questions of human existence without support from a base of science and addressing symptomatology using focused empirically supported methods that may not contact the deep human questions of meaning, self, wholeness, or values.

The disconnection between humanism and behaviorism has been present from the beginning. In the eyes of its advocates, humanistic psychology was fueled in part by behaviorism's refusal to attend to the realities of human existence. Behaviorism's "focus on the commonalties between human and animal behavior" and lack of attention to "any aspects of conscious experiencing" were perceived as drawing "the borders for scientific discourse . . . too narrowly" (Moss, 1999, p. 21). For example, in *The Farther Reaches of Human Nature*, Abraham Maslow, one of the fathers of humanistic psychology, writes,

> I became interested in certain psychological problems, and found that they could not be answered or managed well by the classical scientific structure of the time (the behavioristic, positivistic, "scientific," value-free, mechanomorphic psychology). I was raising legitimate questions and had to invent another approach to psychological problems in order to deal with them. (1971, p. 3)

The "legitimate questions" Maslow was speaking of were such issues as meaning, values, and self — topics that behaviorists of the time largely eschewed. Relying on ideas in existential philosophy, humanistic thinkers found ways to approach these topics.

Contextualistic Behaviorism In order to take a peek at how a modern behavior therapy like ACT can possibly connect with experiential approaches, it is necessary to do a brief historical review of behaviorism. John Watson's classical methodological behaviorism was clearly, as Maslow says, a mechanistic form of psychology. B. F. Skinner's behavior analysis, however, was contextualistic, not mechanistic (Hayes, Hayes, & Reese, 1988). For one thing, mechanists assume that the world is made of parts, relations, and forces, and thus that it is the job of the analyst to model that machinery and test the correspondence between the model and reality. In contrast, Skinner grounded truth in human experience and purpose, not in the correspondence between knowledge and the objectively known world. For Skinner, what was true was what worked, and scientific laws or behavioral principles were rules to guide human action, not ontological conclusions. Scientific knowledge, he said,

> is a corpus of rules for effective action, and there is a special sense in which it could be "true" if it yields the most effective action possible. . . . A proposition is "true" to the extent that with its help the listener responds effectively to the situation it describes. (1974, p. 235)

Although introductory psychology books still mouth the belief that Skinner was only interested in overt behavior, in fact he overturned classical behaviorism's restrictions against consideration of the world within (Skinner, 1945) on the grounds that all scientific observations are acts of individuals, each with their own history and current purpose, and thus any fundamental distinction between an internal and external focus was artificial. In essence, he argued that all knowledge is based on our experience and interaction with the world, regardless of its formal focus (an idea notably similar to experiential and humanistic conceptions). He noted that a public event could be scientifically invalid even if there was good public agreement. For example, a group of teenagers going to see a rock concert could all be certain they just saw the rock star coming out of a store because of their motivation to see the star, not because of the formal properties of the person seen. Skinner noted that a feeling could be like that, too, and thus invalid (e.g., a school child complaining of a stomachache to avoid a math test), or it could be valid if the observation was regulated by the stimulation from the stomach. Thus, the issue was not whether events were inside or outside, or publicly agreed upon, but rather what was the history and context (or in "behavioralese," the contingencies) controlling the observation.

The theoretical and philosophical reasons that this promising opening did not lead to an actual robust behavioral approach to the world within is a sad tale that goes beyond the scope of this chapter, and further has already been related (e.g., Hayes et al., 2001). In a sentence, mistakes in Skinner's analysis of human language led him to conclude that human language and cognition do not alter how direct experiences establish human action, and thus an analysis of thoughts and feelings, while scientifically legitimate, would not help us understand what people do. When that error is put right — as ACT and RFT attempt to do — contextualistic behaviorism and humanistic thought come much closer together.

That would not be possible if the philosophical basis of this form of behavioral psychology was not contextualistic. There is a long list of topics that could be covered in an exploration of contextualism that might be relevant to our current task (see also the case study by Stolorow, Chapter 12). Given our limited space, a few of the key attributes can only be outlined, not fully defended.

Contextualism is holistic. An act and its context are one whole unit, which can be divided only in the limited sense that it may at times be pragmatically useful to focus on certain aspects of a whole event in order to further certain analytic goals. Ripping action from its context — its history and purpose — makes it impossible to appreciate its very nature because purpose, setting, and history are all key functional qualities of psychological events.

Actions are organized by their purposes and goals. Since this is true of scientists as well, it is important for scientists to state their goals a priori (Hayes, 1993).

The stated goals of functional contextualism are to predict and influence psychological interactions with precision, scope, and depth. This purpose is not a conclusion, but a choice, and thus it can only be stated, not justified (Hayes & Brownstein, 1986). It is a purpose that cannot be accomplished by analyses that deal only in psychological dependent variables (e.g., emotion, thought, overt action), because only the contextual aspects of a situated act can be directly altered. The environmentalism of behavior analysis is thus neither dogmatic nor mechanistic, but rather a pragmatic extension of its purpose.

Causality as an actual event is rejected, because any functional relation occurs only in a given context, and that in turn occurs only in a context, and so on, until the unity of totality is reached, and in that moment only silence is possible, since to speak of the totality is to partition it into two: the one and the speaking of the one. Instead, causality is merely a pragmatically useful way of speaking about ways of obtaining certain goals in a given context.

These philosophical issues are reflected almost point to point in ACT. There is a conscious posture of openness and acceptance toward all psychological events, even if they are formally negative, irrational, or even psychotic — the issue is not the presence of any particular event, but rather its contextually established function and meaning. The foundational nature of goals in contextualism is reflected in the great emphasis in ACT on chosen values as a necessary component of a meaningful life (and similarly a meaningful course of treatment). The pragmatic view of truth is reflected in the way that ACT clients are encouraged to abandon interest in the literal truth of their own thoughts or evaluations, and instead to embrace a passionate and ongoing interest in how to live according to their values and to use workability as a guide.

ACT and RFT Clinicians observing ACT therapy for the first time are much more likely to relate it to humanistic, existential, and relational approaches than to traditional behavioral or cognitive therapy. For instance, the pervasive concept of presence in psychotherapy is consistent with ACT's present-moment focus. What is unique about ACT is that it allows these techniques to be addressed not only in terms of clinical language, but in terms of basic science processes without diminishing or oversimplifying profound human questions that therapeutic work can meaningfully address.

If the basic science foundation of ACT is correct, language is at the center of the human ability to suffer above and beyond other creatures, and suffer even in the midst of plenty. The core existential issues of meaning, isolation, freedom, and death are unique to human beings because they are related to language processes. Existential psychotherapy emphasizes human conflicts with the givens of existence, and an awareness of these inherent elements of our shared humanity is at the core of ACT's empathic approach to human suffering as well as its mechanisms of therapeutic change. Within this model, behavioral problems are viewed in terms of common pathological processes related to language, rather than health and disorder, reducing the tendency to stigmatize human struggles. Similarly, these processes are not considered unique to the client, but rather are acknowledged as common parts of the human experience to which the therapist is subject as well, creating additional opportunities for therapeutic intervention at the level of therapist modeling and therapist-client interaction.

From an ACT/RFT perspective, language allows humans to solve problems and plan for meaningful futures, but it can just as easily trap us in self-evaluations that disengage us from our experience and create a way for us to become anxious about future events that have never occurred. The fundamental concept of RFT is the learned ability of verbal humans to relate events, bidirectionally and in combination, under arbitrary contextual control (arbitrary in the sense of created by social agreements). For example, if we learn that public speaking is said to be more anxiety provoking than expressing feelings, and being evaluated by others is more anxiety provoking than public speaking, it can be derived that being evaluated is also more anxiety provoking than expressing feelings. These relationships enable the transformation of stimulus functions, meaning that the psychological functions of one event in a verbal network may alter the functions of the other events. If a client with the above situational relationships to anxiety had a panic attack during an evaluation, he might very well begin to avoid public speaking and emotional expression for fear of having a panic attack as well, even though he had never actually experienced a panic attack in those situations. The simple idea that learned and arbitrarily applicable relations underlie cognition has proven to be powerful in many ways (Hayes et al., 2001). Clinically it has led to several key ideas.

Experiential Avoidance and Loss of Contact With the Present One of the most pathological processes known is experiential avoidance: the attempt to escape or avoid private events, even when the attempt to do so causes psychological harm (Hayes, Wilson, Gifford, Follette, & Strosahl, 1996). RFT suggests that such processes are built into human language and cognition itself, for four basic reasons. The bidirectionality of human language means that pain can be experienced anywhere regardless of the situation, and the predictive and evaluative aspects of language amplify the symbolic contact with negative consequences, even in the absence of actual contact. The arbitrary aspect of language makes these processes devilishly difficult to rein in and, almost in desperation, a person will begin to attempt to avoid pain itself. Unfortunately, many of these means (e.g., suppression) will ultimately come to cue the avoided event because they strengthen the underlying verbal relations between the avoided event and feared consequences.

These verbal processes constantly pull us all out of the moment and into the desired or feared future. As a result, there is a sense of emptiness or loss of vitality as we become increasingly entangled in the verbal war within.

Meaning and Purpose Behavioral psychologists always emphasized purpose, but they analyzed it primarily in terms of the consequences of action.

Verbal relations allow a different kind of purpose: the verbal constructed consequence of action.

Contextual Change Strategies Finally, RFT specifies both that it is terribly hard to modify cognitive networks in their form (since they are learned) and that we can reduce the *impact* of thought via contextual means even if we do not alter the *form* of thought.

Psychological Flexibility and Experiential Liberation It is remarkable the degree to which the goals and processes of ACT and RFT reflect, and in may ways cohere with, existential-integrative concepts. It is particularly remarkable because there was no intention to create such a connection by either party to this conversation.

ACT aims to recontextualize experience through the six processes that create psychological flexibility. The first four ACT processes of acceptance, defusion, a transcendent sense of self, and attention to the present moment are considered to be mindfulness processes that promote engagement with direct experience, as opposed to merely the structured and symbolized world. The second two processes of values and commitment are focused on enhancing the client's choices and effective actions. This enhancement involves using language to construct valued futures that can direct behavior.

The dialectic between contacting the present openly and without needless defense, and channeling that into an organized life parallels the dialectic between expansion and constriction in an EI approach. The core integrative process of psychological flexibility seems quite similar to that of experiential liberation, especially in the ways that it is fostered.

According to Kirk Schneider (2007, this volume), the four therapeutic processes that promote experiential liberation are presence, invoking the actual, vivifying and confronting resistance, and cultivating meaning and awe. Each of these are reflected in an ACT model, although not in a point-to-point manner. Presence and invoking the actual seem to be related to the ACT ideas of a transcendent sense of self and contact with the present moment. ACT principles apply to process as well as content levels in therapy. ACT therapists do not merely discuss ACT principles and guide the client through experiential exercises. ACT principles also guide the therapist and the therapist's interactions with the client. For instance, the therapist's presence in the moment will enable the creation of more psychologically flexible space not only for the therapist, but also in the interactions between the client and therapist. From the present, engaged, and emotionally accepting space created by the ACT processes the client can more freely choose and move toward an experientially liberated life.

Vivifying resistance is similar to the ACT process of creative hopelessness — an acceptance-based procedure that is designed to amplify the client's awareness of how attempts to solve his or her problem have blocked real progress.

Contacting a sense of self-as-context is designed to ground experiences in a continuous process of knowing. As with Schneider's concept of centering, it is thought to foster choice and greater psychological flexibility. Guided defused contact with experience is commonly used in ACT — very much as guided (or embodied) meditation is used in existential-integrative therapy. But perhaps the single biggest overlap is in the area of values.

Values in ACT and in Humanistic Psychology No topic has been more important in humanistic thinking than values. Maslow (1971) emphasized the importance of defining one's own values grounded in direct experience, rather than seeking external advice on choices and behavior:

> What we have learned is that ultimately, the best way for a person to discover what he ought to do is to find out who and what he is, because the path to ethical and value decisions, to wiser choices, to oughtness, is via "isness," via the discovery of facts, truth, reality, the nature of the particular person. The more he knows about his own nature, his deep wishes, his temperament, his constitution, what he seeks and yearns for and what really satisfies him, the more effortless, automatic, and epiphenomenal become his value choices. . . . Many problems simply disappear; many others are easily solved by knowing what is in conformity with one's nature, what is suitable and right. (p. 111)

Maslow regarded this values quest as a central part of therapy that provides the answers to other questions that might otherwise be mistakenly posed to sources other than oneself. In the context of values, the client's challenge was to integrate an ideal self-concept with the perception of the actual self, a process that led Maslow (1971) to refer to psychotherapy as an "ought-is-quest." Maslow believed that facts and values could be united through increased acceptance of one's self and the rethinking of concepts of the ideal self.

Carl Rogers's client-centered therapy similarly emphasized the role of the client's values in therapy, and like Maslow, Rogers fostered the idea of a self within to be uncovered. Rogers was particularly struck by a passage in *The Sickness unto Death* where Kierkegaard claims that "to be that self which one truly is" is the purpose of life, which he interpreted to mean that the greatest tragedy was not the difficulty of becoming what one wants to be, but rather the mistaken desire to be something else (DeCarvalho, 1991, p. 62). Rogers compares the operative values of human infants to the conceived values of human adults, many of which Rogers points out are contradictory and illogical introjections of external sources, but which individuals still regard as their own. Rogers (1964) suggests that the usual adult has allowed these external introjections and "lost touch with his own valuing process," and thus feels afraid to reconsider what his actual values are:

> This fundamental discrepancy between the individual's concept and what he is actually experiencing, between the intellectual structure of his values and the valuing process going on unrecognized within — this is a part of the fundamental estrangement of modern man from himself. (p. 163)

Rogers emphasized the importance of a therapist's genuineness and unconditional positive regard for the client, which he believed would encourage the client's movement toward self-actualization and pursuit of his true values.

Rogers also challenged the idea that science can be value-free. He pointed out that the initiation of any scientific endeavor involves the choice of the value that the enterprise is seen as serving, and thus that science is the objective pursuit of a subjectively chosen purpose (Rogers, 1961). The implication is that one must attend to the subjective goals within which even objective pursuits occur, an idea that applies to psychology in practice as well as research.

> There is no philosophy or belief or set of principles which I could encourage or persuade others to have or hold. I can only try to live by my interpretation of the current meaning of my experience, and try to give others the permission and freedom to develop their own inward freedom and thus their own meaningful interpretation of their own experience. (p. 27)

Rogers's approach to therapy underscores his beliefs in the client's own resources for positive change, resources that include the client's values.

Rollo May interpreted the role of human values somewhat differently, but still emphasized their importance. In his dissertation, "The Meaning of Anxiety," he explained anxiety as a response to threats to human values. May recognized the existence of a state similar to the one Rogers described in "Toward a Modern Approach to Values" (1964) in which human beings have lost touch with themselves and what their values are. May believed that the anxiety resulting from this state could be used constructively as a normal part of growth, but, if left unaddressed, the anxiety could also turn neurotic. May saw the goal of therapy as dealing with this anxiety effectively. In his later book, *Psychology and the Human Dilemma*, May went on to emphasize the importance of using this anxiety to discover an inner center that could be easily explained in terms of values (DeCarvalho, 1991).

Values in ACT are emphasized equally strongly. Values are viewed as choices that in turn give meaning to human action. In accord with contextualistic philosophy it is only within the context of values that action, acceptance, and defusion come together into a sensible whole, because they determine the meaning and purpose of acceptance and defusion. Values dignify the acceptance of specific painful thoughts and feelings, and those painful thoughts and feelings can take on new meaning in a valued context. ACT is not about endless emotional wallowing; rather, it involves "taking in" what one's history offers in the process of living a valued life.

For that reason, ACT therapists often do values-clarification work before other ACT components. ACT therapists often ask their clients, "What do you want your life to stand for?" and provide exercises that take clients into the present moment to develop more clarity about fundamental values. For example, the ACT therapist may ask the client to write out what he or she would most like to see on his or her tombstone, or the eulogy he or she would want to hear at his or her own funeral, or what the implicit values are that are on the other side of painful experience. In essence, this focuses verbal processes away from literal truth toward psychological meaning and motivation. When values are clarified, achievable goals that embody those values, concrete actions that would produce those goals, and specific barriers to performing these actions are identified.

Conclusion

Language makes the human achievements of technology and artistry possible, yet this same language allows us to lose touch with experiencing our very existence. This tension between the creative possibilities of language and the risk of losing awareness of direct experience exists in the process of therapy.

If language is as fundamental in human suffering and human potentials as we conjecture, therapists for whom language is the primary tool must consider some difficult questions. Therapists are required not only to navigate the complexities of processing language with their clients at a rapid pace, but also to make discriminations about function within this processing. The language processing in question occurs not only at the level of the client presenting a target problem, but also at the level of the therapist and in the exchange between the therapist and the client. Any model applied to these processes will, in its very language nature, provide an imperfect mirror and at times separate us from directly experiencing. The structure of a therapeutic model, however, can also provide a compass to navigate the complexities of therapy. Acceptance and commitment therapy is such a compass and, we hope, a compass that will support exploration of meaningful clinical work and meaningful living in the continuing development of therapy as well as its application.

References

DeCarvalho, R. J. (1991). *The founders of humanistic psychology.* New York: Praeger.

Hayes, S. C. (1993). Analytic goals and the varieties of scientific contextualism. In S. C. Hayes, L. J. Hayes, H. W. Reese, & T. R. Sarbin (Eds.), *Varieties of scientific contextualism* (pp. 11–27). Reno, NV: Context Press.

Hayes, S. C., Barnes-Holmes, D., & Roche, B. (Eds.). (2001). *Relational frame theory: A post-Skinnerian account of human language and cognition.* New York: Kluwer Academic/Plenum Press.

Hayes, S. C., & Brownstein, A. J. (1986). Mentalism, behavior-behavior relations and a behavior analytic view of the purposes of science. *The Behavior Analyst, 1,* 175–190.

Hayes, S. C., Hayes, L. J., & Reese, H. W. (1988). Finding the philosophical core: A review of Stephen C. Pepper's *World Hypotheses. Journal of Experimental Analysis of Behavior, 50,* 97–111.

Hayes, S. C., Strosahl, K. D., & Wilson, K. G. (1999). *Acceptance and Commitment Therapy: An experiential approach to behavior change.* New York: Guilford Press.

Hayes, S. C., Wilson, K. G., Gifford, E. V., Follette, V. M., & Strosahl, K. (1996). Emotional avoidance and behavioral disorders: A functional dimensional approach to diagnosis and treatment. *Journal of Consulting and Clinical Psychology, 64,* 1152–1168.

Maslow, A. H. (1971). *The farther reaches of human nature.* New York: Viking Press.

Moss, D. (Ed.). (1999). *Humanistic and transpersonal psychology: A historical and biographical sourcebook.* Westport, CT: Greenwood Press.

Rogers, C. R. (1961). *On becoming a person: A therapist's view of psychotherapy.* Boston: Houghton Mifflin.

Rogers, C. R. (1964). Toward a modern approach to values: The valuing process in the mature person. *Journal of Abnormal and Social Psychology, 68,* 160–167.

Schneider, K. J., & May, R. (1995). *The psychology of existence: An integrative, clinical perspective.* New York: McGraw-Hill.

Schneider, K. J. (2007). The experiential liberation strategy of the existential-integrative model of therapy. *Journal of Contemporary Psychotherapy, 37,* 1, 33–39.

Skinner, B. F. (1945). The operational analysis of psychological terms. *Psychological Review, 52,* 270–276.

Skinner, B. F. (1974). *About behaviorism.* New York: Knopf.

11
EI Approaches to Severe States

The healing of severe forms of suffering is one of the chief concerns of a comprehensive existential-integrative paradigm. Aside from a few formalized studies of existentially oriented mediation with psychoses (e.g., see *The Divided Self*, by R. D. Laing; *Spiritual Emergency*, by Stan and Christina Grof; and the chapter, "Madness Without Hospitals," by Loren Mosher from *The Handbook of Humanistic Psychology*), there has been a paucity of quality investigations. This section is an attempt to redress this tragic gap in the psychological and psychiatric literature. Beginning with his fitful experiences as a young psychiatric resident, Daniel Dorman shows how early on, he valued the understanding of patients' identity development over the disease model for treating severe disturbances. Like his philosophical predecessor R. D. Laing, Dr. Dorman went beyond the standardized armamentarium for patient care and cultivated an attentive authenticity to his clients, neither downplaying nor overdramatizing their personal and practical challenges. In his featured reflection on "Catherine Penney," a 19-year-old "schizophrenic" with whom he worked for seven years, he shows how a nonmedicalizing relationship that included discerning authenticity, loving patience, and dogged persistence can coincide with practical realities (e.g., hospitalization, rehab, etc.) to transform a world.

In the second case, Ed Mendelowitz ponders one of the most perplexing conditions known to human science — the extreme dissociative disorder known as multiple personality. While this case is ostensibly about an extraordinary and rarified condition, it is also about the metaphorical insights offered by that condition. In his riveting study of "Kristina," Dr. Mendelowitz articulates a multifaceted understanding of an internal universe, replete with selves, societies, and spirits. While it is plain that Kristina is extraordinary — just witness her drawings — Mendelowitz does not overemphasize this singularity; instead, he shows how Kristina's individual struggle echoes our collective and indeed human battle to coexist with and integrate our rivaling impulses. Moreover, it is precisely this coexistence — and not the homogenized norm — that is at the heart of Mendelowitz's stance; our object is not to rid clients of their splits, but to help them form new relationships with those splits — or to put it in the words of his patient: to help them "go along with the flow."

Dante's Cure: Schizophrenia and the Two-Person Journey

Daniel Dorman

Daniel Dorman, MD, received his medical training at Indiana University School of Medicine, followed by an internship at Georgetown University Division, District of Columbia General Hospital. He practiced family medicine before his psychiatry residency at the University of California at Los Angeles (UCLA). Dr. Dorman is the author of *Dante's Cure: A Journey out of Madness*. He is an assistant professor of psychiatry at UCLA and in private practice in Beverly Hills.

As I see it, the aim of psychotherapy is to promote or catalyze the experience of existence in the other. Cognitive-behavioral, psychodynamic, and psychoanalytic approaches can all be viewed within the context of adding to one's experience, as can aspects of all relationships. Existence means that my client develops the freedom to experience his self, his *I*.

To this end, some years ago, I set out to discover how a person's *I* develops, and what might have obstructed that development. As a young psychiatrist-in-training at the UCLA's Neuropsychiatric Institute, I had access to those who, I thought, struggled with a diminished sense of personal existence. Despite my medical training, I never bought the medical model explanation of mental distress. Depression, a clinical term for sadness, is seen as a "symptom" of mental disease, as is anxiety (fear), panic (terror), and nearly all the rest of our emotional lives. To conceptualize feeling states only as illnesses or chemical interactions is to equate brain with mind, thus a denial of the human experience.

In order to learn about *I* development, I chose to work with those who seemed to struggle the most — people diagnosed as schizophrenic. I made an assumption that the person labeled *schizophrenic* suffered from a severe disruption of *I* development. I made an additional assumption that since at least a part of *I* development occurs within the context of family life, that is, life with other human beings, perhaps I could enter into the schizophrenic's world in a psychotherapeutic relationship; then I might discover the nature of his developmental arrest and find a way to help him (Laing, 1969).

Before I talk about the details of the successful treatment of a severely schizophrenic young woman, I need to back up a bit and elaborate on what I mean by *I* development.

Creative intelligence, the ability to symbolize and manipulate symbols, was the great evolutionary advance that began with *Ramapithecus* 12 million years ago. *Ramapithecus* later diversified into *Australopithecine* and *Homo* descendants, giving rise to creatures who possessed the ability to adapt to changing environments, thus freeing them from the restriction of life within a fixed environmental niche (Leaky & Lewin, 1977). On a neurophysiological level, creative intelligence is mediated in a way that argues convincingly against the reductive fixed-response medical model of the mind. In *The Origin of Minds: Evolution, Uniqueness, and the New Science of the Self,* Peggy La Cerra and Roger Bingham (2002) talk about the human brain's remarkable capacity to "adapt to on-line experience." Adaptation is accomplished by constant rewiring — experience modifies brain function and anatomy. Neuronal real estate is added when experience dictates. For example, learn to play the piano and the brain areas that represent the fingers of your hand traveling over the keys enlarge. La Cerra and Bingham tell us that even imagining playing produces similar changes in the cortex. But the authors offer us a caveat: The task has to be important to the individual, not merely repetitive.

Since evaluating and managing constant change is the salient characteristic of the great evolutionary advance, how are our brains different? La Cerra and Bingham (2002) talk about the neurophysiological concept of adaptive representational networks, that is, creative intelligence mediated not by individual neurons with fixed responses, but by networks of neurons acting together with the unique ability to modify themselves. In *Blaming the Brain: The Truth About Drugs and Mental Health*, Elliot Valenstein (1998) discusses the integrated action of more than 20 billion neurons, each with as many as 10,000 connections. If we understand these connections as smaller networks, each responding to changes in input from the constantly changing environment and to each other, we can see the basis for a system of monitoring both the external and internal worlds.

These adaptive representational networks allow us to link events and establish causality. One result is a record of our own unique history, a composite picture of ourselves over time, self-representation fashioned at many levels. This self-representation — millions of neuronal networks, representing millions of associations — constitute our ever-changing experience of who we are, our experience of *I*, if you will. Since each person's experiences are different, each, in turn, has a unique *I*. My experience of my self is not just a passive observation of my history of experiences. I can also form new neuronal networks to explain, to make sense of seeming inconsistencies, and more networks to make predictions, resulting in a creative intelligence with regard to my self-perceptions.

Our sense of our unique selves is critical because the self is our reference point against which we assess our perceptions. The potential annihilation of the *I*, that central reference point, is a threat to survival because it is experienced as an inability to narrate or to perceive. Great effort is expended in order to maintain the integrity of the self. Much of that integrity depends on explanatory consistency. In other words, we explain to ourselves inconsistencies in self-perception. An example is the child's explanation that he must have done something wrong in response to observing his mother's distress, a threat to his survival. The child then elaborates upon his explanation, weaving a personal construction regarding his future behavior that might prevent this from happening again. His personal construction derives from his ability to imagine multiple situations at the same time. He chooses the one that seems to best preserve his safety. He seeks an explanation that will bring his mother's distress under his control.

Julian Jaynes (1990), in his book *The Origin of Consciousness in the Breakdown of the Bicameral Mind*, writes about the development of consciousness and the struggle with *I* development. He regards the need to narrate to ourselves as critical. He gives as examples the thief who narrates his actions in the context of poverty, the poet who narrates his writing due to the inspiration of beauty, and the scientist who narrates his work on the basis of a search for the truth. Jaynes (1990, p. 64) states, "A strong fact is narrated to fit with some other strong fact. A child cries in the street and we narrate the event into a mental picture of a lost child and a parent searching for it." Or we narrate, or explain to ourselves, that a cat in a tree was chased there by a dog. Our many explanations are part and parcel of our daily lives. We often do not notice the inconsistencies, or even the falsity of many of them, for that would expose us to further inconsistencies. Consider the many explanations we accept in order to declare to ourselves that we are not helpless: touching a statue of Que Lin, the Buddhist goddess of compassion; the ancient Greek reliance on explanations given by the sibyls at Delphi, Cumae, and a dozen other sites; Mayan human sacrifice, voodoo, the lucky rabbit's foot, and other amulets designed to ward off danger. Politicians capitalize on the explanations people need. Many people are ready to believe that threats to their survival can be warded off by making war on those of another faith or color. Scientists, too, ignore inconsistencies in the interest of propping up their identities. Look at how the medical model of mental life is defended with such ferocity.

If, instead of classifying an individual's explanations as mad or sane, we try to understand him, we gain insight into his state of mind. For example, a woman I see told me that at age 6 she psychologically removed herself from what she experienced as an intolerable family life. From that point on, she experienced herself standing off to the side, an observer of her own life. Since that time she played only roles. She knew that these roles did not represent her true self. She sought therapy not because someone had labeled her as *mentally ill*, but because she was suffering. A registered nurse, she regularly cut her abdomen and also took to inserting a hypodermic needle into the artery at her wrist. I asked her why she did that, and she said, "I have this need to watch the blood spurt out. Then I know that I'm alive."

I replied, "So, you're dead."

"Yes," she said. She experienced herself as psychically dead. Her behavior was her narrative, her attempt to make sense of her dilemma and to reassure herself that she was, indeed, alive.

I am suggesting that the psychotic person's explanations are examples of the very same struggle as anyone else's, namely, his effort to resolve inconsistencies in order to preserve his personal identity, his *I*. His so-called thought disorder is largely composed of explanations designed to relieve his suffering and to make sense of his world (see also Laing, 1969). But why do some people suffer so much? The woman I referred to above knew, deep within, that she was psychically dead, that her *I* hardly existed. I think that we cannot fool our own souls. The suffering individual creates additional explanations to keep his suffering at bay. Either the suffering leaks through anyway, or his explanations become tangled or extreme, which also causes suffering. If we listen to the stories of people whose suffering has reached psychotic proportions, they regularly tell us that they are struggling with the very existence of their personal identities. Schreber, Sigmund Freud's famous patient, talked about soul murder. A schizophrenic man talked about having "no nucleus, no central self." Another said, "Gradually I can no longer distinguish how much of myself is in me, and how much is already in others. I am a conglomeration, a monstrosity modeled anew each day" (Jaynes, 1990, p. 418).

These narratives of psychotic persons often tell us a great deal about the experience of a greatly diminished or even absent *I*. Psychotic people often complain of time standing still. Julian Jaynes has this to say:

> Another way the dissolving of mind-space shows itself is in the disorientation in respect to time so common in the schizophrenic. We can only be conscious of time as we can arrange it into a spatial succession, and the diminishing of mind-space in schizophrenia makes this difficult or impossible. (1990, p. 421)

Jaynes's mind-space is the internal space where *I* resides. The schizophrenic tries to tie his answers to external circumstances. When the schizophrenic says he is commanded by outside forces, the psychiatrist regards it as a delusion, a falsification of reality, but as Jaynes notes, "With the loss of the analog 'I,' its mind-space, and the ability to narrate, behavior either responds to hallucinated direction, or continues on by habit. The remnant of self feels like a commanded automaton" (1990, p. 423).

I wish to emphasize that none of the experiences I have just referred to are exclusive to people suffering from schizophrenia. If we look at people who suffer excessive anxiety, we can see similar phenomena. Anxious individuals are afraid, sometimes of even going out of the house. If you ask them what they are afraid of, they may well tell you about external circumstances — that lightning might strike them or that they will become lost while driving. They fear personal catastrophe. This is the catastrophe that people falling into schizophrenia feel as what is left of their mind-space erodes. Anorexics experience similar processes. It is difficult, nearly impossible, to persuade an anorexic to give up what she calls control, her rigid dieting. But what is she controlling?

Ask most anorexics and you will get the same answer: the overwhelming anxiety of personal disaster, the terror of loss of self. The struggle that is anorexia usually begins in adolescence, as does schizophrenia, and for the same reason. It is at this time of life that one begins to enter adulthood and the larger world. So it is no wonder that the experience of self-dissolution occurs at this time. Anorexia, excessive anxiety, and schizophrenia are not different diseases. They are syndromes that reflect different responses to the same problem.

In order to demonstrate how these syndromes can be addressed, let me return to my schizophrenic patient. I will tell you about "Catherine Penney," who completely recovered from severe schizophrenia through psychotherapy alone. Catherine's treatment lasted nearly 8 years. No medications were used. I saw her 6 days a week during her 3½-year hospitalization, then 5 days a week as an outpatient for just over 2 years, then 3 days a week for another 2 years, a total of 8 years. It is not my intent to declare that a therapeutic context is the only way out of the experience of psychosis. Rather, I wish to demonstrate some very human principles, one of which is how one human being can be of help to another.

Catherine was a shy child, symbiotically attached to her mother. She developed few friends during her elementary school years. At age 17, she began a draconian diet and lost 20 pounds in about 6 months. She began repeating the names of certain foods to herself and ritually stored and nibbled on pies her mother bought for her. At 5 feet 5 inches tall and 100 pounds, she looked all skin and bones. At age 18 she began to hear voices, at first one voice telling her to kill herself, then several voices telling her to kill her mother, and finally a chorus of voices screeching at her to kill other members of her family. Catherine prayed on her knees before a small altar in her darkened room, sometimes for days at a time. She was hospitalized twice, diagnosed as schizophrenic, and placed on the antipsychotic drugs Thorazine and Stelazine. The voices receded, but did not go away. Catherine sat nonresponsive in her senior high school classes, looking down with her chin resting on her chest.

I was a first-year resident in psychiatry at UCLA when I first met 19-year-old Catherine. I saw the use of medication as a means to suppress symptoms, without touching the individual, her core, her meaning, or why she suffered. I thought that psychotherapy was at least worth a try. Catherine rarely spoke, except to complain about her diet and ward life. Our mostly silent hours lasted throughout her three years at UCLA. Once she said, "Why don't you get up and leave?" I sometimes mused aloud about her distress, or what might have led to such a state. In little increments, usually only a sentence or two in any hour, she began to describe the horror of her madness. She seemed disinterested in anything I had to say. She lost more weight, to 85 pounds, and sat catatonic on the dayroom couch. She shut down to such an extent that she did not even swallow her own saliva — she drooled all over the front of her dress, which became so soaked that spittle hung in strands from the hem. She insisted on keeping crumbs of leftover pies brought by her mother on Sunday visits, and she silently repeated the names of a few foods over and over. The hospital staff prodded her to attend occupational therapy and other ward activities. She refused to bathe and often appeared in the mornings with her teeth caked, her hair in tangles, and in yesterday's clothes. The nurses had to scrub her down. Catherine closed her eyes about six months after she was admitted to the hospital. She walked about peering through slits, often bumping into chairs and tables, and was left in the back of a crowded elevator a few times. In the dining room she usually just pushed her food around on the plate, and I had to threaten force feeding if her weight dropped below 85 pounds. She managed to keep her weight at 84½ pounds. Late into the second year of treatment she occasionally asked me for my opinion about her experiences.

I was under enormous pressure from the staff to medicate her. I was accused in open staff meetings of conducting an experiment and of ignoring the Hippocratic oath in that she was so obviously in pain. I had to resist pressure from my superiors to discharge her to a chronic care facility. I answered my detractors by questioning standard treatment (use of drugs) as providing only a cover-up, and asked how it was that the other residents and staff members only saw their patients for a few minutes at a time, hardly enough to gain any understanding of their problems. I was fortunate that the ward chief, although a biologically oriented psychiatrist, respected my work and allowed me to continue. After three years and no visible progress, I did become despairing. I was buoyed only by the fact that Catherine never missed an appointment. She was always waiting for me, leaning up against the wall, her head bowed down upon her chest.

At the end of my residency I transferred Catherine to a private mental hospital. About two months later, she opened her eyes for the first time in nearly three years. I remember the moment vividly. Catherine announced that her eyelids had been "fluttering." Then, pop, just like the sudden opening of window shades, she opened her eyes. She informed me that she was bored, that the same old routine of hiding out and fighting the staff was deadening. She wanted to "see" the world. So, we began to talk of the world and how she might take up her development. Four months later she moved into a small apartment. At this time Catherine became profoundly depressed. She knew how developmentally backward she was and felt that she would never catch up. She thought about killing herself. She persisted, however. Catherine tried to take some classes at the local junior college, failed, and repeated the classes. Her voices went away, never to return. She gradually gained a foothold, eventually graduating and going on to obtain a degree as a registered nurse. Today, 30 years later, Catherine works for the county, responsible for the medical needs of a large indigent population. She has been a member of a county commission on elder abuse and is a consultant to a nonprofit county agency responsible for administering mental health grants. After her recovery, Catherine suggested we write a book about how that occurred. The result was *Dante's Cure: A Journey out of Madness* (Dorman, 2004), so named because Virgil served as Dante's guide to the underworld.

I see psychotherapeutic treatment as helping an individual affirm what is left of his sense of self and helping him expand and develop that self. Affirmation is not empty acknowledgment. It is a learning process. The therapist must learn, truly understand his patient's situation, his experience. The therapist and his patient discover the patient's internal world at the same moment. The validity of experience is what learning is all about. If we sense that another person is truly affected by, or is trying to understand, our experiences, we gain a sense of the validity of our own experience. In the therapeutic context, I am trying to do just that. I was taught during my analytic training to listen for evidence of the oedipal conflict and for psychosexual development. Trying to fit the other person's experiences into our theories is not listening at all. Learning about Catherine meant that I found out that Catherine became catatonic "to get around being violent." She also told me that thinking itself was overwhelming, so she had to "go down inside myself."

Catherine's silence was a reflection of her existential state. It is my job to respect my patient's state of mind and to attempt to understand it. To this end I contented myself with quietly sitting by with occasional queries, such as, "I wonder what your silence means?" She never answered me. Rather, she asked one or two questions about ward life. Frequently she asked, "Do I have to go to occupational therapy?" or "Do I have to eat with the other patients?" I typically answered, "Yes, that is part of ward life here." After her recovery, Catherine told me that she regarded my questions as indicating interest in her condition. In her inner world, she "put up an antenna," meaning that, despite her silence, she responded with a nascent interest in therapy.

I could not help but notice Catherine's posture — she sat hunched over with her hands clasped together on her lap, her fingers in constant motion, twisting and turning upon each other. I tend not to make comments such as, "I can see you are in distress." Nor do I confront patients, because I am careful about the line between attempting to understand meanings and therapeutic intrusion. I prefer not to ask how a patient feels (e.g., "How does that make you feel?") Catherine's long silences and gnashing her fingers, for example, were how she felt. The therapist only reveals his lack of understanding his patients' narratives by asking such questions. I also tend not to declare a patient's state of mind. For example, the comment, "You look like you are in agony," is an example of therapeutic intrusion. Such a comment is redundant and often smacks of trying to force the patient into a discussion of his feelings. He will discuss his feelings when he is ready. I phrase most of my commentary as questions, since I assume all of my understanding as tentative, to be confirmed or denied by my patient. It has served me well to begin with "Perhaps . . ." Early in Catherine's treatment I mused aloud, "Perhaps your silence means a safe and cozy place for you. The world can be a frightening place." Catherine did not answer, but told me after she recovered that she was struck by my attempt to understand her.

The learning process is not one way. Catherine was learning about me, too. As she discovered that I understood her, she began to trust some of my perceptions about her. How did she know that I understood her in the first place? It is a paradox that despite what seems to be a relative lack of self, there is, nevertheless, a self. In the end, I think that the problem is a lack of trust in the self, which is experienced as having little or no self. Catherine could feel whether I appreciated her authenticity. She later told me that she knew that I was authentic, which was important in allowing her to trust my perceptions. In the third year of treatment, Catherine began to share some of her inner world — the horror of the voices, her isolation, and her appreciation of how crazy she was. "I should be sent away," she often said.

I attempted to offer her a context for her experiences, such as saying, "I can see how you would feel futile — you can see no possibility of escape, can you?"

"I'm hopeless," she replied. I did not declare that there was hope, since I did not know that, and it was apparent by my investment in treatment that there might be hope.

There were three phases in Catherine's treatment. I think that these phases occur in any treatment, often mixed up together or overlapping, and not as clear as they were with Catherine. The first was marked by an acknowledgment and addition process (Ver Eecke, 2002). I acknowledged that Catherine was a person whose true thoughts and feelings could be appreciated. She, in turn, began to appreciate my experience of her, including my efforts to understand the origin of her experiences. The combination added bits and pieces of *I* to her individual self-system until she developed enough *I* through appreciation of her own experience to at least partially separate from me.

The second phase, partial separation from me, began when Catherine opened her eyes. She quickly developed a hunger for new experience, her experience. It was during this time that she moved into her own apartment — away from the identity of a "sick" person needing others to help her with many of the basic details of living. She began the process of affirming her independent identity. On one hand, during this phase, I acknowledged the truth of her vast insecurity, and on the other, a truth she could not know, that growth and development were possible.

In this phase, my role expanded from that of a guide to Catherine's internal world to helping her understand the external world. Again, one needs to be careful of therapeutic intrusion. For example, Catherine started to explore the man-woman world. She and a woman friend frequented a local bar where bands played dance music on weekends. Catherine was very naïve, and I struggled with whether to warn her of the obvious (to me) dangers or to wait and let her ask me. One evening she accepted a ride home and was raped in the man's car. Catherine telephoned me at 1:00 a.m., the only time I ever received an after-hours call from her. I asked if she was hurt — she was not. "I burned my clothes," she said. The next day she told me that she was angry at me. It seemed to her that I was not empathic enough on the phone. She seemed satisfied with my explanation that I was, indeed, very sorry for her experience, particularly the invasion that is rape. I told her, too, why I had wrestled with whether to warn her.

Catherine's announcement in our sixth year that she was thinking about stopping therapy marked the beginning of the third phase, the consolidation of her separate identity. It was important that I experienced a sudden diminution in my status when Catherine made her announcement. It was the point where both of us recognized that we were equals. From that point on, Catherine used me as a reality check. She continued seeing me, albeit less frequently, to help her affirm the reality of her perceptual apparatus. Self-confidence can be defined as the ability to trust one's perceptual apparatus. Finally, Catherine reached a point where she could not go forward without the experience of independence.

I think there has been a posttreatment phase, too. Not really a phase — rather, a time during which both of us have been permanently changed. We have come to know each other, and we have developed a deep respect and affection for each other. Each of us, her *I* and my *I*, has been changed by the other. Training programs for therapists often emphasize the importance of the neutrality of the therapist. The therapist's feelings are regarded as countertransference, an impediment to the progress of therapy. I have found that a great deal is lost if the therapist does not feel or experience change as a result of his relationship with his client. An essential part of continuing *I* development is the experience of having an effect on another person, and being affected by others.

There is one characteristic a therapist should be well possessed of — that he knows himself well enough to not be threatened by his client's terror, or by his world. As a supervisor of younger therapists, the most common problem I run across is that the therapist, despite a good heart and a willingness to be helpful, offers up explanations (projections) that are designed to narrate his own anxiety or his own troubled world, and are therefore not an accurate portrayal of his client's struggles. Some experience with the feeling states accompanying the dissolution of self, or at least with the fragility of self, will go a long way.

The dynamics I have referred to as part of a therapeutic process occur on a daily basis in all of our lives. We all depend on the authenticity of the external world to gain an accurate picture of ourselves. For example, there is something centering, real, about a walk in the woods or looking at the stars. Authentic relationships, too, help us define ourselves. Last year I was privileged to attend a meeting of Mind Freedom in Northampton, MA, a self-help group of survivors of the mental health system. I was profoundly moved by the members' understanding and compassion for each other's suffering — this state of mind we call *psychosis* — and how they strengthened each other.

In sum, all human beings struggle with *I* development. I think that the only difference between the psychotic and nonpsychotic person is the degree of developmental arrest. I do not treat a psychotic person any differently than I do someone who is not psychotic. "Symptoms," whether expressions of an individual's suffering or his explanations and personal constructions designed to maintain the consistency of self, will melt away (as did Catherine's auditory hallucinations and odd behaviors) as he develops his authentic self. A more poorly developed *I* does require more elaborate explanations (such as Catherine's projection of her rage as experienced in voices that spoke to her, and her food rituals) to maintain consistency; thus, the therapist will do well to be familiar with these primitive states of self-development. The therapeutic process of helping an individual gradually replace these personal constructions with his authentic self applies to our psychotic and nonpsychotic clients alike.

References

Dorman, D. (2004). *Dante's cure: A journey out of madness.* New York: Other Press.

Jaynes, J. (1990). *The origin of consciousness in the breakdown of the bicameral mind.* Boston: Houghton Mifflin.

La Cerra, P., & Bingham, R. (2002). *The origin of minds: Evolution, uniqueness, and the new science of the self.* New York: Harmony Books.

Laing, R. D. (1969). *The divided self.* Baltimore: Penguin.

Leaky, R. E., & Lewin, R. (1977). *Origins.* London: Macdonald and Jane's.

Valenstein, E. S. (1998). *Blaming the brain: The truth about drugs and mental health.* New York: Free Press.

Ver Eecke, W. (2002). A Lacanian explanation of Karon's and Villamoe's successful psychodynamic approaches to schizophrenia. *Journal of the American Academy of Psychoanalysis, 30,* 633–643.

Meditations on Dissociation: Kristina and the Enigmatic Self*

Ed Mendelowitz

Ed Mendelowitz, PhD, completed his doctoral studies at the California School of Professional Psychology where he worked closely with Rollo May. He serves on the editorial board of the *Journal of Humanistic Psychology* and has presented papers on themes concerning psychotherapy and the arts at annual meetings of the American Psychological Association and European Congress of Psychology. He is, with Kirk Schneider, coauthor of the chapter on existential psychotherapy in

* This narrative has been adapted from various sections of the author's book *Ethics and Lao-Tzu*, a collage-like meditation on character, published by the Colorado School of Professional Psychology Press..

Raymond Corsini and Danny Wedding's *Current Psychotherapies*. His book *Ethics and Lao-Tzu*, a collage-like meditation on character, was published by the Colorado School of Professional Psychology. Dr. Mendelowitz is in private practice in Boston's South End.

Figure 11.1 "The God Mother," November 1998.

My work with Kristina has been, like dissociation itself, many things, with myriad sensations and experiences often arising in quick and commingling succession. It has entailed, above all, an extraordinarily moving and complex occurrence of what is known generally in the literature as the dissociative identity, one in which multiple intrapsychic "systems" or "worlds" emerge within psychotherapy with the passage of time.

There is no way to render a thorough account of Kristina's phenomenology or the course of our work together in a section of this brevity. I have opted, rather, for a few carefully selected fragments meant to impress themselves upon the reader from several directions almost at once — very much the experience one has in working with what has been called, historically, the multiple personality.

Such a procedure is not without precedence. The fragments of the pre-Socratic philosopher Heraclitus that have come down to us through the centuries are wholly satisfying (I dare say complete) in themselves. One could say as much about the perfectly complete incomplete novels of Franz Kafka. As we read Friedrich Nietzsche, we encounter, too, consecutive passages coming at us from varying points of view. "To look now out of this window, now out of that," he writes in his notebooks, "I have resisted settling down." (Nietzsche, 1968, p. 20)

It is necessary at times to embrace the seeming incompleteness, even incoherence, of things in order to approach deeper understanding. ("From the fragments of my broken heart, I will build an altar," exhorts an ancient hymn.) In matters of awareness, less is sometimes more. One precedes best with an intuitive mind and agile ears, and it is incumbent upon therapist and client alike to integrate disparate elements. Let us ponder together the manifold aspects and quandaries of integration.

Resurrection and Providence (Toward a Middle East of the Heart)

1

Figure 11.2 "Her Tears Will Quiet Them," March 1998.

2

On November 24, 1997, my then 20-year-old patient Kristina, a multiple personality, sends me via electronic mail these poetic reflections on memory and psychotherapy, fragmentation and peace. It is the inner guide Cara who writes, dubbing her thoughts "The Inner Ocean":

> Knowing deeply what is lost, the past that brings us closer to knowing despair more fully is directed also at understanding. Accepting what caused this broken connection between heart and mind, emotion and knowledge, understanding and experience.
>
> I am at the shoreline of a wide ocean moved by life. At times it crashes to the shore, breaking and destroying. In wonderment, this power is respected and left alone. Other times, rolling in, the ocean slowly changes the sands and people play happily in its serenity. All is a symphony. In my mind, I hear its rhythm. The waves are the composition, beautiful and breathtaking in their fervor, renewing in their tranquility.
>
> Inside is like this ocean.
>
> Cara Peale

3

Figure 11.3 Kristina's "first picture." Made at the start of psychotherapy, September 1995.

Inner Blueprints

4

On December 4, 1998, Kristina sends me this electronic message entitled simply "Blueprints":

> We stand silenced in awakened understanding. Our souls hollowed out by the noise of others, we lean inward and become a house of people, empowered by necessity. Our resilience becomes the walls. Our hopes build roofs; our anticipation: the doors. Our transparencies become windows. Our reality becomes the ground; our expectations: the sky. Silence becomes the night; our vision: the light. Intuition becomes our roadway; revelation our universe.
>
> Cara Peale

5

Figure 11.4 Untitled, January 1999.

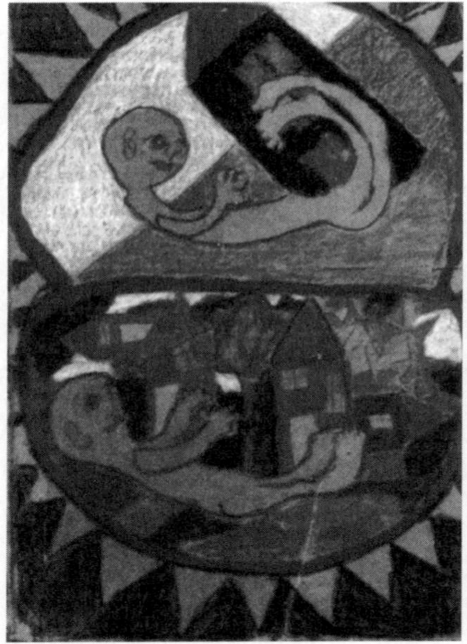

Figure 11.5 Untitled, January 1999.

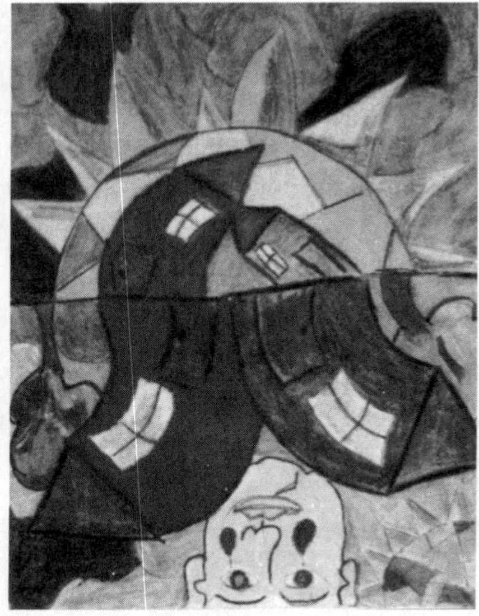

Figure 11.6 Untitled, January 1999.

Figure 11.7 Untitled, January 1999.

Kristina made these drawings during the first of more than 20 hospitalizations. They signal the emergence into relative consciousness of a parallel inner universe of two "houses" or "worlds" of "alters" (orange and purple), mirroring precisely the two extant, more salient systems (red and blue/blood and tears/action and reaction) — the "known worlds" of experience. The pictures were made with crayon on cardboard boxes, the only materials available to Kristina at the time.

Pictures, Voices, and Psychotherapy (Decapitation as Defense Mechanism)

6

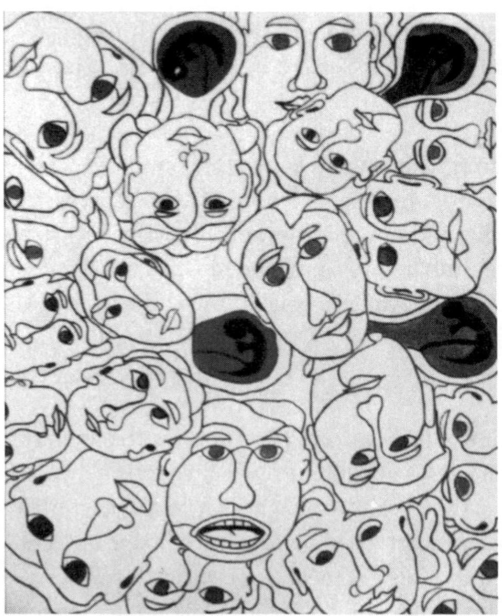

Figure 11.8 "Who to Become?" May 1999.

7

What has this to do with psychotherapy? I relate here the briefest excerpt from a therapy session with Kristina that occurred at the time. Understand that Kristina is someone for whom matters of character (integrity, that is) have always loomed ominously and large:

> During the session, the inner guide Cara picks up a pad of paper and writes:
>
> > Character is the way you behave when no one is looking
>
> I add these words:
>
> > even if you are as solitary as Thoreau at Walden

We are plagiarizing, and I hope not abusing, a line out of Robert Coles that Kristina had come across in a college assignment a year or so earlier, one that she had been moved to share with me at the time. It somehow comes back to us now. Cara reflects and writes further:

Character is looking when no one else is

She pauses and continues:

Character is a way of being when others have a way of behaving

"There are many ways it can go," says Cara, thinking about the sentence but also about character. She is her own proof she is right.

8

Two small children, Sharon and Sarah, are out briefly during the hour, but it is difficult to say just who it is who now draws a representation of the "music-man," a man who had apparently raped Kristina in early childhood at the church that her family regularly attended when they lived in the South. Tears are this time held in abeyance as one of the children scrawls in the disorderly handwriting of a child:

no head

The child attempts immediately to excoriate the memory of trauma with course, heavy lines now abruptly drawn through the words she has just written. It is, perhaps, the infant Sarah who, for all these years, has held this memory and who now attempts to obliterate it, an image that could be contained in childhood only if the face and head were excised from consciousness. Decapitation as defense mechanism, one even Anna Freud may have missed.

9

Many sketches representing the four houses and worlds of Kristina's inner landscape and architecture are drawn spontaneously during the hour. All point to the imperative of connection and movement, the integration of inward forms. Cara writes:

Reinvent yourself.

Each must journey to the other side and find their way back. This is the plan.

Go digging — this is what she means.

Houses become arrows. Each roof must be pointing to another. And then the digging begins.

Kristina is articulating an inner code, her own existential schematic/mathematic. Suddenly, as if self-exploration and character may not be separable, Cara reverts back to her earlier theme:

Why do some people have character and others not?

I say the right thing at times and this time it is nothing.

10

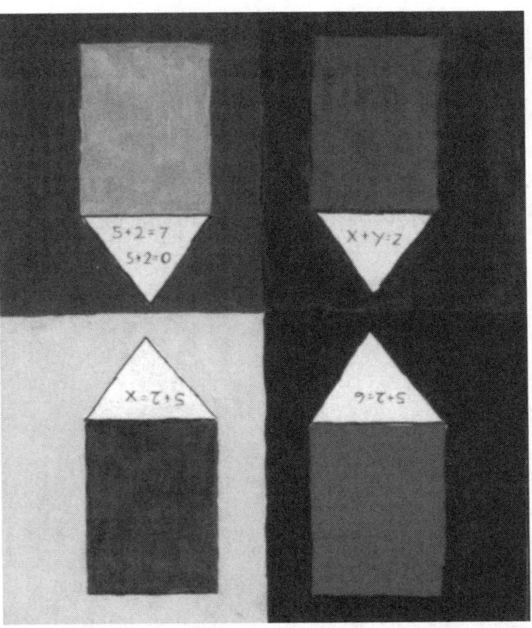

Figure 11.9 "Codes," May 1999.

11

> We need to find a proper balance between the claims on our judgment from our raw, wild, untamed experience, and the claims of objective rationality. Both should be given their due.
>
> *The Voice of Experience* R. D. Laing (1982, p. 27)

> It is a state composed of the recognition of another, a fellow human being like one's self; of identification of one's self with the pain or joy of the other; of guilt, pity, and the awareness that we all stand on the base of a common humanity.
>
> *Love and Will* Rollo May (1969, p. 289)

> There seems to be no agent more effective than another person in bringing a world for oneself alive, or, by a glance, a gesture, or a remark, shriveling up the reality in which one is lodged.
>
> *Asylums* Erving Goffman (1961b, p. 41)

Asylum

12

Figure 11.10 "Brain Pressure," January 1999.

13

Back at her Bible Belt college, Kristina searches restlessly to find clinicians in the vicinity with whom she can effectively work. It has been an exhausting endeavor, as even avowed national experts have not always impressed with their acumen or leads. Our scheduled phone sessions continue, as do Kristina's electronic transmittals — a way for her to feel connected during the course of difficult days. I am aware that this is an extraordinary case, one that flies in the face of a professional Zeitgeist committed to speed and symptomatic cover-up. This is not to suggest that such orthodoxies and objectives do not, at times, also have their place.

On October 5, 1999, I receive an untitled message from a mute system within Kristina's mind that does not interact directly with me. This hidden system is not heard or experienced in any conscious way by Cara or any other representatives of the known systems and worlds. This new set of alters expresses itself in brief, evocative poems or, alternatively, terse statements and is known, collectively, as the Unseen. Here these silent newcomers complain about inner noise (a common, often desperate, complaint of the dissociative identity) before relating a poem about an unidentified man who now, very gradually, begins to enter ominously into intrapsychic view:

> be quiet. be quiet. it's too loud. i don't like them i don't like them at all. make them go away please.
>
> what is seen
> merely a shadow
> a shadow
> merely a reflection
> a reflection
> merely the outline of a man
>
> the unseen

Later the same day, these additional words are received:

> always behind
> the mirror's
> reflection
> always twisted
> reality
>
> the unseen

Still later that day, the poem "unforgotten" is received:

> reading other people's tragedies
> i've forgotten
> i'm just a pile of bones
> wanting to avenge
> another unseen holocaust
>
> the unseen

I am reminded that Kristina had nonchalantly remarked during one of our earliest sessions that she had read many books on the Holocaust during her harrowing adolescence — "kind of a hobby" of hers at that time. These poems, cryptic as they are, tend to correlate, insistently, with dream narratives, also relayed, as well as with themes concurrently emergent in psychotherapy. There is, assuredly, method, if not symmetric simplicity, behind all the chaos and noise. Memories of very early trauma are being gradually called forth.

14

As new systems holding old memories continue to emerge, Kristina's precarious balance begins to falter. Issues surrounding safety and the amelioration of insufferable pain become paramount. On October 29, Cara writes briefly to confirm arrangements for returning to the hospital:

> We're leaving to go back to the hospital now. This should be a better place than the others, though. I really don't know how long they are going to treat me, but maybe you could try to contact them once I am there. Everyone is afraid.
>
> Cara

Upon discharge four days later, Kristina sends this message expressing evident frustration:

> Things are tough. Angry people. Wanted some kind of help in the hospital, but once again it was not there.
>
> Cara

15

The search for an outpatient psychiatrist has also remained a challenge, as the discipline operates these days under the aegis of pharmacological expedience and financial incentive. Psychiatric protocols are heavily oriented in these directions and methodologies — relevant, of course, but in themselves insufficient. Few in general practice today seem particularly knowledgeable or, more troubling, even interested in dynamic or depth psychology, and the insurance companies can hardly be expected to oblige. Literature, philosophy, art, dream, matters of spirit/family/culture/subculture — in short, complexity in very nearly all its forms — seem to have fallen by the wayside as all matters are reduced to symptomatology and the unabashed medicinal cure. The result is a professional bias that militates, necessarily, against precisely the sort of sensitivity and perspective that the complicated individual, especially, needs. I am realizing, further, that we are all a good deal more complicated than we may wish to concede. Kristina, in her essence, is the embodiment of much that the world itself has split off in the interests of adjustment and normalcy: normative dissociation and everyday life's return of the repressed.

16

On January 18, 2000, Kristina forwards this electronic expression of exasperation:

> i am ready to shoot myself and the nearest damned psychiatrist i can find!!!!! i desperately need to find a hospital that i can safely go to in crisis 'cause right now i really could use one … i feel like i've talked with every psychiatrist from my street corner to each end of this state and have not found anyone!!!!!!
>
> cara peale

17

Kristina has been hospitalized more than 20 times during the six years I have known her. Hers, we have noted, is an exceptionally intricate instance of a very complex phenomenon, one that is regularly subjected to a plethora of misdiagnoses and mistreatments. Hospitalizations tend to occur around newly emerging systems (hitherto repressed aspects of the inner terrain/architecture), transitional periods during which Kristina's habitual fragility of being becomes even more precarious and pronounced. Available literature I have seen stresses psychotherapeutic approaches, solitude, creative activities, and amelioration of symptoms with minor tranquilizers as needed during these times. However, Kristina's inpatient stays have been typified by various combinations of far more potent, often questionable, drugs and enforced adaptation to standardized routines. The economic environment in which these conventions become operative is, no doubt, part of the problem. Further, it would take an unusually astute psychiatrist, psychologist, nurse practitioner, or social worker to discern the exquisitely creative, emotional, moral, and spiritual proclivities that commingle here with heartrending disturbance and pain. Laing (1982) was right when he observed that the objective look is, by definition, incapable of seeing that which lies outside its (subjectively determined) objectivity. One is hard pressed, however, to find a clinician these days who has thoughtfully read Laing.

With time, hospitalizations have been avoided as much as possible. It is less the inability to comprehend than the presumption so prevalent among doctors that they must and do that is often the stumbling block. Human beings, the Czech writer Milan Kundera (1998) observes, have a native tendency to judge before understanding. With the makeshift supports of psychologist, pastor, and husband, we have attempted, as much as possible, to create a kind of asylum (a place of sanctuary no less than safekeeping for the avowedly insane) without walls in order to weather crises during which long-repressed systems and worlds begin to make themselves known. Kristina is right when she states that she could use a good hospital right now. Numerous misadventures, however, have inspired caution and restraint. And there never were many Frieda Fromm-Reichmanns in any case.

Kristina's current psychiatrist, Dr. K, is a busy and well-respected man in the Mennonite community in which he lives and works. Although he suggests various pharmacological regimens at various times, he is at least respectful of the patient's feedback when she responds with less faith or enthusiasm than he is used to and, assumedly, would like. However, the patient finds off-putting remarks that she is not cooperating as well as she might when things do not go according to plan, that a misguided understanding of theology perhaps exacerbates her problems (it is the old saw: one ought not think too much), exhortations that she get a job, make more friends, and so on. Really, the list of extraclinical imperatives (and, at times, implied judgments) goes on and on.

As alters and systems bearing intimations of earliest abuse emerge, Kristina becomes increasingly troubled by an excruciating hypersensitivity to sound — an apparent epiphenomenon of inner discord. The noise eventually becomes agonizing. Kristina sends me this electronic message in response to my suggestion that her psychiatrist's availability in the midst of her present duress ought to be borne in mind:

> Do you know that all the craziness feels suffocating? … The noise is so grating for some reason, especially the church bells and the birds. I feel like there are a million insects sitting outside my window for the singular purpose of driving me nuts. I've felt like this before. I know this because I remember talking to K about it once or twice. He always recommends some drug. I get scared to try them because I know they have so many other effects aside from their intended ones. So I suffer with this idiocy and try not to do anything as stupid, justified as it may feel, as my thoughts insist of me. K, I feel, often patronizes me. I'm not sure he suggests things he believes will work. I don't think he knows what's going on with me a majority of the time, and I'd say more often than not HIS perspective needs a new prescription. The noise is overbearing. I feel like I can't breathe. Someday you'll have to tell me how crazy this really is. Right now I wouldn't be amused.
>
> Cara Peale

18

We have glimpsed the manner in which Kristina tends to experience an exacerbation of psychological/physical distress, even outright horror, at times during which split-off selves, systems, and memories begin to surface. It is further clear that her perplexing presentation and polyphonic story are not easily apprehended or assessed. Psychiatric interventions, however, as Goffman (1961a) had observed, operate according to their own set of rules, ones generally inattentive to inner nuance and narratives and to which the patient has ultimately to submit.

Over time, it has become apparent that antipsychotics, administered judiciously, have been beneficial, especially during periods of intrapsychic transition. Although this more circumscribed use of a very potent class of medications is not how most psychiatrists tend to proceed, it is what Kristina has found most useful due to a variety of psychological and, to a lesser extent, physiological and personal reactions and concerns. These so-called major tranquilizers provide both respite and side effects. Their advantages seem to come at the expense of better connections with the more distant and creative parts of Kristina's composite self. "It's a way of exchanging my craziness for yours," observes Cara, identifying me, for simplicity's sake, with the world of the nominally sane. Side effects, furthermore, which vary with individual drugs, become precisely apparent, and hence increasingly oppressive, over time. There is an attention to subtlety in Kristina that standard protocols disallow.

Kristina's current psychiatrist is an interesting compromise. Kristina's sense is that most of his patients feel fortunate to have found him. Further, there seems to have been, in the aftermath of one particular hospitalization, a willingness to entertain a diagnosis and depth in his patient that he, like many of his colleagues, rather tends to avoid. Briefly a window had opened and a sense of curiosity had prevailed. Yet time, the hectic daily round, and the never-ending complexities of the case seem to have conspired quickly to effect a return to habitual clinical protocol and judgment — better, perhaps, than some of his colleagues, but less than what is needed or might have been hoped. The conventional pieties that the psychiatrist presses upon Kristina (meant more to shore up his own comforting beliefs about self and the world) are quickly discerned, thereby working against the very respect he seeks to engender. There is uncommon acuity at work and play in Kristina. One can only admire it without defense or judgment or else feel unnerved.

19

I remind Kristina, once again, at this critical point that her psychiatrist seems to be reasonably well intended, even if pedestrian attitudes limit understanding, leading oftentimes to presumption and even arrogance. Notwithstanding the difficulties involved, I am aware that medication plays an important role in Kristina's care and that more potent ones may be presently indicated. I tell her that her psychiatrist, like people generally, tends often toward patronage because of limitations in comprehension. Following an appointment with her psychiatrist, Kristina writes:

> You are right. There is dignity even for us insanes. K was not patronizing to me, just as understanding as he can be of the situation. In fact, he asks very many questions about the noise and how it sounds. I explain to

> him that it is so excruciating that at times I feel I should take a knife and cut out my ears. He asks if they're the voices I usually hear (the alters). I say no, that it isn't that so much as the external noise that is driving me crazy. For example a bug outside my window might send me into a panic because I cannot find its origin or because the noise makes me feel so upset that I want to hit my head on a wall … At night especially the noises are intense and I am actually afraid of them. I feel they are people trying to come and molest me …
>
> K was sympathetic and told me of a woman he treated who would often suffer from this kind of thing. He said he wanted me to try a new medication. I started to cry and he asked what I was thinking. A moment to compose myself. "You know I have an aversion to taking medication." He said he understood but he really thought it would help. So I will try, more out of desperation for the situation to change than anything else.

Kristina does try and, to her great relief, frustration, and finally horror, finds that this new-to-market neuroleptic not only effects an attenuation of hypersensitivity to sound but also brings, ironically, the side effects of nausea, bodily agitation, and, particularly late at night, profound subjective despair. After some weeks, moreover, there is marked hair loss as well. This last reaction is an occurrence that understandably mortifies her. She has, after all, so little about which she can feel unambiguously good. Dr. K initially dismisses the complaint, somewhat cavalierly, as unrelated to the new medication. It is Kristina herself who, after repeated calls to the pharmaceutical company, is able to finally verify the phenomenon as an infrequent but very real finding among early recipients of the drug. It is both helpful and humbling to regularly consider just how little we "helping professionals" sometimes "know" and "do" for our patients. Presence, patience, and humility are at the heart of it all.

20

Kristina's dream about wards, psychiatrists, multiplicity, psychodiagnostics, insight, and integration:

> I'm in another hospital. The walls are made of thick glass and I can see into other wards. The doctors are arguing, two against one, about my diagnosis. Two say, "she's multiple," trying to convince the doubter of their truths. I'm alone in the room, besides them I mean, and sitting at a brushed steel table. I play with my fingers and look through the glass walls to a room that holds computers and screens. It looks like a war room. The doubting doctor says she doesn't believe in the diagnosis and wants to run her own tests. I am scared of this woman because she keeps walking behind my back as she speaks. The I in my mind says she is standing behind me making faces and, worse, that she is curling

her hands in an effort to strangle me. Whenever she stands behind me, I float up to the corner of the room, like I'm part of the video surveillance system so ingeniously undisguised throughout the ward. From my corner in the ceiling I watch what is happening. I see that the doubter really doesn't make faces at me, but, by the way my hands play, I can see I'm very unhappy to be stuck in the same room with her.

The two doctors finally consent to more tests, and I am allowed to leave the room until they begin. Part of me stays on the ceiling, crawling around up there like a bug, watching myself. When I'm finally left in my own room I can experience sensation in my body again and my vision is through one set of I's. I am unpacking a suitcase. I can see a girl coming down the hallway. She stops at the door and asks, "Are we allowed to move freely here?"

"As freely as you can on a ward," I answered. The girl stood silently, half inside my room and half out. She stood there for so long, so silent, that I stopped what I was doing to stare back. "Over there they lock you in your room," I finally said, pointing at the adjacent ward visible through the glass wall. Somehow the light seemed warmer on our side. The wood trim around the doors and along the floors were [*sic*] painted a cheery green, as opposed to the cold blue trim on the other ward.

The girl finally decided which side of the carpet she wanted to be on and walked to the glass wall, putting her ear flat against it. "I don't hear anything," she said. Everything she said had two meanings.

"That wall is two inches thick."

"To keep someone out or keep someone in?"

"I guess it all depends on what side of the wall you're standing on," I said, crawling under the bed. "I've been over there, and now I'm over here, and I think no matter which side you stand on, it just feels like you're being kept." I didn't see the girl leave, because I had crawled under the bed, but I heard her sigh and walk away after a few moments. I've heard it said, "Freedom has its price," as if imprisonment didn't have any.

I spent a long time underneath the bed thinking of myself as a princess locked in a tall tower. I listened to a story as it jumped between the hemispheres of my brain, growing more elaborate as the moments passed. I couldn't really get the story straight. In my mind I could hear a fight growing between whether to be a princess or a soldier. The one part of the story that I agreed on was that the doctors were the villains and I would call them "The Doctors Three." I giggled, imagining their white coats replaced with black capes and their long noses out-measured by the rims of long feathered caps.

But my story would have to wait because a nurse came looking for me. I didn't budge from my spot under the bed, and soon the whole ward thought I had escaped. If it hadn't been for the shrewd eye of one guard, I would have gone unnoticed. So, finally I was taken to a glass room in the middle of the ward, the same room with all the computers I had seen earlier. The doubter of The Doctors Three spoke to the others as if I weren't even there, and truth be known I sometimes wasn't, although she'd be hard-pressed to know. I never spoke a word, so she thought I was mute or dumb or both.

They hooked up my head to a lot of wires, which fed hungry computers readouts of my brain waves. Well, truth is that I wasn't sure what they were looking for, not that they knew either. Then The Doctors Three let me be, and I was alone in a sealed, silent room. There were toys scattered around on the floor and I began to play with them. One of the computers emanated a sound so loud that I jumped out of my body and clung to the wall again. I could see myself on the floor with my head down and The Doctors Three watching from behind the glass. Surely they could see I had no reaction! But the computer compensated for their lack of insight by spitting out a series of tally marks on a white sheet of paper. They were indeed tricking me, for every time I was on the wall, the computer would print more tallies!

Two of The Doctors Three seemed very pleased to be done with the test when the computer was finished, but Three wanted more. So I was sat again in the room with the steel table. What was this now, an interrogation? "Don't worry. I have a plan," said the I in my head; "I'll have you out of here in no time." The I in my mind was promising an escape to the weary-looking table and chairs. "How long have you been in?" asked the I. Of course, years of confinement had left the table mute, so said the I. I lay my head down.

Three was there, her gaze as hard as the table, trying to penetrate me. "I'm going to show you some pictures, and I want you to tell me what they mean to you," she said.

"Great, a Rorschach," said the I.

She unrolled a large tube of canvases and laid, as flat as she could, the paintings on the table. There on the table were paintings I had seen before. "Do you recognize these?" the doctor asked.

"Some of me," I said.

"Making wise the simple," said the I.

"Some of them?" the doctor repeated incorrectly.

I remained silent, scanning the pictures. There was *The God Mother* and others I had seen before. They were a part of me somehow, and it made me happy to see them. Then my eyes rested on one picture which I did not recognize but which I knew I had done or would do. The canvas was as blue as a spring sky. In the middle of the picture stick figures seemed to float in a downward spiral. In the middle of the spiral was one figure unlike the others. It was painted not only with black but with other colors outlining it. Then I heard the story of I in my mind, and I knew that the painting was a representation of me floating along with others in the doctors [*sic*] world, trying to go along with the flow of all things but always sticking out because I was different.

"What does it mean to you?" the doctor was asking still.

"It's a picture of freedom," I said silently.

21

Kristina's dream is shared by the inner guide Cara with two of the children, Sharon and Meg, each embodying a separate aspect of the composite dreamer and dream. Meg is the central dreamer, while Cara is the one who leaves the body (dissociates) in order to become part of the surveillance equipment in the corners of the ceiling, the bug on the wall. Sharon is the girl who wanders briefly into Meg's room, inquiring about the ability to freely maneuver as she considers on which "side of the carpet" she rather would be. By collating their respective perspectives (a story that jumps "between the hemispheres of my brain"), the fuller dream narrative is reassembled and told.

The partition between wards (transparent in dream consciousness but typically opaque) can be seen in many ways but seems, for the moment, to represent a divide between inner and outer realms: the world of imagination (alternate realities) and the world of hospitals, doctors, and the socially sanctioned and shared. Notwithstanding the difficulty in dealing with skeptics and even well-meaning doctors (who themselves are not sure what they are looking for), it is an auspicious sign that the dreamer finds here a "trim" (one's particular spin or take on life and the world) painted "a cheery green" rather than the "cold blue" border of the inmost domains of confinement. Still, it is only when she is left alone in her own room that the dreamer is able to "feel sensation in [her] body" again and views the world "through one set of I's."

The dreamer is hooked up to "a lot of wires" which feed "hungry computers readouts" of her brain as she finds toys through which to travel back in time and with which to play. Although there are no externally visible signs that the dreamer suddenly dissociates in response to a loud noise, the computer compensates for clinical "lack of insight" by "spitting out a series of tally marks on a white sheet of paper." There are, no doubt, physiological sequelae to the psychological phenomenon of dissociation — an unobserved escape from one world as another is imagined into being. High-tech equipment may render neuroelectrical readings but cannot ascertain the hidden meaning or otherwise explain it away.

Doctor Three, still unconvinced, proceeds now with apparent projective techniques. The pictures that she lays out before Kristina turn out to be, surreally, paintings that Kristina herself has made or is, perhaps, going to make.

These purportedly objective stimuli are creations of the dreaming subject herself! I am reminded here of the metaphorical image of holding up a mirror to oneself while looking into another, such that one sees an infinity of reflections, all receding to a hypothetical vanishing point. Obviously, we have entered the realms of quantum physics and the mysteries of the ineffable self:

> "Do you recognize these?" the doctor asked.
> "Some of me," I said.
> "Making wise the simple," said the I.
> "Some of them?" the doctor repeated incorrectly.
> I remained silent, scanning the pictures. There was *The God Mother* and others I had seen before. These were a part of me somehow, and it made me happy to see them.

We are confronted, here again, with the nebulous borderland between inner and outer domains as the dreamer is "interrogated" with the contents of her own mind. In matters of the self, there can be no wholly accurate method of measurement. It is no wonder that the conventionally trained psychiatrist ("her gaze as hard as the table") is stern and perplexed and has difficulty keeping up.

The final painting that the dreamer sees (yet cannot place in time as past accomplishment or future endeavor) is a moving depiction of multiplicity with its many-hued "outlines" or fringes, an oneiric acknowledgment of the advantages of inner worlds, selves, perhaps even wards. Notwithstanding the many difficulties that inhere, the dreamer discerns that multiplicity has provided a degree of (inward) richness and freedom that, in contrast to a "doctors [*sic*] world" of "stick figures" and monotone clarity, is worth hanging on to in some manner or form:

> Then I heard the story of I in my mind, and I knew that the painting was a representation of me floating along with others in the doctors [*sic*] world, trying to go along with the flow of all things but always sticking out because I was different.
>
> "What does it mean to you?" the doctor was asking still.
> "It's a picture of freedom," I said silently.

It is a sign of progress that the dreamer is now willing "to go along with the flow of all things," her uniqueness always in evidence as she tries to inhabit a middle realm between inward dimension and the world of the commonly accepted and nominally sane. The matter, of course, is infinitely complex. Do you still maintain that there is no such thing as a multiple personality, Doctor Three? And what about those "experts," for example, who find one around every other bend and beneath every stone?

22

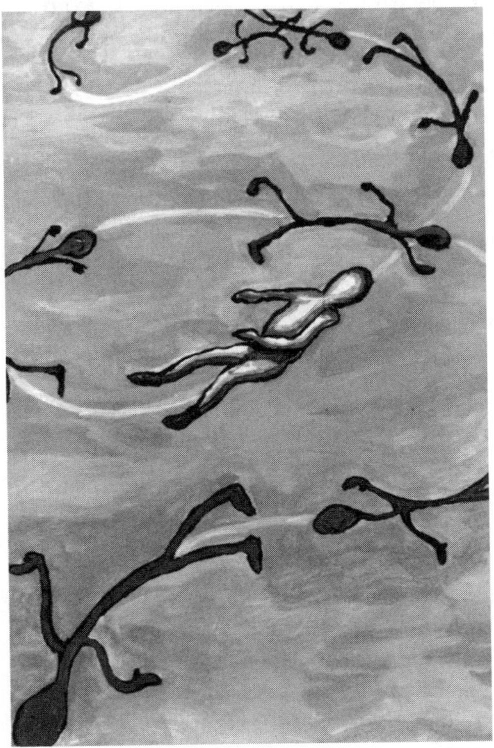

Figure 11.11 "Freedom," May 2002.

23

The dream and painting that close out our meditations evoke the manifold aspects of integration in a manner that is both eloquent and profound. Their psychological richness is expressed poetically and visually and points to the imperative of integrating the systems of, and selves within, psychiatrists and psychotherapists no less than those who enlist us as guides. To the extent that we make headway along these domains, connections are enhanced and suffering ameliorated. Isn't this what it is all about? To the extent that we do not, the client finally stops trying, retreating into the makeshift integrity found within the mind: shelter from the prevailing disintegration/limitation without (what Kafka had called "interior emigration"). We observe by the end of Kristina's dream that she has ceased trying to communicate at all, speaking finally only inside and "silently" — a moving depiction of what happens when the creatively ill can find no worthy interlocutor. Even in the dream narrative, however, and the artwork inspired (themselves stunning integrations of disparate elements), we are left with Kristina's spellbinding exhortations on behalf of what may one day be possible and is too often lost. Gnostic messages, so to speak, for those of us, as Robert Coles would say, "within hearing distance."

References

Goffman, E. (1961a). *Asylums: Essays on the social situation of mental patients and other inmates*. New York: Anchor Books.

Goffman, E. (1961b). *Encounters: Two studies in the sociology of interaction*. Indianapolis: Bobbs-Merrill.

Kundera, M. (1988). *The art of the novel*. (L. Asher, Trans.). New York: Harper & Row.

Laing, R. D. (1982). *The voice of experience*. New York: Pantheon.

May, R. (1969). *Love and will*. New York: W.W. Norton.

Nietzsche, F. (1968). *The will to power*. (W. Kaufman & R. J. Hollingdale, Trans.). New York: Vintage Books.

12
EI Emphases on the Intersubjective

One of the remarkable frontiers in contemporary depth psychotherapy is the convergence of interpersonal psychoanalysis, attachment theory, and neuroscience with intersubjective dimensions of existential psychotherapy. Although the edges of this convergence are just now being glimpsed, their yield is already quite bountiful. In the following, we will examine this yield across three diverse perspectives. Dennis Portnoy sets the context for this chapter with his timely reflection, "Relatedness: Where Existential and Psychoanalytic Approaches Converge." In this commentary, Portnoy carefully sets forth the terms of the convergence, their latest expressions, and their "living" points of synthesis in a dynamic case. Although Portnoy is prudent, he is also quite sanguine that a new era may be approaching. This is an era in which psychoanalytic emphases on mutuality and regulation can meld with existential accents on coexistence and codiscovery.

Following Portnoy's lead-in, psychoanalytic pioneer Robert Stolorow forges new horizons of inquiry with his intersubjective systems theory. This is a phenomenologically based psychoanalytic theory that he and his colleagues have cultivated over three decades. In essence, intersubjective systems theory embraces the context of the therapist-client encounter — and this context encompasses being. To elaborate his perspective, Dr. Stolorow recounts the very personal story of his own breakdown, his wife's remarkable mediation of this calamity, and the resulting integration, both personal and ontological, that resulted. Stolorow's odyssey is, in the end, profoundly existential. Although he attributes language as integral to his healing, he is at the same time mindful of somatic dimensions to which language is "bound" (R. Stolorow, personal communication, November 5, 2006). Stolorow goes on to unpack those dimensions — as well as linguistic structures — in his touching evocation.

In the final contribution to this chapter, Diana Fosha sets forth her Accelerated Experiential-Dynamic Psychotherapy (AEDP) model of practice. In her vibrant illustration, Dr. Fosha lays out the theoretical bases of her approach, compares and contrasts her approach with the EI model, and presents an evocative case to illustrate. This vignette not only animates her methodical formulation, but also vividly intimates parallel stances from within the EI context. Fosha concludes that although they present a slightly different emphasis, together AEDP and EIP can mobilize a potent brew of developmental, neuroscientific, and experiential practices, and that, particularly in the area of attachment trauma, profound healing can result.

Relatedness: Where Existential and Psychoanalytic Approaches Converge

Dennis Portnoy

Dennis Portnoy, MFT, is a marriage and family therapist in private practice in San Francisco. One of his areas of interest is the integration of psychoanalytic and existential-humanistic psychotherapy. He also writes and conducts workshops on the topic of self-care for people in helping roles. He is the author of *Overextended and Undernourished: A Self-Care Guide for People in Helping Roles* (1996).

Overview

Historically, the third force was founded to move beyond what Abraham Maslow and others saw as reductionism in psychoanalysis as well as behaviorism. Existential-humanistic and psychoanalytic psychotherapies have often been regarded as being worlds apart. In this contribution, I suggest that dialogical-existential therapy (derivative of the philosophy of Martin Buber) and interpersonal psychoanalysis have significant common ground, particularly in their emphasis on relatedness as the chief therapeutic ingredient. In the shifting landscape of psychoanalytic theory in recent years, the interpersonal dimension as articulated by Stephen Mitchell and Lewis Aron, and alluded to by Robert Stolorow, have come closest to the dialogical-existential perspective. In even more recent years, trends in the related fields of attachment theory and neuropsychology have added to the dialogue concerning rapprochement. In the balance of this essay, I examine the nature of these developments, illustrate their relevance to practice, and sketch their implications for a broadened theory of therapy.

The Key Change Agents in Psychoanalysis

Psychoanalytic theory has emphasized both intrapsychic and interpersonal factors as central to the facilitation of change. Therapists who view intrapsychic elements as the key change agent in psychotherapy focus on insight through interpretation. Although many analytic therapists have moved away from Sigmund Freud's stress on drive theory and oedipal analysis, they still regard insight through interpretation as the key ingredient for change.

Psychoanalysts have stressed the interpersonal in light of the curative potential of transference. Classical psychoanalytic theory views transference primarily as a re-creation of past relationships. Working through the transference is the main process that enables patients to re-experience and then disengage from their infantile fixations. Aron (1996) acknowledges that several senior Freudian authors have moved away from the detached stance of the analyst and the view of transference as solely a distortion (pp. 11, 199,

256). Aron notes that Hans Loewald was one of the first Freudian analysts to emphasize the analyst's participation within an interactive field (p. 209), yet he also comments on the differences between relational analysts and most contemporary Freudian analysts. "The emphasis is on the analyst as a person and his or her shifting affective experience, mutual influence and the interlocking nature of the transference-countertransference integration" (p. 18).

Mitchell (1988a) addresses the conflicting views that analytic theorists have about the importance of intrapsychic versus interpersonal factors and therapeutic outcomes. He contrasts Freud and Sullivan, stating that Sullivan's emphasis on the interpersonal nature of mental states is very much like Stern's view culled from current infancy research (p. 478). Freud sees free association as shaped by unconscious factors. Sullivan and later interpersonalists see therapy as shaped by the particular situation and by the relationship with the therapist.

Aron (1996) credits Mitchell for viewing intrapsychic factors as interpersonal rather than contrasting intrapersonal and intrapsychic (p. 208).

Relatedness and the Psychoanalytic Tradition

De-Forest (1942) points out that Ferenczi disagreed with Freud's emphasis on the passive, nonreacting analyst. Ferenczi argued that the analytic situation is a human situation that involves the interacting of two personalities and that the real personality of the analyst plays a part in the therapeutic process (p. 121).

Lionells, Fiscalini, Mann, and Stern (1995), in their commentary on the interpersonal tradition of Sullivan, Fromm, and Horney, point out the similarities between Ferenczi and Sullivan in regard to patient and analyst mutuality.

Aron (1996) considers Ferenczi's ideas to be the basis for all interpersonal approaches:

> Ferenczi was the first analyst to consider that the patient's resistance needed to be understood as a function of the analyst's countertransference. Ferenczi rebuked transference as a distortion that needs to be corrected by the analyst. For Ferenczi, the essence of healing comes from the patient's having a new experience in relationship. (p. 168)

Aron critiques Ferenczi's controversial experiments in mutual analysis and concludes, "Ferenczi overidentified with his traumatized patients, and his mutual analysis contains vital elements but is not viable in its extremes" (pp. 174–175).

Clemmens (1984) discusses Karen Horney's break with Freud's mechanistic concept of transference. Clemmens focuses on Horney's belief that Freud's ideas about the entire human race were based on conditions of the upper-middle-class Viennese. He also points out Horney's disagreement with Freud that transference is a rebirth of emotional reactions that are infantile and irrational (p. 311). Clemmens writes, "The meeting between analyst and patient is a unique human encounter in which the individuality of each participant determines the nature and the character of the experience" (p. 314).

Mitchell (1988a), like Horney, emphasizes the cultural backdrop of Freud's theories. He describes how Freud's focus on intrapsychic factors is shaped by Darwin's theory and the Zeitgeist of his day. In clarifying the interpersonal perspective, Mitchell writes,

> The interpersonal perspective is often misunderstood. The human mind is part of a field, not a self-limited phenomenon in its own right. The interpersonal position is sometimes caricatured as a naive environmentalism, a shallow kind of social psychology . . . holding that what goes on "inside" a person's head is either unimportant or else merely a transposition of what took place outside. (pp. 473, 480)

For Mitchell, maximum change occurs in psychotherapy when the emphasis is on the interaction between therapist and patient. According to Mitchell (1988a),

> In the contributions of Jacobsen, Kernberg, Loewald, Sandler and others, drives have gradually been more and more interpersonalized, viewed as appearing not preformed within the organism itself but as arising and shaped in the interaction between the infant and the mother and therefore, inherently dyadic. (p. 488)

There has been an emphasis in psychoanalysis over the past few decades toward a relational perspective. Aron (1996) describes how classical theory, despite significant differences, has moved in the relational direction (pp. 1, 76, 203, 256).

Tobin (1990) and Kahn (1996) credit Kohut (1971) for shifting psychoanalysis from a one-person to a two-person psychology. They stress Kohut's focus away from reality testing, his rejection of psychopathology as being a product of frustrated drives, and his emphasis on the patient's self-object needs. Tobin (1990) points out that Kohut rejected the idea of the therapist being a purely objective observer. Tobin also acknowledged that this stance is not rigidly adhered to by most psychoanalysts today.

Stolorow (1987), who has broadened Kohut's work, sees the patient and the analyst in a "psychological field created by the interplay between the two" (p. 4). He disagrees with the classical analytic stance of neutrality, stating that it further entrenches the original developmental derailments (p. 10). He and his co-authors emphasize the reciprocal mutual influence between therapist and patient and are concerned with how the therapist's subjectivity influences the patient (Stolorow, Atwood, & Brandchaft, 1994, p. 10). Stolorow views the therapist's ability to experience the patient's inner life empathically as a key change agent.

British object-relation analyst Winnicott (1960) emphasized the relationship between infant and mother and believed that the therapist's "good enough mothering" leads to positive therapeutic outcomes.

Deriving from the same tradition, Guntrip (1986) describes his shift away from the purely intrapsychic perspective. When discussing his own analysis as a patient with Fairbairn and Winnicott, he describes the key factors that enabled him to work through his conflicts. He credits Fairbairn for "softening up his repressed material," but points out the limitations of Fairbairn's approach.

Harry Guntrip (1986) refers to Fairbairn's approach as "an internal system of oedipal analysis" and Fairbairn's emphasis on internalized libidinal and anti-libidinal tensions as "a waste of time" (p. 450). Guntrip then praises Winnicott's "holding environment" and profound intuitive insights, stating, "at last I had a mother who could value her child" (p. 450). Guntrip credits Winnicott's interpretations and his being a "good enough mother" as enabling him to work through his schizoid aloofness. In other writings criticizing object relations, Guntrip (1969) sounds like an existential-humanistic therapist:

> The theory has not yet properly conceptualized Buber's "I-Thou" relations, two-persons being both ego and object to each other at the same time, and in such a way that their reality as persons becomes, as it develops in the relationship, what neither of them would have become apart from the relationship. This is what happens in good marriages and friendships. (p. 389)

Throughout the writings of Kohut (1971), Stolorow (1987), and Winnicott (1960), the relatedness theme and its curative value center around the patient's internalizing the caring, reliable therapist.

Stolorow (1987) asserts that patients heal self-object disruptions from childhood by internalizing the therapist's sustained empathy (p. 13). Early empathic failures are re-experienced in the analytic situation and healed by the new relationship. He points out that childhood empathic failures are evoked in the transference and that the therapist's empathic responses directly promote structure formation (p. 44). When clients internalize the therapist's empathy, they develop a capacity to assume a reflective, understanding, accepting, comforting attitude toward their own emotions and needs.

Winnicott (1960) also emphasizes the type of therapeutic environment that enables patients to internalize the therapist as a reliable, stable other.

Mitchell (1987) argues that relational model theories vary, and they differ from one another in many significant aspects (p. 400). (For a detailed description of the similarities and differences among various relational theorists, see Aron, 1996.) Mitchell (1987) points out that Kohut, Fairbairn, and Winnicott share Sullivan's view that the patient's demands for gratification are security based rather than pathological (p. 401) and reflect a struggle for regulation of self-esteem and object needs versus frustrated drives.

Mitchell (1987) believes, however, that Kohut held a monadic view of mind, which regards the self as operating independently of interactions of others. Mitchell takes issue with self-psychologists' (as well as British object-relations theorists') emphasis on internalization and the overemphasis on the past and early relational needs. He comments on Kohut's focus on self-organization (i.e., one's felt needs and self-reflective experience):

> There is no "self" in isolation, outside a matrix of relationships with others. Kohut reduces the complexities of interactions between analyst and analysand to "narcissistic issues," embracing both intrapsychic and interpersonal realms, yet seeing the relationship as ultimately secondary. (p. 406)

Stolorow (1987) takes issue with Freud's concept of the isolated individual mind: "The intersubjective concept is in part a response to the unfortunate tendency of classical analysis to view pathology in terms of processes and mechanisms located solely within the patient" (p. 3).

Aron (1996) notes that many self-psychologists believe that they have moved beyond Kohut's narrow view and embrace a broader relational framework (p. 56). Aron acknowledges that "some of the similarities between the relational approach and Stolorow's intersubjective approach went unrecognized because of the relationship between self-psychology and intersubjectivity theory" (p. 18).

In his critique of the British object-relation model, Mitchell (1987) takes issue with the emphasis on internal presences versus the patient's actual transactions and events: "Winnicott is concerned with the residues of earlier experiences with others; toward the imagery and assumptions about the self in relation to others" (p. 404).

In his critique of the arrested development perspective, Mitchell (1988b) questions the concept of the analyst providing relational experiences as replacements for those that the infant has never encountered (p. 289). He criticizes the notion that a piece of infantile mental life is waiting to emerge and suggested that a child's experience is an active strategy to make interactive connections with, and claims on, others (p. 165). For Mitchell, the genesis of pathology is constricted patterns of relatedness and not missing infantile experiences residing in the patient. He suggests focusing on the "space between" the analyst and analysand (p. 404) and the here-and-now perceptions and interactions in the analytic relationship (p. 405).

> Not because it alters something "inside" the analysand, not because it releases a stalled developmental process, but because it says something very important about where the analyst stands vis-à-vis the analysand, about what sort of relatedness is possible between the two of them. (p. 295)

It is through learning new transaction patterns that clients experience themselves and the therapist in a new way. Richer experiences of self and other become possible, allowing greater intimacy and more possibilities for varied experience and relatedness.

Mitchell (1987, p. 304) captures the essence and importance of what happens between client and therapist in his case of Sam. He asks Sam whether it occurred to him that Mitchell would actually be happy about rather than resent Sam's good mood. Mitchell writes, "Through this and similar exchanges the relationship gradually changed. The here-and-now interactions broadened Sam's relational matrix to allow new experiences of self in relation to others" (p. 295).

Mitchell (1988b) speaks about the therapist's finding an authentic voice that is more fully one's own and is less shaped by the configurations and limited options of the analysand's relational matrix. In doing so, he or she offers the analysand a chance to broaden and expand that matrix.

Aron's (1996) attempt at a definition of relational psychoanalysis captures its essence:

> Relational psychoanalysis is not a unified or integrated school of thought, nor is it a singular theoretical position, but a diverse group of theories that focus on personal, intrapsychic and interpersonal relations.
>
> What unites the many, so called relational schools is not any shared metapsychology, nor is it a shared criticism of classical metapsychology, although certainly this is a common element of many relational contributions. What many relational theorists have in common seems to be an emphasis on the mutuality and reciprocity between patient and analyst in the psychoanalytic process. (pp. 19, 123)

Thus far, I have offered an historic account of psychoanalytic theory and its ideas about intrapsychic and interpersonal factors as the ingredients of change in psychotherapy. I have outlined the relational approach, contrasted the concept of mind as monadic versus interactive, and clarified some main differences among the various interpersonal psychoanalytic approaches.

Existential-Humanistic Psychotherapy

Existential-humanistic therapists differ on what factors are most central in facilitating change in psychotherapy. Dialogical therapists emphasize interpersonal factors as the key ingredient for healing. Others, such as Binswanger (1954), Boss (1963), Bugental (1987), and May (1983), emphasize intrapsychic factors while acknowledging the importance of the genuine encounter between client and therapist.

According to Irvin Yalom (1980), "Existential therapy is based on a radically different view of the specific forces, motives and fears that interact in the individual" (p. 17). In Yalom's study of existential therapy, he concludes that "aside from their reaction against Freud's mechanistic, deterministic model of the mind and their assumption of a phenomenological approach to therapy, the Existential analysts have little in common and have never been regarded as a cohesive ideological school" (p. 17).

For Carl Rogers (1980), mutuality and the genuine encounter between patient and therapist are the central healing ingredients in psychotherapy. Rogers commented on the therapist's stance, stating,

> The therapist is deeply helpful only when he or she relates as a person and risks themselves as a person in the relationship. In rare moments when a deep realness in one meets a deep realness in the other, a memorable I-Thou relationship, as Martin Buber would call it, occurs. (p. 9)

The dialogical approach, which draws from the teachings of Martin Buber, emphasizes relatedness as the central ingredient for change. From the dialogical perspective, what occurs between patient and therapist prepares the patient to accept and really engage others. Buber (1958) considered the I-Thou relationship to be the most mature. The I-Thou relationship involves full respect and mutuality between two persons.

For dialogical therapists, the task is to try to transform the relationship in which I-Thou moments are possible. Buber (1958) stresses that full mutuality is not possible between therapist and patient. Friedman (1985) asserts that moments of real meeting do not require therapists and patients to be equals or therapists to disclose anything about their own lives. Brice (1984) insists that mutuality neither is equality nor fosters transference gratification (p. 122).

Dialogical therapists argue that to internalize the therapist as a positive object puts the emphasis on what occurs inside the patient versus between the patient and therapist. They take issue with the notion of internalization because it places the emphasis solely back on the self (i.e., the internalized effects of I-Thou). The emphasis is on the therapist's function and the type of object the therapist should be. Object-relations theory deals only with mental representations of person and world and does not pertain to any real aspects of a relationship between two persons.

Brice (1984) writes:

> The term object relation does not describe the meeting between person and other. The term is restricted to an internal relationship between self, image of self and internal image of other. Theoretically these relationships exist only within a closed mental system. Buber did not disavow a relationship between self and internal images of self and other. He maintained that such relationships were forever bound to the world of I-It. (p. 119)

I-Thou Versus I-It Relating

William Heard (1993) states that most impairments with patients have occurred in I-It relationships, in which patients have been consistently related to as an object (p. 149). Brice (1984) views I-It relating as the genesis of problems and further explains that the pathological relating of self-disordered patients results from their deep entrenchment in the I-It domain.

> Pathological relating has reduced patients to an it and they become too enclosed in the self, making it very hard to grant to other a status of unique other. . . . These patients typically relate to others as they wish others to be, or cling to insensitive people while totally disregarding their own self-interest. (pp. 111–112)

In my view, Winnicott's (1960) concept of the false self is an example of a way of relating that is bound by the world of I-It. The child becomes compliant when faced with the mother's inadequate responsiveness, hides his or her real feelings, and is forced to live a false existence. Learning to relate in healthier ways through a true self prepares a person for a more genuine dialogue.

Dialogical therapists are also concerned with the ways in which the therapeutic process can reflect I-It relating. They criticize the classical analytic approach to transference and the emphasis on the therapist's neutral stance.

For dialogical therapists, there is an irreconcilable conflict between transference and real relationships. They disagree with the notion that a real relationship between therapist and patient must be sacrificed in the service of therapeutic work with transference. Dialogical therapists also emphasize that patient's reactions to therapists are not solely a repetition of earlier, conflicted relationships.

According to Phillips (1980), "The fact that patients project their past onto the therapist does not detract from the genuineness of present feelings for the therapist" (p. 145).

Friedman (1985) stresses the importance of assessing the patient's capacity for relatedness and the therapeutic task beyond transference, stating "that after transference phenomena are analyzed, the confirming meeting must become central. The therapist must now sense, not only the patient's repressed conflicts, but his unevoked potentialities for personal relationship" (p. 69).

Implications for Psychotherapy

How do we as therapists engage our client as a Thou? How do I-Thou moments relate to transference and countertransference? Consider the following illustration:

"Susan's" eyes slightly squint as she looks past me, occasionally making direct eye contact. I feel her invisible antennae carefully scanning my facial expressions and vocal intonations. Susan often monitors me to gauge her next move. She is protective, strategic, and significantly more alert than she appears. Susan is an intelligent 33-year-old nurse. She is remarkably lonely and isolated and experiences herself as flawed. She is hypersensitive to abandonment/misattunement, which causes her to carefully monitor her environment in order to assess how to fit in. Susan also splits between idealizing me and devaluing me. (Classically, Susan's symptoms are reflective of a high-functioning borderline personality.)

I ask her, "What do you imagine I am thinking and feeling?" Susan tells me that my tone is too harsh and that I am not supportive enough. This is a theme that occasionally surfaces. I encourage her to tell me when she experiences me as unsupportive or too harsh. She tells me that she thinks I am irritated and bored about not getting anywhere with her today. I asked her if she thinks I need her to progress in therapy in order for me to value her and if she feels she is failing me?

We have established sufficient trust for me to ask, "What if you are correct about me being irritated?"

Susan answers, "I will have to do what you want and be compliant." Then I ask her what she imagines will happen if I am irritated and bored yet she does not try to please me or fill my expectations. Susan speaks about her fear of me withdrawing my attention and warmth.

Part of her concern about me not being supportive enough stems from her distrust that no one will be there for her. She also has the tendency to pull for me to fix her and expect me to make everything all better. I realize that I do feel some irritation, particularly with her need to have total control over the direction of the session. I also recognize that sometimes I do have expectations regarding progress in the session that contribute to my frustration. She is picking up on my unspoken affect. I soften and tell Susan that sometimes I do feel irritated, though I am not convinced that I am as harsh as she experiences me. I also tell her that, at times, I feel that I am failing her. This statement can have the potential of bringing out her desire to take care of me; however, in this moment that is not the case.

I tell Susan that I need to sort out to what degree her perceptions about me reflect her issues in contrast to accurate accounts of my behavior. Susan appears to be deeply moved by my response. She looks directly at me, her voice slightly cracking and her eyes teary. "I am realizing how I conclude that my perceptions about you are fact." She is able to access the fragile feelings that are usually covered up by defense. "I am afraid of losing the connection with you and being all alone." We focus on how she experiences my irritation as a break in our connection, which makes her feel that she did something wrong and is not good enough.

I invite her to notice how she sees me as wonderful or as failing her and either finding fault with me or trying to please me by being compliant. She wants to feel that we are always connected, yet not too close. I share with her my belief that she is critical of me when she feels too close. She admits that she is most likely to find fault with me when she is feeling vulnerable and close. Susan has a history of protecting herself from getting too close to people by staying isolated, carefully monitoring and finding fault with them.

Her anxiety about me being bored is related to her vigilance over my reactions and her fear of losing our connection if she is not meeting my needs. I address with her in the moment how she is gauging connection and her value based on my reaction. I frame the discussion in terms of my concern about this pattern being harmful to her (i.e., by limiting her capacity for connection). I am aware, to the degree possible, of how she is impacting me. I also see how my inner reactions contribute to a familiar self-defeating interaction that together we have co-created.

In the months that followed our therapy session, Susan was more willing to reveal her vulnerability, and her propensity toward vigilance and splitting decreased.

Discussion

I-Thou moments do not require that the therapist be congenial and noncon-frontive. The therapist must be willing to allow himself or herself to be shaped by the patient's subjectivity (Wachtel, 1994, p. 102).

It was important that I remained aware of how I was being affected by Susan and that I be open to her perceptions about me as accurate instead of automatically dismissing them as resistance.

Embracing an I-Thou perspective also required that I allow myself to be vulnerable with Susan. I am not suggesting that therapists must engage in uncritical self-disclosure or reveal personal information about themselves.

My responses to her were more than empathic mirroring gestures. Something happened between us, rather than her internalizing me as a good object. Susan has found new possibilities of relating that involve expressing her thoughts, feelings, and needs regardless of how others respond to her.

Stepping out of the realm of I-It required that I become more heart centered than intellect centered. This did not mean that I abandoned intellectual inquiry, but that it played a less central role. There are moments when interpretation is appropriate, particularly when emphasizing the client-therapist interaction in the moment.

Working from an I-Thou perspective requires a shift in attitude rather than an embrace of a specific orientation. An analytic therapist can approach a client with an I-Thou stance. What is important is the therapist's willingness, when appropriate, to let the client know how he or she affects the therapist. The therapist also needs to bracket preconceptions, be open to the genuine encounter between two people, and be keenly aware of how his or her issues/ reactions impact the therapy.

It is not easy to describe exactly what occurs in I-thou moments. What is clear is that meeting is more likely when the therapist holds a particular perspective rather than implements specific techniques. It is not about adopting a particular demeanor such as empathic attunement. The therapist must be willing be moved by the client and, in turn, be ready to explore that dimension in the meeting that ensues. Stolorow makes a similar point (this chapter) using different language.

Clinical Summary

In articulating and defending their perspectives, existential and analytic theorists have often been polarized, embracing either-or thinking. Despite their differences, there is movement in the past decade that suggests more common ground.

Kahn (1996), Tobin (1990), and Hycner and Jacobs (1995) have written about the bridging between the existential-humanistic perspective and psychoanalytic theory. Their emphasis has been on intersubjectivity theory as articulated by Kohut (1971) and Stolorow et al. (1994). In his comparison of Kohut and Rogers, Kahn (1996) states that Kohut and Rogers consider the legitimancy of the patient's view of reality. Both avoid imposing interpretations and value the genuine encounter between therapist and patient. In keeping with the existential emphasis on mutuality, Kahn cites Stolorow's view that therapeutic stalemates are often due to the therapist's lack of awareness.

Tobin (1991) points out that Kohut strove to understand the validity of patients' perceptions in the context of their world rather than adopting the Freudian view that patients are defensively distorting. Tobin sees self-psychology as the bridge between existential and psychoanalytic worlds because self-psychology stresses field theory and a holistic versus reductionistic view. Tobin also offers an illuminating critique of the strengths and weaknesses of both theoretical models.

Hycner and Jacobs (1995) point out similarities between self-psychology and the existential-humanistic approach. They emphasize the importance of the therapist's subjectivity, the self as a self-with-other experience, and feeling what the patient is experiencing from the patient's side of the dialogue. Hycner and Jacobs compare Stolorow's emphasis on empathic immersion with Martin Buber's concept of inclusion. For Buber (1965), inclusion meant a bold swinging of one's being into the life of the other (p. 81).

Hycner and Jacobs (1995) assert that when patients' self-object needs for mirroring and merging are responded to empathically, they acquire skills that are necessary for real meeting. They acknowledge that the primary aim of self-psychology is self-organization rather than living in relation.

My commentary, although covering some of the same ground as Kahn, Tobin, Hycner, and Jacobs, emphasizes Mitchell's and Aron's contribution. It is my view that Mitchell and Aron have brought psychoanalysis even closer to the existential-humanistic position.

Aron (1996) refers to Buber's I-Thou as the mutuality of intimacy and compares Buber's "category of the between" (p. 156) with Winnicott's transitional space. He notes the similarities between Buber's and his own view of mutuality, emphasizing that mutuality does not mean agreement or premature consensus and is achieved through subjective attunement to the patient's subjective world (pp. 150, 151, 156). Aron also points to his and Buber's agreement that the relationship between patient and analyst is not fully mutual and that the analyst must honor the differences between patient and analyst in their roles, functions, power, and responsibility (pp. 124, 157).

The relational approach is compatible with the I-Thou position because of its emphasis on moments of genuine interaction and conviction that the relationship between patient and therapist is the central element for facilitating change.

The dialogical and relational perspectives stress the need for therapists to guard against getting caught in limiting, familiar patterns of interaction while regarding the patient's subjective experience of them as open to and shaped by the interaction between therapist and patient.

Both dialogical psychotherapy and relational psychoanalysis assert that a positive relationship with a therapist does not exist only within the mind, which constitutes a closed mental system. They both emphasize genuineness, and Mitchell (1988b) cautions that approaching patients with a demeanor demanded by doctrine, whether it be neutrality or empathy, can undermine a genuine interaction (p. 296).

Both approaches are concerned with what Mitchell (1988b) calls "constricted interpersonal patterns" and what Buber (1958) refers to as "I-It relating." It is the moments of real and genuine meeting that make psychotherapy work.

Postscript

In the years since this essay was originally written, there has been an increasing emphasis on psychoanalytic neuropsychology, attachment theory, and infant research. Much of the discussion in these areas has focused on the processes by which relatedness (attunement) fosters the treatment of trauma (Portnoy, 1999). Although these new approaches go partially beyond the scope of this essay, they raise many important questions. Among these are: Does a history of secure attachment increase the capacity for I-thou meeting? Do I-Thou moments foster secure attachment or alter disruptive attachment patterns?

It seems likely that Diana Fosha's attention to the details of the moment-to-moment interaction between therapist and client may foster I-Thou moments (see her essay, this chapter). To what degree does she include her subjectivity as contributing to mutual influence in the encounter? Is I-Thou a core affect?

Daniel Siegel (2003) sees therapy as a shared voyage (see Fosha's section). Does this voyage include mutual discovery and influence? He emphasizes the importance of a dyadic form of resonance in which energy and information are free to flow across two brains. How does this resonance correspond to Buber's *between*? Does Seigel go beyond the goal of attunement for the purpose of interpersonal coherence, or integration of neural connections that promote affect regulation? Is the integration of neural networks necessary in order to experience I-Thou moments and true meeting? Or is the perception of people in their wholeness — which is the hallmark of I-thou relating — irreducible to techniques and identifiable properties?

Acknowledgments

This essay is adapted from an article entitled "Relatedness: Where humanistic and psychoanalytic psychotherapy converge," published in *The Journal of Humanistic Psychology, 39,* (3), 1999 (pp. 19-34). The editor would like to thank Sage Publishing company for permission to reprint parts of this article.

References

Aron, L. (1996). *A meeting of minds: Mutuality in psychoanalysis.* Hillsdale, NJ: Analytic Press.

Binswanger, L. (1954). *Daseinsanalyse and psychotherapie* [*Daseinanalysis and psychotherapy*]. Bern, Switzerland: Francke Verlag.

Boss, M. (1963). *Psychoanalysis and daseinanalysis.* New York: Basic Books.

Brice, C. (1984). Pathological modes of human relating and therapeutic mutuality: A dialogue between Buber's existential relationship theory and object relations theory. *Psychiatry, 47,* 110–123.

Buber, M. (1958). *I and thou* (2d ed., R. Smith, Trans.). New York: Scribner.

Buber, M. (1965). *The knowledge of man: Philosophy of the interhuman* (M. Friedman, Trans.). New York: Harper & Row.

Bugental, J. F. T. (1987). *The art of the psychotherapist.* New York: Norton.

Clemmens, E. (1984). Transference and countertransference. *American Journal of Psychoanalysis, 44,* 311–315.

De-Forest, I. (1942). The therapeutic technique of Sandor Ferenczi. *International Journal of Psychoanalysis, 23,* 120–139.

Friedman, M. (1985). *The healing dialogue in psychotherapy.* New York: Jason Aronson.

Guntrip, H. (1969). *Schizoid phenomena, object-relations and the self.* New York: International Universities Press.

Guntrip, H. (1986). My experience of analysis with Fairbairn and Winnicott. In *Essential papers on object relations.* Peter Buckley, ed. New York: New York University Press.

Heard, W. (1993). *The healing between: A clinical guide to dialogical psychotherapy.* San Francisco: Jossey-Bass.

Hycner, R., & Jacobs, L. (1995). *The healing relationship in Gestalt therapy.* Hyland, NY: Gestalt Journal Press.

Kahn, E. (1996). The intersubjective perspective and the client-centered approach: Are they one at their core? *Psychotherapy, 33,* 30–42.

Kohut, H. (1971). *The analysis of the self.* New York: International University Press.

Lionells, M., Fiscalini, J., Mann, C., & Stern, D. (1995). *Handbook of interpersonal psychoanalysis.* Hillsdale, NJ: Analytic Press.

May, R. (1983). *The discovery of being: Writings in existential psychology.* New York: Norton.
Mitchell, S. A. (1987). The interpersonal and the intrapsychic: Conflict or harmony? *Contemporary Psychoanalysis, 23,* 400–410.
Mitchell, S. A. (1988a). The intrapsychic and the interpersonal: Different theories, domains and historical artifacts. *Psychoanalytic Inquiry, 8,* 472–496.
Mitchell, S. A. (1988b). *Relational concepts in psychoanalysis: An integration.* Cambridge, MA: Harvard University Press.
Phillips, J. (1980). Transference and encounter: The therapeutic relationship in psychoanalysis and existential psychotherapy. *Review of Existential Psychiatry and Psychology, 17,* 135–152.
Portnoy, D. (1999). Relatedness: Where humanistic and psychoanalytic psychotherapy converge. *Journal of Humanistic Psychology, 39* (1), 19–34.
Rogers, C. (1980). *A way of being.* Boston: Houghton Mifflin.
Siegel, D. (2003). An interpersonal neurobiology of psychotherapy: The developing mind and the resolution of trauma. In M. F. Soloman & D. J. Siegel (Eds.), *Healing trama: Attachment, trauma, the brain and the mind* (pp. 1–54). New York: Norton.
Stolorow, R. D. (1987). *Psychoanalytic treatment: An intersubjective approach.* Hillsdale, NJ: Analytic Press.
Stolorow, R. D., Atwood, G. E., & Brandchaft, B. (1994). *The intersubjective context of intrapsychic experience: The intersubjective perspective.* Northvale, NJ: Jason Aronson.
Tobin, S. (1990). Self psychology as a bridge between existential humanistic psychology and psychoanalysis. *Journal of Humanistic Psychology, 30,* 14–63.
Tobin, S. (1991). A comparison of psychoanalytic self psychology and Carl Rogers' person-centered therapy. *Journal of Humanistic Psychology, 31,* 9–33.
Wachtel, P. (1994). Behavior and experience: Allies not adversaries. *Journal of Psychotherapy Integration, 4,* 121–132.
Winnicott, D. (1960). *Ego distortion in terms of the true and false self: Maturation processes and the facilitating environment.* Madison, CT: International University Press.
Yalom, I. (1980). *Existential psychotherapy.* New York: Basic Books.

Autobiographical and Theoretical Reflections on the "Ontological Unconsciousness"

Robert D. Stolorow

Robert D. Stolorow, PhD, is a founding faculty member of the Institute of Contemporary Psychoanalysis in Los Angeles and the Institute for the Psychoanalytic Study of Subjectivity in New York. He is the author of *Trauma and Human Existence: Autobiographical, Psychoanalytic, and Philosophical Reflections* (2007) and co-author of *Worlds of Experience: Interweaving Philosophical and Clinical Dimensions in Psychoanalysis* (2002) and of six other books devoted to developing a phenomenological and contextualist perspective in psychoanalysis.

> Language is the house of being. In its home man dwells.
>
> **—Martin Heidegger**

> [In] man's relation to the signifier [are] the moorings of his being.
>
> **—Jacques Lacan**

> *The limits of my language* mean the limits of my world.
>
> **—Ludwig Wittgenstein**

> Language is not just one of man's possessions in the world; rather, on it depends the fact that man has a *world* at all. . . . *Being that can be understood is language.*
>
> **—Hans-G]eorg Gadamer**

Introduction

Intersubjective systems theory, the phenomenologically rooted psychoanalytic perspective that my collaborators and I have been developing over the course of more than three decades (Stolorow, Atwood, & Ross, 1978), holds as its basic principle that emotional experience takes form within constitutive intersubjective fields — systems of interacting experiential worlds. Accordingly, emotional experience is inseparable from the intersubjective contexts of attunement and malattunement in which it is felt. Painful emotional experiences become enduringly traumatic, we have contended, in the absence of a relational context within which they can be held and integrated.

In this illustration, I extend this intersubjective perspective to an exploration of the contextuality of the several varieties of unconsciousness and, in particular, of a form of unconsciousness that I call *ontological unconsciousness* — the loss of one's sense of being. Drawing on my own experience of traumatized states, I propose that it is in the process through which emotional experience comes into language that the sense of being is born, and that the aborting of this process brings a loss of the sense of being. The loss and regaining of one's sense of being are profoundly context dependent, hinging on whether the intersubjective contexts of one's living prohibit or welcome the coming into language of one's emotional experiences.

Emily Running

I begin with a poem about my youngest daughter entitled "Emily Running" (Stolorow, 2003a), which I wrote in September 2003:

My favorite time of day
is walking Emily to school in the morning.
We kiss as we leave our driveway
so other kids won't see us.
If I'm lucky, we have a second kiss,
furtively, at the school-yard's edge.
My insides beam as she turns from me
and runs to the building where her class is held,
blonde hair flowing,
backpack flapping,
my splendid, precious third-grader.
Slowly, almost imperceptibly,
a cloud begins to darken
my wide internal smile —
not grief, exactly, but a poignant sadness —
as her running points me back
to other partings
and toward other turnings
further down the road.

I recite this poem to myself every morning during my daily jog. The significance of this ritual will soon become apparent.

On the morning of February 23, 1991, I awakened to find my late wife, Daphne Socarides Stolorow, lying dead across our bed, four weeks after her metastatic lung cancer had been diagnosed. The loss of Dede, as she was called by loved ones and friends, shattered my world and permanently altered my sense of being. In March 1993, still consumed by emotional devastation, I met Julia Schwartz. We married a year later and were blessed with the birth of our daughter, Emily, on June 3, 1995.

Although Julia, and my relationship with her, lit a candle in the dark world of my grieving, I continued to be subject to feelings of deep sorrow and to recurring traumatized states, the latter being produced by any event leading me to relive the horrors of Dede's illness and death (Stolorow, 1999, 2003b). Julia tried valiantly to be available to me in my sorrow and traumatic states, but her ability to do this for me gradually eroded, as she felt increasingly and painfully erased by my continuing grieving for Dede. Eventually she told me that she could hear my grief no longer, and I responded by deciding to do my best to keep it to myself. I felt a terrible loneliness and, insidiously, my emotional aliveness began to shrink, as my broken heart, unwanted and banished, went into deep hiding. "I die slowly, so no one sees," I wrote in a very dark poem from that period.

Christmases were particularly difficult. The symptoms of Dede's undiagnosed cancer had significantly worsened during our last Christmas holiday together before she died, so Christmas was a time at which I was especially vulnerable to traumatic relivings. In such states I felt painfully isolated and estranged from the holiday cheer shared by Julia and her family. Even now, the words *Merry Christmas* assault me like a thousand fingernails scraping against a thousand chalkboards. I covered my sense of isolation and estrangement with a defensive contempt for the holiday celebrants, much as I had covered the alienation I felt as a boy at Christmastime, being the only Jewish kid in my grade school in rural Michigan. Lacking an intersubjective context within which they could be voiced, my feelings of sorrow and horror lived largely in my body, devolving into vegetative states of exhaustion and lethargy.

During the Christmas of 2004, something different and quite remarkable occurred. On Christmas Eve I remembered something very painful, which, perhaps sensing a greater receptivity in her, I decided to tell to Julia. One morning during Dede's and my last Christmas holiday together, Dede had tried to go jogging with me, but had to stop running because of her worsening cough. As I conveyed this concrete image of Dede having to stop running, and the horror it held for me, Julia was able to feel my state as a retraumatization of me rather than as an erasure of her, and she said she much preferred my real emotional pain to the defensive contempt with which I had been covering it. On Christmas morning, when I was once again picturing Dede having to stop running, Julia held me tenderly as I quietly wept. Later that morning, as I was preparing to go jogging, I sat in near paralysis, unable to put on my second running shoe. In agony, I said to Julia, "I can't stop thinking about Dede having to stop running."

Julia, a psychoanalyst with a fine intersubjective sensibility, said, "Your last poem — its title is 'Emily Running.'"

"Oh, God!" I cried out, and then burst into uncontrollable, hard sobbing for several minutes. In a flash I grasped the meaning of my ritual of running every morning with "Emily Running," reminding myself each day that dear little Emily, unlike Dede, keeps on running. My favorite time of day, I now realized, is seeing Emily running, not stopping.

Julia's interpretive comment was a key that unlocked the full force of my emotional devastation, which now found a relational home with her within which it could again be spoken. When I finally did go jogging on Christmas morning, I felt a sense of vitality and aliveness that had been profoundly absent during the prior Christmases since Dede's death. The blue Santa Monica sky seemed especially beautiful to me as I ran.

Ontological Unconsciousness

Why have I introduced a chapter on ontological unconsciousness with this autobiographical vignette? Ontology is the study of being, and hence I use the phrase *ontological unconsciousness* to denote a loss of one's sense of being. When my traumatized states could not find a relational home, I became deadened and my world became dulled. When such a home became once again present, I came alive and the vividness of my world returned. I believe my vignette provides a powerful illustration of the fundamental contextuality of our sense of being and of the intersubjective contexts in which it can become lost and regained.

The theme of losing and regaining one's sense of being calls to mind Martin Heidegger's (1927/1962) formulations of the inauthentic and authentic modes of existence, the former being characterized by lostness and a forgetting of one's being, and the latter by anxiety and the sense of uncanniness that accompanies the recognition that inherent to our existence is the ever-present possibility of its extinction. Heidegger's conception of authenticity bears a certain similarity to a distinctively Heideggerian description I wrote of traumatized states as I myself had experienced them:

> The essence of psychological trauma . . . [is] a catastrophic loss of innocence that permanently alters one's sense of being-in-the-world. . . . [Trauma] exposes the inescapable contingency of existence on a universe that is random and unpredictable and in which no safety or continuity of being can be assured. Trauma thereby exposes "the unbearable embeddedness of being." . . . As a result, the traumatized person cannot help but perceive aspects of existence that lie well outside the absolutized horizons of normal everydayness. It is in this sense that the worlds of traumatized persons are fundamentally incommensurable with those of others, the deep chasm in which an anguished sense of estrangement and solitude takes form. (Stolorow, 1999, p. 467)

For Heidegger, the inauthentic and authentic modes are given a priori, as necessary and universal structures of our sense of being. As a clinical psychoanalyst, by contrast, I seek understanding of individual experiences of losing and finding one's sense of being, as these take form in constitutive intersubjective contexts. Before discussing this question further, I first summarize the previous efforts my collaborators and I have made to contextualize differing varieties of unconsciousness.

Beginning more than 25 years ago, George Atwood and I (Atwood & Stolorow, 1980, 1984; Stolorow & Atwood, 1989, 1992) have been formulating three interrelated, intersubjectively derived forms of unconsciousness. The *prereflective unconscious* is the system of organizing principles, formed in a lifetime of relational experiences, that pattern and thematize one's experiential world. Such principles, although not repressed, ordinarily operate outside the domain of reflective self-awareness. The *dynamic unconscious* has been reconceptualized as consisting in those emotional experiences that were denied articulation because they were met with massive malattunement and thereby came to be perceived as threatening to needed ties to caregivers. Repression is grasped here as a kind of negative organizing principle determining which emotional experiences are to be prevented from coming into full being. The *unvalidated unconscious* encompasses emotional experiences that could not be articulated because they did not evoke the requisite validating responsiveness from caregivers that would make their articulation possible. All three forms of unconsciousness, we have repeatedly emphasized, derive from specific intersubjective contexts.

Foreshadowing the central thesis of this narrative, our evolving theory rested on the assumption that the child's emotional experience becomes progressively articulated through the validating attunement of the early surround. During the preverbal period of infancy, the articulation of the child's emotional experience is achieved through attunements communicated in the sensorimotor dialogue with caregivers. With the maturation of the child's symbolic capacities, symbols gradually assume a place of importance alongside sensorimotor attunements as vehicles through which the child's emotional experience is validated within the developmental system. Therefore, we have argued, in that domain in which emotional experience increasingly becomes articulated in symbols, unconscious becomes coextensive with unsymbolized. When the act of articulating an emotional experience is perceived to threaten an indispensable tie, repression can be achieved by preventing the continuation of the process of encoding that experience in symbols.

In a later contribution (Stolorow, Atwood, & Orange, 2002), in which Donna Orange joined the collaboration, we borrowed the horizonal metaphor from continental phenomenology in order to capture further the contextuality of unconsciousness. For this purpose, the idea of a horizon is a particularly well-suited metaphor, because we know that visual horizons constantly change as we move about in space from one context to another. Hence, we can picture unconsciousness, of either the dynamic or unvalidated form, in terms of the changing, limiting horizons of one's experiential world. Whatever one is not able to feel or know can be said to fall outside the horizons of one's experiential world. Such horizons of awareness take form developmentally in the medium of the differing responsiveness of the surround to different regions of the child's emotional experience. A similar conceptualization applies to the psychoanalytic situation, wherein the patient's resistances can be shown to fluctuate in concert with perceptions of the analyst's varying receptivity and attunement to the patient's emotional experience.

Unlike the repression barrier, which Sigmund Freud viewed as a fixed intrapsychic structure within an isolated mind, world horizons, like the experiential worlds they delimit, are conceptualized as emergent properties of ongoing, dynamic, intersubjective systems. Forming and evolving within a nexus of living systems, experiential worlds, and their horizons are thoroughgoingly embedded in constitutive contexts. The horizons of awareness are thus fluid and ever shifting, products both of one's unique intersubjective history and of what is or is not allowed to be felt and known within the intersubjective fields that constitute one's current living. Our conception of world horizons as emergent features of intersubjective systems bears a kinship to Gerson's (2004) and Zeddies's (2000) idea of a "relational unconscious" and Stern's (1997) discussion of "unformulated experience."

How might this deeply contextual view of unconsciousness be extended to ontological unconsciousness? In order to explore this question, I must first consider two seemingly contrasting ideas about the foundation of the sense of being that are implicit in my viewpoint. One, which harks back to an early article written with Dede (Socarides & Stolorow, 1984–1985), grounds the sense of selfhood, and, by implication, of being, in the experience of integrated affectivity: *I feel; therefore I am*. The other, to which the epigraphs at the beginning of this article allude, locates the ground of our sense of being in language or, more precisely, in the linguisticality of our experience. When one takes a developmental perspective on emotional experience, however, it immediately becomes apparent that these two ideas about the foundation of the sense of being are not in opposition to one another at all.

One of the first psychoanalytic authors to examine systematically the development of emotional experience was Krystal (1974/1988), who delineated two developmental lines for affect: (1) affect differentiation — the development of an array of distinctive emotions from diffuse early ur-affect states of pleasure and unpleasure, and (2) desomatization and verbalization of affect — the evolution of affect states from their earliest form as exclusively somatic states into emotional experiences that can be verbally articulated. Joseph Jones (1995) refined our comprehension of this second developmental line by emphasizing the importance of symbolic processes in its unfolding. The capacity for symbolic thought comes on line maturationally at the age of 10 to 12 months, making language possible for the child. At that point, the earlier, exclusively bodily forms of emotional experience can begin to become articulated in symbols, for example, in words. Consequently, the child's emotional experiences increasingly can be characterized as *somatic-symbolic* or *somatic-linguistic integrations*.

As Krystal (1974/1988) and then, more extensively, Dede and I (Socarides & Stolorow, 1984–1985) pointed out, this developmental progression takes place within a relational medium, an intersubjective context. It is the caregiver's attuned responsiveness, we claimed, phase-appropriately conveyed through words, that facilitates the gradual integration of the child's bodily emotional experience with symbolic thought, leading to the crystallization of distinctive emotions that can be named. In the absence of such verbally expressed attunement, or in the face of grossly malattuned responses, an aborting of this developmental process can occur, whereby emotional experience remains inchoate, diffuse, and largely bodily.

In the chapter on world horizons in Stolorow et al., 2002, we discussed the case of "Anna," whose early childhood was spent in Budapest during World

War II and the Nazi occupation and whose father was killed in a concentration camp when she was four years old. She described a "nameless terror" that was revived in the analysis when she remembered the horrors of the war years and, especially, her father's incarceration and death. Her mother consistently denied the frightening realities of the war and of the father's death, never openly grieving. Anna perceived that her own terror and grief were unwelcome to her mother, that she must not feel or name her emotional pain, and so her most unbearable emotional states remained outside the horizons of symbolized experience — nameless — until they found a hospitable home with her analyst within which they could be named. As shown in my autobiographical vignette, the aborting of somatic-linguistic integration is not restricted to early childhood. So long as my traumatized states found no welcoming relational home within which they could be given voice, they remained largely vegetative in nature.

I have become convinced that it is in the process of somatic-symbolic integration, the process through which emotional experience comes into language, that the sense of being is born. Hence, as shown in my vignette, the aborting of this process, the disarticulation of emotional experience, brings a diminution or even loss of the sense of being, an ontological unconsciousness. I have attempted to show that the loss and regaining of the sense of being, as reflected in experiences of deadness and aliveness, are profoundly context sensitive and context dependent, hinging on whether the intersubjective systems that constitute one's living prohibit or welcome the coming into language of one's emotional experiences. Consistent with Heidegger's (1927/1962) claim that human being is always embedded, a "being-in-the-world," one's sense of being is inseparable from the intersubjective contexts in which it is embedded and in which it is sustained or negated.

Heidegger (1927/1962) claimed that humans are unique among other beings in that our being is an issue for us; that is, our sense or understanding of our being is inherent to, and fundamentally constitutive of, our being. If Heidegger was right, then for us the loss of a sense of being is, in fact, a loss of being. This can be seen especially clearly in the phenomenology of psychotic states, whose core my collaborators and I (Stolorow et al., 2002) have characterized as an experience of personal annihilation. In such extreme psychological catastrophes, the disintegration of being-in-the-world is so profound and thoroughgoing that the very distinction between the loss of the sense of being and the loss of being, in effect, collapses. There just is annihilation — an eradication of existing as human.

Concluding Remarks

Two themes interweave throughout this essay. One pertains to the profound contextuality of emotional trauma and of the loss of one's sense of being. The second, less explicit theme, which dips into Heidegger's (1927/1962) existential analytic, pertains to the recognition that emotional trauma is built into the basic constitution of human existence (Stolorow, 2007). In virtue of our finitude and of the finitude of our important connections with others, the possibility of emotional trauma is constant and ever present. However, because it is also constitutive of our existence to be "brothers [and sisters] in the same darkness" (Vogel, 1994, p. 94), we are able to form bonds of emotional attunement that render the devastating impact of such trauma more bearable and that help sustain the vitality of our sense of being. It is here, in this emotional kinship, that the existential underpinnings of our calling as psychotherapists can be found, making possible what my soul brother, George Atwood, calls "the incomparable power of human understanding."

Acknowledgments

This essay is an expanded version of an article originally published in *Contemporary Psychoanalysis*, Vol. 42, No. 2, April 2006, pp. 233–241. It was presented by invitation at the International Association for Relational Psychoanalysis and Psychotherapy conference on "Unconscious Experience: Relational Perspectives," Rome, June 23–26, 2005. I am deeply grateful to George Atwood, Donna Orange, and especially Julia Schwartz, for contributing to the development of the ideas in this essay and for helping to make its writing possible.

References

Atwood, G. E., & Stolorow, R. D. (1980). Psychoanalytic concepts and the representational world. *Psychoanalysis and Contemporary Thought*, *3*, 267–290.

Atwood, G. E., & Stolorow, R. D. (1984). *Structures of subjectivity: Explorations in psychoanalytic phenomenology.* Hillsdale, NJ: The Analytic Press.

Gerson, S. (2004). The relational unconscious: A core element of intersubjectivity, thirdness, and clinical process. *Psychoanalytic Quarterly*, *73*, 63–98.

Heidegger, M. (1962). *Being and time* (J. Macquarrie & E. Robinson, Trans.). New York: Harper & Row. (Original work published 1927)

Jones, J. M. (1995). *Affects as process: An inquiry into the centrality of affect in psychological life.* Hillsdale, NJ: The Analytic Press.

Krystal, H. (1988). Genetic view of affects. In *Integration and self-healing: Affect, trauma, alexithymia* (pp. 38–62). Hillsdale, NJ: The Analytic Press. (Original work published 1974)

Socarides, D. D., & Stolorow, R. D. (1984–1985). Affects and self-objects. *Annual of Psychoanalysis*, *12/13*, 105–119.

Stern, D. B. (1997). *Unformulated experience: From dissociation to imagination in psychoanalysis.* Hillsdale, NJ: The Analytic Press.

Stolorow, R. D. (1999). The phenomenology of trauma and the abolutisms of everyday life: A personal journey. *Psychoanalytic Psychology*, *16*, 464–468.

Stolorow, R. D. (2003a). Emily running. *Constructivism in the Human Sciences*, *8*, 227.

Stolorow, R. D. (2003b). Trauma and temporality. *Psychoanalytic Psychology*, *20*, 158–161.

Stolorow, R. D. (2007). *Trauma and human existence: Autobiographical, psychoanalytic, and philosophical reflections.* Mahwah, NJ: The Analytic Press.

Stolorow, R. D., & Atwood, G. E. (1989). The unconscious and unconscious fantasy: An intersubjective-developmental perspective. *Psychoanalytic Inquiry, 9*, 364–374.

Stolorow, R. D., & Atwood, G. E. (1992). *Contexts of being: The intersubjective foundations of psychological life*. Hillsdale, NJ: The Analytic Press.

Stolorow, R. D., Atwood, G. E., & Orange, D. M. (2002). *Worlds of experience: Interweaving philosophical and clinical dimensions in psychoanalysis*. New York: Basic Books.

Stolorow, R. D., Atwood, G. E., & Ross, J. M. (1978). The representational world in psychoanalytic therapy. *International Review of Psycho-Analysis, 5*, 247–256.

Vogel, L. (1994). *The fragile "we": Ethical implications of Heidegger's being and time*. Evanston, IL: Northwestern University Press.

Zeddies, T. (2000). Within, outside, and in between: The relational unconscious. *Psychoanalytic Psychology, 17*, 467–487.

Transformance, Recognition of Self by Self, and Effective Action

Diana Fosha

Diana Fosha, PhD, is the developer of Accelerated Experiential-Dynamic Psychotherapy (AEDP) and the director of the AEDP Institute in New York City. She is the author of *The Transforming Power of Affect: A Model for Accelerated Change* (Basic Books, 2000), as well as of papers on transformational studies, the experiential process, and trauma treatment. A DVD of her AEDP work with a patient has just been released by the American Psychological Association, as part of their Systems of Psychotherapy Video Series. Many of her papers are available through the AEDP website at www.aedpinstitute.com.

Introduction

People have a fundamental need for transformation. We are wired for growth, healing, and self-righting, that is, resuming impeded growth. We have a need for the expansion and liberation of the self, the letting down of defensive barriers, and the dismantling of the false self (Ghent, 1990/1999; Schneider, in press). We are shaped by a deep desire to be known, seen, and recognized (Sander, 1995, 2002), as we strive to come into contact with parts of ourselves that are frozen (Eigen, 1996). Along with needing to be known authentically, we have a need to know the other (Buber, 1965; Ghent, 1990/1999), a profound and undeveloped aspect of attachment.[1] In the process of radical change, we become more ourselves than ever before and recognize ourselves to be so (Fosha, 2005).

Even prior to the need for authentic self-expression and contact, there is the need for effective action on behalf of the self (van der Kolk, 2006), which is why emotions are wired into our brains and bodies: The categorical emotions[2]

THE STRUCTURE OF EMOTIONAL EXPERIENCE PROCESSED TO COMPLETION:
The 3 States and 2 State Transformations of AEDP

STATE 1: DEFENSE
Against the experience of emotion and/or relatedness

FIRST STATE TRANSFORMATION

TRANSITIONAL AFFECTS:
Intrapsychic crises

HERALDING AFFECTS:
Announcing openness to core affect

STATE 2: CORE AFFECT
Categorical emotions, coordinated relational experiences, intersubjective experiences of pleasure, authentic self states, ego states, receptive affective experiences

SECOND STATE TRANSFORMATION

TRANSFORMATIONAL AFFECTS:

- Post-breakthrough affects (relief, hope, feeling lighter, stronger, cleaner, new)
- Mastery affects (pride, joy, competence)
- Mourning-the-self affects (emotional pain)
- Healing affects associated with recognition and affirmation (gratitude, tenderness, feeling moved)
- Tremulous affects associated with the changing self (fear/excitement, positive vulnerability, startle/shock/curiosity)
- The healing vortex of sensations associated with cascading transformations

STATE 3: CORE STATE
Acting adaptively and naturally; calm; flow, vitality, ease, well-being, openness; energy; confidence; creativity; relaxation; empathy and self-empathy; wisdom, generosity; clarity; the sense of things feeling "right"; the truth sense

— fear, anger, joy, sadness, disgust — play a powerful role in survival. Their full expression bestows access to broadened thought-action repertoires (Damasio, 2001; Darwin, 1872/1965; Fosha, 2000; Frederickson & Losada, 2005). Transformational vehicles themselves, each categorical emotion is associated with a set of *adaptive action tendencies* evolutionarily dedicated to bringing about conditions within which the individual's optimal development can unfold.

The existential need for recognition and the functional need for effective action are powerful motives; they are both manifestations of transformance. *Transformance*[3] is my term for the overarching motivational force, operating in both development and therapy, that strives toward maximally adaptive organization, vitality, authenticity, and connection. Residing deeply in our brains are wired-in dispositions for transformance. Naturally occurring adaptive-affective change processes, such as emotion, dyadic-affect regulation, empathic recognition of the self, and so forth (Fosha, 2002), are manifestations of transformance. Accelerated experiential-dynamic psychotherapy (AEDP; Fosha, 2000), the model of therapy that informs my work, seeks to facilitate therapeutic change through actively engaging these affective change processes from the first moments of the first therapeutic encounter. Moment-to-moment accompanied by positive somatic markers, affective change processes effect state transformations and culminate in the positive affects that characterize resilience, expansive growth, and flourishing (Frederickson & Losada, 2005; Loizzo, in press; Tugade & Frederickson, 2004). The positive affects are desired states: As such, they themselves become motivational forces (Ghent, 2002; Sander, 2002).

Transformance is the motivational counterpart of resistance: It is driven by hope and the search for the vitalizing positive affects that accompany all adaptive affective change processes (Fosha, 2002). Resistance, on the other hand, is fueled by dread and the desire to avoid bad feelings — be they deadening or terrifying. Resistance drives processes that eventuate in disorganization, deterioration, and immobility (Frederickson & Losada, 2005; Loizzo, in press; Russell & Fosha, in press; Tugade & Frederickson, 2004).

This essay comprises three parts. In the first, I will introduce some defining aspects of AEDP theory and practice and show how transformance is foundational to both. In the second, I will provide a microanalysis of an initial session with a male patient with a history of trauma suffering from a current relapse of sexual addiction behavior. Work with him will illustrate the transformational spiral that, in less than 45 minutes, takes us from a frenzy of self-loathing and uncontrollability to a moving recognition of the self by the self, and to confidence in his capacity for effective action. It will also allow us to look at the phenomenology of healing. Finally, using transformance as a bridging construct that might help promote the kind of integration to which this volume is devoted, the third part will examine some of the resonances between AEDP and the existential-integrative (EI) model.

Part 1: On AEDP

> ... love and hate are not opposites. The real polarity is between love and fear. Only when there is no fear, love flourishes. (Ghent, 1990/1999, p. 229)

The notion of transformance is part of a larger project of developing a theory of and for therapy that is change based, rather than psychopathology based (Fosha, 2002, 2005). Understanding how healing transformational processes — their dynamics, their phenomenology — work and how they can be effectively and systematically harnessed is central to such an endeavor.

Credo: Basic Concepts and Values In AEDP, the difference between whether the forces of transformance or the forces of resistance are entrained is determined by the attachment relationship. "Attachment decisively tilts whether we respond to life's challenges as opportunities for learning and expansion of the self or as threats leading to our constriction of activities and withdrawal from the world" (Fosha, 2006, p. 570). To entrain transformance forces, and from the first moments of the first session, AEDP seeks to facilitate the co-creation of a dyadic relationship characterized by secure attachment. Evolved to counter fear and protect against danger (Bowlby, 1988; Main, 1999), the attachment relationship is essential for the moment-to-moment regulation of intense emotion, which would otherwise be overwhelming and stressful (Schore, 2001). Through the regulatory powers of the attachment relationship and its subsequent internalization into the individual's self-regulatory repertoire, the individual is able to harness the adaptational advantages conferred upon the organism by the full experience of the categorical emotions. The self can thus benefit from the expanded range of thoughts and behaviors they enable (Frederickson & Losada, 1995).

The therapeutic task is to create a safe environment in which the motivation for transformation can come to the fore. This environment is then buttressed by therapeutic efforts that help the aforementioned motivation grow stronger than the motivation for maintenance of the status quo (which upholds the principle that "the evil you know is better than the evil you don't," a motto for traumatized people everywhere).

Two different pathways are used by treatments that aim for therapeutic healing. The well-established pathway of seeking to overcome resistance, or fix what is broken, characterizes most systems of psychotherapy. Its assumption, articulated cogently by Alexander and French (1946/1980), is that while resistance-driven functioning is inevitable, a corrective emotional experience is achieved when the repetition scenario unfolds but has a different ending.

The road less traveled promotes the activation of healing tendencies — the forces of transformance — from the beginning and not just as a result of having worked through the damage of the past. In AEDP, we do not just seek a new ending, but also a new beginning (Fosha, 2006; Fosha & Yeung, 2006;

Lamagna & Gleiser, in press; Russell & Fosha, in press; Tunnell, 2006). We are on the lookout for glimmers of transformance and resilience, and we focus on these and amplify them. Aiming to lead with a corrective emotional experience, AEDP's pathway entails a stance and a set of techniques, as well as the creation of conditions for the entrainment of the transformance forces always present as dispositional tendencies (Winnicott, 1960). In the right environment,[4] dispositional tendencies toward healing and self-righting that are dormant, frozen, or moribund can begin to emerge. Thus resourced, the patient becomes a partner for the journey ahead. We call this "working with the self-at-worst from under the aegis of the self-at-best" (Fosha, 2000, 2002, 2005).

In addition to its transformance-based, healing orientation, I will focus here on seven other fundamental and holographic aspects of AEDP:[5]

1. *Attachment-based stance sprinkled liberally with intersubjective delight in the patient*: The therapeutic relationship in AEDP aims to be the secure base from which experiential explorations of deep, painful emotional experiences can be undertaken. Key to AEDP's attachment stance is that the patient not be alone with overwhelming emotions. The AEDP therapist, aiming to promote security of attachment and intersubjective contact and to facilitate affective experience, is explicitly empathic, affirming, affect regulating, and emotionally engaged, broadcasting the willingness to help. Such an attachment relationship obviates the fear associated with intense, stressful-when-not-regulated, emotional experience (see dyadic affect regulation below). Similarly, the therapist's delighting in the patient, while in active intersubjective engagement, is a powerful antidote to the patient's shame (Trevarthen, 2001). With fear and shame reduced, the defenses erected to protect the self can come down, yielding access to more somatically based primary emotional experience (Fosha, 2003, 2006; Greenan & Tunnell, 2003, Chap. 2; Hughes, 2006; Lamagna & Gleiser, in press; Tunnell, 2006).

   Two features distinguish AEDP's use of attachment: Attachment is not the *aim of* therapy, but rather the *sine qua non for* therapy. Secure attachment in the therapeutic relationship is what we seek to entrain from the start, so as to optimize experiential work with intense emotions. Second, it is not sufficient that attachment operates implicitly, working as the background hum against which experience takes place. The patient's experience of the attachment relationship needs to be a major focus of therapeutic work (Fosha, 2006).
2. *Dyadic affect regulation*: The goal that the patient not be alone with overwhelming emotions is achieved through the process of dyadic affect regulation. Through the moment-to-moment affective communication between dyadic partners that occurs through nonver-

bal, right-brain-mediated processes involving gaze, tone of voice, rhythm, touch, and other vitality affects, members of the dyad establish coordinated states. The process of dyadic affect regulation proceeds through countless iterations of cycles of attunement, disruption, and then, through repair, the re-establishment of coordination at a higher level. Though invariably accompanied by negative affects, the disruption of coordination, if repaired, is a major source of transformation. Disruption occurs when experiences that are outside the coordinated state burst forth. If attunement is where self and other resonate, disruption is the realm of being on disturbingly different wavelengths. Repair involves establishing a new, expanded state where differences can be encompassed and integrated. "The flow of energy expands as states of brain organization in the two partners expand their complexity into new and more inclusive states of coherent organization, enabling the infant to do what it would not be able to do alone" (Sander, 2002, p. 38). The achievement of the new coordinated state is a vitalizing energizing human experience. It gives rise to new emergent phenomena that transform and expand both dyadic experience and the experience of each dyadic partner, reflecting how being together changes each of them (Fosha, 2001, 2003; Hughes, 2006; Sander, 1995, 2002; Schore, 2001; Tronick, 2003; Tunnell, 2006).

3. *The experiential method — precise phenomenology and moment-to-moment tracking of affective experience:* The aim of AEDP treatment is to provide the patient with a new experience, and that experience should be good. By *good*, I do not mean necessarily pleasant, but rather an experience that, even when painful or difficult, feels right and true, and is accompanied by increasing coherence, relaxation, and flow. We track moment-to-moment fluctuations of the emotional experience of patient, therapist, and the dyad. All interventions are grounded in moment-to-moment experience and aim for phenomenological precision. Thus, they are informed by a sense of where we are and where we (phenomenologically) want to go. The steady somatic focus on the patient's experience and its felt sense (Gendlin, 1981) accomplishes three therapeutic goals: It reduces anxiety; it lets the patient drop from a defensive position to one more connected with emotion; and, finally, it increases access to right-brain-dominated, affectively loaded experiencing (Fosha, 2003; Fosha & Yeung, 2006).

The transformational process is guided by the somatic markers of healing transformational processes. Invariably positive, these somatic markers (e.g., smiles, deep in-and-out breaths, dyadically coordinated head nods, sideways head tilts, upward gazes) signal moment to moment that the therapeutic process is on the right track.

4. *Emotion and the body:* Working with deep emotions to completion — nothing that feels bad is ever the last step. Adaptive, transformational emotional experiences involve the body. Emotion is both the target and the agent of change. The processing to completion of the somatically rooted experience of previously unbearable core affects in the here-and-now of the patient-therapist relationship is the central agent of change in AEDP. After defensive blocks are removed and the inhibiting impact of pathogenic shame and fear has been alleviated, we work to facilitate access to the direct somatic experience of subcortically generated and right-hemisphere-mediated categorical emotions and other adaptive core-affective experiences (Damasio, 1999). We seek to deepen the patient's experience and work it through to completion until his or her adaptive action tendencies are released and the patient's access to resources and resilience opens up (Fosha, 2000, 2004b, 2005).
5. *Focusing on the experience of transformation itself becomes a transformational process*: As all experientialists know, focusing on an experience transforms it (e.g., Gendlin, 1981). Having processed emotional experience to completion, and thus effected a transformation, we do not stop. A major aspect of AEDP is the focus on, and the affirmation of, the experience of transformation itself, particularly the experience of the transformation of the self in the context of a healing dyadic relationship. We call this activity *metatherapeutic processing* since we are experientially exploring what is therapeutic about the therapeutic process, and we call the affects that result from this metatherapeutic exploration the *transformational affects*. Metatherapeutic processing involves alternating between experience and reflection on experience, and then continuing to experientially explore the patient's changing experience upon having articulated something about the experience through having reflected on it. Once each new experience is elaborated through this going back and forth between experience and reflection, it becomes the departure point for the next round of exploration. Thus we unleash a cascade of transformations (Fosha, 2004b, 2005, 2006; Fosha & Yeung, 2006; Russell & Fosha, in press).
6. *Receptive affective experiences*: It is not sufficient that empathy, care, love, or help be given. To work their potent magic, they must be taken in and used. Receptive affective experiences of feeling seen, held, understood, helped, or recognized are also rooted in the body, and have a felt sense specific to them: Exploring them allows us to know whether, and how, what is relationally given is received. Thus, we explicitly explore the patient's experience of receiving empathy, or care, or delight. Once we address defenses and fears that stand in the way of the patient's capacity to take in and use good stuff, we then

work to deepen the patient's receptive capacities. Being able to receive emotionally is necessary if the vitality and security that are the aim of attachment and joyful intersubjective contact are to become integrated mainstays of the patient's core identity and sense of self.

7. *Vitalizing positive somatic markers associated with transformance*: A felt sense of vitality and energy characterizes transformance-based emergent phenomena. AEDP, along with others interested in exploring the progressive motivational forces of transformance operating in development and therapy (e.g., Buber, 1965; Eigen, 1996; Gendlin, 1981; Ghent, 1990/1999, 2002; Sander, 1995, 2002; Schore, 2001; Trevarthen, 2001), recognizes these very positive phenomena as energizing developmental growth, glorious development, and expansive, enriching exploration. Rooted in the body, they mark transformational processes on an optimizing path: Going beyond symptom relief and stress reduction, we are in the realm of thriving, flourishing, and resilient functioning (Frederickson & Losada, 1995; Tugade & Frederickson, 2004; Russell & Fosha, in press). Moreover, these positive vitalizing experiences are the affective correlates of a neurochemical environment in the brain that is maximally conducive to optimal learning, development, and brain growth (Schore, 2001).

The Three States and Two State Transformations

> The existentialists teach us that both [creatureliness and godlikeness] are . . . defining characteristics of human nature. . . . And any philosophy which leaves out either cannot be considered to be comprehensive. (Maslow, 1968, quoted in Schneider & May, 1995, p. 92)

In AEDP, we leave out neither creatureliness — that is, biologically based processes like emotion and attachment, rooted in our mammalian brains and bodies — nor godlikeness — that is, the transcendent aspects, equally biologically based, of our selves-at-best. The two are organically and inextricably connected in the transformational process by which emotion in the context of attachment safety is experientially processed to completion (Fosha, 2005). Three states bridged by two state transformations (see page 291) characterize that process:

State 1: State 1 functioning is dominated by defenses and inhibiting affects, such as shame and fear, which block the person's direct contact with his or her own emotional experience. Interventions here aim at building the experience of safety through establishing relatedness, bypassing defenses, and alleviating fear and shame. The secure attachment bond obviates the need for defenses through undoing the patient's aloneness.

First State Transformation: The first state transformation reflects the disruption of old and dysfunctional patterns as a result of the new experiences generated by the therapeutic dyad. All the while staying with the patient, so that he or she does not feel alone, we seek to amplify the glimmers of affect that herald previously warded off intense emotional experiences. Here, dyadic affect regulation is achieved through right-brain-to-right-brain communication: Through eye contact, tone of voice, gaze, tone, rhythm, and the use of simple, evocative, sensory-laden, imagistic language, we seek to entrain (and facilitate nontraumatic access to) right-brain-mediated, somatically rooted emotional experience. The secure base is co-constructed as old patterns are deconstructed.

State 2: With defenses and inhibiting affects out of the way, the patient is viscerally in touch with bodily rooted emotional experience, most notably, the categorical emotions, the essence of creatureliness. Again, the key here is the attachment relationship: Once it is in place, emotional processing work can be launched. State 2 dyadic affect regulation has patient and therapist working together to help the patient access, deepen, regulate, and work through subcortically initiated and right-brain-mediated emotional experiences, so that the seeds of healing contained in such experiences can be released.

Second state transformation: What in most therapies is often seen as a natural endpoint of experiential work, that is, the completion of a round of processing of emotion, is for AEDP the herald of another round of work. In metatherapeutic processing, the focus shifts to the patient's experience of transformation. Using alternating waves of (right-brain-mediated) experience and (left-brain-mediated) reflection, here the goal is to integrate the fruits of intense emotional experience into the personality organization. Through exploring the experience and meaning of what has just gone on for each partner, we also further strengthen attachment security, which is rooted in difficult experience, successfully traversed together.

The dyadic affect regulation characteristic of metatherapeutic processing entrains the integrative structures of the brain, that is, the corpus callosum, the prefrontal cortex (especially the right prefrontal cortex, which is shown to mediate emotionally loaded autobiographical narrative; Siegel, 2003), the insula, and the anterior cingulate (van der Kolk, 2006). These structures have been shown to be adversely affected by trauma (Teicher, 2002) and to play a significant role in the healing from trauma through the coordination of left-brain and right-brain aspects of emotional experience (Lanius et al., 2004; van der Kolk, 2006).

Entraining them through metatherapeutic processing is both a one-brain process and a two-brain process: While the dyad supports the integrative work that takes place within the individual's neural processing, it also supports a dyadic brain-to-brain communication process involving the integrative brain structures of the dyadic partners. The result is the patient's nascent capacity to generate a coherent and cohesive autobiographical narrative, the single best predictor of security of attachment and resilience in the face of trauma (Main, 1999; Siegel, 2003).

The focus on the experience of healing transformation evokes one or more of the six types of phenomenologically distinct transformational affects identified to date (Fosha, 2006):

1. *Post-breakthrough affects*: feeling relief, as well as feeling lighter, clearer, and stronger, after an intense emotional experience processed to completion
2. *Mastery affects*: pride and joy that come to the fore when fear and shame are transformed
3. *Emotional pain*: the transformational affect associated with the process of mourning the self
4. *Healing affects*: gratitude and tenderness toward the other, and feeling moved within oneself in response to affirming recognition of the self and its transformation, as well as of the role of the other in the process
5. *Tremulous affects*: fear/excitement, startle/surprise, curiosity/interest, and a feeling of positive vulnerability, associated with traversing the crisis of healing change
6. *Healing vortex*: oscillating and vibrating sensations, associated with how the body proper processes quantum transformation

State 3: The processing of an emotion to completion ushers in a third state. In *core state*, the patient has a subjective sense of truth and a heightened sense of authenticity and vitality; almost always, so does the therapist. As in State 2, defenses and anxiety are absent in core state. But whereas the turbulence of intense emotions defines State 2, calm, clarity, confidence, centeredness, curiosity, compassion, courage, and creativity — Schwartz's (2003) eight C's — capture the defining qualities of core state.

Work with core state phenomena culminates in the assertion of personal truth and strengthening of the individual's core identity. In this "state of assurance" (James, 1902/1985), the patient contacts a confidence that naturally translates into effective action. The patient's true self declares itself (Osiason, 2006). A strong sense of self and the capacity for effective action on behalf of the self are inextricably intertwined.

In core state, the patient experiences a sense of expansion and liberation of the self, as well as openness to and capacity for deep contact and interrelatedness. Fully able to move back and forth between compassion and self-compassion, between wisdom and generosity, True-Self–True-Other relating — AEDP's equivalent of I-Thou relating — is a quintessential core-state phenomenon. Thus, the transcendent qualities Abraham Maslow (1968) associates with "godlikeness" are front and center in core state.

Processing intense emotion to completion describes an *arc of transformation* (Fosha, 2005). It goes from (1) defenses against, and anxiety and shame about, both creatureliness and godlikeness, to (2) creatureliness — that is, the bodily rooted, subcortically initiated categorical emotions — to (3) godlikeness — that is, core state, where through a sense of the sacred and the effective, we become most deeply human and most ourselves. The time-honored dichotomy between creatureliness and godlikeness is bridged in one fell continuous moment-to-moment experientially tracked swoop.

Part 2: "Wheels on the Pavement": A First Session

I have chosen to use a single session, the first initial contact, to show how healing is possible from the first moment. The session illustrates how, in this case in less than 45 minutes, we can get from the depths of despair and self-loathing to a resilience that feels authentic and real. The patient is a man who, before being able to engage in I-Thou relating, first has to become an *I*. By the end of this piece of work, his *I* is firmly in place — so much so that it evokes the patient's own sense of awe with respect to himself.

In this example of AEDP work, all clinical choices are informed by an overarching goal: to buttress and foster the forces of transformance, while minimizing the forces of resistance. The clinical material shows how the focus on the experience of transformation solidifies, deepens, and fosters its ongoing emergence. The transformational process is not finite: The sense of self and effectiveness keeps on evolving and changing. True to the existential moment, not only can we have "a world in a grain of sand, eternity in an hour" (Blake, 1863/1987), but also the treatment in a session.

The patient is a 30-something professional, a recently married man whom I shall call "Lee." Lee recently relocated to the city where I practice and seeks therapy following a relapse of his sexual addiction suffered over the course of a week preceding this session. As I learned subsequent to the session, which is presented below, the patient's early history is notable for emotional and sexual abuse, as well as emotional neglect, in his family of origin, and a 10- to 15-year history of struggling with a sexual addiction, which had been under control for over a year prior to the current episode.

Vignette 1: Achieving Safety Through Honoring Defenses, Counteracting Anxiety and Shame, and Inviting Deeper Bodily Based Emotional Experience The session begins in the waiting room. Without even waiting to come in, while we are walking toward my office, Lee tells me that his being more than 15 minutes late is evidence of his tendency toward self-sabotage:

Therapist (T): [*Welcoming, smiling*] I am eager to hear why you were late.

Patient (P): [*Fidgety, uncomfortable smile*] I think purposefully not on purpose I didn't leave myself enough time because I think I was nervous about coming here and starting. . . . I had a very good working relationship with "Dr M." and initially I was looking at coming to New York as an opportunity to take a break from therapy, and kind of trying it on my own and quickly realizing that was not a good idea . . . and I guess I had a lot of hope about coming to New York, but also a lot of anxiety. And all of that sort of came together so that at 2:00, when I could have gotten up and left my office and gotten here with 15 minutes to spare, I instead decided to leave and not wait until 2:30. . . . I looked at the clock at the time that I could have come, but I guess I even said in my head, "That's too early," or something like, "What are you, a goody two shoes, showing up 15 minutes early?"

T: [*Big smile*] First of all, I'm very impressed. . . .

P: [*Giggles, taken aback; sweating; shallow breathing*]

T: . . . with your self awareness and openness with me. [*Surprises the unconscious," disconfirming patient's expectations of being met critically*]

P: Thanks.

T: That's the first thing that's very striking as we launch in. But secondly [*concerned tone*], that you have a lot of anxiety.

P: Yeah.

T: And had a lot of anxiety about being here [*Shifts focus from defenses to anxiety powering them*]

P: Yeah.

Here we see a combination of affirmation, on one hand, and keeping the pressure toward deepening experiencing, on the other. If the deepening is to take place, then anxiety has to be regulated.

T: Tell me what you're aware of, what you're experiencing [*experiential focus*]

P: Ummm, I guess it's more like I'm kind of insulating myself from the experience, to an extent.

T: Pushing back, pushing away. [*makes motion with hands of pushing away from oneself; therapist's right brain speaking to the patient's right brain*]

P: Yeah, like thinking of cute things to say, you know, questions that would be irrelevant like, "Where did you get the mike?" and dodge 'em type things which I know are not emotions. . . . You know, I've seen a lot of therapists and first sessions have gotten kind of "old hat" for me. . . . Not that I am a pro or anything, but it's very easy to come in and rattle off my little script and that is another way of . . . not being in the moment. But as to the original question of "What am I feeling, anxiety-wise?" you know, I am not feeling the anxiety, which is probably the problem. [*Insight is hard to separate from his self-criticism, or intellectualization, or anxiety*]

T: What are you aware of feeling? [*going for what he is feeling, rather than for what he is not feeling*] Let's stay with that because the issue of coming here is very loaded.

P: Yeah . . . yeah. [*Looks away, looks perplexed, confused, at a loss*]

T: Just when I said that, what was your experience? [*entry point into experiential exploration of relatedness*]

P: [*Uncomfortable smile*] Umm . . . expectation, like "come up with something to say," [*Intervention evokes more harsh self-judgment, projected outwards*]

T: Is that what the smile is covering up? [*away from the head, focus on the body*]

P: No, that was uh . . . What did you say? [*anxiety interfering*]

T: I said, "It's very loaded . . . You have a lot of feelings about coming here."

P: Oh yeah. [*Sweating, wiping his brow, holding his head*] . . . Ummmmm . . . I think . . . the laugh was like . . . "Tee-hee, I got a lot of problems" [*more self-deprecation, shame*] and uh . . . I think some of this is nervousness about working with you. . . . Dr. M was a very good experience for me. Easily my best therapy experience. Most progress, most work [*explicit focus on anxiety and the therapist's willingness to help with confusion bring down anxiety; can now articulate his basic conflict*] She . . . So, I kind of think I am missing that. I mean, this is like a funny dynamic here, where you pay someone to help you.

T: No, but what you are saying here is very very important [*honoring the patient's true communication; cutting through defensive subterfuges, self-deprecations*]. That you had a very positive experience with her, felt very helped by her, did a lot of work. . . . And that, in a way, coming to see me brings home that you are not going to see her anymore.

It is seven minutes into the session and we have shifted the focus from self sabotage and what is bad about what the patient is doing, to starting to elaborate the context in which the patient's efforts can be understood as adaptive.

P: Yeah.

T: [*Very empathic tone*] So that, right off the bat, there is an experience of the loss of something very precious.

P: Yeah, absolutely … Ummm … Yeah … She … I think I was aware while I was doing it of how helpful it was, but also … [*His anxiety visibly less, he is looking sad*]

T: And you know, I just feel . . . I feel your feelings about it. That there's a lot of sadness [*Pressuring toward core affect; anticipatory mirroring; already feeling the affect the patient is struggling against*]

P: Yeah [*sighs deeply, twice*]. Yeah, yeah and that's a lot of . . . I mean she was kind of describing some of your techniques, I don't know how fairly she can represent them, and I was thinking, "Oh, probably that wouldn't work for me," you know, so I was kind of figuring out ways of not doing this and just sitting around and missing not working with Dr. M [*very clear articulation of dynamic; rise in therapeutic alliance*]. Mmmm …

T: Mmhmm …

The aim has changed from first undoing the patient's self-deprecation, and then regulating his anxiety. Now with a clear dynamic emerging, the aim is to get past defensive blocks and help the patient access a core affect, which, at this point in the session, appears to be his sadness over loss.

P: And it was weird . . . in the lead up to the end, I didn't really . . . We did some end closure-type things, but I didn't go into the last sessions with this kind of mentality.

T: Of missing or sadness?

P: Yeah . . . it was there some . . . and she kind of expressed like, you know, the professional version of having a patient leave or whatever. . . . It was weird. . . . It was almost like … I didn't just let myself feel it. . . . I had to use that as a cue to like, "Oh yeah … this is ending, so I should probably feel something about it."

T: [*Not taking the bait of all the negative self statements, but going after the gist of the communication, refocusing on the here-and-now in the context of what was just elaborated*] … In a way, I could understand why you wouldn't want to come to see me. . . . You put it in terms of sabotage … but there is this kind of a huge loss of a very important relationship with someone who has helped you a great deal [*i.e., a positive attachment figure*].

P: Yeah [*head nods*].

Dyadic affect regulation is now in operation: There is an entrainment of our respective rhythms as the oscillations of our head nods become increasingly yoked and synchronous. Also, the tempo of our speech has slowed. There is a lot of space between the words. We pick up the action eight minutes later.

T: Now, you said to me you felt very insulated from these feelings about really having a loss in your life.
P: Yeah.
T: I don't know what you're experiencing, but you look mighty sad to me.
P: [*Laughs, nods his head, pauses, looks away, bites his lip*] Yeah . . . I might be more depressed than sad.
T: You laughed again. . . .
P: [*Shoulders shrug*]
T: What was your reaction to my saying that [*i.e., that you look sad*]?
P: Uh, I don't know . . . I don't know [*seems shy; is giggling*].
T: Go ahead [*encouraging tone*].
P: It just seemed funny, you know . . . your therapist telling you you look sad. . . . I know that it would be a valuable thing for me to feel. . . .
T: When you say, "It's a funny thing for your therapist to say," in what way? [*Note that I have become* his *therapist and not just* a *therapist.*]
P: From the point of view of trying to feel better and get better, it's, like, ironic. . . . You want your therapist to say you look good, or that you're doing better. . . . I mean, I know I've been here [*looks at his watch*] all of 20 minutes, so that would be a stretch, but . . .
T: So my saying that you looked sad felt like something negative. . . . See, to my mind, sadness, though it's a painful feeling, is very adaptive. . . . I mean, if you have a loss, you feel sadness. . . . It's not a failure, it's not a weakness, it's not a bad thing.
P: [*Smiles*]
T: [*Empathic, curious*] That smile tells me the entry points, about how this is getting in and how you're reacting to it. Tell me . . . [*inviting*]
P: [*Sobering, thoughtful*] Now I actually feel like there is a lot of sadness, like I want to cry or something. . . . It's like a relief. . . . You know, it's very easy to come and sense the expectation, not from you, but just in my own head, of me needing to do something or perform here or do whatever. . . . It's almost like a relieving giggle . . . like oh yeah . . .
T: [*Encouraging*] Uh hmmm.
P: Like this is safe or something, you know?

The patient begins full of self-attack, defensiveness, anxiety, and shame, with no access to the deeper experiences motivating his behavior. Instead of pointing out various destructive aspects of his moment-to-moment behavior, and getting hooked into an enactment where attachment figures tend to respond to his vulnerability with criticism, I consistently attend to the glimmers of transformance: I offer support and empathy while simultaneously maintaining a tight experiential focus, encouraging Lee to attend to his internal experience. Lee's belief is that getting connected with me as his new therapist means needing to relinquish his attachment to his previous therapist. As that assumption becomes increasingly articulated and clarified, he is able to relax into being in the session. We go from detachment and sabotaging of the new therapeutic relationship to an implicit acceptance and settling in, as he talks about "you want your therapist to tell you that . . ." implying that I have become his therapist. A few minutes later, he spontaneously declares, "This is safe or something," a strong green light for proceeding to deep affect work.

Vignette 2: Dropping Down: Sadness, Grief, and Unbearable Loneliness This vignette illustrates the process of working with intense emotion, using the attachment relationship and dyadic affect regulation to help the patient through suffering. Here the therapeutic work consists of (1) somatically accessing the previously feared-to-be unbearable affective experiences, (2) holding them and dyadically regulating them until they can be (3) worked through to completion and (4) their adaptive action tendencies, resources, and resilience are released. In the process, the experience of unwilled aloneness in the face of feared-to-be unbearable emotions has been procedurally alleviated: Lee feels not only not alone, but safe, and emotions, far from being unbearable for him, when processed together, turn out to lead to good stuff (Fosha, 2004b).

P: I cried some with Dr. M. . . . I cried a decent amount . . . but then, you know. . . .

T: But in a way, if you let yourself . . . just . . . more than anything else, if you allow something to happen. . . . And I am glad that you're feeling some sense of safety [*The language of permission*].

P: Yeah.

T: That some of the performance aspects have at least for the moment been allayed or . . .

P: Yeah.

T: So, if you were to imagine . . . let yourself from this place, from here, say goodbye to Dr. M, and put into words to her what she meant to you and what you're giving up and what you're losing.

Here, I am using the technique of portrayal to deepen and elaborate Lee's experience of grief (Fosha, 2000). Our attachment relationship is implicit and is what allows him to do the work he needs to do, that is, grieving the loss of his previous attachment figure, while being himself and having my support.

P: I tried to write something, I did write something when I sent her the last payment. . . . Yeah . . . it was very valuable to me. . . . I could . . .

T: What would you say to her? [*Keeps focus, redirects*]

P: I would say, "Thank you for getting me as close as I have ever been to the real regular old normal me." I was close enough to see it and be it for a little bit.

T: Um hmmmuh.

P: And you know . . . yeah . . .

T: [*Empathic tone*] So, it's upsetting to have to say goodbye to that.

P: Yeah . . . yeah . . . she was . . . she knew how to . . .

T: [*Making very supportive sympathetic noises and sounds as the patient is talking*]

P: She never, like, gave up on the whole thing [*left- and right-brain integration: the articulation deepens the feeling, and the deepening of the feeling allows for the deeper meaning and significance to emerge*] . . . which is frankly something.. . . It may sound very trite . . . but I think I find the ways in real life to get people to give up on me.

T: [*Echoes the patient, repeating some of his words*] . . . to give up on you.

P: Yeah.

T: So can you tell her . . . that?

P: [*With a giggle and looking away, but still very very sad*] Yeah. "Thank you for not giving up . . . [*trying to hold back sobs*] and just always helping me realize that . . .

T: . . . and always . . . [*helping: dyadic affect regulation*]

P: . . . and always kind of bringing back to this focus on realizing a lot of what I am doing is to get off track, to give up on myself. . . . Yeah, I mean, I think I basically tried to spend two years to get her to give up on me and she never did.

T: Mmmmm [*appreciative*].

P: So I thank her for that. "Thank you for that."

T: How does that feel to acknowledge that? I mean, it's very moving to me. . . . [*Metaprocessing remark, i.e., having done a piece of work, here saying goodbye to the former therapist, how does it feel to have done it?*]

P: Mmm . . . Yeah, it feels sad . . . it feels lonely and scary. . . . [*Crying deeply; as the meaning of the affective experience emerges, it further deepens the experience*]

T: Um huh [*Nonverbally being with the patient*].

P: Coming up here and some of the things I want to do . . .

T: Stay with lonely and scary [*Gentle redirection to remain connected to deep affect*].

P: Like . . . at this stage, you're a very nice person but the alternative of me just trying it on my own doesn't feel very different than this at this second. . . . It kind of feels like . . .

T: . . . kind of feels like . . . [*Helping, being with, empathic*]

P: . . . like I am totally alone [*crying, voice breaking*].

Paradoxically, by Lee's being able to share with me his experience of aloneness, Lee is not alone; the secure attachment and dyadic regulation are operating implicitly as he is finally feeling held and helped enough so that he can articulate this true experience, which is of tremendous loneliness.

T: [*Very sympathetic, sad, nonverbal communication through sympathetic noises*] That's a very old feeling.

P: Yeah, I felt that for a long time [*crying, but calmer*].

T: Mmmmm [*more sympathetic noises*].

P: [*Deep sighs, more crying*]

T: It comes from a deep, painful place.

P: Yep . . . I've been alone for my whole life, basically, and just trying to make it . . . and now I have a couple of major things that mean that I am not alone but . . .

T: But I am so struck that this touches this level of deep, lifelong loneliness [*Refocus on deepest affect*].

P: Frankly, I've worked with not-so-hot therapists where I still felt lonely afterwards because you get used to it [*Voice cracks again*]. . . . To work with someone who was . . .

T: . . . really there. . . .

P: Yeah . . . good and productive it makes it a lot more difficult. You know, I am married now, and that means I am not alone, and, you know I don't have tons and tons of friends, I could have a lot more friends, but I figured out ways to reinforce this lonely feeling because that's what, like, normal is to me.

T: So then with Dr. M, in a way, there, for a couple of years you weren't alone [*De facto, procedurally refocusing the patient*].

P: Yeah, absolutely [*Vigorous head shaking in emphatic assent; declarative tone of voice*].

T: You had someone on your side.

P: [*Vigorous head shaking in assent*] Totally . . . [*long pause*]. So yeah, it is sad, and lonely and scary [*An integrative statement, with patient clear voiced and no longer crying; declarative and feelingful, a marker for me that we had reached the end of one wave and that we were starting to come up*].

T: The more I am feeling what I am feeling [*touching heart/chest area*], the huger the loss seems.

P: Yeah.

T: Can you tell her, in your mind . . . If you were to imagine yourself talking to her from this place [*Having reached a plateau and worked through the unbearable feelings of aloneness, we return to a second round of the portrayal of grief with patient more resourced and resilient*] . . . tell her what it means losing her, what it means saying goodbye to her, what you will most miss about her? [*Helping the patient not be alone with previously feared-to-be unbearable feelings; using the technique of portrayal to work through the previously warded-off grief*]

P: [*Lighter now, head nodding*] It . . . Yeah . . . I'm not always good at the "pretend you're talking to her" thing . . . but uh . . . [*Very sad again, young voice*] I just feel like I had training wheels that are gone . . . that, you know, . . . I very much felt like I was doing the work but it was a lot different than being alone.

T: Uh huh.

P: So . . .

T: And I gather that other people in your early life did not make you feel that way?

P: No, no . . . I guess that's another thing. With her I realized the depths of how absolutely chaotic my life has been and f'ed up [*sic*] everyone around me was and continues to be. . . . I guess it is an interesting dynamic that the one who . . . that I am now losing the person who has helped me go all the way down to the real brass tacks or whatever of what I've been going through [*Coherent, integrated narrative. Takes a deep breath, looks down, takes another deep, cleansing breath, looks like he's absorbed in thinking something through, and then comes up: His gaze comes up and he makes eye contact with the therapist as he smiles*]

T: You smile. . . . What?

P: I guess now I am ready to do something else.

With a big, genuine, easy smile, the affect wave is over. Having worked through his mourning, the patient is ready to now engage the world. It is very important to read this as a marker of completion of the wave and support the rise of the adaptive action tendencies and transformational affects, and not treat this as a defense against the depths.

A beautiful and profound moment, somatically marked by two deep exhaling breaths and a lifting of the eyes to make clear, direct, open contact. The essence of the mourning process is that when a wave of the grief is processed to completion (Freud, 1917/1958; Lindemann, 1944), the self emerges out of its absorption in the loss ("The shadow of the object falls upon the ego"), and energy is once again available for life — for engagement with the world, and more specifically, for engaging with others.

The focus in this vignette is exclusively on the patient's emotional experiences, which he was previously unable to process on his own. Dyadic affect regulation through right-brain-to-right-brain communication — nonverbal, attunement, affect sharing, echoing, and empathic elaboration — helps him stay with the deeply painful experience. As Lee is able, with help, to stay with and surrender to the experience of emotion, his anxiety over the emotion decreases; the emergent phenomenon is integration. As one wave of emotional experiencing is completed, another comes forth. The worked-through grief, first inaccessible and then emergent, is now the new achievement. It becomes the platform for the next level of emotional processing, which involves the emergence of frightening feelings of loneliness, poignantly expressed: "I just feel like I had training wheels that are gone," an evocative image suggesting loss of control and loss of support, coming from a very young self-state (circa age 3 to 6, whenever kids learn to ride a two-wheeler). And again, once that experience is processed and transformed through sharing, we see the upswing of the wave; the wave over, the patient comes up, so to speak, and liberated from under the yoke of unprocessed emotional experience, the adaptive action tendencies kick in. Deep sighs, uplifted gaze, and positive affect are the somatic markers that signal a state transformation is in progress.

Having dealt with the there-and-then, Lee is ready to be in the here-and-now. I take his statement of "Now I'm ready to do something else" at face value. So we do.

Vignette 3: Metatherapeutic Processing: The Transformational Spiral

> The notion of self here . . . is intensely alive and active. . . . It is experienced in an aura of power. The respite here is not passivity in the womb, not asleep, but an active seeing stillness, compact and electrifying. (Eigen, 1973, quoted in Ghent, 1999, p. 220)

Now that the two waves of core affective experience have been processed fully, and that we have a green light to proceed, we can begin the metatherapeutic processing of the just undergone therapeutic experience. Alternating between experience and reflection, we move toward further deepening, solidification, and integration of the gains we have made and the gains we will make along the way. We deflect the soft defenses that come up (see Fosha, 2000). They need to be minded and attended to, for they are important, but, like a good parent, we pay attention to issues of timing and set limits — de facto saying something like, "Not now, later." If these obstructions, which are nothing more than heralds of what further needs to be addressed, are honored and respected (Schwartz, 2003), the process can continue to unfold.

There are three parts to the balance of this case study, capturing different aspects of the metatherapeutic process. In the vignette below and the next two to follow, patient statements that are underlined document the progression of the transformational spiral.

Vignette 3a: "The Real Me," "Innate," "Natural," "Wheels on the Pavement"

T: How are you feeling?

P: I feel some of the release of having felt that emotion [*Post-affective breakthrough affects*].

T: Tell me.

P: It's a little freeing [*Post-affective breakthrough affects*].

T: A little more relaxed.

P: Yeah [*Head nodding; the head nodding is a somatic marker of being on the right track, of being in sync*]

T: How does it [*i.e., the work we have done*] make you feel about you?

P: [*Long, reflective pause; moved, with tears*] Kind of reminds me of the real me [*Healing affects: affirming recognition of self by self*].

T: Mm huh.

P: That the real me is like not necessarily this performer,. . . has all those attributes and skills, but is a little more incisive than just always trying to be jokey.

T: So what's it like to make contact with the real you? [*Further metaprocessing, the next rung of the spiral; having reached a new experience, "the real me," that experience becomes the platform for the next wave of exploration*]

P: That always feels really good [*Nice, relaxed smile; vitalizing positive affective marker associated with healing adaptive experience*]. . . . There is something very real about it. You're right there. . . .[*The language of affective transformation tends to be simple, from the heart*]

T: Right.

P: Kind of like getting pissed at people, you're feeling it and you're doing it [*Motions with his fists in a muscled motion*] and there is something empowering about that [*Declarative expression of experiencing an adaptive action tendency; vitalizing positive affective marker*].

T: Right.

P: [*Declarative tone*] The wheels are on the pavement. [*Very significant statement, given that he described his experience of loss and aloneness as "the training wheels came off": This current experience is a direct healing of that experience*]

T: Which means what? [*The spiral of transformation: more exploration of newly articulated experience of "The wheels being on the pavement"*]

P: Yeah [*Big, strong, declarative "yeah"*] . . . yeah . . . cuz the wheels haven't been on the pavement for about the last seven days.

T: And from this place of the real me, when you say "I'm in touch with the real me," again it touches something deep in you [*Positive affects are also deep inside, not only negative affects like grief and rage*], there's a sense of the real me, there's a sense of control, the wheels are on the pavement, what's the feeling that goes with that? Because there's a lot of relief, you say it's good. . . .

P: Mmmmm . . . [*Pause*] mmmm. . . .

T: Hmmmmmm . . . Just let yourself notice [*Encouraging inner exploration*].

P: Notice?

T: Notice. . . .

P: It feels good. . . . It's the real me, but there is still . . . It's all still very new. . . . I still feel some skepticism about the real me version sitting here, which is like the first real me appearance kind of thing. . . . But, uh . . . [*The newly achieved experience of a positive sense of self is followed by the appearance of some old defenses*]

T: But if you put the skeptic to the side for a little bit, I mean we will address that part of you too, because there's something to that part of you too — but if the skeptic doesn't mind stepping aside for the moment and just allow you to have this experience, and share it with me, — again, it touches something . . . inside you [*Honoring defenses; respectfully asking them to step to the side*].

P: [*Deep breath*]

T: [*Deep breath, matching and mirroring his*] Yes . . . yes . . .

P: It feels good. . . . It feels trite. . . . See, the skeptic has a hard time stepping aside. . . . But, that said, I feel confident and uh . . . [*Moves past his defenses on his own*].

T: [*Affirming*] Mmmhuh . . . you feel confident [*mirroring, echoing*] . . .

P: I feel confident and uh . . . like, ready to act . . . [*Declarative expression of experiencing an adaptive action tendency; vitalizing positive affective marker*]. This is like 50% genuine.

T: OK, so within this kind of 50%, staying with that first, and then we'll address the other 50%, . . . but to just stay here, because it feels very important. . . . When you touch this and when you feel and when you have the sense of authentic, the sense of *real me* inside, there's release, there's relief, it feels good, and then you say something else that's very important . . . that you feel confident . . . confident, wheels on the pavement, ready to act.

P: Yeah.

T: And what does that feel like?

P: It feels good. . . . It feels . . . it almost feels like I don't need to describe it, I know that that's the helpful thing to do, but it just feels innate [*Core state assertion of experiential truth: state of assurance*], it just feels like . . . you know. . . . I think it's the basis of something that makes me go off in not the greatest direction all the time but . . . [*Sits up straight*] . . . I feel like I got a lot of strong abilities and qualities that I am still trying to get on the pavement and when I feel this way, in touch, all that just feels . . .

T: Natural.

P: Natural and doable and, like . . . [*Voice shifts to a more certain tone of voice; declarative assertion of subjective truth; state of assurance; translating into confidence about being able to take effective action on behalf of the self; the declaration of self by self and its accompanying positive consequences*] . . . being creative [*direct, declarative here*].

T: So that's the part that feels base, rock solid — like this kind of innate, natural kind of native creativity.

Through the transformational process, the sense of self is becoming increasingly positive and solid (Fosha, 2006; Russell & Fosha, in press). When the patient says "innate," it is like he has been reading the AEDP manual, except of course for the fact that he is, so to speak, writing the manual. Innate, natural, confident, ready to act. Indeed.

Vignette 3b: "More Like Myself, Rather Than Less Like Myself" This vignette begins with the therapist summarizing what the patient has said about his feelings about working with Dr. M, and about having said goodbye to her.

T: Even though you haven't used the word, I sense your gratitude toward her.
P: . . . Yes, I am [*Moved to tears*]. . . . And I am also having this feeling of appreciation of myself, too [*Healing affects of feeling moved by spontaneous recognition, affirmation, and appreciation of self by self*].
T: Yes, yes. [*A few minutes later*] Uh huh . . . but that in recognizing Dr. M and what she's meant to you and what she has contributed to your life, you're also recognizing what you have done . . . that you, too, have participated . . . and that it's something that you've done together . . . that she may have been a wonderful guide, and wonderful in unprecedented ways.
P: Totally.
T: But that you, too, worked with your sleeves rolled up, side by side with her. . . .
P: Yeah . . . yeah [*Deep affirmation*].
T: . . . and that acknowledging that sort of puts you in touch with your feelings [*Patient nods*]. . . . What's coming up for you?
P: More of the same.
T: Well, then, let's stay with it.
P: I never . . . I kind of never thought I would get that close. . . . There were certain days and certain points that I could see it really happening and I could see me as a fully actualized person . . . still coming to therapy, or not . . . you know, being the way I am in a good session, like as a normal thing . . . like that would be my regular life . . . and that just feels like constant home runs. . . . The whole critical thing goes away [*Moved, tears in his voice*] . . . because when I am in one of those moods, there is no critical [*He is aware that core state being is pure: no defenses, no self-attack*]. . . . Everything can be figured out in some way [*Assertive declaration of competence, mastery, adaptive action tendency*]. . . . Yeah, I used to use this example with her . . . I used to smoke cigarettes. And there was a point where I didn't think I was going to be able to quit. I just . . . and I was disap-

pointed by that. . . . When I imagined quitting, I imagined waking up and being a different kind of person . . . and you know, realizing that I was the same person, I just didn't smoke. Which is kind of a good thing.

T: So that you succeeded.

P: So I wouldn't be something different, I wouldn't have to necessarily reinvent myself. . . . It's not like the fixed me is going to feel different or . . . or think about things differently.

T: But, rather that it's finding you, more than . . .

P: I guess I would be more like myself, rather than less like myself [*Declaration of self, more recognition of self by self; core state truth*].

This vignette illustrates the clear link between effectiveness and self-efficacy, and core positive self-identity — and the dialectical amplification between the two.

The patient goes back and forth between the theme of control, competence, and mastery, on one hand, and the solidity of himself as an authentic person, on the other. When fully in contact with these experiences, the critic does not have anything to say: In touch with "the real me," there is no critic.

It is interesting to note how this comes about: As we do a last round of processing his loss of a positive attachment figure, acknowledging her contribution to him and exploring his gratitude toward her, he spontaneously asserts that he also appreciates himself, a beautiful example of what I mean by an emergent phenomenon. Through the other arises the self. Finally, in the next vignette, one last round of metaprocessing yields another wave of healing affects, expressed with an almost biblical eloquence.

Vignette 3c: "The Gratefulness of Me"

T: So far, just how does it feel to share this with me?

P: It's definitely a relief. . . . Yeah, I mean, like, all the things we've been saying [*Notice the "we"*]. I really felt sad. . . . I kind of feel this gratefulness of me kind of thing . . . [*Healing affects, stated with extraordinary, spontaneous eloquence*].

T: That's beautiful.

P: It's still new, I'm still in New York, for 10 minutes in there I was, like, hanging onto myself, so like, . . . OK, we're still there kind of thing.

T: [*Low, deep, moved voice*] The "gratefulness of me" . . . that's wonderful.

P: [*Pleased, touched, serious*] Yeah.

The Phenomenology of Healing The sequence that is to follow, a summary of the phrases underlined above, documents the phenomenology of healing. Once the healing transformational process is activated and supported, its progression has an inexorable quality. Note the simplicity of language, whether straightforward, direct and declarative, or elegiac.

> I feel some of the release; it's a little freeing → Kind of reminds me of the real me; that always feels really good → You're feeling it and you're doing it, and there is something empowering about that → The wheels are on the pavement; it feels good → It's the real me → I feel confident, ready to act; it feels good → Innate → Natural and doable → Creative → I also feel an appreciation of myself → Obviously I do have a great deal of control over exactly how I do all of this stuff; it's very empowering → Everything can be figured out in some way → More like myself, rather than less like myself → This gratefulness of me

As a result of not being alone, and a relentless therapeutic focus on his own capacities for healing, Lee is able to process his grief about an attachment loss and share his deep feelings of aloneness, thus paradoxically transforming them. The foundational process by which changes become self is almost palpable.

Following this session, the patient regained his control over his sexual addiction, which he has maintained, with only very occasional mild, and largely mindful, single-episode lapses.

Part 3: Discussion, Summary, and Conclusions: AEDP and EI Therapy

We are living in exciting times. Body, mind, heart, attachment, identity, and healing are being seamlessly integrated into a discourse where practitioners of affective neuroscience, psychotherapy, philosophy, and mindful Eastern practices are actively engaged in lively interdisciplinary exchanges. Integration is not something we strive to achieve but is a condition of the very phenomena and processes with which we as psychotherapists are concerned. Our models of mind, body, and development, of suffering and stress, and of treatment and healing, are finally catching up with their intrinsic rich complexity.

This narrative has been concerned with describing the arc of transformation that characterizes the processing of intense emotion to completion in AEDP. It naturally links creatureliness with godlikeness through a moment-to-moment experiential journey taken together with a caring, affirming, affect-facilitating true other. I also wanted to document the unfolding phenomenology of the process of healing: once previously disowned emotion is processed and (re-)owned.

Being invited to contribute an essay to this august collection was not only an honor, but also an opportunity to learn, a gift for which I am grateful. In reading the works of existential writers, the experience I have had has been one of unbroken head nodding (cf. rhythmic oscillation as a marker of dyadic resonance) at the extraordinary resonance between AEDP and the writings of existential clinicians and philosophers, with, of course, the powerful vitalizing energy that accompanies experiences of recognition (both recognizing and feeling recognized). My first reaction was, "How uncanny!" My second reaction was, "How validating!" And my third reaction was, "Of course!" The "of course" has to do with a shared passionate interest in and humbleness before the power and richness of healing transformation. My contribution here is an ode and a testimonial to that power.

We are not in the realm of invention here. We are in the realm of mining what is there and learning how to best access it. It is not surprising that phenomena (a phenomenological bent and a respect for phenomena is deeply shared by both AEDP and existential therapy) carefully focused on and respected should yield their secrets to different explorers. The gold is there and it has certain properties. Seeking it, many of us have found it. Some of us have found it looking for gold, for others of us, it has been serendipitous, finding it while looking for something else, as often happens with progress in science. The phenomena will continue to instruct us and guide us, as our ability to see and inquire becomes more sophisticated as we gain experience and learn from one another.

I chose the session presented above because it is a wonderful illustration of how we can swing from the depths of despair and self-loathing to the accessing of deep resources that feel like the fundamental essential self. But since this is an integrative-experiential psychotherapy casebook, I also chose it to foster the explorations between AEDP and integrative-existential therapy as I am beginning to understand it.

The dialectical tension between opposite poles of existence and experience — between the individual and the dialogic/dyadic; between the anxiety and dread at the root of human existence and the actualization of potential equally at the root; between biology (and thus the body), on one hand, and the spiritual and the mystery of being, on the other — is deeply and broadly acknowledged by existential writers (Schneider, this volume). I am well aware that the efforts to bridge these dichotomies are precisely what the integrative-existential spirit is about and I hope to learn more. And yet, it seems to me that while in theory the idea of dialectically connected opposites is strongly held, in clinical writings different writers tend to focus on and identify with one pole or the other. The embrace of either hope and healing potential or the inevitability of dread tends to be differentially emphasized, and rarely are the two connected together through the transformational arc where these phenomena are intrinsically linked through how we are wired and what happens when emotions can be regulated and processed to completion. Similarly, the tension between the individual's personal quest and the realm of mutual discovery appears more polarized in practice than in the dialectical existential theory.

What I hope to contribute to the discussion is yet another integration and transcendence of these dichotomies by shifting to a complementary conceptual framework, one that mother nature provides in an already integrated form. And that is the attachment and emotion and transformation model that informs AEDP theory and practice. AEDP embraces both aspects of all these polarities and does so organically, and not as a result of integrative effort. What allows it to do so is an attachment-based stance, a grounding in the bodily rooted experiential method, the focus on the dyadic regulation of intense affects within a dyadic relationship, and the notion of working with the self-at-worst from under the aegis of the self-at-best.

There are two aspects of AEDP that I offer as possible ways of promoting the integrative dialogue that this volume seeks:

1. The idea of dyadic affect regulation of intense emotions within an attachment relationship bridges the dependence/independence dichotomy: A central tenet of attachment theory, and one that has received robust empirical validation from countless studies, is that the safety of attachment promotes an expanded range of exploration. The safer we feel, the more we are willing to take growth-promoting risks. Another unnecessary polarization, that between positive and negative affects, is also seamlessly bridged. As discussed above, optimal dyadic affect regulation is not achieved via uninterrupted blissful attunement, but rather is the result of countless cycles of attunement, disruption, and hard-won repair. Like K. J. Schneider (personal communication, November 27, 2006) says, "The temporary and often inadvertent suspension of safety — disappointment, terror and the like — can often be gem-like in their power to transmute and to heal." It is precisely through actively engaging these moments dyadically that expansive growth takes place. The safety of the firmly established, and re-established, therapeutic bond allows the exploration of emotional experience in a much deeper way than leaving the individual, a fortiori the traumatized individual, to his own devices.

   The dyadic experience contributes to the greater coherence of the self-organization of each dyadic partner. In turn, the expanded consciousness of each dyadic partner contributes to the richness of the dyadic interaction and its emergent phenomena. At any one moment, one of these elements is in the experiential, exploratory foreground, while the others are in the background, but they are all in operation — integratively — moment to moment and at all moments. Dyadic affect regulation is a way by which the dyad can help the individual process intense, otherwise overwhelming and potentially traumatizing, emotions. But through the dyadic processing of emotion, as I discussed at some length above, the bond between dyadic partners is strengthened, deepened, and enriched. Thus, the dichotomy between the relational/interactive/dialogic/intersubjective dimension (a horizontal dimension) and the emotion/depth/exploratory/intrapsychic

dimension (a vertical dimension) is bridged through the intrinsic properties of the dyadic affect–regulation process.
2. The moment-to-moment processing of emotional experience to completion, guided by somatic transformational markers, in the context of dyadic safety, empathy, and help, describes a transformational arc, as we saw above. This arc naturally and organically links suffering and flourishing, pathology and healing, action and grace, and biology and transcendence. In addition, through the further metatherapeutic processing of transformational experience, we are able to deepen and expand transformation and organically promote integration from the inside out.

In closing, the idea of transformance as the healing motivational counterpart of resistance can function as an organizing construct for the various strivings — be they dialogic or identity questing, biologic or transpersonal, emotional or relational, for meaning or well-being — by which we seek to transform ourselves. The construct of transformance, in other words, gathers under its aegis progressive motivational forces that, when engaged, promote authenticity in relation to ourselves and others and foster effective and meaningful lives.

Notes

1. I am developing this idea in an upcoming paper: *On Being Known by and Knowing the Other* (Fosha, in preparation).
2. The term *categorical emotion* refers to dispositional tendencies we share with our animal predecessors, wired in by evolution, that serve our survival. The categorical emotions are universal (Darwin, 1872/1965): Each has a specific identifying brain landscape, bodily signature, and characteristic arrangement of facial musculature.
3. Ghent, in his beautiful, deep, and brilliant (1990) paper, uses the term *surrender* to mean something very akin to what I mean by the term *transformance*, also choosing a term to denote the opposite of resistance. I opted not to join him in the use of the term *surrender*, which seems to me more appropriate to adult psychotherapy, where one has to let go of some organization (i.e., surrender it), so as to reach something more primal, more basic, more organic. I am looking for a term to apply to both therapy and development. Moreover, the ordinary-language connotations of *surrender* are, I think, hard to overcome, hence *transformance*.
4. By *environment* here, I mean the human environment that any dyad co-constructs. In a therapeutic setting informed by an attachment perspective, however, the therapist has a greater role in setting its tone and parameters. As Lachmann (2001) has said, in caregiving dyads, be they mother-infant or therapist-patient, the bidirectional process of influence characterizing such dyads is indeed mutual, but asymmetric. A similar point is made by Daniel Hughes (2006).

5. Because of space limitations, I can only provide a thumbnail sketch here, and since each of these aspects of AEDP has been extensively written about, in parentheses at the end of each paragraph will be the references where the interested reader can explore these ideas in a more fully developed fashion.

References

Alexander, F., & French, T. M. (1980). *Psychoanalytic therapy: Principles and application.* Lincoln, NE: University of Nebraska Press.

Blake, W. (1987). Auguries of innocence. In A. Ostriker (Ed.), *William Blake: The complete poems* (pp. 506–510). New York: Penguin Books. (Original work published 1863)

Bowlby, J. (1988). *A secure base: Parent-child attachment and healthy human development.* New York: Basic Books.

Buber, M. (1965). *The knowledge of man: Selected essays.* New York: Harper Torchbooks.

Damasio, A. R. (1999). *The feeling of what happens: Body and emotion in the making of consciousness.* New York: Harcourt Brace.

Damasio, A. R. (2001). Fundamental feelings. *Nature, 413,* 781.

Darwin, C. (1965). *The expression of emotion in man and animals.* Chicago: University of Chicago Press. (Original work published 1872)

Eigen, M. (1973). Abstinence and the schizoid ego. *International Journal of Psychoanalysis, 54,* 493–498.

Eigen, M. (1996). *Psychic deadness.* Northvale, NJ: Jason Aronson.

Fosha, D. (2000). *The transforming power of affect: A model for accelerated change.* New York: Basic Books.

Fosha, D. (2001). The dyadic regulation of affect. *Journal of Clinical Psychology/In Session, 57,* 227–242.

Fosha, D. (2002). The activation of affective change processes in AEDP (Accelerated Experiential-Dynamic Psychotherapy). In J. J. Magnavita (Ed.), *Comprehensive handbook of psychotherapy: Vol. 1. Psychodynamic and object relations psychotherapies* (pp. 309–344). New York: John Wiley & Sons.

Fosha, D. (2003). Dyadic regulation and experiential work with emotion and relatedness in trauma and disordered attachment. In M. F. Solomon & D. J. Siegel (Eds.), *Healing trauma: Attachment, trauma, the brain and the mind* (pp. 221–281). New York: Norton.

Fosha, D. (2004a) Brief integrative psychotherapy comes of age: Reflections. *Journal of Psychotherapy Integration, 14,* 66–92.

Fosha, D. (2004b). "Nothing that feels bad is ever the last step": The role of positive emotions in experiential work with difficult emotional experiences. *Clinical Psychology and Psychotherapy, 11,* 30–43. (Special issue on Emotion, L. Greenberg [Ed.])

Fosha, D. (2005). Emotion, true self, true other, core state: Toward a clinical theory of affective change process. *Psychoanalytic Review, 92,* 513–552.

Fosha, D. (2006). Quantum transformation in trauma and treatment: Traversing the crisis of healing change. *Journal of Clinical Psychology/In Session, 62,* 569–583.

Fosha, D. (In preparation). *The cascade of transformations and the fountain of youth.* New York: The New York Academy of Science.

Fosha, D. (In preparation). *On being known by and knowing the other: An attachment perspective on transformation and emergence.*

Fosha, D., & Yeung, D. (2006). AEDP exemplifies the seamless integration of emotional transformation and dyadic relatedness at work. In G. Stricker & J. Gold (Eds.), *A casebook of integrative psychotherapy*. Washington DC: APA.

Frederickson, B. L., & Losada, M. (2005). Positive affect and the complex dynamics of human flourishing. *American Psychologist, 60*, 678–686.

Freud, S. (1958). Mourning and melancholia. In J. Strachey (Ed.), *The standard edition of the complete psychological works of Sigmund Freud* (Vol. 14, pp. 243–258). London: Hogarth Press. (Original work published 1917)

Gendlin, E. T. (1981). *Focusing*. New York: Bantam New Age Paperbacks.

Ghent, E. (1999). Masochism, submission, surrender: Masochism as a perversion of surrender. In S. A. Mitchell & L. Aron (Eds.), *Relational psychoanalysis* (pp. 211–242). Hillsdale, NJ: The Analytic Press. (Original work published 1990)

Ghent, E. (2002). Wish, need, drive: Motive in light of dynamic systems theory and Edelman's selectionist theory. *Psychoanalytic Dialogues, 12*, 763–808.

Greenan, D. E., & Tunnell, G. (2003). *Couple therapy with gay men*. New York: Guilford.

Hughes, D. A. (2006). *Building the bonds of attachment: Awakening love in deeply troubled children* (2nd ed.). Northvale, NJ: Jason Aronson.

James, W. (1985). *The varieties of religious experience: A study in human nature*. Penguin Books. (Original work published 1902)

Lachmann, F. M. (2001). Some contributions of empirical infant research to adult psychoanalysis: What have we learned? How can we apply it? *Psychoanalytic Dialogues, 11*, 167–185.

Lamagna, J., & Gleiser, K. (In press). Building a secure internal attachment: An intra-relational approach to ego strengthening and emotional processing with chronically traumatized clients. *Journal of Trauma and Dissociation*.

Lanius, R. A., Williamson, P. C., Densmore, M., Boksman, K., Neufeld, R. W., Gati, J. S., & Menon, R. S. (2004). The nature of traumatic memories: A 4-T fMRI functional connectivity analysis. *American Journal of Psychiatry, 161*, 1–9.

Lindemann, E. (1944). Symptomatology and management of acute grief. *American Journal of Psychiatry, 101*, 141–148.

Loizzo, J. (In press). *Optimizing learning and quality of life throughout the lifespan: A global framework for research and application*.

Main, M. (1999). Epilogue. Attachment theory: Eighteen points with suggestions for future studies. In J. Cassidy & P. R. Shaver (Eds.), *Handbook of attachment: Theory, research and clinical applications* (pp. 845–888). New York: Guilford.

Maslow, A. (1968). Toward a psychology of being. Excerpted in Schneider, K. J., & May, R. (1995). *The psychology of existence: An integrative, clinical perspective* (pp. 92–98). New York: McGraw-Hill.

Osiason, J. (2006, November). *It's all there: The when and what of empathy*. Paper presented at the Monthly Seminar Series of the AEDP Institute, New York.

Russell, E., & Fosha, D. (In press). Transformational affects and core state in AEDP: The emergence and consolidation of joy, hope, gratitude and confidence in the (solid goodness of the) self. *Journal of Psychotherapy Integration*.

Sander, L. W. (1995). Identity and the experience of specificity in the process of recognition. *Psychoanalytic Dialogues, 5*, 579–594.

Sander, L. W. (2002). Thinking differently: Principles in process in living systems and the specificity of being known. *Psychoanalytic Dialogues, 12*, 11–42.

Schneider, K. J. (2007). The experiential liberation strategy of the existential-integrative model of therapy. *Journal of Contemporary Psychotherapy.*

Schneider, K. J., & May, R. (1995). *The psychology of existence: An integrative, clinical perspective.* New York: McGraw-Hill.

Schore, A. N. (2001). Effects of a secure attachment relationship on right brain development, affect regulation and infant mental health. *Infant Mental Health Journal, 22,* 7–66.

Schore, A. N. (2003). Early relationship, disorganized attachment, and the development of a predisposition to violence. In M. F. Solomon & D. J. Siegel (Eds.), *Healing trauma: Attachment, trauma, the brain and the mind* (pp. 107–167). New York: Norton.

Schwartz, R. C. (2003). *Being the "I" in the storm: Staying centered with different trauma clients.* Paper presented at the conference on Phase-Oriented Treatment of Psychological Trauma: Developmentally-Informed, Time-Effective Treatment of Complex Trauma Disorders, Harvard University Medical School, Boston, MA.

Siegel, D. J. (2003). An interpersonal neurobiology of psychotherapy: The developing mind and the resolution of trauma. In M. F. Solomon & D. J. Siegel (Eds.), *Healing trauma: Attachment, trauma, the brain and the mind* (pp. 1–54). New York: Norton.

Teicher, M. (2002). Scars that won't heal: The neurobiology of child abuse. *Scientific American, 286,* 68–75.

Trevarthen, C. (2001). Intrinsic motives for companionship in understanding: Their origin, development, and significance for infant mental health. *Infant Mental Health Journal, 22,* 95–131.

Tronick, E. Z. (2003). "Of course all relationships are unique": How co-creative processes generate unique mother-infant and patient-therapist relationships and change other relationships. *Psychoanalytic Inquiry, 23,* 473–491.

Tugade, M., & Frederickson, B. L. (2004). Resilient individuals use positive emotions to bounce back from negative emotional experiences. *Journal of Personality and Social Psychology, 86,* 320–333.

Tunnell, G. (2006). An affirmational approach to treating gay male couples. *Group, 30* (2), 133–151.

van der Kolk, B. (2006). When you stop moving you're dead: Clinical implications of neuroscience research in PTSD. *Annals of the New York Academy of Sciences.*

Winnicott, D. W. (1960/1965). Ego distortion in terms of true and false self. In *The maturational processes and the facilitating environment* (pp. 140–152). New York: International Universities Press.

13
EI Child Therapy

Too often, child therapy caters to adult needs and forgets the needs of the child. The child's inner life — her subjectivity — is considered peripheral in such instances, and measurable behaviors reign supreme.

In the case to follow, Stephen Curtin describes a subject-centered, integrative approach to child therapy. Through play, metaphor, and encounter, Dr. Curtin helps "Joey" to adjust herself to her physical and social environment, to immerse herself in therapeutic play, and to find the capacity to transform this play into liberating and constructive action.

Joey presents as hyperconstricted — fragile, tense, vulnerable. Her father appears to be the catalyst for these dispositions, but they are suffused throughout Joey's world. Her expansive acting out — bed-wetting, soiling, aggressivity — may be ways to counter her sense of smallness and attract the support she requires.

Dr. Curtin cultivates an atmosphere of gentle challenge for Joey. The approach he takes, the games he offers, and the creativity he encourages all bespeak opportunities for Joey's self-renewal. In the final stages of her therapy, Joey is able to talk about her fears directly ("My dad really is mean") and to directly explore her role in restraining her father.

In sum, Dr. Curtin is able to invoke the actual with Joey, to vivify and enable self-encounter, and to catalyze her resources to cope.

The Inner Sense of the Child: The Case of Joey

Stephen Curtin

Stephen Curtin, PhD, is a licensed psychologist. He is a credentialed teacher, school counselor, and school administrator. A graduate of Saybrook Institute, he trained extensively with James Bugental and is a member of the American and California Psychological Associations. Dr. Curtin is a founding member of the Existential-Humanistic Institute.

What is an existential child case? If I search for such a case in my notes, I cannot find one. There are no notes that start with "he is struggling to discover his subjective self." Yet, as I think about individual child clients, most of them have experiences and relationships that foster a diminished awareness of themselves.

A child's emerging sense of self can be negatively affected by the forces of cultural expectation (Pipher, 1996; Pollack, 1998), verbal and nonverbal messages from parents (Miller, 1981), or the influence of reductionistic images of the human condition (Kagan, 2006). We live in a society heavily influenced by marketplace forces using simplistic metaphors to explain our distress (Olfman, 2006). Children who behave outside the societal norm are labeled as *neurologically* or *affectively ill*. This promulgates the view that emotional or behavioral disturbance lies solely in an individual's biological structure, thus ignoring the impact of social and historical forces on an individual's development.

The existential-integrative (EI) model of therapy exploits the child's naturally occurring developmental drive. What parent or teacher hasn't complained that even the most conforming child will test limits, break rules, or stretch the truth? Even the most compliant child can stray from the norm when expressing his or her unique individuality. This exploration of one's environment and relationships is described by James Bugental (1987) as a "search process." This process is clearly evident when a child enters my office. The eyes move, scanning the toys and drawings. Fingers touch plants or surfaces. The nose sniffs for odors left in the air from lunch, coffee, or previous clients. The candy jar is noticed and eyes question my nonverbal messages regarding access to the contents. The dance of learning what is expected and permissible in that space begins. My response is designed to limit my influence over what is possible for the child in that space. My attention is focused on how this search process unfolds. Therein lie the clues as to how the child constricts, expands, and centers his or her experiences in the world. As I observe the child I discover how his evolving worldview hinders or assists in his development.

Emmy van Deurzen-Smith (1997) has criticized American existentialism for believing that this search process evolves with the sole purpose of seeking happiness or joy — so that only optimism results from this process. This is a misunderstanding. The evolution resulting from the search process leads to increased freedom and authority over one's life. This result does not always bring joy; rather, it leads to a life that cultivates the self and world construct (or meaning structure of one's life). The self and world construct can bring joy and happiness, but it also brings recognition that life is inherently challenging, difficult, and distressing. The American concept of liberation is centered not on achieving happiness per se, but on the recognition that one has agency even in the most distressing moments.

A young child's self and world construct evolves largely without language or intent. It is guided by experience within developmental limitations. While one can observe the strategies a child uses to meet his needs, the same child has a limited capacity for insight or analysis of his own behaviors. Children develop an array of strategies that are utilitarian rather than cognizant. What parent when asking a young child to explain his actions or intentions has not received a wide-eyed stare and a look of complete befuddlement? That child knows he did something, but he cannot describe his intent or decision-making process.

Many children utilize patterns and habits that distort or limit an awareness of self. These habits and patterns make it difficult to have a view of self that is not moderated by experiences or relationships. For example, children often take responsibility for experiences and behaviors they did not initiate, such as divorce, illness, or neglect. These experiences get incorporated into a self and world construct. Within this construct are attributions of worth and meaning that vary based on the child's temperament, relationships, and environment. To sustain self-value, the child acquires, often without intention, a variety of coping strategies. These coping strategies are incorporated into a self and world construct that informs the child's life. When this construct goes unchallenged, he begins to believe that these strategies define him. For each of us, our strategies become an expression of who we are. We become objects rather than individuals influenced by multiple factors (Bugental, 1987).

In working with a child who experiences abuse, it is easy to see how her perception of the abuse distorts her view of herself. The adage that "children are to be seen but not heard" encourages children to forget or overlook physical and emotional trauma. All children have moments where they are rebuked, ridiculed, or punished for exposing internal feelings and thoughts. Caught between the urge to voice his own feelings or acquiesce to authority figures, a child learns to ignore some degree of internal experience.

Every child struggles with the dilemma involved in sorting internal cues from external cues. "Did you really want that toy, or did you want it because your brother had it first?" This is a common question from a parent, to which most children reply, "I don't know." Sometimes parents are relieved that the child has no pressing need or wish. Others require the child to search further within, to try harder to know the meaning of his actions.

The focus of the existential therapeutic process with children is to heighten their awareness of being in the world. When the therapist describes aloud the child's words and behaviors, the child becomes conscious of how he appears to others. Simple questions like, "What is your hand doing?" draw the child's attention to the choosing of his actions. As the child becomes more aware of his agency, it is possible to explore intention. This heightening awareness allows for inquiry into the meaning of the child's behavior. For example, a child may resist drawing or seek explicit direction. When describing this behavior, one can attach a question such as, "You only want to draw if I tell you exactly how to draw the picture?" or "If you refuse to draw, do you think you won't have to?" The child usually answers simply by agreeing or disagreeing. The therapist can feign lack of understanding to encourage the child to elaborate on the meaning of his action.

When I read psychology textbooks I am sensitive to any effort to make a child's actions fit neatly into a psychological theory or treatment plan. As these actions are translated to conform to an adult definition, the child's perception of his experience is lost. The child's behavior or act is now understandable to me, the adult reader, but often in language that no child has the developmental capacity to verbally express. The importance of focusing on the phenomenological elements of the therapeutic process is that it grounds both parties in the meaning the child brings to the encounter. Respecting the child's perspective validates the process the child uses to acquire and reflect on the meaning he gives to each lived moment.

To the extent that subjective experiences are brought to awareness in the relationship with the therapist, the child becomes cognizant of his "inward sense" (Bugental, 1978). With this awareness, the child has some experience of choosing his behavior, what Bugental (1978) calls "subjective sovereignty." For the child, the awareness of choice often results in a sense of empowerment. For example, a child who flees conflict has a different felt experience if she experiences herself as choosing to run away instead of seeing the environment as causing her to run away.

There is no perfect case. Every therapeutic encounter brings with it a multitude of interdependent factors that muddy the waters of therapeutic progress. Any one session or fragment of a session can be viewed in many ways. In the case that follows, the therapist's attention is directed toward facilitating the child's awareness of internal feeling, and sensations. None of the techniques used in existential therapy are exclusive to one school of therapy. As Rollo May (1983) stated, "Existential analysis is a way of understanding human existence rather than a system of 'how to's'" (p. 151). Thus, the therapist uses strategies that help the child shift from "detached, impersonal statements" (or behavior) to "more emotional and uniquely personal elements" (Bugental, 1987, p. 13).

"Joey," the child in this case study, demonstrates a striving for personal agency. During the course of therapy Joey demonstrates significant anxiety of annihilation. As therapy proceeds, she focuses on external forces to protect her from this annihilation. Joey becomes increasingly aware of how her choices leave her dependent on others she may not trust or see as powerful. As dependency on others only temporarily relieves her anxiety or constricts her independence, she seeks another means of relief. When choosing to explore her own power, she tries strategies of allaying her fears. As she tries a variety of behaviors, she increases her attachment to behaviors that activate her personal autonomy. Joey is unwilling to sustain relief from her anxiety only with external resolutions. Instead, she continues experimenting until she is able to use resolutions that give her personal agency.

Kirk Schneider (Schneider and May, 1995; this volume, Part 2) describes six levels on which an individual can discover liberation. During the course of therapy, Joey displays movement toward liberation on three of these levels: the physiological, the environmental, and the interpersonal.

Initially, Joey tries not to exist physically in the presence of danger. She closes her eyes, pretends not to hear, or tries to make herself still. She tries to numb herself or restrict her awareness of her senses. By constricting her awareness of her physical experience, she is attempting to avoid annihilation. Any expansion from this restricted state increases her awareness of the danger. She cycles between awareness and constriction of her experience of her fear. It is her body, and not the object of the fear, that signals she is fearful.

When she is unable or unwilling to constrict her senses, she uses the environment to alleviate her fear. She seeks safety in the environment, hiding under a chair. As she expands her environment, she finds corners, tables, and a piece of cloth to hide behind. She then leaves the room on the pretext of using the bathroom or looking for her mother in the waiting room. Joey uses her mom or the therapist as an object to hide behind. At this level, they are only useful for their physical size. Joey alternates between hiding (hyperconstricting) and running away (hyperexpanding) from her environment.

As Joey expands her search for relief from her anxiety she begins to use interpersonal resources. The mother has a social obligation to protect her child. She is not merely a large object, but is now socially defined. Policemen and judges have a socially constructed role and a socially defined obligation to protect Joey. In light of her experiences with the court and police department, she constricts and expands her trust in their agency. In the same manner, Joey alternates between complying with the demands of the judicial system and resisting the demands of other authority figures. She attends a supervised session with her father, communicates with his court-appointed counsel, and attends multiple interviews with Child Protective Services. She also misbehaves at preschool, test limits with her mother, and is uncooperative with her grandparents.

When watching Bugental demonstrate his therapeutic work, I am struck by his unrelenting faith in the individual's capacity for agency. He has great faith in an internal drive that seeks a path toward integration. When working with clients, he attends to and gives voice to the client's experience of this agency.

What is important is not the child's history of agency, but how it emerges in the therapeutic moment. In the case of Joey, I am attending to and giving voice to those moments. Without prompting, encouraging, or directing, I sit with similar faith in Joey's drive for agency. The therapy environment provides materials and support to facilitate Joey's search process in her play, drawings, and interactions. In the therapeutic moment this faith allows me to set aside my assumptions and focus on the meaning Joey brings to her experiences. I am immersing myself in the child's search process, which I believe is directed toward acquiring and modifying meaning in the self and world construct. I am giving voice to the child's efforts to form and construct her identity.

The Case of Joey

This case involves a three-year-old child who was brought in by her mother because of concerns that she was not adjusting well to her parents' separation.[1] Joey was expressive, intelligent, and artistic. Her presenting complaints included soiling her pants at preschool, wetting her bed nightly, masturbating when playing alone, aggressive behavior with other children, and inappropriate affection with adults other than her parents.

In cases involving custody disputes, the therapist must clarify with both parents the therapist's role and relationship with all parties, including the court and attorneys. In Joey's case, a written document clearly stated that therapy was to be focused on reducing the symptoms that led to treatment. Joey was in therapy solely for her own benefit, and therefore treatment would not include her family or conjoint sessions. The document also stated that the therapist would communicate with all other parties in writing or under oath only when required by judicial order, and that the focus of therapy was the behavioral and affective health of the child, not forensic investigation. For therapy to benefit the child client, the therapist must be attuned to the child and not the pressures of a custody dispute.

When I met this child, she was clinging to her mother and would not separate from her. She sat in a corner of my office and watched me from a distance. As I directed her attention to the surrounding games, puppets, toys, and art material, she showed little response. She huddled close to her mother's side and watched me. Her mother prompted her to play with the toys, but to no avail.

In his art of therapy courses, Bugental cautions therapists to take small steps. In the context of child therapy, "small steps" involve engaging the child in the familiar. In the office, many objects (games, puppets, toys, books) are familiar to children. Children are drawn to these objects and use them without prompting. Their natural curiosity begins the engagement process. With Joey, these objects provided a means of establishing her presence in the room. Therapy began when she was able to separate her attention from the avoidance of being in this setting to something in the room. Often the very presence of the therapist, a stranger to the child, prevents the child from engaging in play or interaction. Familiar objects can begin to focus the child on the therapeutic space.

To meet Joey, I began to place puppets on the couch next to her. At first she ignored them. As I moved the puppets, nodding heads and wiggling arms, she looked at them from the corner of her eye. Often the initial action of such children is to push the puppets away, and that was Joey's response. This action can evoke several responses in the therapist. In this case, I chose to deepen my presence by making a noise of surprise and pushing the puppets back. After several pushes, Joey picked up two of the puppets and had them fight with one another. The struggle between the puppets was half-hearted and brief. Following this action, she sank further into her mother's side and hid from me.

Quietly, I asked if she was hiding from the fighting or from something else. Her response was to kick the puppets onto the floor. My response was, "Oh, it has to do with the puppets. Is it what they did, or is it something else about them?" Joey turned further away from me. I got some plain paper and colored pens. She looked at the pens with obvious interest. As she reached for them, I asked her to draw something about the puppets. She made a number of marks on the paper with the black and red pens. When asked to talk about the drawing, she described it as "the mommy bunny [nursing] the baby bunny." She then presented the drawing to her mother. I asked her, "How's the baby bunny feeling?" "Good." "What does the baby bunny feel about the puppets?" "Bad!" "What kind of bad?" Her response was to curl up on the couch in the fetal position.

By the next session, Joey was able to walk to my office from the waiting room unattended by her mother. She asked to check on her mother frequently, but she always returned from the waiting room without prompting. Much of her play in this session was exploratory. She opened all the cabinets and touched everything. She picked things up and played mostly with the objects that were familiar to her. When she found something unfamiliar, she attempted to discover its properties on her own. She made no attempt to engage me directly and clearly avoided asking me for help in identifying the unfamiliar objects.

In our third session, she spontaneously placed all the puppets other than the wolf in a corner and hid there with them. As she cowered there, I asked her to tell me what was happening. She pointed to the wolf puppet and said, "That's the big bad wolf!" I asked her what she felt about the wolf. She visibly shivered. Speaking about the other puppets and her, I said, "You all look scared. Is anyone *not* afraid of the wolf?" She got a female adult doll from the toy basket and placed it on the floor between the wolf and the hiding spot. She continued to shiver. "You still look scared," I said. She nodded and left the room again to check on her mother. Upon returning this time, she turned her attention to the dollhouse.

All of my focus with thematic material is to follow the client's lead. While this seems like a simple idea, in the moment it is easy to lose attention and wander into psychological speculation and analysis. Sustaining concentration on the therapeutic moment, one is attuned to the child's exploration of the thematic elements rather than attaching psychological significance to it.

With Joey in this early stage of therapy, some limited interventions toward diverging or expanding were possible. The meaning of this material became more evident when I was slow to respond to Joey's cues or pretended to not understand her cues. This behavior on my part usually results in the child further elaborating on a thematic element.

Later in the third session, Joey played with the dollhouse. She used only the adult female doll and a boy doll. The play was not remarkable other than that the two dolls were inseparable. Her play was quiet, and the drawing she made afterward consisted of lines with no description. Joey's behavior reflected movement toward constriction and avoidance of fearful themes.

Rather than focus on why she was afraid and attempt to allay those fears, I used the existential approach, focusing on her internal attempts to come to grips with the fear. Living involves fear. It is what we do in response to the fear, not necessarily its basis, that sets up lifelong patterns and habits. Existential therapy focuses on how the child experiences fear, not necessarily its source. Avoiding the content trap allows the therapist to focus on the larger dilemma of how the child will cope with fears present in any lived experience.

During the sessions that followed, the "big bad wolf" was always present. Dolls, puppets, and Joey were all afraid of the wolf. The child felt vulnerable all the time. Therapeutic efforts were made to focus Joey on the experience of fear rather than on what was fearful. "Interpersonal press" (Bugental, 1987) was used to influence the child to try on a variety of "personal" resolutions to her crisis rather than restrict her search to the first resolution that offered relief. Emphasis was placed on reflecting back to Joey her human predicament, with increased attention on the strategies she used in attempting to contain her fear.

The evolving theme for Joey was how she would attempt to control her fear of extinction. Over time, Joey moved from relying on external forces to finding internal forces. Thus, in the initial play, Joey struggled to have various puppets, dolls, and the therapist control the wolf.

At times, Joey was content with each of these external strategies. In one session, a puppet was made into a judge and the wolf retreated. In another session, a doll became a police officer and killed the wolf. In the next session, the wolf returned and Joey was forced to confront the wolf on her own. When she failed, she sought protection from a maternal doll and left the session sucking her thumb.

In this kind of play, the child identifies individuals in her real world whom she expects to protect her. These may include her mother, her grandparents, officers of the court, uncles, or other adults from the child's daily life (perhaps her father's new companion, the mail carrier, a neighbor, or friends of her parents). Reliance on these external forces provides temporary relief.

After four months of weekly therapy and a series of sessions focused on flight, in which dolls were used to enact physically distancing from the threat, a new strategy emerged. Joey split her self into three figures. One of the dolls became the "real Joey." This doll was a twin of another doll except that the other one had a few more scratches. This second doll she named the "other Joey." This doll was always given to the father doll when visitation was reenacted. The third doll was a girl doll who Joey named after a real-life friend,

"Amy." Amy was not afraid of the wolf and was able to yell and confront it. Amy and the real Joey were constant companions.

The therapeutic effort was aimed at heightening Joey's experience of this splitting up of the self. Each time this strategy was acted out in the play, I explored with Joey how each of the facets of the triad felt inside as events moved forward. In order to clarify with Joey the advantages and disadvantages of splitting, I attempted to elicit from her what it was like to feel separate from the others in the triad.

The Amy doll, meanwhile, yelled at the wolf each time he came to take the other Joey. Amy tried to protect the other Joey as the real Joey watched. In each session, I pressed Joey to describe what it was like for the Amy doll to confront the wolf. She would describe feelings of anger and hostility toward the wolf. The power of these feelings would often be described with clenched fists and angry facial expressions. Joey could sense the energy in her hands and face. It made these body parts solid — "like rocks that can hurt but can't break," as Joey put it.

The other Joey was frequently described as "holding" the fear. She was described as a fugitive from danger (external and internal). She did not want to feel anything except safe. This safe feeling was felt when the wolf was vanquished. At the same time, however, Joey described the other Joey as feeling nervous about her safety, not quite assured.

The real Joey doll was described as a watcher who often exhorted the Amy doll to express anger at the wolf. From a distant and detached place, the real Joey was feeling anger while being protected from the threat the wolf symbolized.

Over the next three months, Joey continued to alternate between the triad and adult figures. Slowly the real Joey doll joined the Amy doll in confronting the wolf. It was always Amy, however, who initiated the confrontation. Over time, the difference between the experience of the real Joey and Amy diminished. The attempts to use adult figures (the "judge" and "mother" dolls) to contain the wolf diminished in frequency as real Joey and Amy merged.

I pressed Joey to experience the judge and mother. Role-playing these figures increased her sense of what it feels like to be them. In the role-play, she felt taller and had more resources (such as calling the policeman) to cope with her feelings of fear. Joey talked about what she would do when she got bigger (bigness represented a state of fearlessness).

In the next series of sessions, Joey used the experience of bigness to make her own attempt to control the wolf. In one session, she placed the wolf in a jail she had made of fences and placed army men outside the enclosure. The wolf broke free. In another session, Joey took a rock, stoned the wolf, placed the wolf in the garbage can, and announced that it was dead "for good." When she left the session, the wolf was still in the trash. This effort to control the wolf directly was repeated over several sessions.

With each session, Joey displayed less energy in the process of killing and throwing away the wolf and took less time doing it. More of her energy was directed toward playing with the dollhouse and with other figures. Her focus turned toward the "family" of dolls, who acted out daily tasks and events. She made drawings that reflected an interest in the emerging self. The drawings were primitive, consisting primarily of lines and spirals, but Joey identified herself, and occasionally her mother or a friend, in these drawings, sometimes paired with hearts or flowers. She also made drawings that she labeled the "mean dad." These drawings had only one figure in them.

Up to this point, Joey's fear was projected onto the toys and drawings. In the next series of sessions, she began to act out containing the fears in several skits. The first of these skits involved "hearing a noise outside the door of the office." First she hid, then we slowly opened the door and searched the office building for the big bad wolf or the mean dad. This search was extensive, and Joey was relieved when the wolf was not found. The emphasis was placed on the strategy of finding safe places.

With this change in strategy, Joey became actively involved in containing her fear. Her whole being — body and mind — was engaged in this struggle. The focus was on real time. The threat was in the here-and-now. The sessions seemed longer as the child tried out her strategies in the moment. Now the therapeutic effort was toward Joey's experience with these individuals. Paraphrasing and gentle challenges were used to support Joey's expression of her real feelings and needs with three powerful people: the dad, the mom, and the judge.

These feelings were evident as Joey devised a skit that used a play phone to call the judge. One significant theme was consistently present in these conversations: She was telling the truth. She said, for example, "My dad really is mean." The effort was directed toward establishing that her words or perceptions had validity. Joey's inherent need to be validated slowly outweighed the other strategies. Joey told the judge secrets that she thought would make the judge jail the father. The child was using the strategy of telling the truth to gain protection from the authority figure.

During this same series of sessions, a "ghost dad" emerged in her drawings and in her play with the dollhouse. This imaginary dad made the family acceptable. In the mind of the child, there had to be a dad in order to have a real family. In the process, the three dolls (real Joey, other Joey, and Amy) became modified. Real Joey and Amy became siblings who lived with the mother and father. Other Joey was present only when contact with mean dad occurred. Other Joey was becoming an artifact. Joey described other Joey as "just there." It appeared, from Joey's description, that both mean dad and other Joey were not felt in the body but were in the head, as memories.

With her emerging inner strength, Joey shifted her attention from the intrapersonal to the interpersonal world. We saw this child start with hoping that forces in the material world would protect her. Over time, she turned to her own personal resources. Initially, these resources were fragmented and detached from the self, but as she gained confidence, she developed strategies that reflected greater personal power. Finally, she voiced her intentions to the others in her world. She finally saw herself as an agent for change in her world rather than a helpless figure.

Summary

When I met Joey, she was difficult to engage. Using familiar objects with attention to mirroring her actions, I was able to forge an alliance. As Joey demonstrated her strategies for coping with her fear, I pressed her to continue the search process. Her willingness to share the search process with me allowed for a deeper appreciation of Joey's experience. Included in that experience were Joey's feelings, strategies, and worldview.

Being with a child in that deeply felt experience allows the therapist to support any movement the child makes on behalf of agency. Joey's journey from external to internal resources and her newly developed courage represented an effective use of the existential-integrative model. Joey has total ownership of her progress. Faith in an inherent drive toward agency and integration of that agency allows the therapist to follow rather than compel the child's growth. In her willingness to voice her needs, it was clear that Joey was acting intentionally (Bugental, 1987).

Put simply, Joey's therapeutic efforts led to expanded awareness of her hopes, dreams, and wishes, coupled with the courage to voice them to the court and to her parents.

Note

1. Some changes were made to protect the identity of the child. Also, the therapeutic contact with this child extended over several years and involved more material than presented here.

References

Bugental, J. F. T. (1978). *Psychotherapy and process: Fundamentals of an existential-humanistic approach*. Reading, MA: Addison-Wesley.
Bugental, J. F. T. (1987). *The art of the psychotherapist*. New York: Norton.
Kagan, J. (2006). *An argument for the mind*. New Haven, CT: Yale University Press.
May, R. (1983). *The discovery of being*: *Writings in existential psychology*. New York: Norton.
Miller, A. (1981).*The drama of the gifted child*. New York: Basic Books.
Olfman, S., (2006). *No child left different*. Westport, CT: Praeger.
Pipher, M. (1996). *Reviving Ophelia*. New York: Ballantine Books.
Pollack, W. (1998). *Real boys*. New York: Henry Holt.
Schneider, K. J. & May, R. (1995). *The psychology of existence: An integrative, clinical perspective*. New York: McGraw-Hill.
van Deurzen-Smith, E. (1997). *Everyday mysteries: Existential dimensions of psychotherapy*. London: Routledge.

14
EI Encounters With Death and Dying

There are few areas of life that are as jarring — yet elusive and ethereal — as dying and old age. In this concluding chapter, Drs. Elizabeth Bugental and Tom Greening meditate on the day-to-day details of death preparation, as well as the enigma of demise. In the first illustration, Dr. Bugental awakens us to the wisdom of eldership and of the need to harvest that wisdom. She writes in terms that are especially relevant today, as the baby boomer generation moves rapidly toward its developmental peak. In a trailblazing commentary, Dr. Bugental outlines the emerging movement that she has helped to steward — existential group process for elders. She elucidates the rationale for this group, the challenges that are broached, and the rewards that are reaped — for both members and the culture of which they are a part.

In the next — and final — essay, Greening looks back at his work as a youth with a dying client. In spite of (or perhaps even in light of) his traditional training, he shows how "being there," "not panicking in the face of the pathology," and "holding out a positive vision" enabled his dying client, "Carol," to reclaim her freedom. Dr. Greening was successful with Carol precisely because his process of relating to her superseded his technique. Like many young practitioners, Dr. Greening learned to be present precisely at the points where more conventional means failed and "doggedness," as he put it, palpably shined through. By the end of his work with her, Carol began to die, and yet inside she began to thrive. She made peace with her cruel constraints and found hope. Dr. Greening, for his part, found inspiration — and his concluding poem is both tribute and commemoration.

Swimming Together in a Sea of Loss: A Group Process for Elders

Elizabeth K. Bugental

Elizabeth K. Bugental, PhD, spent her 20s and 30s as a Catholic nun in Los Angeles. She has taught on all levels and was for over a decade the chairperson of the Department of Theatre Arts at Immaculate Heart College in Los Angeles. Her second career, lasting into her 60s, was as a psychotherapist in the San Francisco Bay Area, in private practice and working jointly with her husband, James Bugental, noted psychologist and author. She holds a doctorate from Stanford University in speech and drama, a master's degree from Catholic University of America, and is a licensed marriage and family therapist. She is the author of *AgeSong: Meditations for Our Later Years*. For the last three years Dr. Bugental has been a full-time caretaker for her husband, who suffers from dementia and partial paralysis as the result of a stroke. She is now working on a sequel to her book.

Loss is the existential given of old age. We wake every day to face a way of being for which we are never prepared. Our minds, our bodies, our loved ones, our surroundings, our habitual ways of dealing with difficulties, our place in our social network, our status, our work, our self-definitions disintegrate in our hands as we struggle to hold them together. Younger persons talk to us, but despite our best intentions, on the everyday level we may not hear and understand as well as we wish. We hold in our memories not only our own life history, but such life-changing events as the Great Depression, World War II, the Korean and Vietnam wars, and the beginnings of radio, television, the computer, space travel, and the United Nations. A younger generation cannot experience us as we experience ourselves any more than we can feel completely comfortable in the high-tech world they intuitively understand, no matter how hard we all try.

Nevertheless, here we all are, stuck together in the challenging, maddening, stimulating *present*. And there will be 70,000,000 of us old folks very soon. Even if we did not have much to give one another across the generations, we are stuck, whether we like it or not, with one another. All generations have seriously conscious work to do as we decide whether this cohabitation will become our joy or our burden. And we have barely begun even to notice the task.

Eager as we might be to begin before the tide takes over, being good existential realists, we know we can never jump over the *now*. Before we can give or take from each other's stores, we have to acknowledge where we are, our differences, our unique tasks, the water we swim in every day, which is so obvious we hardly notice. While you behind us head for the lights of shore, build your muscles to fight the current, keep your eyes on the horizon, we struggle to keep moving, remind one another that sinking is not yet an option. You grab the flotsam and jetsam to enhance your nests; we grab whatever we can reach to stay afloat. And yes, it is vital to most of us that we continue to be of use to our children.

In the words of Gabriel García Márquez, "The old are younger in one another's company" — *younger*, as I interpret it, meaning that we call out to one another in the same language, laugh suddenly and spontaneously, understand each other's silence. We share the taken-for-granteds; the reference frame holds us in place.

My experience leading groups of elders has poured riches over me in this last phase of my life, riches I might have missed if I had not been fortunate enough to be in the right place at the right time, looking for the wealth I sensed was all around me. The youth culture, inside and outside us, tamps down our warmth, can smother us into submission.

What I have to share here is an introduction, in theory and practice, to the possibilities of this last aging swim in the waters of a long life. A group of elders provides us with a space and time to acknowledge where we are in life and what is possible in these late years. We have created a form and a process for awakening our consciousness to the existential issues arising at this apex of life. Meeting together with others of similar age arouses camaraderie and enriches us all. We celebrate our differences as we challenge one another's habitual assumptions.

The Beginning

After an initial phone call, usually made on the basis of a friend's or therapist's referral or of some publicity about the program, the potential group member is sent a brochure detailing the topics to be considered in the group and the place, time, and cost of the meetings.* Each is asked to call back after he or she has read the information to let us know if they are still interested in joining the group. Needless to say, there is a self-selection process going on since the topics clearly indicate the direction the group will take.

Following this second call, an initial interview is arranged with one of the two facilitators. The interviews are 45 minutes long and are welcoming and casual. However, since we are not focused on therapy, we refer persons with obvious therapeutic needs to other groups or individual therapists. One woman, 85, suffering a very recent loss of her schizophrenic son, for whom she was the caretaker, was referred to a grief group, and after completing that six-week program she was able to join one of our groups. This was necessary, not because we do not deal with grief, but because her grief was too recent and overwhelming. Another person with a long-continuing history of mental disorder was referred elsewhere. Generally, however, the interview is a simple step toward becoming acquainted with one of the two facilitators and a way to impart information and answer questions about the nature of the group. We also ask prospective participants to commit to the eight weeks so that, short of emergencies, regular attendance is assured.

In general, we operate on a "first come, first served" basis. However, because we have more women than men applying for the groups, we have asked men to wait until we have enough to make the group somewhat equal in gender. Eight

* The AgeSong program has been offered by Family Service Agency of Marin since 2005, facilitated by Elizabeth Bugental, PhD, and Ann Coffey, PhD. To protect confidentiality, names have been changed, identities sometimes combined, and recognizable details altered.

elders between the ages of 65 and 90 meet once a week for eight weeks. The sessions are 90 minutes, and the cost is minimal.

Content and Process

Each session has a particular focus, although we make it clear that the group belongs to the participants and their own needs take precedence. In the brochure each member has received we have listed the themes on which we will focus. These themes are presented in the form of questions or unfinished statements, such as "How did I get to be this old?" "Creating a new old age," "Who am I now?" "Staying connected," "Filling our lives with beauty, truth, goodness, wonder," and "The courage to find new possibilities in the midst of loss."

Each session begins with a short orientation and a two-minute reading followed by silence. The readings are chosen from my book, *AgeSong: Meditations for Our Later Years* (Elders Academy Press, 2005) and meant to offer a stimulation and focus to the meeting, as well as to encourage personal reactions. The facilitators model self-revelation and careful attention to each person as she or he makes the effort to reveal impressions, thoughts, or pertinent anecdotes. At the first meeting we set ground rules for staying as much as possible in the present, for listening and responding to one another with empathy and *I* messages, for allowing spontaneity and humor. We explain that this is not a therapy group, although it might well be therapeutic, and that what will result will resemble "more an art-form than a legal document."

By an art-form we mean that it will unfold as each of us plays our part and helps create the environment we want in order to experience new awakenings in ourselves. Our goals and expectations may change and expand as we verbalize our thoughts and feelings and listen to one another. We welcome differences, which will lend interest and expand our thinking. How does each of us personally choose to live this final life segment? Our hope is that we will be helpful to one another simply by being present here with what is going on in each of us in the moment. Ideally, we will form some lasting relationships in the process.

We come back often to these principles and model acceptance and active listening as well as personal sharing. We remind the group that every age needs peers, and we are no different. It helps to have others who are going through some of the same crises, who are handling familiar problems in various ways, who come with different expectations and life experience but arrive here and now with many of the same difficulties and surprising pleasures. In a very short time, people begin to say their particular truths and share their dilemmas.

We have very deliberately not asked anyone for an autobiography recital. Each is given a name tag with their first name in large print. What is shared is therefore in the present around large issues familiar to everyone.

Biographical "facts" emerge in a context. On one occasion we learned that one of our most positive and creative members had — in addition to the recent loss of her husband — also lost two other close family members in recent years and was caring for an adult child with severe brain impairment. She told us she waited to speak of this until she was sure we had a sense of who she is and would not see and treat her simply as a "sad person, because I'm not." Biographies can get in the way of fresh sight. One of the advantages we have in a group of elders is that age and life experience actually transcend academic degrees, occupations, and even life choices such as marriage, children, geographical locations, and what sometimes might be called life-changing events. Most of us are no longer in "striving" mode; competition has given way to searching for connection.

As we speak our spontaneous thoughts around, for instance, "What surprises you about being this age?" remarks include "I never wanted children, now I wish I had some," or "I counted a lot on my looks, now I see an old lady in the mirror I don't even recognize," or "I was so busy getting graduate degrees and building my reputation, now it doesn't seem to matter very much," or "I have six children and only one of them really seems to understand me now." The facts sneak out with immediate and emotional meaning attached and become bridges with others rather than creating barriers.

Likewise, without our personas to defend or hide behind we can roll up our sleeves and compare the black bruises on our fragile skin and laugh at how they embarrass us. One woman in the first meeting pulled up her shirt to show us the scars from all her operations, which leave her in pain and discomfort much of the time. It was obviously a relief to her to put herself out there for all to see. It also gave everyone permission to metaphorically show their scars. Much later we learned that this woman had traveled the world, spoke several languages, adopted a foreign-born child, and lost her husband much earlier than she expected. Currently, she was visiting and transporting several even older people to meetings and doctors' appointments because she was still able to drive and had a real desire to be useful. In this gradual way, who people are speaks much louder than what they might say about themselves.

As we move on to "Creating a new old age," members share the changes they are making in their lives. Almost every change involves loss, but almost always there is in the mix of emotions some excitement or surprise. "Joe," 79, with more time now, writes every day; the would-be journalist of his youth gets to come out and play with his new computer. "Jane" returns to her music and the piano she never gave away through all the years of child-rearing and teaching. "Emily" laughs about "getting my body back, a little more battered, but still working," as she joins an African dance group. "Susan" has moved her garden into containers so, even with an arthritic back, she can still grow flowers. "Peter" has become a peer counselor. "Claudia" has turned to "mindfulness meditation" after many years dedicated to a religion she no longer espouses.

By the time we reach the third meeting, "Who am I now?" we are ready to talk in more depth about the "sea of loss" and what we need at this moment to keep moving. Mourning, spoken and unspoken, inhabits the room. We use an analogy here of the game of pick-up sticks. We have to look carefully at which piece in our life will move most easily. We may have to just look for a long time. Trying to move the whole pile, thinking too globally, or looking too far ahead might bury us in life fragments, cause an earthquake to our carefully constructed foundation. What will move most easily and naturally?

Instead of deciding now, 10 months after her husband's death, whether she will sell the family home, "Jennifer" decides to invite a friend to live with her to help assuage the loneliness and pay the bills, and allow her grief time to change or subside so that she can experience herself as a separate person. We encourage her to listen to what she wants, to her own needs, to resist the push of her caring, but impatient, children to make a decision before she is ready. Another group member, who has cleared out her home and feels "freer" because of it, says she knew exactly what she wanted to do after caring for her husband for several years. We agree together that there is no one answer, and as this becomes obvious, participants relax and begin to try out possible next steps, knowing they are the only ones who can know what is in their best interests. Having decided to move, "Melanie" needs to look through every single box and drawer and say goodbye to each item. "Lisa" tosses everything on the Goodwill truck or in the trash without a backward glance. "Howard" needs to consult one specialist after another about his back. "Jim" listens only to the physician he has consulted for years. As they hear one another, group members also may gain new insights, but it becomes increasingly obvious that there are no "one size fits all" answers.

As group members learn to respect their own feelings and those of others, more insights emerge. One participant responded to a longish rumination from another member, "Would you like to hear some suggestions here, or would you rather just have us listen?" This question, reinforced by the facilitator, became familiar to the group and gave permission for refusing "advice" or, on the other hand, requesting ideas.

Another issue, especially among older women, "fading beauty," elicits varied responses: "Sally" rushes to cosmeticians and plastic surgeons. "Anna" says she has "made friends with the older woman I have become." Neither woman is "right," since each must live with herself in the way she is most comfortable. At the same time, they hear one another and are, perhaps, better able to see their options as personal choices.

The fourth meeting, "Staying connected," when combined with continued discussion of "Who am I now?" brings the participants to an awareness of the importance of relationship in the redefining of self. Time is short. Putting off decisions is no longer open ended. Each time elders talk with one another about the decisions facing them in their sea of loss and are given permission to consider various possibilities in a personal and immediate environment, their awareness is expanded and, at the same time, they are allowed to consider options unique to them as individuals. "Elvira" considers spending some money traveling to Asia while she is still physically able to fulfill this lifetime wish. "Susan" says she wants only to be settled, comfortable, and alone in a small apartment. "Fran" fantasizes about moving into a Quaker residence where she can have support for her social activism. "Lisa" tries out a Zen community.

By staying with the larger questions we are able to include the personal and specific in a context that allows more perspective and often bypasses embarrassment and shame. When we get to the topic of "Connections," we are ready to address it in its broader implications: from our long-term love relationships to the momentary adherence to an idea, or a beautiful vision of one kind or another. "Lana" told of stepping out on her back porch and being caught unaware by a bright orange moon just slipping over the horizon. "Jeb" described catching sight of an ancient automobile, which brought up all sorts of memories of family outings as a boy. "Mary" recounted her weekly phone conversation with her childhood friend and how they laughingly moved from subject to subject and from past to present. Other participants moved deeper into shared conversations with spouses or children in moments of crisis. We acknowledged together the twin emotions of love and pain in relationship, of attachment and letting go. The ache of losing a loved one to dementia or death lies palpable in the room, and through it all we maintain our immediate connections with one another by listening and responding in the moment.

Moving from the larger notion of connectedness allows everyone to participate, and those who are now more isolated can begin to see possibilities in everyday events for staying in touch with life as it goes on all around us. Whatever our current situation, we can say to one another, "Where will the new juices come from?"

One of the blessings of late life is broader perspective. After years of experience, older people can appreciate the efforts of others, knowing what it takes to achieve success and to be responsive to the demands of work, children, and dependent adults. However, it is also true that many elders, frightened by their own increasing needs, changing mores, and an unknown future, may respond to younger people with exactly the opposite demeanor. A group meeting is an opportunity to become aware of unconscious attitudes. By the fifth meeting we can pause to appreciate and celebrate one another directly, and explicitly value what each contributes to the meetings. Habitual appreciation of one another, fostered in the group, can help bring hidden feelings to the surface. A 78-year-old cries over the mistakes she made in bringing up her son; another member reaches out to her, describes similar feelings, and reminds her of all the sacrifices she made to support her child. "Serena" apologizes for her lack of education, and "Ted" reminds her that she was working to support her family all the years she might have been in school. "Ella" tells "Maria" how beautiful she looks today. "Nancy" expresses gratitude to another group member for giving her a ride to the meeting.

Negative feelings and actions are also sometimes appreciated. "Cassie" gathers support to express anger at her son for pushing her to move out of her home too precipitously. "Donna" holds up a hand facing another group member, warning her not to interrupt. "Gerry" expresses hurt at "Ron's" dismissal of his interest in art. The group learns that it is possible to object or protest without alienation. Some begin to see they can respond honestly when negative feelings are directed at them in or out of the group; others learn they have many positive feelings hiding behind their negativity.

We remind one another that, as we become more dependent on others, "thank you" may well be our most frequently uttered words, so practicing gratitude becomes a necessity. Somewhere around the fifth meeting of the group we take time to acknowledge and appreciate one another directly. Quieter, more introverted members are often surprised at the effect their comments or even unspoken gestures have on others. As each person speaks, it becomes clear that much more is going on in the room than the content of conversations. This affirmation of the personal influence an older person may still wield is important for this life phase when so many of society's messages are dismissive or patronizing. To see one's self as still potent brings renewed energy and opens possibilities for becoming involved in some meaningful action.

When we begin to talk about truth, goodness, and beauty in our lives, each person's personal experience and even definition of these terms creates a sense of possibility among the others. "Vera" lies in bed and memorizes a poem first thing every morning. "Angela" takes a walk in the bird sanctuary. "Jane," childless and prone to depression, describes herself walking around town chatting with people she meets and especially "getting my fix" from animals and babies. The group encourages her to get the cat she cannot quite let herself have.

When we talk about truth we personalize it to "our truth." Out of that discussion, many particulars of individual lives begin to emerge: religious beliefs that have come and gone and often return under new interpretations, life experiences that have enhanced or discouraged beliefs, spiritual practices that are no longer important and others that have taken their place. In this atmosphere there is respect for "Lila," who loves to dance with the Sufis, and "Ray," who teaches and practices the 12-step program. "Ken," who says he "just doesn't get spirituality," reveals his early childhood with abusive parents who "talked a lot about God." Another man talks about his years in a seminary, and "Miriam" shares her anxiety about a son who, along with his wife and children, has joined a cult. "Sally" recites the Sermon on the Mount from memory. In some cases, discussion falls easily into views on an afterlife. One person looks upon his religion as his anchor, another sees it as a myth.

Usually, at this point, participants are ready to share more details about the deaths of their loved ones, and the group has become close enough to one another that this recounting is a shared experience rather than a lonely recital. Tears come easily. Some participants fall silent and, for their own reasons, remove themselves from this experience. We do not insist that everyone respond in the same way. Three persons have left groups entirely.

By this time, the remaining sessions take on a life of their own. Although we follow the same pattern of a reading followed by silence and conversation, group members arrive with unfinished business and words flow easily. People bring their own poems and quotes to share and introduce their own wishes or topics into the meeting. Books and movie lists come out. Of course, some members are more deeply involved than others, but the prevailing sense of attentiveness remains constant.

Follow-Up (In Progress)

By the time the last session arrives, conversation turns easily to "What now?" and how to continue with one another. Some groups have elected to continue meeting in one another's homes and several members have formed ongoing relationships.

For the past year we have introduced the group members who have completed the eight-week course to other completed groups in a monthly meeting. This was part of our original plan since we were fairly certain that the groups would want to continue meeting. This proved to be the case. However, we have learned that if these monthly meetings will continue without our involvement, a new form has to be invented for this larger group and, in spite of strong intentions, no persons have emerged willing to lead such an endeavor. We are now considering another possibility, which is to form an ongoing group with our most recent members who wish to participate and allow others from former groups to join as openings become available. Meanwhile, groups or individual members who wish to meet are free to do so. Everyone has a complete list of names, addresses, phones, and e-mail addresses.

One given, in these later years, is *attrition*. We become ill or die, or spouses need care, or we are forced to make new living arrangements. Change is inevitable. At this stage, our plan is to stay with an ongoing group that is constantly in flux, while training former group members to begin new groups. In true existential fashion, we are learning as we go and growing organically from within.

Summary

I have chosen a narrative style to inform and describe this approach to facilitating a group for elders because I feel it most accurately depicts the unfolding nature of the process. Emphasis on existential questions rather than a factual and problem-solving approach encourages remaining in the present with questions rather than preconceived answers. Everyone is equally engaged in thinking and feeling in a larger context out of which tentative solutions to current issues may emerge holistically. Expanding awareness through the introduction of larger questions for which there is no right answer reduces defensiveness and encourages spontaneity and creativity. Personal revelations are offered and heard in a context large enough to allow perspective. This process, exactly suited to this final phase of life, mirrors and magnifies the challenges and possibilities inherent in aging.

Suggested Reading

Bugental, E. (2005). *AgeSong: Meditations for our later years.* San Francisco: Elders Academy Press.

Erikson, E., & Erikson, J. (1997). *The life cycle completed: Extended version with new chapters on the ninth stage of development.* New York: Norton.

Morrison, M. C. (1995). *Without nightfall upon the spirit* Wallingford, PA: Pendle Hill Publications.

Tornstam, L. (2005). *Gerotranscendence: A developmental theory of positive aging.* New York: Springer.

Reflections on the Depressed and Dying: The Case of Carol

Tom Greening

Tom Greening, PhD, has been a psychotherapist in private practice for 48 years and was the editor of the *Journal of Humanistic Psychology* for 35 years. He is also a professor of psychology at Saybrook Graduate School in San Francisco, the author of *Existential-Humanistic Psychology*, and a published poet.

"Carol's" childhood, adult life, psychotherapy with me, and dying were all full of pain. Was there any value to all that pain, and to her and my attempts to heal it, numb it, ignore it, share it, confront it, transcend it?

She came to me for help in 1959, when I was just out of graduate school. I had been hired by James Bugental and Al Lasko as a staff psychologist in their Los Angeles group practice. I was not prepared for a client like Carol. At first, she appeared to be a fairly well-functioning, if neurotic, young woman. She was my age (28), an attractive, intelligent grade school teacher who loved folk music. In spite of my help, or perhaps because of it, she deteriorated into an overweight, depressed, suicidal, accident-prone victim.

She often phoned me for emergency support. One time she called because the skeleton of her dead mother was coming out of the closet of her apartment to grab her and take her to hell. Carol had already swallowed a lethal dose of pills and was surrendering to her mother. She had called me in a final attempt to clutch at life. I was indignant, outraged. I told her that was a terrible thing for her mother to do and ordered Carol to tell her mother that I said so and that I demanded she go back in the closet and stay there. Carol did this, her mother retreated, and Carol threw up the pills.

This was not the turning point I hoped it would be, however. We went on like this for eight more years. Finally, Carol felt somewhat better and concluded we had done all we could together. I was relieved to be free of the burden of trying to help her. I did not see her for 12 years.

Then, in 1979, she called to congratulate me on a book I had published, and we agreed to meet to review and reflect on what we had done together. She was still overweight and sad, but she was also strong and wise. She felt our psychotherapy work together had been successful and was grateful for it. I told her I supervised psychologists in training and asked her what had worked in our struggles together that I could pass on to others. She immediately answered, with clarity and conviction: "Tell them to do three things: (1) be there, (2) don't panic in the face of the pathology, and (3) hold out a positive vision of what can come from the pain."

I confessed to Carol that, based on my experiences growing up and in graduate school, when I first saw her I had not the faintest idea of what it meant to "be there." I'd read Carl Rogers on congruence and heard Martin Buber and Rogers discuss the I-Thou encounter in their famous 1957 dialogue at the University of Michigan, but I had never had an actual experience of myself or anyone else "being there." Instead, I had tried to do things, including psychotherapy, with Carol. In the process of failing with her, I learned, unwillingly and inadvertently, to be there with her.

I admitted to Carol that I had certainly panicked in the face of her pathology (graduate school had not prepared me to combat skeletons), but I had doggedly refused to let my panic or her dead mother dominate my relationship with her.

I do not know what positive vision I had held out for Carol during her therapy. In 1959, I was still imbued with reductionistic, pathology-oriented models from psychoanalytic training and academic psychopathology courses. Rollo May's book *Existence* was published in 1958, but I did not read it until a few years later. In confronting nothingness with Carol, I could only draw on the knowledge of existentialism I had acquired from reading novels by Jean-Paul Sartre and Albert Camus. The positive visions of Abraham Maslow, Bugental, and others that led to the development of existential-humanistic psychology also did not come to my attention until I had been working with Carol for several years.

When we talked in 1979, Carol's emphatic prescription of the three things therapists should do impressed itself upon me as a reminder of what I have taken so long to learn and what I have often learned more with help from clients than from teachers. I currently have a client who is giving me an advanced (or remedial?) course in Carol's principles of psychotherapy, and we are both indebted to her more than she will ever know.

That is because she died in 1989. She got cancer, had surgery, had severe and mismanaged postoperative pain, took control of her pain management and recovery, elicited support from caretakers, went home to recover with her playful dog, found the continuing pain and daily struggle too hard, and gave up.

And in the process, she and I went one final round with the lessons she had taught me. I spent time being there with her, and we connected in a deep and peaceful way, sitting, talking, reminiscing, sharing jokes, playing with her dog, listening to music, and doing some more psychotherapy. She had never heard music on a compact disc player, so I played blues and folk music for her, some of which she knew and some of which she learned to love for the first time. There are times in life when Bessie Smith is the best doctor. And even if you do not hear Gabby Pahanui until you are on your deathbed, he is worth waiting for.

Carol's niece and nephew lovingly cared for her to the end. Her nephew is the son of her brother, whom she hated for abusing her as a child. Her love for her nephew, and his love for her, helped heal those old wounds. She died peacefully, "being there," not panicking in the face of the final pathology, guided by a positive vision of living — and dying.

I wrote four poems about Carol. The following, "Postponed Remembrance," is one of them:

Driving to a deathwatch by the beach
a memory I don't want tries to reach
into my mind; I twist away —
I cannot deal with it today.
One death at a time, that's enough.
More than enough, actually —
As the bumper-sticker says,
"I'd rather be sailing."
I've brought a rare guitarist's record
to entertain my friend.
Our tastes get very specialized
when we get near the end.
And so the beat goes on;
there's still a song for her to sing,
and rhythms in the dusk
to help us both defer
the silence that will come.
Today's visit over, I drive inland
along the hamburgered boulevard,
away from the coastal fog and

the part of my barnacled brain
that sank there.
I'll be back again
until her song ends
and the ebbing evening tide
reveals what I would hide.

Summary and Conclusion

This book places psychotherapy on a new scale. This scale stretches beyond physiology, environment, cognition, psychosexuality, and even interpersonal relations, and toward being.

Existential-integrative psychotherapy is one form of the *being* orientation. By existential-integrative psychotherapy, I mean a ground or context out of which other therapeutic standpoints arise. I also mean immediacy, kinesthesia, and affectivity as they inform living experience. The basis for existential-integrative psychotherapy is phenomenology — a richly descriptive, qualitative method for investigating human experience. Although phenomenology was formalized by Edmund Husserl at the beginning of the 20th century, it has a profound literary and artistic heritage.

The core existential-integrative position is that human experience (or consciousness, in the full sense of that term) is both *free* — willful, creative, expressive — and *limited,* environmentally and socially constrained, fallible. To the extent that we deny or ignore this dialectic, we become polarized and dysfunctional; to the extent that we confront (or integrate) it, we become invigorated and enriched.

The freedom-limitation dialectic is characterized clinically by the capacities to constrict (draw back, make oneself small), expand (burst forth, make oneself great), and center oneself. (The freedom-limitation dialectic, in other words, is the range within which we can constrict, expand, and center ourselves.) Dread of either constriction or expansion (across many psychophysiological dimensions) fosters equally debilitating counterreactions to those polarities; confrontation with (or integration of) the modalities, on the other hand, promotes dynamism and vitality.

What are the implications of this aforementioned framework? The key implication, I believe, is that existential psychology is wider (theoretically and clinically) than is generally assumed. For example, while it is true that the existential-integrative model stresses experiential domains of functioning (i.e., affectivity), the approach also acknowledges the import of biological and mechanical levels of our being — the engagement of the world through chemistry, nutrition, reinforcement contingencies, and Aristotelian logic. Correspondingly, while the EI model indeed emphasizes immediate and kinesthetic dimensions of experience, it concurrently appreciates the interpersonal antecedents to those dimensions — childhood separation/attachment issues, for example, or the traumas of sexual/aggressive imbalance.

Finally, while the EI perspective acknowledges its compatibility with traditionally privileged clientele (or participants), it also recognizes its value for a broader and more diverse population. This is a population with which students and practitioners increasingly interact, and it is one that is significantly more amenable to life exploration than is generally accepted — as we have seen. For example, who among this population would not benefit from attunement to the preverbal, openness to the spiritual, and acknowledgment of life's tragedies? Who among them would fail to profit from attention to their constricted or expanded worlds, or cultivations of aliveness, emergence, and even awe at appropriate junctures?

Indeed, who among them would be unable to benefit from encounters that reach them personally, not merely objectively, and from fundamental opportunities to invigorate meaning, purpose, and fresh perspective into their lives?

Few, I believe — on all counts.

This book is but a "shot across the bow." Yet it is an essential one, I believe, for the many practitioners animated by psychotherapy's expanse. To the extent that this book has captivated these providers and enabled them to consider existential methodologies anew, it has amply realized its task.

Index

U

V

W

Y

See: useful refs for EHTx

p. 10 • Norcross, 1987